# A Blessed Life UPDATED

## Autobiography of a Traveler to Emmaus

LINDA ANNE MONICA SCHNEIDER

AuthorHouse™
1663 Liberty Drive
Bloomington, IN 47403
www.authorhouse.com
Phone: 833-262-8899

This book is printed on acid-free paper.

ISBN: 979-8-8230-2564-5 (hc)
ISBN: 979-8-8230-2549-2 (sc)
ISBN: 979-8-8230-2550-8 (e)

Print information available on the last page.

Published by AuthorHouse  04/25/2024

authorHOUSE®

# A
# *Blessed Life*
# UPDATED

*Autobiography of a Traveler to Emmaus*

# OTHER BOOKS BY THE AUTHOR

Available from Author House, Bloomington, IN

Novels:
*The Unbroken Circle* A love story of a princess, a unicorn, and her kingly beau.
*Diary of an Unwitting Explorer* Science fiction tale of astronauts stranded on an inhabited asteroid.
*Heir to the Dragon King* A story of the last possible interactions between humans and real, benign dragons.

Poetry Collection
*The Ivory Pyramid*

Short Story Collections
*Slice of Life*
*A Second Helping*
*Cream Puffs and Other Goodies*
*A Walk in the Park with friends*
*Flights of Fancy and Food for Thought*
*Tying up Loose Ends*
*Diamonds, Nuggets, and Pearls: New Stories and Old Stories Retold Amazon, Available March 2024.*

Autobiography
*A Blessed Life: Autobiography of a Traveler to Emmaus (earlier edition superseded by this present book)*

# DEDICATION

For Jesus,
My Lord, My God, and My Best Friend
With all my Love and Profound Thanksgiving!

You died for me; I'll live for you!

For Janice Morton, who encouraged me to write this account of my life!

# AUTHOR'S ORIGINAL NOTE

Over the years, teachers, friends, and critics have sometimes advised me to "write about what you know," as opposed to trying to write, by fact or fiction, about experiences, circumstances, or subjects that I have neither experienced nor researched. Following this advice has often led me to write about fantasy or imaginary circumstances or to integrate into my fiction elements of my own personal experience. [1] For once, I intend now to write strictly about what I do know, my life and its circumstances. I want to tell the story of what it has been like for a middle-class American descended from Italian and German immigrants. It is the story of a girl who grew up and found her law vocation during the 50's through 70's and who happens to be blind and hard of hearing, and who now has used a series of wonderful guide dogs as traveling companions.

I first want to explain the title. I have referred to my life as blessed, because, as the ensuing pages will reveal, the hand of Divine Providence has been at work since my conception, both directly and through the human beings in my life, in shaping me and promoting whatever goodness or success I may have attained. The imperfections and errors that remain, which I hope to continue to remedy with His help, are the evidence that this Divine work is, as Benjamin Franklin said in his epitaph, a work in progress, being continually revised and corrected by the Divine Author. The sub-title comes from the theme of the discussion group in which I participated during my Cursillo retreat: Travelers to Emmaus. Like the two discouraged, disillusioned pilgrims who fled from Jerusalem after the death and still disbelieved resurrection of Jesus, I am still in the lifelong process of finding the Lord. Although the truths taught by the church and the support and example of other people

---

[1] Although some of the descriptions and events in this autobiography may tempt readers to infer that they are the source of some of the fictional characters and events in my previous books, I do not intend to explicate my earlier works by detailing where the idea or details for specific characters or events originated in my life experiences, unless it is relevant to the discussion of my life.

of faith have been guiding lights in my life, each of us needs to internalize our own personal faith experience, as viewed through the circumstances of life.

This book is not meant to be either a strictly chronological narrative or a detailed account of every jot and detail of my life, because my memories often clump themselves by themes instead of a running day-to-day review. Rather, I have tried to focus on the highlights and to emphasize the positive aspects of my experiences. I also have not attempted to go back and do research about the details and specifics of past events that I have forgotten. I do not want truth to get lost in trivial details, and I will leave all the fact-finding and documentation to any accuracy hounds that may wish to do their own snooping and fact-finding after my death. I have often refrained from giving the full names of some of the people in my life to protect their privacy and sensitivity, in case some of the details are not always complimentary.

Moreover, this work is, by definition, incomplete, since I cannot return from the Great Beyond to write of the denouement. The Lord's kindness and loving Providence have been evident throughout my life, and I trust that He will see me to a safe landing in my heavenly home and destination.

As far as acknowledgements are concerned, I gratefully acknowledge the prayers of Mary, Joseph, all the saints, and my family and friends on both sides of the great divide, as well as the loving care of my guardian angel. I also gratefully acknowledge the assistance of the folks at Author House with this book and my previous works. The remainder of this work, in telling my story and the influence on my life of many important people, is an acknowledgement in itself. I gratefully acknowledge the help of Debbie Abernethy in formatting the manuscript of the previous edition, as well as Eileen Badie and Judy Gechter in reading it for content and possible errors.

Incidentally, a Chinese friend told me that 1951, the year of my birth, was a year of the rabbit. I have relied on this version of the calendar, although I understand that other cultures use different years for the rabbit sign. As I approached my sixtieth birthday in November of 2011, another rabbit year, it seemed like a good time to tell this story.

In going back in memory and trying to reconstruct the details of my life, I am struck by how ordinary and commonplace much of it is. I also sometimes digress from the narrative to draw conclusions and state lessons that I have learned from my experiences. I am appalled at how long it has taken me to grasp some very fundamental things, and I am eternally grateful to the patience of God in giving me time to work out these learning experiences. The saying, "Too soon old, too late smart," comes to mind here. I hope that, by telling my story, other readers may be helped to speed up the process and to learn some of these things without going through the dear school taught by experience.

Looking at the strange weather and disquieting human behavior of our times, some people say that Jesus may be coming back in our lifetime. Two thousand years ago, folks also thought that He was coming back in their generation, and He did not. I therefore am cautious about assuming that His coming is imminent, but we still need to be ready. It is just possible that individually and collectively we have less time than we would like.

Linda Anne Monica Schneider
July 4, 2011

# ABOUT THE REVISED EDITION

Linda Anne Monica Schneider

October 16, 2021
Revisited and augmented, March 19, 2024

*I*n 2016, I brought out a fifth collection of short stories, *Flights of Fancy and Food for Thought, with Author House,* as well as a delayed revision to Heir to the Dragon King. I completed and published the sixth collection of short stories in 2021, T*ying up Loose Ends, still with Author House.* In the meantime, it occurs to me that, of necessity, my autobiography was unfinished. However, it might be useful to my readers or other interested persons to know as much of the outcome as possible.

Time has a way of inexorably marching along. I don't want to wait too long to start putting the second part together or revising and correcting inaccuracies in the original book or this update that came to my attention. For that reason, I revised the 2011 version and have augmented the one that was published in 2022. I consider myself fortunate in remembering so much of the first seventy-two years of my life, and the review after that length of time conveyed a certain perspective. However, I do not want to assume that thirty or forty years from now, I will be able to assemble the necessary information and details. I therefore decided that this revised edition needed to be completed. Otherwise, the accuracy hounds will have to accumulate whatever information or conclusions they wish after I have departed for the great beyond. If we are fortunate enough that Jesus comes back before then, it may all be moot in the end. With the upheaval in the previous presidency of Donald J. Trump and the discord and animosity that now prevail, as well as the travail, tragedy, and the turmoil of the COVID19 pandemic, we still are in very unsettled times. It would seem that the remarks I made in my previous introduction are still valid. However, as President Joe Biden said in memorializing the victims of this pandemic, in order to heal, we have to remember!

In reviewing this latest updated edition of my autobiography, I suggest that my readers pay attention to the footnotes. In addition to giving references for some of the comments I made, I also used them to augment my thoughts and include additional information that readers might find helpful, explanatory, or interesting. I put these nuggets in footnotes to avoid distracting from the flow of the overall narrative.

I gratefully acknowledge the help of Ruben and Judy Gechter in reviewing this manuscript for obvious errors and formatting issues and inserting pictures where they belong, including new ones. Debbie Abernethy also was very helpful in catching spacing errors and formatting issues, as well as describing the inserted picture of my friends and me at lunch in Thunder Grill. I also appreciate the help of Marty Suydam with technical, computer, and formatting matters.

I also want to thank my family and friends for their constructive criticisms of the earlier version of this autobiography and for bringing some inaccuracies and omissions to my attention. I hope that the present book will be better as a result. As I said in the earlier introduction, any errors that remain now are all mine!

# CONTENTS

# ORIGINS OF THE BEGINNING

*I*n a TV adaptation of the story of Heidi that Papa recorded on reel-to-reel tape years ago, Peter and Heidi are climbing up to Echo Ridge. Precocious Heidi keeps wanting to find "the beginning," which means going higher and higher. She keeps asking, "Where is the beginning of the beginning?" until Peter irritably tells her, "Oh, shut up with your beginnings!"

In my case, as with all of life, the ultimate beginning is God. I don't presume to go back that far, but I think it is relevant to sketch the background of the two sides of the family, to lay the groundwork for the individuals who met, fell in love, married, and, by the grace of God, generated me, my brothers, and my sister. These details will also provide background for events and people discussed later in the book. Readers who may not want to follow these details may try skipping to the next chapter, *The Beginning*, and referring back to this chapter if later references seem not to make sense. Others may find it interesting to see how events transpired that later resulted in the family that I knew.

My father was Carl Frederick Schneider, (December 21, 1909—July 17, 1982). He was born, I believe, in Pittsburgh, PA. His father, John Schneider, emigrated from Germany when he was around sixteen.

My paternal grandfather's mother, Margaretha, married twice; the first marriage was to a Schneider, and the offspring from this marriage were my grandfather and, I think, another brother, named Carl. Among the children of this uncle were young Carl, (known as Carli), Maria, and Amanda. He also had a daughter, Elfriede, to be discussed later in connection with a trip to Germany. Margaretha's second marriage was to a man surnamed Guileman, and he had two daughters. One of them was the mother of Hilde (who died young) and Dr. Walter Sterzinger, whom we visited on the German trip. The other daughter was the mother of other relatives to be discussed later.

Upon arriving in America, at some point my grandfather, John Schneider, went to work for Westinghouse Corporation, where he may have worked for as long as seventy-five years. He married three times. The first wife, Tilly Helscher (spelled phonetically) was the mother of Robert and Hilda Schneider. Robert married a lady named Agnes, who happened not to be a Catholic (which I think may have caused some familial estrangement.) In any event, I lost track of that side of the family altogether, and I don't know anything about them. Hilda eventually went into the convent of the Sisters of Mercy, and she became Sister Loreto. Because she was my aunt, though, I often called her Sister Hilda.

After Tilly died, John Schneider, my grandfather, married Annie (or is it Anna?) Miller, my paternal grandmother. She was the mother of my Aunt Margaret Schneider Dean, (wife of Uncle Jimmy Dean), my father, and Aunt Maria Schneider, whose husband was Raymond Nolan. The Deans had four children, young Jim, Alice Ann (who entered the Sisters of Divine Providence and became Sister Margaret James) [2]Gretchen, and Tim. Jim married Connie Schneider (no relationship known,) and had two children, Jeff and Molly. Jeff has Down's syndrome and lives in a group home near his father. Molly is married to Steve Bitner with two young boys, and they live near Richmond, VA. Gretchen married Ted Johnson and had two children, Erich and Sara. Molly, Erich, and Sara all have children who are fast growing up and whom I have not met yet. Ted has died. Gretchen lives in Plano, TX, and her daughter, Sara, lives nearby with her three children. Erich is in Oklahoma, and he and his wife, Kit, teach at a law school. They have two boys. Tim married Doreen, with no children.

Maria and Ray had two sons, Paul, (who married Pat, had three daughters, Dianna and twins Lisa and Lyn, and is now a grandfather living in Indiana). Paul's younger brother is Terry Nolan; as far as I know, he isn't married.

Anna Miller Schneider, Papa's mother, was one of other brothers and sisters, but I know little about this side of the family. The only vague reference that I remember is that one of the Millers on Papa's mother's side had twins, because Papa remembered his mother helping to take care of the twins. That fact has some relevance, inasmuch as I understand that the tendency to twin can be inherited, and I was one of triplets. One of my paternal grandmother's sisters-in-law, whom we called Aunt Naim, was the mother of my father's cousin, Al Miller. He married a German lady, Sigrid, from West Berlin, and lived in Vienna, VA, with his wife and four children. As described more in other chapters, they came to visit us in Arlington from time to time. Another cousin on Papa's mother's side of the family was a lady, Lucille Miller, who lived in Washington, DC and whom we visited sometimes.

After Anna died when Papa was a teenager, John Schneider married a third time. This lady we called Gross-Mum, the German word for Grandmother, though she wasn't my grandmother as such. She survived her husband, and I met her on a couple of occasions during family visits to Pittsburgh.

---

[2]  One of James Dean Sr.'s sisters was also a member of this order. I think that she went by the name of Sister de La Salle. I met her on a few occasions during family visits to Pittsburgh.

I never met or knew either of my paternal grandparents. When John died, many of the possessions of my grandmother were passed down to Gross-Mum, which caused a lot of resentment on the part of my aunts, but Papa stayed on speaking terms with that side of the family, even after Gross-Mum died. Gross-Mum had a daughter from a previous marriage, Emma, who married a man named Paul Stasiak. They continued to live on in the family house on Campania Avenue in Pittsburgh for a number of years. I have lost track of them, but one or both of them may have died. They had no children.

My father was in the Coast guard as a photographer during World War II. He sailed back and forth across the Pacific on a troop transport. As far as I knew, he didn't see direct action, although there was danger (necessitating drills) of Japanese attacks. He took pictures of much of what happened on shipboard, many of which found their way into a family album. Among the pictures were photos of Neptune rites of initiation on crossing the equator, touching photos of Polish refugee children, and other events, which I do not now recollect. While he was on the ship, he took pictures of a shipmate's watercolor paintings. In return, the shipmate did a watercolor portrait of my father. Papa didn't know what happened to the portrait, but many years later, after Mama had died, we got a letter from the Coast Guard in the mail, asking if he was the right Schneider, and did we want the picture? The answer was yes on both counts, so they mailed the portrait to us, and it now hangs over the mantle above the fireplace in the living room.

My father was granted compassionate leave to return to Pittsburgh at some time during the 40's for the death of his father, I think between 1943 and 45.

My paternal grandmother had a reputation for being warm and outgoing, with a happy disposition and a good sense of humor. Papa said that one of her favorite hymns was "Amazing Grace."

On the other hand, John Schneider had the reputation for being a stickler for getting things just so and being good at electrical projects. He wired an old oil lamp to make it electric, and it is still in my living room. Actually, I'm not sure whether Grandfather John or Papa did the wiring: like father, like son in some ways. The last time I visited Pittsburgh with Papa quite a number of years ago, my grandfather's old chicken coop (built on a stone foundation) was still being used as a tool shed in the old homestead.

Until later years, Papa didn't talk much about the details of his growing up, except that he slept in a room near the top of the tall house. Also, there was a statue of a knight in full armor, which his father had also modified into a lamp, at the bottom of the main staircase on a newel post. Papa said that they called it "The Man." The last person into the house at night turned off The Man. It was still there on the last occasion that I visited the house many, many years ago. Papa said that for years there was a sign in German above the mantel that said, "In diesem Hause wird Deutsch gesprochen." Or something to that effect, until it was deemed unpatriotic to have that sign up during the two World Wars. My paternal grandfather also had the reputation for being stubborn and "One way as hell," as my father might have put it. He may have had trouble with his feet, because Papa would talk about how Aunt Maria and I inherited "the Schneider feet." My grandfather had a tendency to not walk a straight line when he was walking along the street, and I unfortunately have definitely inherited this trait. Only my guide dogs keep me going straight!

Papa did recount one story reinforcing the fact that my paternal grandfather could be stern and difficult. The family house was on a hill; the house, too, was reached from the street by a great number of steps. For obvious reasons, such a location would accentuate the force of the wind on a windy day. Papa said that one morning the folks from Sears or Spiegel or where it was bought delivered the phonograph. When they brought it into the house, the wind blew the glass-pained front door open and it banged against the wall of the house, breaking the glass. Papa said that his mother frantically called friends and relatives and desperately worked at finding a way to get the glass repaired in the door before her husband came home from work.

After World War II, Papa ended up in Washington, D.C., where he met my mother. He worked for over 30 years as a government employee. He retired from his job at the Pentagon as a photographer with the Army Signal Corp before I entered Law school in the fall of 1974.

My maternal Grandmother, Eva Amelia Novelli Calabro

(December 5, 1889—April 23, 1988) whom I shall generally call Nana, was born in Vermont, although I'm not sure whether it was in Barre, as it may have been somewhere else. For years, Nana thought that her birthday was December 6, which happens to be the Feast of St. Nicholas, bishop of Myra, AKA Santa Claus, but when we needed to get her birth certificate for some legal reason or other, it turns out there is a discrepancy in the records between December 5 and 6, and she probably was born on December 5. She liked to say that, when she was born, there was six feet of snow on the ground.

Her father, Samuel Giovanni Baptiste Novelli, was a sculptor and a statue cutter. He immigrated to America from Italy. The story goes that he was born in Carrara, the source of good marble. I know very little about his background, except that his mother may have been a cook, and his parents supposedly had enough money to send him to study at Oxford.

One of the few works that can specifically be attributed to him is a statue of Robert Burns sculpted in granite that still stands in Barre, Vermont, on top of a pedestal decorated with sculpted scenes from the poet's poems. My great-grandfather's friend, Elias Corti, did the sculpting on the panels. According to Nana, these two were as close as brothers. They started out working in somebody else's stone shed, but eventually they went into business together for themselves.

From the stories that Nana told, it seems that Sam Novelli did well enough when the children were growing up. Because of the cheap hydroelectric power available from the Manusky River, electricity was available in Vermont long before it came to other places. The house had electricity, telephone service, and possibly indoor plumbing, although Nana did mention some large outhouses with multiple seats. As she put it, up in Barre, every shack by the railroad track had electricity. The house also had a kitchen in the basement, where the children often ate, and a dining room on the first floor. Food was brought up from the kitchen on a dumb waiter. It sounded as though the house had at least two upper floors above the main floor, and it seemed that the house had a room at the top that was used as an infirmary if somebody got sick. Nana spent time in that room as a child, because she survived bouts of scarlet fever and diphtheria. A nurse, whom the family affectionately called Grandma Connelly, nursed her through her illnesses. Nana said that, when she was very sick with the scarlet fever, she dreamt that the Blessed Virgin, Mary, appeared to her and told her to run. Nana said that she woke up and tried to get out of bed to run.

"Where do you think you're going?" Grandma Connelly asked.

"The Blessed Virgin told me to run," Nana said.

"Well, run in bed," the nurse answered.

Nana always ended this story by saying that, "I've been running ever since."

Nana said that she only survived the diphtheria, because the anti-toxin arrived on time by train. She said that she remembers getting four injections, two on each side of her backside. The family friend who saw her through these crises was the doctor, Jack Jackson. Nana called him "Uncle Jack" and his wife "Aunt Martha." Nana quoted Dr. Jackson as saying that he walked with a spade on his shoulder but never said die. Nana said that Aunt Martha played the harp in the Protestant church that she and her husband attended.

Nana's stories were possibly part family legend, and I have not attempted to document them, but it seems that part of Vermont in those days was rather a turbulent, violent place. Sam Novelli and Elias Corti were, she said, good friends and in business together, but they didn't do all the work themselves, and they employed other artisans to work with them on projects and monuments. Corti supposedly went into a gathering in a hotel in Montpelier looking for a stone carver to do some detailed work. Nana said that the Bolsheviks or some group were having a meeting, and some kind of dispute was in progress. Poor Mr. Corti walked into the middle of it, and he was shot and fatally wounded in the abdomen by a bullet intended for somebody else.

Nana was the oldest surviving child of seven. Supposedly, there was a firstborn baby boy who died. The story goes that, when the second and now surviving oldest child turned out to be a girl, Sam Novelli got drunk that night. He was so disappointed at not having an oldest child that was a son, to carry on after him. Nana said that, before he died, he told her that she was worth many sons and apologized to her for his attitude.

Nana supposedly was, as she put it, a beautiful, blond longhaired tomboy with a fair complexion and steely grey eyes, who liked to climb up into the apple tree and sit and look around. (By the time I knew her as Nana, she had snow-white hair, which she wore short.) Because of eye problems caused by a childhood bout with measles, she wore thick glasses all of her life. As a young girl, she also had a pony, named Frankie, that she rode bareback (with just a quilted pad in lieu of saddle that her mother made for her). As a girl, and into her nineties, she also had a good pitching arm. When I was growing up, Nana made lunch for me to take to school and another sandwich for Papa to take to work. Sometimes, Papa would forget his lunch. Nana would open the cellar door and call, "Carl, catch!" I would hear the package make contact with his hand. She would shut the door and assert confidently, "I'm still a good pitcher!" She only lost that ability after her breast on that side was removed to combat cancer. [3]

The other six Novelli children were Almo, (who eventually settled in Massachusetts and married and had one surviving daughter, Mildred; the little son died partly in grief after his father.) Gemma Olga, (known to the family as Janie) Mary Edna (Called Marie or Riri to distinguish her from her mother, Mary), Gino, Sam Jr., and William, known as Billie. Aunties Janie and Riri never married, but they were my favorite aunties, because of their patience and sympathy for a little girl who was often bored among adults with all their adult talk. Gino went to sea and joined the Navy, and he married a lady from Wales named Elsie. He had two daughters, Margaret (who died of breast cancer) and Jeanne, with whom I corresponded until her death after I retired in 2014. Gino retired from the Navy as a Commander, and he at one time raised apples in California. They say that he and Aunt Elsie came to visit when I was a baby, but I don't remember that. I do remember that he sent us big wooden crates filled with his apples. When the crate came, it sat in the living room, waiting

---

[3] 3 Nana told other stories about throwing baseballs as a child, and being cheered on and asked, "Blondie, do you want to be on the team?" I don't know which arm she used, and I forgot which breast was removed.

for Papa to come home and open it with his tools. We would all walk around, sniffing the delicious aroma of the apples, with our tongues hanging out! We couldn't wait for Papa to get home! We ate some of the apples, and Nana made pies with the rest. Gino's daughter, Jeanne, and one of her two sons, Ken, lived in Redwood Valley, CA. Jeanne had to go into a nursing facility before her death. I don't know what happened to Ken after she died. Her other son, Clifford, and his wife, Toni, lived in CA, too, and they had three grown children, but I don't have any idea where they are now.

Sam Jr. went to sea, also, and he joined the merchant marine. He never married, like his two maiden sisters. In their later years, all three lived in a tiny little flat, crammed with mementos and old furniture, in Quincy, MA.

William, known as Uncle Bill or Billie, married Katherine, and had a daughter, Eleanor, who has Denise and other offspring and descendants. This part of the family probably is still in Massachusetts, though I have lost track of them.

Sam Sr.'s wife, the mother of the seven, was a high-strung, talented dressmaker named Mary Josephine Novelli. Nana's story was that her mother eloped with her father and had a civil marriage service, before ultimately getting married in ST Monica's church.

Nana's mother seems to have augmented the family income by doing dressmaking work. Nana said that she could look at dresses in fashion magazines and then copy a particular dress for somebody, without a pattern. It sounded a little fantastic to me, until my long-time housekeeper, Leleet (AKA Patsy) Edwards, exhibited similar talents and abilities.

Nana told other stories about growing up in Barre. She said that one of her father's friends, who happened to be a sea captain, brought the family three pets. They were a German shepherd dog, named Leelo, a big, fluffy Persian cat, probably called Kitty, and a canary. Nana said that Leelo and Kitty didn't know each other during the daytime, but they slept on the same rug at night. Nana said that on one occasion, Leelo was out walking and cut his foot. A man found him, and saw the address on the collar. He hired the express wagon and put the dog in it and sent him home, after bandaging up the paw with one of his handkerchiefs. When her father found the handkerchief with the monogram and initials on it, he recognized them as belonging to one of his friends from his Oxford student days. It was the first he knew that this friend was also in Barre. Another one of her father's other friends, who kept a butcher shop, borrowed Leelo for a few nights to help to catch a burglar who was breaking into the store. In return, he sent choice cuts of meat and steaks over for

Leelo. Leelo often sat behind Nana's chair, so that she could give him what she didn't want off her plate. Even in those days, Nana apparently was a fussy eater.

Kitty looked huge with his fluffy fur, but Nana said that he was very skinny when he had a bath and his fur was flattened out. He was very territorial, and he would beat up other cats that came into his yard. Nana liked to play with Kitty with a string. As she put it, sometimes his paws were quicker than her eyes, and he would scratch her. If her mother found out, she would give both of them a swat. The cat would turn around and look at Nana and say, "Meow!" as though to protest that it was Nana's fault. Then he would run upstairs and go to sleep on the window seat in her parents' room, while Nana's mother took her off to put salt water on the scratches, despite her cries and protests.

The canary apparently was allowed to fly around the kitchen sometimes. Nana said that one day, they were trying to get the bird back into the cage, and one of her brothers accidentally hit the bird with a broom and killed it.

I will discuss one particularly tragic part of family history here, because it left its emotional scars on Nana and the rest of her siblings, and it probably accounts for some of the emotional upsets and hard feelings over the years. As Nana put it later, two good-looking people ought not to get married, because they could end up being jealous of each other. Mary Novelli was apparently very insecure of her husband, and there may have been other things going on. Nana described her as high-strung and emotional, with a temper. For example, according to Nana, her mother used the back of her wooden hairbrush to spank her as a child. Nana said that her mother died when Nana was a teenager, that she was thrown from a horse and died instantly. Nana said that she didn't go to the funeral, because she was emotionally too upset. Even as a child, I thought that was strange. Nana did say that, before she "died", her mother and father had a stupid argument about something, possibly a coalscuttle! She used that story as an illustration that it didn't pay to get upset over minor things. Whatever the dispute was about, it probably was a front for something much more serious. That story, it turns out, was a big cover, meant to save face and maybe shield Nana from the emotional impact of the truth.

What probably happened is that her mother shot off a gun, by accident or design, and the bullet hit her in the head. No, she didn't die, which might have been a mercy. Instead, she languished in a nursing home in Massachusetts for years with probable severe brain injury. I didn't discover this outcome until years later, when Jeanne told me of her father, Gino, going to visit his mother (and Jeanne's grandmother) in the nursing home. Apparently, Mary Novelli was kind of frozen in time, and she asked about her children as babies.

Subsequently, as Nana reluctantly succumbed to senility and its relaxing of inhibitions, she made the remark, "They say that my father shot my mother. He did not! She shot herself."

By this time, I knew the truth of this reference, but I decided not to stir up something painful, and just said, "I know." And then I tried to change the subject.

After his wife's incapacity, which the family treated as a death, Sam Novelli apparently tried to carry on for a few years, with the help of Tilly, the Swedish descent family housekeeper. At some point, though, Billie, who was a baby, was entrusted to the care of the wife's maternal aunt in Massachusetts, known as Old Aunty to the family. However, Sam Novelli paid dearly for his sculpting work. He apparently became the victim of silicosis, a disease caused by granite dust in the lungs. Nana said that, at the dedication of the statue of his dead partner, Corti, on the man's grave in the cemetery, Sam fainted. According to Nana, that statue was the last thing that her father did. [4]

After Elias Corti died, his widow farmed out her husband's share of the stone shed that he and Sam had together to a man named Calcatni. Calcatni apparently didn't feel comfortable with his position, especially after Sam Novelli went to Italy to seek a remedy for his health and maybe to see his father. When Sam died, possibly from a heart attack, listening to a recording of Ave Maria on a phonograph, they found a letter from Calcatni on his person. The letter supposedly said that Sam should either come back to Vermont or buy him out, as he couldn't continue in Sam Novelli's absence without full authority to make decisions. I think that Nana said that she was sixteen years old when her father died. That would put his death around 1905 or 1906.

According to Nana and Mama, after Nana's father died, the states of Vermont and Massachusetts assumed that the seven children would be best cared for by the mother's relatives, a maternal aunt, to whom Billie had already been entrusted. Old Aunty, however, apparently took the money that was supposed to be for the Novelli children and spent it in part for ne'er-do-well nephew (Mary's brother,) Peter and his family, neglecting the Novelli children. This filled Nana with frustrated rage; she even wrote to her grandfather in Italy, but apparently to no avail. Nana said that she could have stayed in Vermont, with Uncle Jack and Aunt Martha, the family physician and wife, who offered her to stay

---

[4] Nana claimed that her father sculpted this beautifully detailed statue/monument on the grave of Mr. Corti. It depicts the man sitting, with the tools of his trade around him. When Papa and I visited Vermont in the summer of 1975, we met two surviving daughters of Eli Corti. One of them, Lelia Commolli claimed vehemently that her mother's brothers did the statue. Nana was incensed when I told her what she said. We finally managed to calm her down by pointing out that Ms. Commolli only knew what her mother told her, and maybe the mother's brothers worked on the lower parts of the monument, where the implements are.

with them (not relatives, but dear friends.) She chose, instead, to accompany the younger ones to Massachusetts and their vicissitudes with Old Aunty. Eventually, when Old Aunty died, she left half of what remained to Billie, and the other half to one of Peter's daughters. Although Grandpa and a supposed Aunt Mary, not a real aunt but a family friend, tried to hire a lawyer and seek to get some money back, they were unsuccessful. No other success could be obtained in getting any other restitution for the Novellis. Nana was grateful that, at least, Billie got something out of the old lady's estate.

Meanwhile, when things got too difficult at Old Aunty's, Nana moved in with Aunt Emily and helped look after her children. Nana's mother's sister, Emily Josephine Abbiatti, was the wife of Jeremiah Abbiatti, whom Nana called Uncle Jerry. They had four daughters, with Biblical names: Tecla, Naomi, Ruth, and Edna. As grown women, Ruth and Edna became schoolteachers, and, I think, school principals, before they retired. None of them ever married; after their father died, they took care of their mother until she died as a very old lady in her nineties, and then they spent the rest of their lives looking after each other. Edna was the last to leave this life. I very much enjoyed my visits with them in Quincy as a child and teenager.[5]

The unstable situation of the Novelli family probably prompted the younger boys to go to sea. The younger sisters, as I said, never married. After Nana married Grandpa, they moved in with her for a while. Eventually, Janie went to work as a telephone operator, and to her dying day, she had a plain, clear voice, wonderful to hear on the telephone. According to Nana, she had brown hair before it turned gray in old age and big, soulful brown eyes. Nana always said, petulantly, "My sister, Gemma, could make my brothers do anything she wanted, with those big brown eyes of hers, like a cow!"

Marie eventually went to work for a long career as a teller in the South Shore National Bank. Her big story of those years was surviving a bank robbery. Poor Aunt Riri had to go into court to identify one of the robbers. She told us that she said that she wasn't sure. He was a young man, and she felt sorry; she also had in the back of her mind that this fellow was going to get out of jail at some point, and she didn't want him coming after her!

Only young Bill was relatively unscarred by the family tragedy, because Old Aunty was the only mother he ever really remembered, and he wasn't told that she was not his mother until he received

---

[5] I discuss the Abbiattis in later chapters. I am grateful that I happened to call Edna about two weeks to ten days before she died. We had a most pleasant conversation, as always. After her death, someone who answered the telephone, possibly the lady who had looked after her, told me that Edna had gone to the doctor's that morning, came home and had lunch, and then went to her eternal sleep in her favorite easy chair! We all should be so lucky.

First Communion. He became a fireman in Quincy Massachusetts, and he retired from the Fire Department after a long and probably distinguished career.

The only inkling I had of the plight of the great grandmother was that when I was a child Nana went back to Massachusetts for a funeral of a supposed family friend, called Aunt Mary. This "Aunt Mary" supposedly wasn't a real aunt, according to Mama, but had tried to help get restitution for the seven children. That may have been the case, but from the benefit of hindsight, I wonder. As I understand that my poor stricken great-grandmother didn't die until the early sixties or late '50's, this trip to Massachusetts may have been occasioned by Nana's mother's death. It was the first time that Nana had been away from me, and I missed her terribly, so the event is fixed in my mind. The other reason that I remember it so well is that Mama had to cook, instead of Nana, who was an excellent cook. I'm sure that, given enough time, Mama would have become a good cook, but one night she tried to fry chicken, and the crusty skin and meat fried on the bone and were inedible. I told Nana the story when she called from MA, remarking that Papa was "as hungry as a bear."

I also eventually came to understand that Nana harbored a deep anger at her parents, although I didn't know why as a child. She said that, as the oldest child, she was often expected to take care of or look after the younger siblings. She said that she once asserted to her father that, when she had children, she would take care of them herself. Even though I was an only child, I could understand how she might have felt some resentment, but it didn't seem to provide an adequate explanation. Another manifestation of her resentful feelings toward her parents was that, supposedly, she had the oil painting portraits that were done of them. She said that, after her husband died, she took the paintings down to the basement of the Quincy house and burned them up in the coke-burning furnace! My Uncle Joe, Mama's younger brother, confirmed this statement. After I found out what happened to her mother, I had a much better understanding of the root of her feelings.

Nana eventually met and married Anthony Thomas Calabro, (December 21, 1883-August 26, 1943) most often called Tom. She said that they met at a dance, where both of them were sitting down, because neither of them could dance. Nana said that she never did well at dancing, because she was "stiff as a board." Tom Calabro was one of many children of a baker and a midwife. The story goes that they lived in Detroit, Michigan. When the great-grandfather's horse fell on him and broke his legs in four places, he was laid up for a while, and his wife tried to run the bakery, with the help of an associate. It seems that the associate had his hand in the till, and the wife was too trusting of customers with bad credit, and the business failed. Eventually, after traveling around the world, (children were born in different places, and my grandfather was born in Italy,)[6] and the failure of the bakery, they settled in Massachusetts, in the vicinity of Quincy. Apparently, when he had too much to drink, Tom's father didn't scruple to remind his wife that he lost his business because of her. Many of his children, including my grandfather, Tom, didn't drink because they saw the effects of alcohol in how their father treated their mother.

Tom's mother apparently was very good at patiently helping mothers and delivering babies. Her son, Tom, feared that she would get into trouble with a difficult birth, on account of not being licensed as a midwife in Massachusetts, but she never refused anyone who needed her, including people who couldn't pay her. Mama said that even the doctors liked having her participate in deliveries with them. She helped to deliver my mother, Estelle Marie Calabro Schneider, (November 12, 1910—September 3, 1965), who was born in the home at 15 Clarendon Street, Quincy, MA. Nana said her mother-in-law would "plaster you with Vaseline" and then wait until the head emerged, then take it with her hands with their long, skinny fingers, and then she would deliver the baby. The story goes that my mother was about five pounds. When she was born, she was very white and pale, and didn't seem to be moving or breathing. According to Nana, they tried everything, including putting her in cold water. Eventually, said Nana, "Her grandmother said that she was moving, and spanked her on the backside, making her cry and breathe." My mother supposedly was tiny and delicate growing up, but very precocious and intelligent.

Nana's second child, Joseph Stephen (Uncle Joe) was born five years later, I think in a hospital. Nana said that she wouldn't go through childbirth without her mother-in-law's help again. [7] My great-grandmother, the midwife, was apparently very good at what she did.

As for my great-grandfather, Mama said that he was a quiet man, but the kind of quiet that you still felt good having him around. The story went that when he went to bed, he disdained normal nightclothes and wrapped himself in light cotton blankets, like an Indian chief. Nana's mother-in-law was aware of the problem that his recriminations caused for their children. Mama told me that her grandmother's prayer was that her husband would go home to the Lord first, because she

---

[6] One complication from being born abroad was that Grandpa had to be naturalized as a U.S. citizen, which he was when my mother was little, possibly in 1919.

[7] Nana's husband may have had brown or dark hair. When friends teased him about having two blond children, Nana quoted him as saying, "The lambs born in the fold belong to the shepherd!" I can imagine St. Joseph saying something similar if asked why his wife, Mary, gave birth to Jesus early after they were married.

knew that her daughters would look after her, but she feared that they might neglect her husband if he were a widower. Her prayer, I'm told, was answered.

Grandpa had a number of brothers and sisters. I'll say a little more about them later, but for purposes of this situation, it suffices to point out that Grandpa and his brothers took turns sitting with their father during his final illness, to relieve their mother. On one occasion, Grandpa went with Nana to visit the old man. He supposedly whispered to her, "Blondie, I left you a million dollars!"

Nana told Grandpa on the way home, and he supposedly laughed and said, "Well, Mal, (the nickname the family used for Nana), "if that's true, you had better take the next train for parts unknown!"

The implication was that all the rest of the relatives would want their part of the million. Nana would conclude that story by saying, "I'm still waiting for those million dollars!" (Of course, her father-in-law didn't have the million dollars.) The real point of that story was that he valued Nana enough to leave her the million if he had it!

Aside from the family strife described above, moving from Vermont to Massachusetts was a bit of a shock for Nana in other ways. Before she met Grandpa, she apparently tried at one time to study nursing, but she didn't make it through the program, because some aspects of it were too uncomfortable for her. In those days, for one thing, nursing apparently involved much more physical hard work than it does today, including scrubbing out bedpans. After failing at nursing school, Nana went to work as a file clerk, for a dollar a day. She stopped working after she married Grandpa. Grandpa worked for many years as a leather cutter in a shoe factory.

I'm sure that Nana loved Grandpa, but she sometimes said that they were not well suited, because, as she put it, they came from different sides of the tracks. Nana wouldn't let Grandpa give her a diamond ring, saying that "we could put that money down on a house," which they did. Grandpa did buy her a gold pendant watch, which went to Uncle Joe's side of the family, as discussed later. He did give her a thick gold wedding band, and he apparently wore a wedding ring himself. I think that my cousin, Tom, got his watch and wedding ring, but I got Nana's wedding ring and the porcelain Bavarian cookie jar that Grandpa bought for Nana after they were married. I also have the little opal ring that one of Nana's friends gave her. I guess that her friend thought that she ought to have something, instead of the diamond.

Unlike Vermont, Massachusetts, or that section near Quincy, didn't have the benefit of swift waters. The house that my grandparents bought together had gaslight and appliances for years, before electricity finally came to their street.

Ironically, like my paternal grandfather, John Schneider, Grandpa also had a reputation for doing things just so, and wanting everything very neat and tidy. Nana said that, if he didn't like how the house was kept, he would put on an apron and start doing things the way he wanted them done. She said that made her feel worse than if he had complained about it. He, like my paternal grandfather, raised chickens during World War I. He had four different kinds, with four roosters and separate runs for the different groups; he had white Leghorns, black Ancones, Rhode Island Reds, and Plymouth rocks, which supposedly were grey and pretty.

Nana apparently inherited her mother's temper. She said that, sometimes, she would say that she should have gone into a convent instead of marrying. Grandpa's answer supposedly was that she would have taken the roof off the convent sometime or other when she got angry, and she would not have been a suitable nun. Nana admitted that, one time, she had a bad day, and the kids were bothering her, and her husband did or said something that was the last straw on the proverbial camel. Well, Nana tore the shirt off his back. She said he just stood there looking at her, with this funny expression on his face, like he couldn't believe it. By way of apology, the next evening, she put the children in the dining room near the window and told them to stay there until she came back. She went to meet her husband at the train station, when he was coming home from work on the train, with his hat, raincoat, umbrella, and galoshes, because it was pouring down rain and he would have been soaked walking home. According to Mama, her father didn't stay angry. When things got tense, he would put on his hat and go for a walk. He often would return later with ice cream or some other treat. From what I know, neither of the two sets of grandparents had cars while the children were growing up. I seem to recall Papa mentioning an old Edsel, but I don't know whose car it was or when they bought it.

Mama told me many stories of growing up in Quincy with her younger brother. They attended Catholic school, but it was a mile away, and they had to walk it four ways each day. They came home for an hour to have lunch. Uncle Joe had braces and problems with his teeth, and going through the braces and dental procedures was a painful ordeal. I grew up with the stories of the three family dogs.

Jackie, the collie, was protective of Mama as a baby; whichever parent put her in the carriage had to take her out. He was a good watchdog but also a thief who stole bones and other items. He got into other mischief, like going into an uncle's house and getting into his bed all wet. My poetic bent surfaced early in response to the stories about Jackie. There was a childhood poem about a rascal, named Tabby, who was a watchman and a thief. I took that poem and made up the following about Jackie.

Jackie was a watchdog.
Jackie was a thief.
Jackie came to my house
And stole a piece of beef.

I went to Jackie's house,
But Jackie wasn't there.
Jackie came to my house
And unraveled my dolly's hair!

I went to Jackie's house,
But Jackie was out with Skipper!
Jackie came to my house
And chewed my bedroom slipper.

I went to Jackie's house.
Jackie was out alone.
Jackie came to my house
And stole a soup bone!

I came home to my house,
Found him curled up in my chair!
He looked so cute
I gave him a hug,
And told him I didn't care!

Brownie, the water Spaniel, went romping with the children and helped them to find their way home when they got lost picking blueberries in the nearby woods. Brownie and his father, Pal, (owned by Uncle Bill) liked to tag along with a mailman on his routes.

The family's last dog, Teddy, was Uncle Joe's dog as a young man, a coal black dog with a long tail and floppy ears. My uncle helped a woman by repairing her car; she couldn't afford to pay him, but she offered him the pick of a litter of puppies. Mama thought that they were Doberman Pincher puppies, purebred, and Teddy was the only black one in the litter. I've been told that this breed rarely has all-black dogs, so maybe they were mixed with some other breed. Unfortunately, when he was almost a year old, a woman driving to church killed this promising canine. He had gone out the front door, instead of being in the fenced backyard; Uncle Joe called him, and he tried to return, but, as Mama described it, the sun was in his eyes and he didn't see the car. She said that nobody ate dinner that night. Her father said firmly that they wouldn't have any more dogs.

All Nana's stories emphasized the intelligence of these dogs, and the old childhood one, Leelo. She also told a story about a dog that cut his paw while out walking. He could have gone home, she said, but instead he walked through the doors into the next-door hospital emergency room, so they could bandage him up, which they did. As Nana put it, maybe he saw other people go into that door who were limping or on stretchers, and then they came out again.

I also heard stories of the intelligent, bratty parrot, Polly, that the family had for a few years, when Mama was little. They eventually had to find a new home for him, after he developed a swearing habit and exhibited strong jealousy of my Uncle Joe, as the new baby in the family. According to Nana, they gave him to a schoolteacher and husband, who didn't have any children.

I also heard of Nana stitching up the head of a little chicken that the others almost pecked to death. He became a pet, named Petey, and grew into a big rooster, but with a small comb on account of the scarring on his head.

Nana told a funny story about her peach trees and grape arbor. She had grape vines in the yard growing on an arbor, with a picnic table underneath. She also had planted three peach pits, which grew into seedlings. They grew into at least two big trees that bore humongous peaches. The peaches on one tree were so numerous, heavy, and big that during one year the poor overloaded tree split! Nana said that Grandpa and the neighbors had to use old shoes, ropes and anything else they could find to hold the tree together long enough to harvest the peaches. Then the tree had to be cut down.

Nana said that Grandpa would put peaches and grapes down at the end of the driveway, so that children and others could help themselves. However, some neighborhood children and boys still came into the yard to pick peaches. A little after her husband died, Nana had gone to her parish church, St. John's, for a potluck supper. As usual, she brought one of her pies, which disappeared almost immediately. A priest came over and caught her by the wrist.

"Hey, Mrs. Calabro, remember me?" he asked Nana. She was wondering what he could possibly want. Then he added, "I'm one of the boys who used to come steal your peaches!"

That priest was a member of an illustrious company. In his Confessions, St. Augustine, later a bishop and doctor of the church, repentantly told of climbing into a neighbor's pear orchard as a boy with some of his friends to steal pears!

My mother studied piano, and thought of making a career of it, but didn't. She said that she "wanted to play on the radio" but was too nervous. She retained her love of the piano and of music all of her life. She taught me to love them, too, but more about all that later.

Mama attended at least a two-year college. She took some creative writing courses, and she wanted to be a writer. Although she never got anything published, to my knowledge, she could tell good stories that she made up from scratch; at least, I as a child thought that they were wonderful. She could also put inflection and dramatization into books that she read aloud. Years after her death, I went through her creative writing efforts, and included one of her stories in my first short story collection, *Slice of Life.* [8]

Mama continued to be somewhat delicate growing up. In her early twenties, she had a bad infection, either in her sinuses or her ears, and she became so ill that they had to do surgery, hollowing out the mastoid bone behind one of her ears. As she told me, "I woke up, and saw my parents at the foot of my bed, and I thought that I was going to go up to see St. Peter." They couldn't get a night nurse, so Dr. Braveman, the family physician, stayed with her all night. He told Nana that he went home in the early morning, when the milkman was coming to make deliveries. Mama was eventually diagnosed with allergies, and she may have been treated with injections. She also suffered from nosebleeds, and she had surgery to correct some problems with the bones in her nose.

In her early twenties, Mama learned to drive and had her first car. She said that she was very proud of it, and she loved to come home from work and spend time polishing and waxing it. When Mama was growing up, they called her Tutee, because about that time, King Tut of Egypt's tomb was opened, and things involving King Tut were in vogue. I don't know if she liked the nickname, but she really didn't like being called Stella instead of Estelle, because, as she said, so many negative and bad characters in literature were named Stella. She also had the nickname of The Lamplighter, because she had a habit of turning lights on as she went through different parts of the house, such as her bedroom, the kitchen, or the garage.

Mama went to work as a secretary, first in MA, but later she moved to Washington, DC with some friends. She was very good at taking shorthand dictation, and I often made use of that skill when I was a student and trying to compose creative writing assignments.

---

[8] See "Lost and Found," *Slice of Life*, Linda Anne Monica Schneider, Author House, Bloomington, IN.

Mama's father died on August 26, 1943, of some kind of blood disease or infection, possibly leukemia. He died at home after a long illness that wore Nana out nursing him. His last words supposedly were that he loved his home and everything in it. Nana said that he was unconscious for only twenty minutes before he died. When Nana realized that Grandpa had died, she said that, as she put it, her mind went for a walk for a minute, and she turned around and hit her brother, Bill, who was standing just behind her. I imagine it was the shock of her husband's death. She said that Bill just grabbed her hands and said, "Mal, it's me."

When Grandpa died, Mama said that a breeze swept through the house, and pushed all of the front and back doors open, including the inner hall doors! She thought that it meant that his soul had left his body. He liked to whistle, "Return to Sorrento" in the bathroom, they say. Nana said sometimes that maybe his soul went to Sorrento en route to heaven. After her father died, Mama said that she dreamt about him for a while, but eventually it stopped, and she thought that it meant he had gone to heaven from Purgatory. [9]

Grandpa was buried in Quincy MA, in a protestant or secular cemetery, Mount Walleston cemetery, because there wasn't any space in the Catholic cemetery. Grandpa made Nana promise to be buried beside him. A carved granite headstone marks the grave. Uncle Joe is buried there, too, and the plot had space for my Aunt Irene to be buried with him after she died.

After her husband's death, Nana carried on in the family house for a while. She sold the house eventually and came down to Washington to be with Mama and "the girls." Mama and a couple of her friends had an apartment together. I think that the address was 1 Sunderland Place, in Washington, DC. Nana was living with Mama and her friends, and she was around when my father began courting Mama. From some things that Nana said years later, she may not have been too thrilled when Mama decided to marry Papa. I don't know how seriously to take her remarks, but, in any event, Mama was determined, and it all worked out for the best.

---

[9] For the information of readers who are not familiar with some of the beliefs of Roman Catholics, I offer the following brief explanation of Purgatory. Unlike most Protestants, who believe that, after death, the choice is strictly between heaven and hell, Catholics believe that there is an intermediary state for those who have some minor sins for which to atone, or other unfinished spiritual business, called Purgatory. After spending the necessary interval there to resolve whatever leftover issues are involved, the souls of the just go to heaven. Of course, saints and others without such issues go straight there. Note that Dante, in the second section of *The Divine Comedy* puts Purgatory inside the gate of St. Peter.

I'm not sure whether this operation happened in MA or Washington, but at some point, Nana had surgery on one of her legs, to correct a problem with varicose veins that resulted from her pregnancy. She said that her surgeon was a very competent, capable fellow, named Dr. Hildebrand. He only did one of her legs, but she would have preferred that he do the two of them. When she asked him why he didn't do both, he supposedly said that the other one didn't need it. The operation was a little difficult, inasmuch as they got her off the table to walk around, to make sure that the legs were the same length, when the anesthetic had barely worn off. It seems that they tied up the veins, and I understand that this procedure is no longer done. Nana had trouble with repeated cellulites infections in one of her legs in her old age, the one that was not done.

Two of Mama's friends with whom she kept in touch in later years were Shirley Thomas, who eventually married a man named Frank Biberstein, and Betty Lally, who married Charles Gorday and had two children who were my contemporaries, young Charlie and Louise. When I was growing up, I called the parents of these children Aunt Betty and Uncle Charlie.

Before his father's death, Mama's brother, Joe Calabro, became a plumber. Because of some accidents on the job, he sustained serious back injuries requiring a couple of back operations. I don't know how successful they were, but my uncle had chronic back pain all of his life. He married Irene Cirilo, and he had two children, young Tom, known as Tommie, who married Arlene and has no children, and Nancy, who is married to Dick with two grown married children with children of their own and even some grandchildren. Uncle Joe died a few years ago. Aunty Rene sold their house in Taunton, MA, and she moved to San Antonio TX, and she lived with Nancy and Dick. She was a great-grandmother before her death, after a long struggle with arthritis.

# THE BEGINNING: A TIME TO BE BORN AND A TIME TO DIE

As I mentioned in my introduction, I have not attempted to do research to document facts in family history. I have tried to piece together circumstances and facts based on what my parents and other relatives told me.

From what they said, my parents had other loves before they met each other. Mama had a childhood sweetheart with whom she grew up, named Eddie. Eddie planned to go to or had entered medical school. At some point he became ill, possibly from pneumonia, and died. They must have been very close. Nana said that some folks were kidding around, and one of the fellows said something to the effect to not get ideas about Estelle Calabro, because she was Eddie's Girl. Eddie supposedly responded, "You bet your life! She's Eddie's girl!"

After Eddie, and before my father, Mama said that she dated a man, named Paul. They almost got serious, but Mama said that he was a Lutheran, and Mama just wasn't comfortable with the idea of having a husband who didn't share her faith and wasn't a Catholic.

For his part, my father had women friends before Mama. After Mama's death, he mentioned a couple of them to me in passing. I met one particular lady, Ida (Polly) Pollard, who lived in Connecticut. I found her very pleasant and charming, and we corresponded for years, until she became unable to write letters any more.

I don't know how my parents first met, or precisely where. I always assumed that it was in Washington, DC. My uncle Joe said something to me years later that Papa courted Mama in Connecticut or Massachusetts, during or after the war, but he may have confused Papa's seeing Polly, or he might have confused Papa with another suitor, or –who knows? From what else I know of their circumstances, it doesn't seem possible or probable to me.

Mama didn't say much about the courtship, except that she remembers seeing this tall, handsome man getting on or off a bus. Papa gave Mama a gold engagement ring with a single diamond, a little over half a carat, with a matching wedding band. He didn't have a wedding ring or diamond from Mama. He wore a gold snake ring, with a diamond in the head, which I assumed for years, as a child, was his wedding or engagement ring. After Mama died, Papa told me the history of the snake ring. It seems that one of his shipmates wanted to sell a gold cuff link set with a diamond and a gold snake ring. Papa asked to have them checked, and he took or sent them to Bill Ritger, who had a jewelry store in Pittsburgh, to have them evaluated. Bill said that the diamond was good, but it had a small chip in it; He said the price that the man was asking was reasonable. He proposed to Papa that, when he bought the items, he should use the old gold in the cuff link to mount the diamond in the head of the snake, and that's what Papa did. Bill helped Papa select the engagement ring and diamond and matching wedding band for Mama.

Unfortunately, during the trip to Ocean City, MD, that Papa and I took in 1978, Papa lost his ring somewhere between there and coming home. We looked and looked, but we couldn't find it. I helped Papa with the decision to mount a tiger's eye stone that he brought back from India in another 10-carat man's ring that he had left over from my star sapphire ring. This tiger's eye ring came to me when Papa died. I wore it on a gold chain sometimes, because it was too big for me to wear it as a ring. Eventually, I had part of it, including the tiger's eye stone, mounted in a pin composed of other similar keepsakes.

Either before or after they were married, Papa gave Mama a gold watch, which she wore all the time when I was growing up, and a gold bracelet set with jade stones that he brought back from India. He also gave her a sandalwood box that he bought during the war, when the ship stopped in India. The lid has a carving of the Taj Mahal on it, and Papa had put Mama's nickname that he gave her, Babe, on the front in gold letters. I still have the box.[10] Among other things to be discussed later, he also brought back a teak carved wooden elephant, with real ivory tusks. Because Nana liked elephants so much, a partiality that I share, she got and kept the elephant. After she died, I made him the head of my elephant collection.

My parents married in a simple wedding, in street clothes, in St. Matthew's Cathedral in Washington, DC, on September 19, 1948. I still have the wedding album with the pictures. The wedding picture of them together that is framed on our mantelpiece is on the first page of this chapter. Years later, Mama told me, by way of advice, that she thought that having a big wedding was a good idea and very advisable. I'm not sure whether it was because she missed having one of her own.

When I was growing up, Papa used a self-winding Rolex watch, but he had one with a wind-up movement and a regular watchband as a backup.

My parents had good and difficult things in common, and they were opposites in many ways. Papa was about six feet two inches tall, with brown hair that tended to wave and hazel eyes. After the marriage, and for the first couple of years of my life, he smoked. They tell me that he gave it up, because, as a little kid, I kept imitating his coughing, and it helped him to realize that it wasn't a good idea to keep it up.

Like his father, John Schneider, Papa could be stubborn, determined, and a little "one-way" at times. He had a good, sometimes outrageous, sense of humor.

Sometimes, I didn't appreciate the humor of some of the things that Papa said. He would say, "Laugh, why don't you?" Then he would add, "You'll get it in church!"

Sure enough, in the middle of the sermon, I would suddenly understand what he meant, and I would try so hard not to laugh. Then Papa would nudge me, making it worse, and say, "You got it, didn't you?"

Papa had a temper sometimes, but, when not angry or upset, he generally tried to project a cheerful, upbeat personality. He tended to be practical and to emphasize things that worked, as

---

[10] On one visit to Pittsburgh, after Mama Died, Sister Loreto gave me another similar sandalwood box that Papa had given her, before he met Mama. Papa told me afterwards that he was very relieved that I didn't blurt out that I already had a box like that.

opposed to pretty and fancy or popular brand names. As he often said, "It doesn't have to be gold-plated to be good." Conversely, he had a good color sense and an appreciation for some of the finer things, including good jewelry and diamonds.

Papa inherited his father's propensity to be talented with electrical or electronic things, and he had an engineering, scientific frame of thinking and analysis of problems and their solutions. This tendency sometimes resulted in his making a project out of something that should have been simple and straightforward. He loved his photography and always had a camera around for family occasions, offbeat pictures, and photos of scenery. He liked to have different cameras and lenses. To avoid taking glasses on and off, once he needed them, he used bifocals, so he could see close and far away. The result was that, even though I cannot see them, I have a house full of pictures and a case of negatives stored in the cedar closet upstairs. As discussed in more detail later, I keep the albums full of Papa's pictures, because I appreciate all the care, skill, love, and art that he put into them.

Ironically, when Mama needed reading glasses, she ended up with the same reading lenses that Papa needed. After she died, he kept her little glasses, with their aluminum frame and the lopsided shape on account of the hollowed-out bone behind her ear, in his desk drawer at work, in case he forgot his other ones.

Papa was a good driver, but he tended to keep the steering wheel in one place when traveling on a straight road. In contrast, Mama liked to turn the wheel ever so slightly to "feel the road." Her driving made Papa nervous, and he would kid about women drivers, which irritated Mama very much!

Papa believed that rules were meant to be broken, in a good cause, but he believed in strict adherence to church teachings and religious observances. He loved babies and children. I later observed him lift babies high up in the air, to make them laugh.

Mama was five feet two inches tall. I guess partly on account of this, she liked spiky high heels. One of my vivid memories is of hearing her come walking, going "click click click." To this day, when I hear someone with snappy high heels, I find myself wishing that it could be Mama. Mama said that, when she was younger, Aunt Janie sounded even snappier when she was walking in high heels. By the time I knew her, she was wearing more sensible shoes with wedge or lower heels.

Mama had blond hair and large green eyes. She kept her hair somewhat short, and liked it curled in wavy cuts. She complained that it was turning grey at the temples, and she used rinses to try to keep it looking blond. She liked dainty, pretty things and wanted the best brands. She had a more romantic, poetic view of things. She could be very possessive, especially because she was oversensitive and could be hurt very easily. Papa perceived this as jealousy, but I don't think that it was. I think that, instead, Mama was insecure and had a need for the more romantic, tender attentions that maybe didn't always fit into Papa's scheme of things. Nana sometimes got on Mama's case for getting upset over little things, and for being jealous. Nana would say to Mama at such times that she had big green eyes, like a cat. These remarks hurt Mama's feelings. I think that she felt especially bad, because Mama knew that I couldn't see her and judge for myself about her eyes. I remember her crying to Nana, "I do not have eyes like a cat!"

Mama, too, had a quick-flaring temper, but her storms were fast and furious and her contrition was just as quick and intense. She did have a fun-loving, playful nature and a good sense of humor, but she didn't always find the same things funny that made Papa laugh.

Mama, like Papa, was religious and loved the Lord. She carefully taught me my catechism and how to say the rosary. We would go and sit down at the dining room table, for Mama to tell me stories of Jesus, go over the little child's catechism, or read me stories from the children's Bible books. After I got a little older, she started reading me the actual Bible, beginning with Genesis. Besides their faith, the other thing that my parents definitely had in common was that they loved children.

Nana lived with them after they married. Until after I was born, they lived in an apartment in Virginia. Papa was working as a photographer in the Pentagon. I think that Mama was doing secretarial work, possibly also at the Pentagon, but I don't know the details. It was over two years after they were married when Mama found out that she was pregnant. Mama was going on forty-one, and Papa was going on forty-two, years of age. The parents were happily expecting one child.

In terms of the confusion about the number of babies, I know only what Mama told me when I was growing up. She said that she suspected that she had more than one, because, when she was lying down, she could feel the round heads, more than one. Although she apparently tried to tell the doctors, each of them listening to her abdomen only heard one heartbeat, but each heard a different rhythm. They all concurred that she was carrying one child.

Mama said, looking back, it turned out that my brothers were together in one sack, lower down. They were, after all, identical twins. I was apparently higher up, and under her ribs. She said that was what kept her from breathing at night, but then she would add that I was, "Up under Mama's heart!"

Although the doctors still were expecting one baby, they noted that my mother was getting very large, especially considering that she was a petite woman. The doctors began to fear that uremia poisoning would develop. They decided to induce labor prematurely. Mama said that it was two weeks ahead of time; according to Papa, it was two months.

The day that my brothers and I were born, November 1, 1951, was the Feast of All Saints, a Holy Day of Obligation. Mama said that her feet were so swollen that she couldn't get her shoes on, so she went to church in the snow in her stocking feet. That day, she went into Garfield Hospital, in Washington, DC, and the doctors induced labor.[11] Three babies were born, two boys and one girl, weighing around two pounds each. In the hospital, they told our parents to come up quickly with three names, because they did not know how long we would live. We were Carl Frederic, John Robert, and Linda Anne Schneider. A nurse baptized all three of us. Although the ceremonial baptism was repeated for me, to be official, in church, this hospital baptism was the beginning of my life with the Lord. When I was a teenager, after Mama died, one Sunday, after Mass, Papa said that he wanted to introduce me to someone. It was the nurse who baptized us. I feel a special bond with her, and that was a great moment. I'm sure that she was glad that one of us did survive.

They say that my brothers were blond like Mama. I was a brunette with blue eyes, who had some of Mama's features but favored my father in looks. We all ended up in the premature nursery in incubators under oxygen. According to Nana, at some point the doctors did a complete blood change on me. They fed me with a feeding tube that went through my nose into my stomach, and they probably did the same with my brothers. However that might have been, within two weeks the boys developed complications with their breathing, possibly hyaline lung disease, and they went home to heaven within a few days of each other. As Nana told me afterwards, "They left their sister to fight the battles."

The two little saints were buried in a common burying place for little babies. After Mama died, Papa tried to have their remains moved, so that they could have been buried in the same cemetery with Mama. He was told that their remains could not be separated or identified. I renewed the effort after Papa died, and I ended up finding out the same thing. I have information in the file as to where they are, and I was told that I could come out to visit the place, and that it is a peaceful place. I thus am one of the few people who can say, with absolute conviction, "I have two brothers, who are saints."

Years after my father's death in 1982, Nana said that she dreamt of my brothers.

"Two fellows came to the front door, and they were looking in through the screen at me. They were tall, like your father, and blond, like your mother. They were about thirty-five years old. One

---

[11] Old Garfield Hospital, as I understand, has closed and probably has been torn down. I have no idea who, if anybody, still has the old records.

of them said to me, 'I'm Carl, and he's John, and we're Linda Schneider's two brothers.' I was afraid to let them in, but I said to them, 'Well, if you are her brothers, then who am I?' 'Oh, we know who you are,' they said. 'You're our grandmother!' After that, I woke up. I went out into the living room, to look, and make sure that they weren't still there."

Patsy, the housekeeper, and I both agreed that it wasn't a dream. As I told one of the weekend caregivers, Margie, I hoped that those two boys would come and get Nana when her time came. They probably did.

They say that the night that we were born, Papa twisted all the buttons off his jacket! Here he was, thinking that he would have three babies on his hands. For her part, when the parents went to the hospital, Nana said that her nerves started her nibbling on little licorice candies. She overate on them, and eventually her stomach rebelled and disgorged all the surfeit of candies!

By the end of the first two weeks after our birth, Nana and my parents were wondering if they would end up with me. I apparently inherited some stubbornness and willfulness from my parents. For one thing, I didn't like the feeding tube, and I kept pulling it out. Because it was, for those days, new technology, it had to be put back by a doctor, not the nurses. Dr. Scalessa didn't appreciate having to get out of bed to put this feeding tube back in this tiny baby. For another thing, Mama said that I kept trying to get away from the place where the oxygen came into the incubator. When I was born, I was the smallest of the three. Eventually I got up to almost five pounds.

On New Year's Day, January 1, 1952, my father came to get me out of the hospital. He was quoted as saying, "I've come to take my baby out of hock." Two months in hospital was a long time in those days for a baby, and it had run up a considerable bill. My parents brought me home that day, with no idea about possible vision or hearing problems.

The story goes that Mama and Nana were still a little frightened by my small size and fragility, and they were afraid to hold or handle me. They say that Papa took charge and said, "Babies are tough! She won't break." As I said, Papa was at home with babies.

The sequence of the following events isn't very easy to reconstruct. I think that I was brought home to the apartment. In April of 1952, the four of us moved into my present home at 808 S. 26th Street, in Arlington, VA. Papa had the brick house with wood trim built.[12] The first floor was

---

[12] After Papa died, we found the papers in the files, showing that Nana loaned my parents some money for the down payment on the house. The record also showed that they repaid the loan. Nana also loaned Uncle Joe money for a house of his own, but it was many years before he bought his first house in Norton, MA. He later sold this one and bought the home in Taunton. According to Mama, he didn't repay these loans, but I have no direct knowledge of the paperwork.

finished completely, but they ran out of money before the second floor was fully finished off, but more about all that later.

At some point, Papa and Mama "tried again," and Mama was pregnant again. Meanwhile, when I was around one and a half years old, Sister Loreto (My father's half-sister, Hilda) came to visit. In those days, religious sisters were not allowed to spend the night in family members' homes, so she visited with my parents in the daytime. At night, Papa had to drive her to a local Sisters of Mercy or some other religious convent to spend the night. Anyway, she supposedly was sitting in the living room and I was on the couch, and she looked at me, and asked my parents what was wrong with Linda's eyes. It was the first clue that they had of my vision problem.

What my parents learned was that I was almost totally blind, from what was then called retrolental fibroplasias, damage and detachment and scarring of the retina. It was thought that the high oxygen levels in the incubator caused the condition, but we now know that it can result from prematurity. It is now referred to as retinopathy of prematurity.

Mama claimed that she was very upset by all this bad news about my eyes, and wanted to cry. Supposedly, people tried to comfort her and told her not to cry, and she held in her emotions. At this time, maybe around August or September of 1953, my cousin, Tom, came to visit. According to Papa, Mama was uncomfortable telling her mother that she was pregnant, and Nana didn't know. However that might be, Mama started hemorrhaging while sitting at the dining room table. They rushed her to the hospital. It was, depending on how far along it was, either a stillbirth or a miscarriage. My sister, who they say looked like me, was born dead. Mama could have died.

Mama said that she thought that holding her emotions inside caused the cord not to conduct enough oxygen and strangled the baby. The doctors told Papa a different story, which he told me after Mama died. They agreed that the placenta didn't give enough oxygen. They called it "old woman's afterbirth," and they blamed it on age. Mama said that she couldn't bear to look at the little dead baby girl, but Papa had enough scientific detachment to see her. The doctors took Papa back and showed her to him, including the dried-up placenta. My mother was, after all, forty-two going on forty-three. They told him that any other attempts would end up this way, because Mama was too old to safely bear children. I was to be their first, last, and only. I can only guess at what difficulties this state of things meant for my parents' marriage!

The loss of my sister had other consequences for Mama. Mama said to me that she was especially grieved at losing this baby, because she was hoping that I might have had a sister, who could have been my eyes. In any event, losing a child after the long anticipation of pregnancy is a wrenching thing, and it left Mama emotionally upset. She tried unsuccessfully to go back to work. After Papa died, we found the correspondence in the files. I think that mama may have requested a leave of absence, not granted, or ended up being fired or having to resign. I found the letters in which Papa went to bat for her. After finding them, I understand now why he became so concerned during my turbulent high school years, when I needed psychotherapy and counseling. He was all too aware of the stigma and difficulty that reputations of emotional or mental instability could cause, as exemplified by Mama's experience.

However, all this, in retrospect, turned out to be a blessing in disguise. God is so wonderful at making lemonade out of lemons! I grew up with a stay-at-home Mama and with a live-in Nana, under circumstances in which I needed both. It did impose more stresses on Papa, who ended up adding a second job to his full-time work as a photographer at the Pentagon, to pay the bills and especially for my education expenses.

Some feminists like to deride housewives and other non-working house-spouses, but the reality is that, during the time when I was growing up, the stay-at-home moms were the pool of people able to do things for their children and to volunteer in the community. Their availability meant that they could provide the delicious home-cooked meals and nursing of sick family members. Today we suffer the effects of the diminishing number of people with the time and energy to reach out to others.

# EARLY MEMORIES

*H*ow do you search through the fog of infantile memories for one's early recollections? Very carefully, I say, with a strong sense of humility. I have a very vague recollection of someone putting an undershirt on me. I remember being brought into a house and into a room with a rocking chair, and maybe that was the new house. I remember Mama and Nana. I had very bad stomachaches, and Mama made me feel better by putting her hand on me. Her fingers felt firm and cool, and very soothing and healing. I recall the time that Mama wasn't there for some reason, and I was crying, because my stomach ached. I wanted Mama, but Mama wasn't there. Nana kept saying, "Can't I put my hand there and make it better?" She tried, but it didn't work, and I cried and cried. I didn't know how to tell her that it just wasn't the same.

Mama was very demonstrative and affectionate. She would hug me and kiss and cuddle me. I would say, "I love you, Mama," and she would say, "I love you, too." Mama was very gentle and sympathetic if you got sick, and she would sit and read to you.

Mama also rolled my hair in aluminum curlers every night. Papa fussed about how much trouble she took, but what he didn't understand was that the time that Mama spent rolling my hair was our special time together.

Nana wasn't very much into hugging and kissing, but she showed that she loved me by the cooking, cleaning, and nursing of me that she did. She had a wonderful, musical laugh, a good sense of humor (including a dry, Yankee wit,) and a good singing voice and ability to carry a tune. Nana often said to me that God left me here, because she had to have someone to love. Although Mama favored curling my hair in ringlets, Nana sometimes braided my hair, securing the ends of the braids with elastic rubber bands.

Nana was an excellent cook, but we did have to be alert about how she handled the gas stove. Sometimes, she would turn on the burners and not be aware that they weren't lit. I became attuned early to the smell of gas and to alert Mama or Nana about it. Among Nana's delicious dishes were her roasts, fried chicken, casseroles, and butter cut-out cookies, apple, cherry, blueberry, and lemon pies, and delicious cakes, particularly her blueberry tea cake. She cooked wonderful, scalloped potatoes with butter and milk. She made homemade soup with marrowbones and learned to make it also with ox tails, at Papa's urging.

Although I had to stay away from dairy products on account of allergies, all that bone-made soup provided good calcium. Despite my other health troubles, I was relatively fortunate at the dentist. I didn't develop cavities until I was in high school. I also was spared braces. I had an under bite, but the wise orthodontist that we consulted gave me a solution, provided I had the discipline to undergo it. He told Mama to get some wooden tongue depressors. While I was sitting around doing quiet things, like listening to music or talking books, I should bite on the tongue depressors and force the jaw to go forward, so that my lower front teeth would be behind my upper front teeth. It hurt a great deal and made me cry, but I made myself do it. I heard all the horrid details from my girlfriend, Vickie Reece, about braces, and I didn't want them or the "blocks" that the dentist said would be necessary if I didn't succeed!

In addition to French fries, which she called potato sticks, Nana made German fries from leftover boiled potatoes and potato pancakes with leftover mashed potatoes. Whether the potatoes were fried or oven-roasted, she always drained them, as well as fried fish, chicken, and bacon, on paper towels. Nana made delicious pasta with tomato sauce and mushrooms. In our house, this dish was a side dish, served with a vegetable and some kind of meat. We only ate it by itself on Sunday evenings as a leftover. For some reason, it always tasted even better warmed over.

During one memorable winter during my grade school years, Nana baked homemade fresh bread for us. She would mix flour, yeast cake, and water to make the dough, and she would knead it in a wooden bowl. She often let me help her, and it was very satisfying to take out one's frustrations on that dough! After it was mixed, Nana would put it under a blanket near the heating vent to rise. She would punch it down with her fist after it rose the first time, and let it come up a second time. It's amazing how quickly all that air goes out of yeast-raised dough! Then she would divide it into loaves and let it rise in the loaf pans before putting it in the oven. When she first mixed it, and after it was in loaves, she would put a cross on it with the side of her hand and ask God to bless it. If some of the dough were left over, she would make two or three rolls with it. The bread was delicious, with wonderful, big slices, and it was wonderful toasted.

I remember Nana's strong will and fearlessness. If bees found their way into the house, she would grab them in a tea towel, paper towel, or anything else she could find to get between her hand and the insect, and she would take them to the nearest door or window and put them outside. "I'm bigger than they are!" she would say.

Nana tended to take a fighting, stubborn attitude toward sickness. Her first line of defense, for illnesses considered minor enough not to need the intervention of a physician, were laxatives, soap and water enemas, ginger ale and Amatone gas pills for indigestion; aspirin, cough syrup, and hot water bottles for fevers; and pushing liquids for everything. The hot water bottle was nicknamed Soggy, and he was often a favorite bed pal during illness.

Nana would keep asking, "Don't you feel better now?" Eventually, one would get so angry that you would yell, "Yes," just to make her stop asking. Maybe making you say "yes" was part of the mind over matter thing.

Unlike Mama, Papa wasn't so sympathetic and affectionate in a demonstrative way, and he tended to be brusque and abrupt if you weren't feeling good. Nana said that he worried and got nervous if I got sick. He could give wonderful back massages with his big, strong, gentle hands. He also took care of cutting my toe and finger nails. Cutting my toenails wasn't easy for him. For some reason, I had great sensitivity in my big toes, and I really didn't want anybody touching them. It didn't hurt as such, but it wasn't very comfortable. It took years for that sensation to go away. I now know that it probably had something to do with my needing interventions as a premature baby that my body remembered, even if my conscious memory did not.

Mama and Nana also had to use similar patient persistence to get me comfortable with warm water poured or sprayed over my head to rinse my hair. Now I very much enjoy that wonderful warm water on my head; it relaxes me and makes me feel pampered!

Papa was also brave enough to take a calculated risk sometimes to let me learn things the hard way, so that I would remember them and learn caution. For example, on one occasion, he was reading the newspaper in his big rocking chair. I noticed that the floor lamp behind him was missing a light bulb in one of its sockets. I asked Papa a couple of times what was in the place where the light bulb used to be, but he was either preoccupied with the paper or decided not to answer. I grew tired of waiting for an answer, and I stuck my finger into the socket. I got a shock.

"Did you get tickled?" Papa asked.

Needless to say, I never did that again. It was a good way to learn about the problems of live electricity and its dangers.

Papa had a practical, hardheaded attitude toward helping yourself. On one occasion, I had a bad stomachache, and all the usual remedies, including "playing ostrich" on Nana's bed weren't helping.

Papa said, "Either you can lie there and suffer or you can get up and come out for a walk."

Fortunately, I listened and went for a walk, and afterwards I felt better.

Papa also promoted the idea that you needed to believe in yourself and put your talents forward. He liked to quote the following saying, whose origin I don't know:

> The man who whispers down a well
> About the things he has to sell
> Never reaps the shining dollars
> Like the man who lifts his head and hollers!

Papa, Mama, and Nana were all different, but they loved me very much. In future, I shall refer to them collectively sometimes as "my parents." I will try to make it clear when I mean this word to refer only to Papa and Mama. My parents' voices and manner of speaking were different, too. Mama had a crisp, pleasant, expressive voice. She tried to speak regular American English, without any New England accent, but if she were tired, she would lapse into earlier pronunciations once in a great while. When she laughed, she sometimes made a little hissing sound between her teeth, which meant that she found something funny. She liked to talk to the canary, Dickey, to coax him to sing, and sometimes she whistled to him. Mama's nickname for me was Tweetie.

Papa had a strong, decisive voice, and a very pleasant laugh. He gave some words a pronunciation similar to the manner often used in Pennsylvania that involved saying the "ow" sound like a. Windows became "windas", and pillows became "pillas." Sometimes, Papa would playfully give me a little swat and tease me by saying, "That's for nothing! Just do something, and see what you get!" His nickname for me was Peanuts.

Nana had a lighter pitched voice than Mama, and on the telephone she almost sounded like a little girl. She had a New England accent in her way of pronouncing her R's. She liked to say that her accent was nothing compared with the way the old Vermont Yankees used to talk. Sometimes she called me Lindy, instead of Linda, in a nice, musical ringing way.

Going back to early childhood memories, I also remember when my parents began to put panties on me, instead of the diapers. I didn't make it to the bathroom. Papa laid me down on the couch, and began to try to put diapers back on me. I remember kicking, fighting, and probably screaming about it. It was the last "accident".

After all this, I seem to remember my third or fourth birthday party. Along with my parents and Nana, Uncle Charlie, Aunt Betty, young Charlie, and Louise were there, having driven over from their home in Clinton, MD. The next-door neighbor, Ellen Reece, was at the party, along with her niece, Vickie, who was my childhood best friend. Vickie was Ellen's brother, Billy Reece's younger daughter, and she lived a few blocks away. Ellen's other brother, Cal, lived in the neighborhood, with his wife, Mary, and they later had two children, Beth and Johnny, but they weren't born yet at the time of this birthday.

For this particular birthday, I remember getting some kind of stuffed doll with a pasteboard face (that I think I Named Vickie), a miniature Bissell sweeper, and, either this birthday or another, a cute stuffed monkey, dressed in a little suit and hat, that I called Bobo. I guess we had cake and ice cream. The canary bird sang.

Yes, we had pets. The most prevalent, recurring pet was a canary bird. I thought it was all the same bird, named Dickey. In retrospect, we had three birds, because the first two died. I remember that they didn't tell me that they died. They just said, "Dickey had to go to the bird hospital to get better." At least, that's what they told me the two times. The reason that I know that the bird changed the first time was that the singing changed, for some reason, and I wondered why. Dickey wasn't gone very long the first time, but the second time, Dickey was gone a long while. I remember waking up and crying to Mama one night that I missed Dickey, and couldn't he come home. I guess that they decided that we needed another bird, because Dickey did come home. Nana said that they had to play the piano for him where he was, so that he would get better and sing. I think that the third bird was the one that we had a number of years, until after Mama died. Also, they told me at first that Dickey was yellow. The last Dickey was cinnamon color, or brownish.

Mama was very patient about cleaning out the bird's cage, every other day, and putting powder on him to prevent mites, and clipping his toenails when they got too long. After she died, Papa had to take over these chores for a while. He fussed and complained, but he was very gentle with this little tiny bird in his big hands.

In addition to having a consistent canary bird, I had other pets, but Mama was the one who mainly took care of them. We had goldfish, at one time as many as five or six. It's hard to "feel" goldfish, so what Mama did, she would have me help her feed the fish and change the water. She would fill a big basin, and then transfer the fish, one at a time, with a net, into the basin, change the water, and put them back in the bowl. While they were in the basin, I would make a bridge of my hands, so that they could swim under them. We named all the fish; the last one to die was Frisky, so-named because he fought the net and flopped around vigorously in it. He was also the biggest, fattest fish in the bowl.

Before the goldfish, we had pet turtles, one at a time. Mama would show me how she fed the turtle, and she would take him out of his bowl and let me feel him, and let him walk up my arm with his little prickly claws that tickled. I found out later that, when the turtles began to get too big for the bowl and accommodations that we had for them, Mama would turn the turtle loose in the backyard. Some of those turtles survived. Once in a while, one of these larger turtles would turn up, and I would get to play with him/her for a little while in the kitchen, before he would be turned loose again. On one occasion, one of the turtles bit me on the finger; I guess that I was a little too rough. He was a very forgiving turtle, because he let me go on playing with him and didn't bite me again. I tried to stay clear of his head, and I suspect that I was much more gentle. Later that evening, Mama washed off the sore finger and put a Band-Aid on it. "What did you do to him?" was all that she said. It was a lesson well learned.

I will digress here to tell a funny story about the turtles and the denouement. One of the neighbors who lived across the street for many years was a wonderful couple, Helen and Winn Alley. Years after Mama died, Mr. Alley and Papa were talking about the troubles they were having with their gardens, especially their attempts to raise tomatoes. Papa asked Mr. Alley what was eating the tomatoes, taking bites out of them.

"Oh, Carl, it's turtles!" Mr. Alley told him. "Don't you know? They love tomatoes."

I had a silent, private laugh. I decided it might not be a good idea to tell him that they were probably my pet turtles from childhood days, or maybe their descendants, that were ravaging the tomatoes!

These pets were all very nice, and of course, I especially enjoyed Dickey filling the house with wonderful song, but I really wanted something furry to hold and cuddle and call my own. Nana told me, and I seem to remember, that we went for a walk, and the lady up the street had a cat, and oh! How much I wanted to play with that cat! Nana tried hard to get hold of the cat for me, which was difficult, because the cat ran up the steps toward its house. Nana said she fell down once while trying to wheel me in the baby carriage and broke her arm and had it in a cast for a while. She didn't want to break another arm over a cat. What I really wanted was a dog, with all the stories that I heard, but that didn't seem possible for a while, especially when I later tested as allergic to dogs and cats.

Other events punctuated those early years. As I said already, Mama went to MA, to be there for Uncle Joe, for one of his accidents or back surgeries. I don't remember it very clearly, but there were letters in the file found after his death that Papa wrote Mama while she was gone.

In one of them, Papa said, "Baby misses you. She says we don't talk loud enough. Something is missing." The clue to the later-discovered hearing loss was there at this early stage.

Mama may have gone more than once,[13] but on one occasion, she brought me back a little pocket sized baby doll, that I named Tina. It was one of my favorite dolls, until the elastic broke; Mama put it away to restring it, but Tina got lost, and I had to make do with another one that I still have as a keepsake. On the second occasion, she brought me a little six-inch stand-up storybook doll that I still have.

I had many, many dolls growing up, eventually almost a hundred. One of the originals was a rag doll, called Susie, with a pasteboard face and cloth body, arms, and legs; no, this wasn't the one I remember from the birthday party. Another doll was a cute one with a hard jointed body and a soft vinyl head and face with two little pigtails that I called Bonnie Braids. Papa had to repair the arms on that doll when they came off. Relatives and friends, as well as Nana and my parents, often gave me dolls. I remember one Christmas when many of the gifts were dolls, which I really liked to receive. As I grew older, I received more serious dolls, including two dolls dressed in religious habits. One of them was a "prize" for selling a couple of subscriptions to *The Catholic Standard*, the Catholic newspaper for the Washington Diocese, which my grammar school was encouraging our students to promote. I named this doll Sister Dorothy, after my first and second grade teacher.

Mama told me about a German imported doll that she had when she was a girl. It had a bisque porcelain face, movable brown eyes, and real hair. Mama said that she gave this doll away when she thought that she would never marry and have any children, I guess before she met Papa. She promised to try to find such a doll for me, but she wasn't able to do it during her lifetime. Her prayers probably still helped me, because I later found such a doll at a doll show in the DC Convention Center, which I bought.

For Christmas and birthday gifts, I preferred dolls and books to clothes. Mama's friend, Shirley, often sent me a dress for Christmas or my birthday. I didn't like these gifts, because they were usually the wrong size. Mama would take me to the store and try to exchange the dress for the right size, but it often wasn't possible, and she would have to send them back to Shirley, so that she could do something about it herself. I would have appreciated the thought much more if Shirley had come

---

[13] As mentioned again later, Mama also had trouble with anemia. On one occasion, I think she went to the hospital to get her blood count back to normal. This episode is merged in my mind with the trips to MA.

to visit and spend some time with us. I would have come to know her that way, and she wouldn't have just been this person that Mama described, who sent all those bothersome, tiresome dresses!

My aunties in Quincy and my Uncle Joe often sent money to me as a gift on holidays or my birthday; the Abbiatti cousins did, too, but sometimes they put a little pin or some other gift in the envelopes. As a child, my problem with money was that Mama usually wanted to put it in the savings account. As a teenager and later an adult, I now know the value of this account, but it didn't seem very practical at first to a little kid.

One of my first lessons in dealing with anger came when, for some reason that I don't understand myself, I took my rag doll, Susie, into the living room, turned her face down behind the front picture window draperies, and banged her head on the floor. It broke a place on her head, which had to be taped up.

Mama and Nana asked me why I did it, but I didn't know; they did impress on me that I was not to do that kind of thing ever again to poor Susie or my other doll children, and I don't think that I did. I'm glad that it was the doll, and not something alive, that taught me that lesson. In fact, over the years that followed, I often tried to repair or patch up dolls that other people wanted to throw away.

In addition to the dolls, I enjoyed many of the other things of normal childhood. Vickie came over sometimes, and we enjoyed play acting, playing with play dough and modeling clay, and playing with jungle and farm animal sets, as well as dressing and making up stories about our dolls. Vickie especially liked to give my dollies new hairdos. Mama sometimes would play children's Roulette and Parcheesi with Vickie and me. I could play Roulette if Mama told me the numbers that came up and helped me place the bets with the children's chips. Concerning Parcheesi, the "men" were different shapes for the different sets, and I could tell them apart. The cardboard game board was punched with holes, but I had trouble following the prescribed path without Mama's help. The dice had holes that I could feel.

Other games were usable by blind children. Some games, like Topper and Stadium checkers, could be played without modification if someone told me the colors of the disks or the marbles. Other games could be used if one got creative. We had a game with a metal tray with depressions for wooden balls to be rolled into from the floor. Papa used a ruler as a guide, so that I could roll the balls. Mama Brailled cards for other children's games, like Rummy, Old Maid, and Rack-O. Other cards came in sets that were already in Braille, like the regular playing cards and another deck called Rook. These cards, and other modified games like Parcheesi, checkers, chess, and Chinese checkers, could be bought from places like The American Foundation for the Blind.

Concerning the playing cards, Vickie taught me to play games like Fish and Crazy Eights. Papa taught me a little about playing poker. He had a set of real poker chips. I never mastered the game, but I learned some of its fundamentals. Papa also played checkers with me, and sometimes I beat him when I was little. As I grew older, I lost my knack for playing checkers, probably because I became fearful of risking my checkers to try to win. In *Around the World in Eighty Days* Mr. Fog played Whist. I understand that this game is played with two decks of cards and four people. I'd like to learn to play that game someday, as well as Chinese checkers and chess.

Mama and I played a fun game with twelve little cubes that had letters on the four sides. We would put them in a cup and mix them up, and then throw them on the table. The object was to take turns doing this and making words with the letters that were face up. The letters weren't raised, and Mama had to tell me what showed up when we emptied out the cup. When it was my turn, I would tell her what words I wanted to make with the letters. Mama bought me a Braille Scrabble game from AFB for one Christmas gift, but for some reason, I had trouble mastering Scrabble and putting the letters in a crossword puzzle format. I really had more fun with the little letter cubes!

I enjoyed playing with clay and play dough with Mama or Nana. Mama taught me to make turtles and fish, and she showed me how to use coils to make a cup or vase. Sometimes, when we were playing with clay, I would try to make a mouse. Nana would come along and take the clay and make a big old rat with it. She probably had some of her father's sculpting gifts, and maybe I inherited some of them, too. Years later, as a grown woman, I made a mouse from wax and had it cast in bronze; I also did a smaller one, and had it made into a silver pendant, all in memory of Nana and those days of making clay mice.

I did watch some TV; we had black-and-white TV's, and it was a big deal when color came out. Papa would go down to the hardware store or drugstore to test the tubes and try to keep the old sets going for a while. Eventually, we bought our first color TV. The only difference the color made to me was that the newer TV had a better sound quality.

I cannot speak for all blind or visually impaired people, but for myself and others in the visually impaired group, it's perfectly OK to refer to watching TV or looking at or seeing things. After all, we "see" with our hands, ears, and other senses, including our imaginations. The programs that I watched included The Romper Room and such programs in early childhood, Fury, (the story of a black horse and his boy master, Joey) Copter Patrol, Lassie, Rin Tin Tin, National Velvet, and later Raw Hide. Even then, I had a big soft spot for dogs. No, I didn't go very much for cartoons.

The action in them is very fast, too fast for Mama to describe to me what was happening, and the voices didn't sound natural to me; they sounded artificial, like typical Donald Duck, and I had trouble understanding them or distinguishing who was who. The first cartoon piece that I ever really appreciated was the old Disney movie, *101 Dalmatians*, the black-and-white version in which the dogs and other animals "talked" with human sounding voices. Mama took me to see it in the theater. In any event, watching TV was considered a privilege. One time, when I misbehaved in school, I was punished by having to forego TV for a week or two.

One of my favorite records, as you can imagine, had a recording of organ music with canary birds singing and accompanying the music. I had lots of records; at first, they were mainly '78's, with stories and music. I gradually progressed to the "long-playing" records, 33 1/3rpm. When I started receiving "talking books" through the National Library Service program, they originally were on 33 1/3 rpm records, then 16 2/3 rpm records, eventually four-track cassettes, and more recently digital cartridges. Some other libraries, such as Xavier Society for the Blind, went from two-track cassettes to CD's with MP3 audio files on them. They recently are starting to use the same kind of cartridges that the National Library Service (NLS) now uses.

I did listen to music and some news on the radio, especially when being driven to and from school. We had to leave the house a little before eight o'clock to arrive at school by eight-thirty, and we would hear the eight o'clock news on the car radio followed by classical music on WGMS, which was the classical music station in the Washington area. On the way home, we would listen to WRC and the more popular music and singers. As I grew older, I started hearing the evening news broadcasts and other special programs, such as coverage of the space launches and political conventions.

In addition to the records, Papa started making reel-to-reel tape recordings of some of the movies on TV that dramatized children's stories, including the Shirley Temple movies in which she acted as a child and the Shirley Temple Story Book series in which she narrated other stories as an adult and sometimes played an adult role. I learned to operate the tape recorder to play them back later. I kept many of those old tapes, and enjoyed listening to them again as an adult. Papa also used reel-to-reel tapes to correspond with Sister Margaret James in Pittsburgh or Detroit, wherever she happened to be stationed as a teaching sister. We would make tapes together to send her, and she would send her answers back on the other side of the tape. Sometimes, Mama would talk on these tapes, but she resisted being involved in this correspondence for some reason. Maybe she thought that it was something that Papa and I should do together. Sometimes, Mama read stories onto other reel-to-reel tapes for me to enjoy.

However, my favorite things were stories, and later poems. There were, of course, the usual children's stories in books that Mama and Nana read me. One story that I especially remember was Nana reading me *The Drugstore Cat*, and Mama reading me *Make Way for Ducklings*, a book sent to me by the Abbiatti cousins about a family of Mallard ducks in Boston. I still have her reading of that book on tape. I remember on one occasion, Ellen was visiting and trying to talk about neighbor things, and I kept saying to Nana, "Read, Nana, read."

I would collect my children's books and pile them up for Nana to read. She would read until she started to cough and her voice became tired. I would send her off to the kitchen to get a drink of water, and then pile up some more books while she was gone, for her to come back and read some more!

However, the stories that Mama and Nana told were as much fun as the printed books. I have summarized some of the stories that they told of their childhoods in the earlier section. In addition, one of my favorite stories was Nana's version of "The Three Little Pigs," and I included this story in *Slice of Life*. I also included it in my latest book, the sixth short story collection, *Tying up Loose Ends*.

In addition to the stories, Nana sometimes sang Italian songs. There was a song about Marianina, who went walking on Sunday with her hair curled in ringlets; another song about a chimney sweep coming down from the mountains to make a living and the little children who were frightened of his black face; a song about a girl whose boyfriend painted pretty pictures of her and made her a star, and a song about sailing on the ocean.

Papa didn't read too many books and stories to me in those early years, but sometimes, as I grew older, he would call me over to sit beside him, and he would read me interesting articles he found in the newspaper. We subscribed to *The Washington* Star, and he was especially fond of articles by Mary McGrory. We didn't start taking *The Washington* Post until the Star stopped publishing years later.

Papa and I did play together. We liked to play trains. We would get into the upholstered rocking chair in the living room, and we would pretend that we were on a train going to different places. Papa also bought me a set of electric trains with which I played by myself and sometimes with him. He also would "play horsy" with me, by crawling around the floor on all fours, with me on his back. One other thing that he did for me, which was particularly important for me, because I couldn't see, was to put me on his shoulder, and carry me around the house. In this way, I could feel the tops of the doorframes of the various rooms and the shape of the archway between the dining room and living room, and I could also feel the way the light fixtures were mounted on the walls and ceilings.

Sometimes, Papa and I went for walks in the neighborhood. We enjoyed gathering hickory nuts that dropped from the neighbors' trees in the fall. These walks were a good way for me to learn about my surroundings, and who lived where.

I will discuss here some of the neighbors at the time that I was growing up, because they figure in some of the later events in my life. I am not attempting to tell how things ended up for everyone. It suffices to say that Mrs. Patterson, Barbara Sheehan, and I were the only old timers who remain for many years. I don't remember when Mrs. Patterson eventually died or moved away. I don't know the people who currently occupy the house they had. As discussed in more detail later, Barbara died on May 2, 2019, at the venerable age of 103.

As I said, Ellen Reece lived next door on the left, with her father, Mr. Tom Reece, who was Nana's contemporary. As far as I know, Ellen never married or had any children. She and Mama were good friends. Ellen couldn't drive, so Mama often took her with her when she went shopping at the grocery store or ran other errands.

On the right, Karl Marcy (who worked on Capitol Hill), his wife, and their two children (older than I), Eric and Karen, inhabited the house on the corner of 26th Street and Hayes Street. The Williams family lived next to the Marcies on the Hayes Street side. Their youngest son, Tony, sometimes came over to visit and play with me, but he was older than I was. The house next to Ellen on her other side changed hands often, but the Sheets family lived there for a while. Their daughter, Mary, who seemed like a big girl to me, sometimes came over to play with me. I think that this family was the one who owned that cat that I wanted Nana to catch for me.

Across the street, Holland (known to the neighbors as Dinty) and Vivien Moore owned the house on the corner where Yves Street dead-ends in S. 26th Street. They also owned the lot next door, which had no house on it while they were living there. They spent their summers in Arlington, but they often went to Florida for the winter. They were very kind and generous neighbors. Mr. Moore, in particular, could often be counted on if you needed something done or help with something. For that reason, he was known in the neighborhood as "The Mayor of 26th Street." He was always going around picking up stray branches and litter, especially from the green island in the middle of the wide street. After Mama died, he sometimes helped by driving me to school.

Although he was good at tidying up the neighborhood, Mr. Moore was a bit of a packrat where his own personal belongings were concerned. When he was straightening up his house, preparatory to selling it, he went to Ellen and asked her if she and her father could use some doors. In case I didn't mention it already, Ellen's father was a carpenter. He used his skills to improve his own house, including building a nice sunroom on the back. Ellen told Mr. Moore that, yes, she thought that Daddy could use a couple of doors. Mr. Moore proceeded to bring over doors and more doors: house doors, a garage door, storm doors, and all kinds of doors that I have forgotten! Ellen chose a couple, and she told him he would have to take the rest back!

When the Moores finally decided to sell the lot and the house and move to Florida to stay, the neighborhood gave The Mayor a big send off. At that time, we found out that this gentle, courteous man, with his pronounced Tennessee accent, who liked to tell corny jokes, was a lawyer with a law degree.

A couple of houses down from the Moores, the Pattersons lived with their two boys and girl, who were older than I was, and next to them were Helen and Wynn Alley, who also had older children. Helen Alley's sister, Barbara Sheehan, who had a boy and girl, lived with her husband, Don, about a block away, on the opposite side of S. 25th Street. She became one of my dear friends after Mama died.

Milton and Alice Bennet, whom I called Aunt Alice and Uncle Milton and who had no children, lived on the corner opposite the Marcies. Like the Moores, they often went to Florida for the winters, and they often brought back oranges and grapefruit from Florida. They also brought me seashells, and one time, a stuffed real baby alligator. I named him Al, and I played with him, including wheeling him around in my doll carriage, until he literally fell apart. I really liked being able to stick my fingers in his open mouth and feel his sharp little baby teeth. Aunt Alice also gave me a baby doll with curly hair, called Misty Eyes. She was the second "drink and wet" doll that I had. Nana gave me the first one for a birthday, Betsy Wetsy. I still have Betsy. Eventually, the Bennets went to Florida to stay, and we missed them.

The Filers lived on the corner across Hayes Street from the Bennets.

All the folks across the street and the Filers had hickory trees. Ellen had them, too, but you couldn't get to hers from the sidewalk. Hickory nuts have an outer green shell, which peels off readily when the nuts dry and ripen. Inside, the inner shell that protects the delicious meat is thick and very hard. You can't crack hickory nuts with a regular nutcracker. Papa would crack them with two bricks, and then use picks to get out the delicious meat.

Admiral Murdaugh and his wife lived in the house behind us. Mama and Mrs. Murdaugh would often visit across the fence. The Murdaughs often gave me interesting or educational Christmas presents. Mrs. Murdaugh liked to talk about the places that they had visited during her husband's duty time in the Navy.

Next to the Murdaughs, I think a couple of houses up the street, lived the Heedalls. They moved there after I started school. They had a swimming pool dug and built in their yard. In fact, they did much of the construction themselves. While they lived there, they encouraged children to come up there to play, and Mrs. Heedall tried one summer to teach me how to swim, with some limited success. A family surnamed Bean moved into the house after them, but we didn't know the Beans very well. They did a great act of charity by bringing inner city kids to use their pool in the summertime. For years, many of the neighbors complained about the noisy children who swam in the pool, and about the flooding of their yards that resulted from the pool not being drained properly and through the property instead of directly into the front street. After the house changed hands yet again many years later, the new owners filled in the pool.

My parents and Nana all believed in saving money. Some of my dolls and clothes came from children relatives who had outgrown them. Mama and Nana would go through the ads in the paper, looking for things on sale in the grocery stores, and Mama would go from store to store to get the best buys in groceries. We also collected TV stamps and S&H green stamps, and we would put them in the books on rainy days. When they had enough books, Mama and Nana would go through the stamp store catalog to see what to buy. Among other things, we bought our big soup tureen with those stamps. Eventually, stores and gas stations stopped giving out the stamps. Meanwhile, when Mama died, we found some stamps that weren't yet in books. We put them in books, and I bought a couple of jewelry items with them.

Sometimes, taking advantage of the sales resulted in a surplus of a particular item. I remember that, one summer, we had a lot of little boiled potatoes on the menu at dinner. Mama played games with me about how we could have those little boiled potatoes in different ways. We tried them without butter, with butter, cut in squares, cut in slices, cut in quarters, and with skins on and off. The result was that I never complained and never got tired of them until we moved on to something else.

We were a one-car family. We had a number of cars over the years, one at a time, and we gave them playful names. The first one that I only dimly remember was a red Dodge, damaged in an accident that I only vaguely recall, that we called The Cannonball express (after the train in the Casey engineer train story.) Then we had a green dodge, named Green gussy; next came a blue Dodge, the Blue Bird, that I remember for its pretty, tapered, fluted tail fins. The last car that we bought, just before my mother died, was a Pontiac. We were thinking of naming it the Fawn. She only drove it once, from the driveway to the garage. After Mama died, we stopped naming our cars. After the Fawn, we had a Ford LTD with black nylon upholstery and factory-installed air conditioning, our first air-conditioned car. We needed the air conditioning in that car. The nylon material was cold in the winter, but its black color caused it to absorb the sun's heat in the summer and made the car very hot. After the Ford LTD, we had a Ford Torino for a little while. They were all second-hand used cars, until the Ford Grenada that Papa bought when I finished law school.

A few years after Papa died, I finally sold the Grenada and bought a Mitsubishi Gallant. After that one, I bought my present car, a 2004 Toyota Prius. It has been my dream car. I only wish that I could drive it myself, instead of having to depend on others. Someday, I'd like to have an all-electric car, or at least a plug-in hybrid, and it would be nice if the self-driving technology could work for someone like me. It might not happen, but it's sweet to dream!

When I was growing up, Mama used the car during the daytime, because Papa either walked or took the bus to the Pentagon to work. He generally had the car for his second job activities during the evenings and often on weekends. Often in the weekday evenings, at 5:30, I would go with Mama when she drove to the Pentagon to get my father. She would park in Lane 18, and we would sit and wait for him.

"Oh, where's your father?" she would ask me rhetorically, tapping the brake pedal in impatience and exasperation.

"Turn off the motor, and he'll come!" I'd say.

When he came, he would open the driver's door, Mama would crawl or scoot over or around me and get in the passenger side of the bench front seat, he would get into the car, and they would kiss each other over my head. However the evening evolved afterwards, that generally was the way it began.

Sometimes, I was able to go to visit Papa at the Pentagon. His office was on the fifth floor. The building was amazing, with elevators, ramps, and escalators to go between floors in different locations. It had such long corridors that, according to Papa, the maintenance folks rode around on little electric carts with their paints and cleaning supplies. Downstairs, the concourse had a bakery, a jewelry store, a dry cleaner place, a movie theater in which Papa and I watched some memorable movies, (including *Operation Petticoat, The Poseidon Adventure,* and *The Russians Are Coming,*) and a small Woodward and Lothrop's department store branch. There were other things that I have forgotten; and there were snack shops and hamburger stands all over the place. It was like a small world unto itself.

I met some of Papa's co-workers, who shall remain anonymous for the most part. One secretarial lady, who became a lifelong family friend even after she retired, was Charlotte Frease, known to me as Miss Frease. She had a booming, vivacious voice, and a good sense of humor. Often, if I called Papa at work, she would answer the telephone. Especially after Mama died, she was the one to whom I went to get my knitting fixed when I made mistakes. Eventually, over many years, I have learned to fix most of my own mistakes myself. However, catching over a hundred stitches after a needle broke is something that Miss Frease could do, and I would even now find daunting. Patsy, my later housekeeper, was also good at rescuing such catastrophes.

We had other experiences with the military when I was growing up. Sometimes Papa would take us to army reviews, such as Prelude to Taps, at Fort Meyers or other places. On one occasion, when we attended such a program, they wanted us to park a long distance away. Nana was with us, and Papa raised the roof with the folks that they were going to make this old lady who could not walk very well hike miles to get to the seats. As I said, Papa believed that rules should be broken for good reasons, like looking out for somebody vulnerable.

One Sunday, Papa and I went to Arlington National Cemetery to visit some of the graves. We met there a very nice gentleman, named Mr. Tom Keehoe. Mr. Keehoe walked around with us and showed us the different graves, some marked with crosses and some with the Star of David. He became a friend of ours, and he later introduced us to a friend of his, Colonel Pitt. The retired colonel couldn't talk, because he had surgery to remove his larynx on account of throat cancer. He had good thoughts and may have been a poet. He communicated by writing. One of the things that I remember his writing to us was that, if people would follow God's laws, peace among nations would follow as naturally as night follows day.

When we moved into our house, the first floor was fully finished, with plaster walls and oak hardwood floors, and linoleum in the kitchen and tile in the bathroom. The house relied on a gas forced-air furnace and hot water heater and window air conditioners in the summer when I was a child. Eventually, in 1979, Papa replaced the original furnace, and in 1981, he had central air-conditioning installed. Nana said that it was about time we got rid of the window units, which she called "hen coops."

The house had on this first floor the living room, dining room, kitchen (which was small until I enlarged it and put down ceramic floor tile in 1995), and the hall with the closet for coats and hats; at the end of the hall it divided, like the Three Little Pigs' roads: to the left was my parents' room; straight ahead was the bathroom, and to the right was Nana's room that I shared with her.

After I was big and old enough to be able to sleep in a single bed instead of the crib, Nana and I slept in twin beds, side by side. Mama was often eating or nibbling on something, including ice, carrots, celery, peanut bars, or little coffee candies, and she liked to have toast at night before she went to bed. Nana and I nicknamed her Crunchy. At night, we could smell the aromas of the toast drifting into our room. I would whisper to Nana that Crunchy was eating something. I would often go to sleep holding hands with Nana. If I was distressed or wanted her, I would bang on her mattress with my hand to get her attention. I called Nana "My Old Pal," or "the Pal of my baby days." Sometimes, if I were sick or upset, Mama would come into the room, kick off her shoes, and get into bed next to me. She would hold and cuddle me until I went to sleep, and then quietly leave.

I somehow understood that it was OK to go rummaging in the chest of drawers and bureau and night table that Nana and I shared. After all, nobody had to worry about my snooping and reading old letters. If I found interesting things, I would bring them out, and ask Nana or Mama what they were, which was especially likely to happen with pictures in frames. One of the things that I remember finding was a stuffed, bolster-style dog, with yarn hair and button eyes. When I asked Nana, she said that he was called Pete, but I don't know anything more about him. Among her keepsakes, Nana also had a powder-box type music box that played The Marseillaise, and sometimes she would wind it up and let me hold it while it was playing. The box had a lid with a wind-up clock mechanism in the center of it.

Nana and I enjoyed ourselves on the rare occasions that my parents went out together without us. We would ignore the usual bedtime, and stay up to read and talk. When Nana heard the garage door opening, she would hustle me into bed, saying in a stage whisper, "Shut your eyes and go to sleep!" As though we could fool them!

If Nana and I were pals, Mama and I were also close, and we were friends. I don't mean that she wasn't my Mama and didn't discipline me, but we had a lot of things in common. We both liked reading; we both liked to make up stories, and to write them down. We both appreciated poetry and music, including later playing the piano, and we enjoyed shopping for pretty figurines, dolls, miniature models of old-fashioned cars, and jewelry together. We usually drove to stores, but sometimes we would park the car at our nearby bus stop and take the bus downtown to Washington, DC to shop in the big department stores. We walked between the stores, and we usually had lunch in the Tea Room at Woodward and Lothrop's (also known affectionately as Woody's.)

Mama was also very generous and giving about her personal things and thinking of my welfare. One day, when it was cold, I forgot my gloves when I was going to school. Mama lent me her gloves, which worked, because our hands were of similar size. When she came to get me that afternoon, she had bought me a new pair. I tried them on, but I told her that I liked her gloves better.

"Fine. Keep the ones you like," she said, which I did. She liked the new ones, because they had leather on the palms and were good for driving the car.

I didn't go rummaging in my parents' drawers, but sometimes Mama and I would go through her jewelry and other trinkets, and she often shared her treasures with me. When I was old enough to wear rings her size, she gave me her topaz ring to wear all the time. We were both born in November, and we shared the same birthstone. She also told me that I could start wearing her gold ring with the blue sapphire-colored glass intaglio of a soldier's head after I started high school. After Mama died, most of her goodies came to me. I would have given much to have her with me, instead, through my difficult teen years!

Downstairs in the house, the basement held the laundry room, doors to the backyard and garage, Papa's workbench and tools, and all kinds of fascinating things. He kept some of his pictures and camera things there, along with the equipment used for his second job, to be discussed later. The basement had asbestos tile on the floor. I later had to replace it with ceramic tile. The old tile started coming unstuck after the basement flooded, something that hadn't ever happened before.

Papa used Navy terminology in ordinary speech, so the words seemed every day to me. Upstairs was "up topside," and downstairs was "Down below." The floor was "the deck" and the bathroom was "the head." Throwing something away in our house meant to "deep six it." When John Erlichman made headlines during the Watergate scandal by using the term "deep six" I got a big laugh out of it.

Upstairs the second floor was at first unfinished, with just the sub-flooring and wall frames. Eventually, 5/8-inch dry wall went up. I didn't go up to the second floor alone as a little child, because it was a vast open space, with no banister around the stairwell and no railing to go up the uncarpeted stairs. Sometimes, I would go upstairs with Mama, so that she could get the Christmas things down from the cubbies under the eaves, or we could rummage through memorabilia stored up there in the cubbyholes under the eaves. Mama really liked Christmas and the other holidays, and she taught me to really enjoy celebrating them.

Over the years, as money and time allowed, the banister was installed around the stairwell, a hand railing was put on the stairs, the room was finished off and the bathroom was equipped with tub, sink, medicine chest, and a commode, with tile floor in the bathroom and a pine floor on the rest. They closed off the biggest of the side rooms and lined it with cedar to make a cedar closet, where everybody's wool coats and other woolens were stored during the summer time. Ironically, the bedroom didn't have a real ordinary closet until long after Nana's death, when I paid Bill Sutton to close off a closet area. Before we had the closet, I used one of the cubbies as a closet or hung clothes on a bar on the bedroom door.

When the room was finally finished, Mama helped me pick out the colonial-style, cherry wood furniture and the carpeting for the room and the stairs. The leftover carpet from the stairs was used to partially cover the floor in the largest part of the areaway outside the bedroom, which became my office. My desk and learning supplies were moved up there.

In theory, I was to work and study upstairs, and Papa had the bedroom and downstairs for camera equipment and working on pictures. However, maybe because it was less lonely, everybody seemed to migrate into the dining room. Nana couldn't understand it.

"You have your office upstairs, and Papa has his room and downstairs to do things. How come everybody and their projects always land in the dining room on the dining room table?" she would ask, but she really didn't mind.

I moved into the bedroom upstairs with Nana eventually when I was in the sixth or seventh grade. Papa installed intercoms between the basemen, first, and second floors to facilitate communication and avoid long-distance shouting. After Mama died, Papa made Nana move back downstairs, and I had the room to myself. In the late 1990's, I had the office area on the second floor enlarged to accommodate two desks and the computer tables for my house and the telework SEC computer while I was still working. Now, I consider this second-floor suite to be my Penthouse. In 2017, I renovated the stairway going up to the second floor to eliminate the turning stairs near the bottom, create a straight first three stairs, add a landing, and leave the straight stairs going up to the second floor. Fortunately, we had a large enough piece of the leftover original rug to carpet the new stairs and landing.

As I said before, I clearly remember Nana going away for "Aunt Mary's funeral". It seemed that she was gone a long, long time, and I missed her so much. Mama tried to cook in her absence, as I said, with some disasters and some limited successes.

Nana's return was also memorable. I should explain that I began to suffer from some asthma –like symptoms after I was taken off the baby formula. I was put on medicine for it, eventually, but finally it was discovered that I had allergies, and the treatment was changed. Like Mama, I was also prone to have nosebleeds and sinus infections. The nosebleeds have been another lifelong nuisance. They are probably caused by a hereditary condition, known as Osser Webber Rendu (after the people who found it) or by a medical term with the initials HHT. It results in superficial blood vessels that form abnormally in different parts of the body and which can bleed if subject to disturbance or irritation.

The underlying problem is that veins and arteries connect directly in the affected areas, instead of going through a capillary system, which can result in the ready bleeding. In my case, I consider myself fortunate that these blood vessels are primarily in my nose, where they are easily accessed and treated, instead of the intestines, the gums or tongue, or the brain. When I was scanned prior to my hip surgery in 2018, we discovered some *AVM's*, abnormal venous malformations, in the lungs, which need to be checked periodically but so far are stable. Allergies and dry conditions can cause or aggravate the bleeding in the nose. I learned early to pack the nose with cotton until the bleeding stopped, usually fairly quickly. Sometimes, Nana would use ice on the nose or the back of the neck to cool down the blood flow and cause the nosebleeds to stop earlier. A few times, I have had cauterizations or packing in the emergency rooms, but I try to avoid them if at all possible. These treatments don't get to the root of the problem, and they can be uncomfortable. Doctors recently told me that cauterizations aren't recommended or effective. They consider the bleeding situation was aggravated during my menstrual cycle years because the tendency to bleed increased as the periods approached. After my second guide dog, a yellow Labrador retriever, called Mikki, was successfully treated with homeopathic remedies, I sought advice from a homeopathic physician. The upshot was that we discovered that a homeopathic remedy made from poison ivy, *rhus tox*, (the full Latin name rhus toxicadendrum means poison leaf,) could help to stop the more severe bleeds. I keep the little pellets in my purse and available at all times. Among the other problems caused by this condition is that screwing up the face when crying can open these delicate vessels. For this reason, both Mama and I have paid the penalty for our tears.

I will describe more about my nose situation and my allergies later, but in the early stages of all this, they tried different things. For a while, I was drinking goats' milk, because it seemed to agree with me better than the milk from the cows. To this day, I still like goat cheese, when I can find it at a farmer's market or other store.

At any rate, when Nana came home from that trip to Quincy, MA, she was bearing gifts. She brought me a record with the story of Jack and the Beanstalk, from Aunts Janie and Riri, and a box of coconut macaroons, cookies loaded with almond paste. Of course, they were delicious, and I was busily eating them. My parents said that I didn't eat very well as a little child, and I'm sure they were glad to see me like something. In any event, after dinner, I began to choke up, and to itch terribly in various private places. Even playing the trains game with Papa wasn't too much fun. At last, they called the doctor, and they had to get me medicine. It seems that I am allergic to almonds and almond paste, among other things. I try to avoid it to this day, because it nearly killed me then. Supposedly, I don't test as allergic, but I'm afraid to take the risk.

In addition to the allergies, I had the usual childhood illnesses and sore throats, including measles and Rubella. sometimes they were an occasion for pleasant memories. When I contracted the mumps during my early years at school, I fortunately had a mild case. I stayed home to recover and avoid infecting anyone else, and Mama read to me during the day. The girl Scouts were selling shortbread cookies, and I enjoyed nibbling on them.

Usually, however, my sicknesses were hard and unpleasant. Mama often had to sit with me and hold me during illness and the breathing difficulties. She would wrap me up and try to help me calm down, to ease the spasms, and she would try to sing to me. She said that her voice got ruined after her tonsils were removed, but I still liked to hear her sing to me. One song that she sang that I remember well was, "I Love You Truly."

Nana sang many songs to me, too, including "I'll Deck my Brow with Roses," and other good oldies. She could carry a tune well into her old age, and she could actually sing "The Star Spangled Banner."

Mama had allergies, too, and she often got sinus infections. On one occasion, she became severely anemic and was hospitalized for a while to deal with it. Mama would get bad headaches from time to time, some of which were migraines. Papa also had his physical trials. He sustained a back injury while he was in the Coast Guard; he had a big, heavy, corset-like back brace that he would wear sometimes, if his back bothered him, until it calmed down again.

Although Nana had problems with her legs and calluses on her feet, she was very strong and healthy for her age. She did develop arthritis in her hands, which didn't seem to bother her too much, except for her wrist. She was always washing fruit, meat, or vegetables in cold water while she was preparing meals, and the cold water might have helped to minimize the inflammation. She would come out of the kitchen, and tease us by putting her cold hands on us, to make us complain and ultimately laugh.

Sometimes, if Mama got sick when I was, Nana would be running back and forth between us. I would say to Nana that I didn't want her to get sick, too.

"I'm not going to catch it!" she would retort defiantly, as though daring the germs to even try to get to her, and she usually didn't get sick!

I should mention my doctors here. Dr. Scalessa was my initial doctor, involved with the feeding tube and other things that doubtless helped to save my life. I have a vague memory of him, particularly that I wasn't comfortable with him doing things for me, especially if they involved needles, like shots and vaccinations. I liked Mrs. Kelly, his nurse, much better. I remember the doctor saying that Mrs. Kelly should do whatever it was that I needed on this particular occasion, because he wasn't going to have me fight him.

After Dr. Scalessa, Dr. Robert Bregmann became my pediatrician. I liked him so much better. He and the other doctors in practice with him could make you feel better by just walking into the office to see you. He also used to come to the house if necessary, even in bad weather. He recommended honey-sweetened candies or hot, sweet tea to break up congestion. I thus was one of the only students in grade school to carry sweetened tea in my lunch thermos bottles. When my mother was stricken with the final attack that paralyzed her lungs, I instinctively called Dr. Bregmann, and he went to the hospital to comfort my father. I stayed with him as his patient during my teen years, long after most girls would have changed. I finally had the sense of growing up on one of my last visits. When I was a child, my parents would come into the examining room with me. On this visit, probably one of my last, Dr. Bregmann ushered me into the office, and closed the door. To my surprise, I noted that Papa wasn't there.

The doctor understood. "Oh, we can't have him in here with you anymore," he said. "My goodness!"
I realized with surprise that I really was becoming a woman!

Besides the pediatrician, of course, I saw Dr. Lynden, the ear, nose, and throat specialist that I shared with Mama, Dr. April, the allergist, and others that I don't recall.

Eventually, my frequent sore throats resulted in the doctors deciding that my tonsils should be removed in Children's Hospital. I found that experience an ordeal, even though they tried to explain to me that I would go to sleep, and then it would be over. I wasn't prepared for having my arms pinned at my side, and then waking up in horrible pain. The medicine that they tried to give me to relieve it only made me sick. It taught me that sometimes the so-called medical remedies just don't work. Being distracted by stories helped more than the medicine, but the recovery was a long ordeal.

The tonsil surgery was one occasion that I was in the hospital as a child. The second occasion happened on a pleasant summer evening. I had gone out to play, and then I came in and played with Papa. I went to bed and went to sleep. Nana said that she came in and went to check on me, and I was impossible to move, like a stone. I remember being aroused. I remember the flashlight being shown into my eyes –I still had some light perception at that time—and Papa saying, "Stick out your tongue." All I wanted to do was lie back and go to sleep. What I didn't know was that I was having convulsions. I woke up in Arlington Hospital, wondering where I was and wanting Mama.

That was when the doctors finally decided that I was not a chronic asthma sufferer, to be treated with theodral, the medicine in vogue at that time, and the medicine was causing my problem. I was tested for allergies. They confirmed that I was allergic to wet molds (that meant no penicillin), dust, pollens, ragweed, feathers, and dogs and cats.

I was put on allergy injections, and now we see another example of Divine Providence in my life. The day after I received my first injection, we went to visit Ethel and Ed Stanulis. Ethel was a member of a volunteer Braillist group that was helping to provide books for me in school. The couple had a lovely, big house in the countryside in VA, with spacious grounds around it. They gave us a tour of the house, but at one point, Mama and I ended up going outside, and walking down their lawn to the parallel-bar fence at the end of it. With my parents' consent, I started climbing on the fence. Fortunately, I never got onto the other side. On the other side of the fence, hidden by a rose bush, was a hornets' nest. They came out after me. It was like being pierced with hot needles. I received 37 stings. They took me to the doctor to be checked, but I was going to be OK, although in pain. Mama and Nana had to keep baking soda poultices on me for a few days. They said that it was a good thing that I had my first injection for allergies the day before. The second time that I was stung was from a yellow jacket that came out of a crack in Ellen's driveway while I was standing and talking to her. Mama had called me, and I was dawdling. She said that it was meant to teach me to come when I was called.

Meanwhile, the allergies were prompting changes in the household. The feather pillows went away, replaced by foam-filled (and later fiber-filled) pillows; strenuous activity was a no-no, as well as ice-cold foods and drinks (they can increase mucus production), milk, chocolate, and almond-extract. I had to learn to live with more limitations.

# COPING WITH DISABILITY AND LIMITATIONS

Sometimes it seems to me that my life is a story of learning to cope with limitations. Of course, the most obvious one is my blindness. Many well-meaning people ask me if I was born blind. Most of the time, I just say, "Not exactly," because the reality is a little complicated to explain on casual acquaintance.

Retinopathy of prematurity sets in over a period of weeks or months after birth, so I must have been able to see at one time, for however short a period. As I have already described, my parents didn't discover my loss of sight, until I was around one and a half or two years old. I vaguely remember hearing my parents discuss Dr. Parks, the eye doctor who supposedly was the expert in this condition. I remember being examined by him, too.

My blindness meant that Mama and Nana had to teach me with hands-on methods to do many of the things that children take for granted, such as getting dressed and brushing my teeth, bathing, and using eating utensils. I learned to tell time with the help of the Seth Thomas mantle clock that chimed on the quarter hours and struck the hours. Uncle Johnny and Aunt Murff, close family friends discussed in the next chapter, bought me my first Braille watch in 1960 for an Easter gift. The watch had dots to mark the numbers and a hinged crystal that opened.

Concerning money, my parents taught me to distinguish coins by their size and shape. Dimes and pennies were the most difficult, because they are close in size. Fortunately, dimes are thinner than pennies, and, unlike pennies, they have milled edges if they aren't too worn. Later my blind piano teacher taught me to differentiate between different denominations of paper currency by folding them in distinct, consistent ways.

I did pretty well with most basic tasks, but I found it hard to master tying a nice, neat bow. Mama and Nana also taught me to help with household chores, such as washing and drying the dishes and making the beds. Nana, in particular, taught me to tuck in the sheets and blankets in nice, tight hospital corners. She said that she learned that from her nursing training days. She also said that her brother, Gino, was taught to make neat beds in the Navy. The instructor said that he wanted to be able to bounce a quarter on the nice, smooth made beds. The gas stove scared me, and I was always a little afraid of hot flames. Unfortunately, Nana wasn't a good cooking teacher, because she didn't have the patience, and she wasn't good at hands-on instruction.

I don't know whether this trait resulted from my blindness or if it's just my way, but I seemed to take longer than anybody else in the house to do things, including eating. Papa would tease me about being a "slowey." Sometimes, he would snitch or take away something that I was eating and hadn't finished, to try to encourage me to eat more quickly. He also would tease me by saying, "Last one upstairs (from the basement or the garage,) is a rotten egg."

As I said, I didn't have a good appetite when I was little. I remember Nana and Papa persistently trying to feed me soft-boiled eggs in the morning. For some reason, I just didn't want to eat, but they managed to get those eggs down me, which probably saved my life. Now, I'm very fond of those incredible, edible eggs. Nana also made fresh-squeezed orange juice in the morning, but she left the pulp in the juice. I still prefer it that way. Now I like to eat the juice oranges in their entirety, even if they are a little messy on account of the juice.

However, when I was little, everything came to a head when I was recovering from one childhood sickness or other. I couldn't seem to get rid of the "butterflies" in my stomach, and I was delayed going back to school for a couple of days, when I should have been better. I missed the Halloween Party, for which I had my costume all ready. I was taking some bitter green medicine to help my stomach. I don't know if these symptoms came from some anxiety about going back to school that I couldn't really understand or articulate.

The following Monday, I went to school, still not feeling quite right. On the way home that afternoon, Mama told me, "I called Dr. Bregmann today, and told him about your problem. He says there's nothing wrong. Just ignore it and go ahead and eat."

I believed him, and I acted on his advice. Unless I'm upset or under great stress, I've been eating with a good appetite ever since that day.

When I was little, I remember having light perception. I could see the sunshine, and sometimes I could tell that an electric light was on in a room. This light perception was a source of hope to my parents for a while, because they thought that, if some light perception remained, some hope for recovering sight might exist. I think that Mama and Nana clung to these hopes more than Papa. They would test me sometimes by moving their hands or an object back and forth against a light. If the light were bright, I would sometimes see the light "flash" if the object passed between it and me. No, I never really saw objects or shadows. At night, when I said my night prayers before going to sleep, after asking God to bless Papa, Mama, and Nana along with the other relatives, Mama taught me to ask God to heal my eyes so that I could see. I think that Papa was more of a realist about the situation. As I said, he concentrated when I was little on teaching me about my environment. Out in the yard, Papa put poles with rope or wire strung between them, to guide me in walking around, so that I wouldn't fall down the outside stairs to the basement or into the window wells. He also used flagstones to mark the path and to make steps going up the hill to the backyard.

Even as a little kid, it eventually dawned on me, that my situation was not likely to change. I came to understand that, although God can work miracles and do whatever He wills, He often does not divinely intervene to change the crosses that He helps us to carry. Sometimes, one of my little playmates in the neighborhood or school would get all excited, telling me about a family member or friend who had an operation to restore his/her eyesight. Of course, I told Mama about these ideas, and they always went nowhere, because the other person's situation was entirely different from mine. Now, I find it very annoying, although I try not to show it, when relatives, friends, or acquaintances mourn over the fact that I can't see. Except for not being able to drive, which I find to be a royal pain, my blindness has evolved into a nuisance, and I try to ignore, endure, or compensate for it and get on with my life. I don't have time to mourn over what I don't have and am not likely to get in this life.

When I was little, I wanted always to be facing the light, which meant that I didn't like sitting facing away from windows, and I sometimes had a tendency to crane my head back as though I were looking up at the sky. I also had a childhood habit of putting one hand up to my left eye. My parents worked hard to break this habit, and I eventually succeeded.

Gradually, as the years have passed, the light perception has faded. I still can see the sunshine if it hits my eyes at the right angle, but I no longer can tell whether the lights are on or off in a room. If people ask me, I generally just say that I'm totally blind, because I don't want anybody to get the erroneous idea that I have usable vision.

I found the last examination that I had with Dr. Parks very upsetting in this regard. I asked him about the diminishing of my light perception. It turns out that now the eyes have cataracts. Apparently, he didn't consider it important enough to see if any precaution should be taken, such as wearing sunglasses to protect from ultraviolet rays. He said bluntly that there was no vision to save. I resented his assumption that the little light perception that I had wasn't important to me.

I suffered a big disappointment when I was in the sixth or seventh grade. Mama took me to a hearing specialist, because she was hoping that an operation could help my hearing. I was devastated to learn that nothing could be done. In many ways, I find my hearing difficulty to be more of a problem than my blindness.

Once I joined Papa in the camp of the realists, I concentrated as much as possible on making the best use of, exploring, and enjoying my world as much as possible. Papa was always trying to get exceptions to the rules about "don't touch" so that I could experience as much as possible, feel things, and get an idea what they were like.

One vivid summer memory was of our local lightning strike. I don't remember how old I was, somewhere between six or seven, I guess. That summer was hot and humid, but we seemed to get a great many thunderstorms in the afternoon. They usually quit soon after the sun went down. That evening, they continued into the night, and I went to bed in the room that I shared with Nana, as usual. In the early morning, a horrendous clap of thunder woke me, even without my hearing aids. I seem to remember seeing a big flash (I still had some limited light perception) before the big thunder clap. After I was up and dressed, while we were having breakfast, we learned that lightning had struck the locust tree in Mr. William's yard. After breakfast, Papa and I walked to the end of the block and turned the corner to walk up Hayes Street, past the Marcies house, to the Williams' yard. Debris and pieces resembling driftwood were scattered all over the place. I'm sure it looked as though someone had taken an inept axe to that poor tree! Papa and I took home a couple of pieces, (handle gently on account of splinters,) for souvenirs! That didn't even include the shattered part of the tree still in the ground that professionals probably had to remove! It was an awe-inspiring exhibition of the power of lightning! I subsequently learned that locust trees are more prone than many others to be struck by lightning, but I don't know why.

On one pleasant summer evening, Papa and Mama caught a good number of fireflies. They put them in a glass jar with holes in the lid overnight. I understand that their being in the jar lit up the jar, like a little lamp, and the jar actually grew warm to the touch. In the morning, we let them go.

On one memorable Fourth of July, Papa bought a whole bunch of home fireworks, and we set them off in the backyard. We had sparklers, most of which my parents stood up in the ground, planting their wires in the earth. I was allowed to hold a couple of them, one at a time, by the end of the wire, under very close supervision. They took them away as they started to burn down. They had some little things in the box, but when they lit one of them, we decided it was a bad idea, because the smell was terrible! They lit up the rockets and the fountains. I liked the fountains best, because of the whooshing sound that they made, almost sounding like water. Maybe that's why they call them fountains. Finally, there was a pinwheel affair, with wicks connecting the divided thirds of the circle. Papa nailed this one to a tree trunk before lighting it. It was lots of fun, and the only time we did the whole works. Maybe we were living a little dangerously, but it was nice to have the experience. The next day, after the dawn's early light, Mama and I went out and picked up all the debris from the yard to throw it away, including all the sparklers with their charred ends. If we had that much to pick up from our yard, I can imagine the clean up on the Mall after the public display must be immense!

I also remember one particular Halloween. Papa went with Vickie and me "trick or treating." We visited Ellen's house and the neighbors across the street. I don't remember what costume I wore. Vickie greeted everybody with "Guess who I am!" and I probably tried to chime in, too. The wonderful adults played along with our games and made us feel valued and important. Their empathetic interaction with us was more important than the candy that they gave us. I couldn't eat most of it anyway, because it was chocolate.

Another year, I had a fairy costume with a wand and a crown. Perhaps that was for the Halloween party at school. I always wanted a cat costume: not the frivolous, childish kind, but the type that zipped up around you, with fake fur, kitty ears, and a kitty face.

Years later, my friend Dottie and my housekeeper, Tina, helped me to get a child's version of a cat costume. It had a kitty mask and a headband with ears. As an adult, I wore it that year to greet and hand out goodies to the children who came to my door. I'm afraid that I didn't do so well as my kind neighbors did with us. For one thing, I couldn't see their costumes to speak intelligently and admiringly about them. For another thing, I was distracted by the need to keep my working and retired guide dogs calm, away from the door and the candy, and safely inside the house. It probably would have been better if someone had been with me to describe what was happening, but Tina was out that evening.

When I was a little girl, for a while, I thought that the tooth fairy brought me coins in exchange for lost baby teeth, but I soon figured out that Papa was the tooth fairy. Getting the six-year old molars wasn't fun; it was painful and a bother, but it was good to have them when they were completely developed.

Mama also tried to explain colors to me, which is hard, because color is so intangible. She said that green was a cool color, and I tended to associate it with plants and trees, although intellectually I understand that not all greens are forest green in shade. She said that red was bright and hot, and I tend to think of fire trucks in connection with this color. Pink was lighter and softer than red, but some pinks were considered to be "loud" or "hot pinks". Blue had shades ranging from very light pastels to navy blue that is almost black. I don't have a good idea about purple, except that it is sometimes between blue and pink. I associate yellow with being bright and cheerful, and it makes me think of canaries.

Mama also told me that some colors did not go well together, or did not look right with my complexion. To this day, nothing irritates me more than finding a pretty dress or piece of jewelry that feels good and fits right, only to be told that the color won't work for me or that it isn't the right shade!

I could navigate pretty well inside my house. As I already discussed, when I was little, everything was on one floor. I found my way around by using clues from the position of rugs and furniture and getting familiar with the floor plan and how rooms related to each other. For these reasons, I'm not one of those adventurous souls who change the layout of their house, because they are tired of looking at the same thing. Familiarity of furniture and environmental clues is definitely my preference and my friend. Sometimes it drives me crazy if people move things around and don't put things back in their familiar places. Inside the house, I generally walked with hands outstretched, to avoid bumping into walls or higher objects. Nana put ice and witch hazel and brown paper on many bumps on my head when I was little.

The stairways in the house had doors to close them off. I especially learned to be careful of the stairs going down to the basement, because sometimes the door was left open. I remember taking a couple of headers down those stairs. At that time, they were open-backed and uncarpeted, and the basement floor was hard. I am grateful to Divine Providence that I was not hurt beyond big bumps on my head. If I did walk downstairs, I held onto the handrail on the left side near the wall. I don't know whether it was related to the hearing loss or caused by a fear of falling or both, but I do not have a good sense of balance on stairs. I don't like walking up or down stairs without a railing. In recent years, I had two railings put on the basement and the upstairs staircases for balance and support, as discussed in a later chapter. If no railing is available, I now often use my dogs to help me balance on stairs. My previous dog, Teddy, and my present dog, Ives, are especially good about helping me this way.

The stairs that went upstairs were also closed off with a door, but it is hard to fall up stairs, although you can trip on the step and hurt your knees. As I previously discussed, I didn't go up there alone as a little girl. When I put in the landing described in the earlier chapter, the door was removed for the staircase to the second floor.

In addition to my blindness, I inherited feet difficulties from both grandfathers. Grandpa Tom Calabro is said to have had narrow feet, and I do, too, with small heels. It is often difficult to find shoes that fit well across the ball of my feet and don't slide up and down in the heels. From Papa's father, I inherited trouble with my arches. The podiatrist calls it "compensated flat feet," because the arches look fine if the feet are elevated, but they drop when I put my legs down and try to put weight on them. I have needed supportive shoes, usually Oxford-style, with strong arches and supplement arch supports or orthotics all my life. I consider myself still fortunate. My poor Aunt Maria had to wear specially fitted and made orthopedic shoes that were not very attractive that she called space shoes. I recently am trying arch supports from The Good Feet Store, and I can use different ones with different shoes. I think that they are helping, although it will take time to strengthen what arches my feet have.

I gradually came to regard my blindness (and eventually my hearing impairment) as nuisances and inconveniences. The disabilities made it harder to find my way around. They meant that I couldn't go out and run around the neighborhood on my own, like other children. Although I rode a little tricycle when I was very small, I never was able to independently ride a bicycle, because I wouldn't have been able to see where I was going. I learned to find my way across the yard and through the bushes to get to Ellen's driveway and her basement door and to walk down the block to the corner mailbox on my own, but otherwise outside the house I had to rely on someone else to guide me. I eventually learned to use a long cane for mobility as a teenager, but, as discussed later, I never found cane travel very comfortable or practical outside, because the hearing situation made street-crossings a problem and potential danger.

Even inside the house, I had some problems in playing. If I dropped my toys, I couldn't locate them by sound, and they didn't make a noise if they fell on the rug. Nana often had to help me pick things up or find things for me. I also liked things that weren't necessarily toys that had interesting shapes. One of my favorite places to rummage for unconventional playthings was the broiler drawer under the gas stove in the kitchen. The broiler either didn't work or was seldom used, so this drawer was used to store pots and pans, cake tins, and many neat things, like hand-beaters and little strainers. I can remember marching out of the kitchen with one strainer in each hand, going "choo-choo!" For some reason those strainers reminded me of trains, maybe because they suggested the cowcatchers on the model trains.

Mama did everything that she could to help me get a good attitude toward my situation. On the one hand, as she explained to me, she tried to love me all the more, not because she felt sorry for me, but because of the needs that I had and to try to make up for the problems I had in some way. However, she also tried to impress on me the fact that I was no different from anybody else on account of my blindness. As a little child, I remember arguing with Nana and Mama about this, not because I disagreed with them, but because I was very aware of my own unique individuality. I was a child, and I couldn't explain what I meant.

Even before it was discovered, the hearing loss was causing its own set of problems for me.

I remember the silences, when I was little, and I remember talking, listening to the sound of my own voice. Some might have said that I was "talking to myself." I spoke aloud to listen to myself; I talked out loud to act out stories that I had in my head, and, later on, I prayed out loud.

The impaired hearing also affected the way I perceived sounds and music. As I already said, I liked to listen to records, including some older records that Papa had that had musical tunes on them. The song Bali Hai from South Pacific made me cry and get upset. It doesn't now, of course, because I hear it better and understand the words, but when I wasn't hearing it right, the sounds I did hear were disturbing to me. I also remember getting very upset over the children's record, the story of Mickey Mouse and the Wonderful Candy Mine.

I also had problems with speech and pronouncing words correctly. Much of my hearing loss is in the higher pitches, which are where the soft sounds of consonants are articulated. I now listen with a sense of awe and chagrin to some of the tapes of my little childish voice, and I marvel at the patience and persistence of my parents in coping with what they didn't completely understand for a number of years. What I did hear also triggered some reactions that must have been puzzling to my elders and teachers. For example, the sound of plastic disks hitting the floor made a bouncing, sharp noise that I found very funny. I liked ordinary noises, so long as they weren't too loud. It's a good thing that I enjoyed noises and didn't mind the ones that weren't appealing, because Nana was a very noisy operator in the kitchen, dropping pots and pans, and clattering pots, pans, and dishes. As a teenager and adult, this reaction to sounds now manifests itself in my liking Spike Jones music and some electronic music.

I enjoyed listening to singing birds outside, as well as to Dickey inside the house, and I tried to imitate and "talk" to some of the outside birds, with limited success. I guess I'm best at imitating the distress calls of blue jays and the cawing of crows.

I wasn't the only one trying to adjust to all the problems and behaviors related to my disabilities, of course. They affected my Papa, Mama, and Nana, and they aggravated what would have been a tense situation under any circumstances. The old saying goes that "Two is company, and three is a crowd." That must have been true with my father, mother, and maternal grandmother trying to coexist in one household. All three had tempers and vented their emotions by a good deal of "yelling, screaming, and hollering," as Papa used to say. All that furious sound invading the silence could be overwhelming and frightening, even when I was too young to understand what it was all about. Although they rarely got physical, emotions often ran pretty high.

On one occasion, during a three-way argument, Mama told me afterwards that Papa became so angry at Nana that he picked up a chair to throw it at her; Mama said that she just stepped in between them, and nothing happened. On another occasion, Papa became furious about something, and he stormed out of the house, slamming the doors behind him. Mama locked herself in their bedroom, and I was screaming at her to come out and crying to get in there with her. Mama and Nana had a great deal of trouble calming me down afterwards. Those exceptions proved the rule: that generally, despite everything, my parents ended up at night in the same bed.[14]

Sometimes the anger was directed at me, if I misbehaved or broke something by being careless. I remember Mama getting furious about some mistake I made, and shaking me by the hair and crying, "Stupid, Stupid Linda!" The funny thing was that I knew she didn't think that I was stupid, just that I wasn't using my head and should have known better. On the other hand, if I did something wrong, deliberately or otherwise, one thing that I didn't want to hear Papa say was, "Tonight, we are going to have a meeting!" A meeting meant that there would be a sit-down, and I would be told to "straighten up and fly right," and maybe privileges would be suspended.

I began the story of my life with the pleasant memories and stories, because I prefer to emphasize them, but I also have to acknowledge that growing up in a house frequently beset by tensions was often confusing and very upsetting to a sensitive child. Sometimes, in her anger and frustration,

---

[14]  After my parents' death, we found in the file some of the little homemade Valentines that Mama sent Papa, before I was old enough to start making birthday, Christmas, Valentine's Day, and Father's Day cards with Mama's help for Papa. In one particular card, Mama wrote, "We try each other's patience, I know, but I love you like the devil!"

Mama would, in my hearing, threaten to divorce or leave Papa. All three of my parents said things in my hearing that, in retrospect, I'm sure that they didn't mean or thought better about later. How I wish that adults would learn not to say what they don't mean, especially in the hearing of their children! They little understand what a devastating emotional effect such careless, loose talk can have!

Abraham Lincoln is quoted as saying that he often ended up on his knees, because there was nowhere else to go, so did I. I came to see God, including His Son and the second person of the Trinity, Jesus, as my Best Friend, the only one that I could go to with my problems, knowing that the confidentiality of what I said would never be broken and the love was unfailing. I knew that my parents and Nana loved me, but I sensed that their love was imperfect, although very wonderful, and I realized that God's love must be even greater, especially after I learned that Jesus died for the whole world but also for me personally.

I learned early that human help was often temporary and fleeting. At one time, I tried to confide my concerns about my family troubles to Ellen, but Mama made me understand that it was not a good idea to discuss home things with the neighbors; Aunt Betty sometimes came to visit, and she and Mama would trade promises to pray for each other and confidences about family woes (Uncle Charlie wasn't a Catholic, which probably caused some tensions in that household connected with bringing up the children as Catholics), but eventually Aunt Betty went home, and we had to deal with family matters on our own.

On one occasion, when I was crying, Papa tried to comfort me. As he dried my tears, he said, "The father takes care of his kid."

Papa was talking about himself, of course, but I made the parallel connection with God's love.

I have heard that some children, especially those with disabilities, may feel guilty, because they think that somehow they are causing their parents' problems. I don't think that I ever felt guilty in this way. I somehow understood that all of these troubles and emotional scars resulted from the frictions and difficulties of living with difficult situations. Although I heard my parents say some very angry, hateful things when they were upset, I never heard any of them say that they wished that I had not survived. As discussed later, however, I did often wish that I could have these loving people with me in a more ideal family situation, like the ones described in the children's classics that I read.

My nerve-type hearing loss in both ears was eventually discovered. My first-and-second grade teacher, Sister Dorothy Raney, became convinced that my not following the class and not having my place couldn't all result from just not paying attention. An audiologist at Children's Hospital in Washington, DC, probably what we now call Children's National Medical Center, tested me. The man's name, as I recall, was Mr. Rotollo. They tried a body hearing aid model on me, but eventually I was fitted with a Zenith battery-powered behind-the-ear hearing aid in the right ear. Later, as a teenager, I finally consented to get a hearing aid on the left side. I have gone through many pairs of battery-powered, behind the ear hearing aids, but I still prefer the analog aids to the digital. Digital aids are fine for older, sighted people, who want to screen out environmental noise and focus on conversation. However, to function in a world that I do not see, I need to hear the ceiling fan, refrigerator, and automobiles. Also, the older models of digital hearing aids did not transmit music so well as the analog aids. Fortunately, because the analog aids are no longer being made anymore, as discussed in a later chapter I now have been fitted with a pair of digital aids that function like mini-computers and solve most of the problems I had with earlier models. The upshot is that, with the hearing aid, I do pretty well with spoken conversation on a one to one basis or in a small group if people project their voices and speak one at a time. I cannot converse very well in a crowd or in a place with high background noise. The new digital aids may help with this problem, but I haven't been able to test them on account of not getting out in busy places with pandemic precautions. Time and technology are catching up with me, and fortunately my present pair of digitals may offer a solution to my aging analog aids. With or without hearing aids, the other consequence of the hearing loss is that I cannot localize sound. The hearing loss is unequal in the two ears, and even adjusting the volumes on the two hearing aids doesn't create balance or true equality. To follow or localize sound, one orients toward the direction of the ear that hears the sound first and loudest. However, in my case, the ear that hears it loudest may not be where the sound is. For these reasons, I absolutely hate it when mobility people, and other well-meaning folks only tangentially familiar with blindness, say, "Follow my voice," or "It's over here," banging on something to make a sound that I theoretically should be able to follow. It doesn't work for me. You need to tell me, by left or right directions, how to find the person or object in question. In the press of the moment, it's so hard to get folks to understand.

Nana understood even less. She was no good at left and right, and always said, "Over here," or "right there." She probably was pointing, too, although I couldn't tell.

Some people say to me that they can't imagine how I cope with my situation. In some ways, I perhaps was blessed in not having a long period of remembered sight, because I didn't have the pain of missing what I lost, except for losing my light perception discussed already. However, the fact remains that the things that other people do or omit doing either augment or mitigate the impact of my disabilities on me. I have gradually learned that I have a responsibility to educate others about the do's and don'ts and about my abilities and desire to assert my humanity and individuality. It's wonderful when other people intuitively understand the right and empathetic thing to do, but I can't count on this happening very often. Although I am grateful for such people, I have the ultimate responsibility to reach out to others and try to make the world and the path better for others with disabilities. Believe me! Sometimes I get tired of being this kind of a teacher!

# FAMILY, FRIENDS, AND VOLUNTEERS

My being blind caused another major inconvenience. It gave my parents a dilemma concerning my education. The first decision confronting them was whether to try to get me into a regular school, or to send me away to the VA State School for the Blind, in Stanton, VA. Some of my contemporaries went to this school, and I heard some of the details about mistreatment and difficulty from some of them that made me glad that my family decided not to send me away. My parents chose to try to get me into a regular school. It was harder than it sounded.

As discussed more fully in the next chapter, our Catholic parish church, Our Lady of Lourdes, was only three blocks away from my house, but our parish doesn't have a parochial school connected with it. Had I not been able to get into a Catholic school, I would have to receive my religious instruction from Confraternity of Christian doctrine (CCD) classes on Sundays.

When I was four, going on five in November, my parents succeeded in getting me to a local, probably private, kindergarten near my house, taught by a very nice lady, named Mrs. King. I think that I was there only for half-days. We had some fun times there, including field trips to a farm and a bakery. I made friends there with a little boy my age, Robin Russell, who came to visit and play at my house during the afternoons or on weekends. Nana said that he also helped me sometimes to get into my snowsuit and such. He was very nice. Sometimes, his older brother, William, came to visit us, too. Their father may have been in the military, and they moved away. I lost touch with them.

The following year, I was home again, and Nana only told me that it was because I actually had to be six to get into the first grade, and that turning six in November of the next fall meant that I was too young. That may have been true on its face, but the reality, as revealed by the correspondence that we found in the files later, was different. My parents were busy trying to mainstream me, long before that concept was even recognized as such, and they were running up against refusals and obstacles by the public school systems, and even rejection by some Catholic and other Christian schools.

Meanwhile, Nana kept me assuming, as a matter of course, that I would get an education. When I asked her when I would grow up to be a "big lady," she would answer this way.

"First, you have eight years of grammar school, then four years of high school, then four years of college, and you'll be a big lady."

It seemed like a very long time to me. I have always had to work to be more patient. Had I been born into a Puritan household, they probably would have named me Patience to cure me of this fault of being so impatient.

For that post-kindergarten year, all I knew was that, from time to time, I was taken to meet priests, sisters or other people, and that it had something to do with where I would go to school. I remember that they tried one school with me -- I think that it was the Holy Name School, -- but not sure, but the classes were too large, and I only lasted a couple of days. My father also wrote to the Lutheran bishop, asking to have me admitted into one of their schools, without success. I think that Papa concluded that a Christian education was the main thing, and my parents could deal with doctrinal differences and issues at home and in church.

Meanwhile, another fact of life connected with my blindness was the role of the VA Commission for the Blind or later known as the VA Department for the Blind and Visually Handicapped. They had to do with trying to provide information and resources for parents of blind children. I came, rightly or wrongly, to resent this bureaucratic presence in my life. I accepted what Mama said inside, and I just wanted to live my life like anybody else. Mama started teaching me Braille with flash cards with the letters, but eventually Sarah, the home teacher, was sent to my house to continue the teaching. She taught me to write Braille with a slate and stylus, a cumbersome method that involves writing from the opposite side of the paper, right to left. I didn't like it. Also, in future, folks at the Commission and others automatically assumed that Sara taught me Braille. While she did have a major part in the teaching, even as a child, I resented the fact that nobody gave enough credit to Mama for all that she did to help me.

My parents also tried to network with parents of other blind children, especially those who had become blind from the same condition. I particularly remember twin girls about my age, and another girl, Jane McIver, and we got together once in a while when our parents did. I developed a lifelong friendship with Jane. However, I wanted to like and be friends with someone because I liked them as a person, not necessarily because they are blind. Papa tried to urge me to compare blind people to bricklayers and other union people who stick together to achieve their goals. Blind people should do the same thing, because they have many interests in common. My parents also sent me to the day camps and other summer programs provided by the Columbia Lighthouse for the Blind in Washington, D.C. I learned some arts and crafts there, and played some games with the other children, but what I really wanted was to do the same things that other children who weren't necessarily blind did. All of my life, I've had to try to balance the need for people with disabilities to stand together to defend their common interests with our rights to be individual people.

During one of those day camps, we almost lost Dickey while I was away for the day. On the way home, Mama asked me to pray for a special intention. She wouldn't tell me what it was, but it turned out to be that Ellen, her father, and Nana would somehow catch Dickey. It was a very nice summer day, and Nana put him out on the front porch in his cage on the stand. She didn't notice that the door of the cage hadn't closed! Dickey got out and had a good time flying all over the place, including up into the oak trees. Ellen's father, Mr. Reece, finally had the idea to put Dickey's cage on his porch between two of his canary birds in their cages; one was a male, and the other a female. They put seeds and treats in Dickey's cage. Eventually, Dickey went down to investigate and went into his cage. Ellen had to creep quietly up the bank to get behind him and shut the door. By the actions of good friends and Divine Providence, we had our bird back! It turned out to be a happy ending and a good story!

Apart from day camp, of course, I had childhood hobbies, which tended to emphasize things that I could do by touch and could be used to combat boredom. I liked to make things, and I started by enjoying playing with pipe cleaners, but there's only so much that you can do with them. I learned to make potholders and place mats with potholder looms.

I had one unique hobby that involved trying to draw raised things on paper, using the various combinations that I could make with the six-dot Braille cell and the Braillewriter. It was fun to see what I could design. Among other things, I did a floor plan of my school, a drawing of a Christmas tree with packages, and a pear tree with a bird sitting on the top. This talent proved useful for making homemade Christmas, Valentine, and Easter cards for my parents.

Mama and my aunts tried to interest me in crocheting, but I didn't do very well with it. When she was young, Mama crocheted the squares for an Afghan, but she never found the time to put it together. She showed me the squares that she kept in a box.

Mama taught me to knit when I was in grade school, and I did better with that. I started by making simple things, like scarves and baby doll blankets. I knitted a scarf and earmuffs for Papa, but he didn't use them, because he didn't like the scratching of the knitted material against his skin. Now, I use the scarf sometimes. During my teenage years and as an adult, I knitted a couple of Afghans, lap robes and throws, some hats, a couple of capes, and a sweater. I also, through trial and error, learned to make doll dresses for my larger dolls and Barbie dolls, and I sometimes dress dolls for sale at church bazaars and for other worthy causes.

To try to use this hobby as a way for me to make friends, one summer Mama tried to get some girls in the neighborhood interested in joining me in a knitting club once in a while at my house. It didn't work out, because the other girls didn't have the same interest in it as I, and they were on the go and doing other things.

Sometimes, in the heat of discussion, I've heard people say some very hurtful things to me, such as, "You can't see, so you don't understand…" or "If you could see, you would think differently."

No, folks, it doesn't work that way. While the fact that I cannot see limits my perception of physical things, such as colors and the way physical objects look, and while my blindness has given me a unique perspective on the world, to be discussed later, Linda A. Schneider can have right, wrong, stubborn or bullheaded opinions because of who she is as a person, not because she happens to be blind!

Finally, in the late summer of 1958, I went to meet two more sisters. They were Sister Mary Joanne, the principal of Immaculata, and Sister Dorothy, who became my first grade schoolteacher. This time, the answer to my parents' request that the school accept me was yes. Years later, Sister Dorothy told me that she woke up at 2 O'clock in the morning, wondering what she was going to do with me.

"Did you wonder very long?" I asked her.

"No, not after I got to know you," she answered.

I was accepted in a private, Catholic, all-girls school, Dunblane Hall, Immaculata. Dunblane Hall was the eight-grade elementary school, but the complex included Immaculata High School an all-girls high school, and Immaculata College, a two-year women's college. It was located on Wisconsin Avenue in Washington, DC, and it was taught by the Sisters of Providence, out of St. Mary of the Woods, in Indiana. My going there required sacrifice on the part of my parents. Papa had his second job, to be discussed in this chapter. The school was 10 miles away from my home, and my mother drove the distance back and forth four ways through the rush-hour traffic for the first few years. The school was on a hill, and it was especially difficult to get the car up the steep driveway in bad or snowy weather. Sometimes we had to leave the car at the bottom of the hill and hike up to the building through the snow. The winter of 1960-61 was especially snowy. In 1965 or 1966, we had such a big snow that the school was closed for a few days. Sometimes, Mama would bring Nana in the afternoons when she came to get me. Nana had a black coat with a piece of Persian lamb fur on the shoulders. I always knew she was there when I reached over in the front seat and felt the curly sheepskin. I would tease her by going, "Bah." [15]

Mama tried sharing the driving during one or two years with the mothers of some other students, but it was still a lot of driving for her. Some people have told me, in jest or seriously, that I was spoiled. I wasn't spoiled in the sense that my parents and Nana tried to make sure that I learned to love God and do the right thing, but I did get used to having their undivided attention most of the time. Having so much love and care focused on me was wonderful, but it also could be a burden. So much love and many hopes, dreams, and expectations from these three people rested on me!

When I was driving with other girls in the car, I had to learn to share. I also couldn't discuss anything private with Mama on the way to or from school while they were with us. Sometimes, it could be fun. Nana sent bags of popcorn with Mama when she came to get us during one snowy afternoon. It took hours for us to get home in the pokey traffic, and meanwhile we nibbled on that delicious popcorn!

After school, Mama read for me what wasn't in Braille and helped me with the homework. After I went to bed, she would be up late doing Braille. Sometimes, while she was reading, she would get so tired that she went to sleep, and her head would drop onto my shoulder.

Concerning Papa's second job or income, I should say at the outset that he was involved in recycling long before it became trendy or popular. Our second income came from Papa's getting silver from the process of x-ray development and sending it to a refinery for money. Early in his endeavors, he did this by collecting the used fixer, also known as hypo solution, from various doctors' offices and hospitals. When X-rays are developed, they release silver into the fixer. Papa would take the used fixer home to our basement. He would use electrolysis to remove the silver, which would come out and form on the plates in little rough pieces. When he had enough of this silver, he would send it to the refiner, Handy and Harman. When I was little, I went with him on some of these trips to collect fixer solution. On one memorable trip, one of the big glass bottles in the back of the car broke, and I had to keep my feet up off the floor all the way home. Papa also hurt himself on another occasion when he dropped one of the big heavy bottles that contained the solution on one of his big toes.

We did something fun with some of the silver. With the help of one of our dentists and a mold made from the material used to make impressions of teeth, we made a couple of silver birds

---

[15] When the coat wore out, Nana cut the lambskin off the coat and gave it to me. I had it lined with satin, and sometimes I wear it over my winter coats when going to church on Sundays.

modeled on some glass and plastic figurines. I may have used the last remaining pieces for one of my own casting projects after Papa died.

Eventually, during my grade school years, the doctors and hospitals started using companies to handle their fixer, and maybe the process changed. At any rate, this relatively easy source of income was no longer available. Papa turned to the backside of the process. When the films are developed, some of the silver remains on the films. After a period of years, when X-ray records are discarded, the used films are no longer required to be kept. Papa started collecting the discarded films. He would bring them home, and either remove them from the boxes with papers in between (the easy ones) or take them out of the big X-Ray envelopes. We threw away the envelopes. (No paper recycling was available at that time.) Often I would help him to take films out of envelopes, which I found to be a very tedious, boring process. Once the film was collected, Papa would take it out to an open place, a pipe factory that one of his friends allowed him to use on weekends, --we called it the Pipe Place--and he would burn it in metal barrels. When the films were finished burning, and the ashes had cooled, Papa would put them in a container. When he had enough, he would send this material away to the refinery. The process was much harder, and the percentage of silver in the ash was lower than what came out of the fixer. I only went with Papa to the Pipe Place once or twice, and I can say that the acrid smoke was horrible. I do not know how he stood it! This is the act and shape of great parental sacrifice and love. He continued this effort, I think, through my High School and my college years. I was very relieved when it was no longer possible for him to continue, for reasons that I don't know the details. Papa paid a horrible price for this avocation. When he was dying of lung cancer in 1982, he said that he wanted to know how his condition came about. I did not have the heart to say it to him at that time, but I'm sure that this work, especially the film burning, was a major contributing factor, involving as it did exposure to toxic chemicals. The tobacco smoking didn't help, either, but he quit that bad habit when I was a baby.

Fortunately, my parents still found time to do some pleasant things together. They both liked flowers and plants. Papa's big effort was in multiplying azaleas through cuttings, and trying to get as many colors as possible. Mama would go out with him to water them in the evening. That way, they had some private time together doing what they liked. Nana and I stayed inside. Nana would complain that, "They are going to come in crying, after they get all bitten up by the mosquitoes!"

When Mama watered plants in the daytime, she liked to take the hose and play with the sunshine, to see if she could get rainbows. She also sometimes shook rose petals on me, in fun, when they were getting ready to drop petals and she was getting ready to cut off the rose hips. Papa always said that St. Patrick's Day, March 17, was the right time to trim the rosebushes.

Looking back, Dunblane Hall was a pretty unique place. The grade school students wore uniforms. Except for my first year, when the uniform was a jumper with a white blouse, the uniform consisted of woolen skirt and waist-long jacket, with a short-sleeved white blouse with a round Peter Pan collar. Eventually, as the years progressed, we were allowed to buy a specific skirt and blouses to go with it from J. C. Penney's to wear when it began to get hot in the summer, instead of the wool. The elementary school did not have air conditioning.

The elementary school was in an old stucco building that may have gone back as far as the revolution. All of the grade school activities were on the first floor, except that the music room with the piano was on the second floor. The school had four classrooms, a library, and a little room used as a candy store on the first floor. It also had a locker room in which two students each had a locker to store boxed lunches and coats and hats. Two classes shared a room. The first and second, third and fourth, fifth and sixth, and seventh and eighth grades were paired together. The two grades in each room had some subjects together, such as religion, but for other subjects the teacher taught the grades separately. While the teacher was working with one grade, the students in the other class were supposed to be studying or doing their homework. Sometimes, it was more interesting for me to listen to what the other grade was doing than to do my own work, especially if it was the grade ahead of me.

I got around my grade school the same way that I did at home, by feeling my way and relying on physical clues. That school had a student body of around one hundred students, so everybody knew everybody pretty much. Of course, more people knew me than I recognized by voice. It isn't true that all blind people know everybody instantaneously by their voices. I did recognize family and close friends by voice, but otherwise, I found it helpful for other people to identify themselves.

For some reason, all of my life, in addition to the special friends I have made in my classes, I find that I make friends with folks older and younger than I am. When I was in grade school, I remember the "big girls," in seventh and eighth grade, who were very kind to me in first and second grade. They sounded like "big ladies" to me, with their more mature voices. When I was in the fifth or sixth grade, I became friends with Mary Anne McCabe, a girl a few years younger than I was. She was very kind and helpful, and we had much in common, including mothers who cared enough to yell at us sometimes. Mary Anne came to visit me at home on occasion, including for one of my birthdays. Papa took us that day to National Airport (called that before it was named after Ronald Reagan) to watch the planes take off. The airport is near my house.

I think that some of my classmates didn't understand my friendship with Mary Anne, but I tend to blaze my own trails. You have to do the right or comfortable or good thing, regardless of what other people think.

Mama was more popular with the students than I. Sometimes, Nana would come with her when she came to get me, and Nana told me that often a group of girls would gather around Mama. They knew how much she loved children, and she was a good listener.

During my grade school years, I still kept up with Vickie on weekends and in the summertime, but she was now in local public school. She also often was away on weekends and in the summer, because her family had a country house in Culpepper, VA, where they spent much of their spare time. During one summer, Vickie did something wonderful for me. Using a stylus, she punched dots in paper to trace the outline of letters, and she taught me to write my signature. It was a very useful thing for me to know. I think that she also worked with me on other letters in the alphabet. Later, in 1974, at the Virginia Rehabilitation Center in Richmond, VA, a teacher named Bobbie finished the work that Vickie began and helped me to perfect my signature. She also helped me to learn to print capitals for the rest of the alphabet and to write some of the cursive letters.

I had my friends at school, of course. But, like me, they came from different places and got to school by car. It wasn't easy to continue fostering our relationship outside of school hours. Occasionally, one of my school friends would come to my house to spend the day, if parental transportation could be arranged. Sometimes, I attended birthday parties at my friends' homes. The family of one of my classmates, Denise, also invited me to go with her and her friends to a theme park called the Enchanted Forest, to celebrate Denise's birthday. It was a fun day, and Denise's mother gave us all redheaded Barbie-type dolls as souvenir gifts. I named this doll Hannah. Papa had to repair Hanna's arm when it came off, and he made a little chair for her, and he cautioned me that the doll would be fragile after that.

A few months after I received Hannah, Mama and I went to one of the five and ten stores, and Mama bought me a redheaded Barbie-type doll, with her hair pulled into a twisted queue and soft arms and shapely hands. For the next couple of Christmases, she and Nana bought me outfits for this doll. I named her Suzanne.

Denise's mother and father were divorced. Her father, Dr. Bruner, married again. He and his wife lived in Virginia, not too far from me. Denise was with her Dad during the weekdays and with her mother on weekends. At school I learned, through the experiences and lives of my classmates, that the ideals taught by the church are often not lived in practice. It made me grateful that my family was still together, despite their difficulties.

At my school, we had students of all races, some non-Catholics, and some students of different nationalities. In my first grade year, there was a girl from Turkey, named Ilhahn, who needed to learn English, so she sat in on most of the classes, to listen and absorb. I remember her whispering to me to "move over" so that she could sit next to me. A few years later, we had a little send-off for Sylvia, who went back to somewhere in South or Central America.

For the first few years, the school accepted students who needed to board during the week, and who lived in the rooms upstairs. Eventually, the fire marshals said that it wasn't safe, so they had to stop taking borders.

In addition to the four regular teachers, Sister Mary Lord came once a week for special music classes to supplement the regular music instruction by the class teachers, and Miss Von Wald came once a week for speech and language work. Madame Bernier came every day to teach French to all grades. Miss Von Wald also gave me additional one on one time to help me with my speech, so that I would learn to stop saying F's for TH's, and to say s's cleanly.

Once a week, we went down to the Little Theater in the high school/college building for dance classes in the early grades. I was introduced to ballet steps, but I didn't do very well with it. When I was in pre-school years, I took tap dancing with a group of blind and partially sighted children from a partially sighted teacher, Miss Ann Chapman. I liked tap dancing much better than ballet. We ended up putting on a little program for our parents. I was dressed in tights and a little costume. After our part was over, I got to sit in the audience next to Mama, while she tried to describe the little dramas that the ballet students were performing. It was fun.

At school, once a week we went down to the gymnasium used by the high school and college for our gym classes. In good weather, we had them outside on the hockey field. Once a year, we had a Field Day on the hockey Field, with picnic lunches of hot dogs, hamburgers, cool drinks, and sports activities and friendly competitions. Sports wasn't one of my strong suits, but my friends often asked me to hold the prizes that they won while they went back to compete some more. On one occasion, I ended up sitting on the sidelines on a grassy hill, holding a water balloon, a crucifix, and various other items. My friend, Gail, also asked me to hold the camera that she was using to take pictures of the activities. Others of my friends kept coming along, and playfully taking these things away and giving them back, just to tease, which upset me mightily. I was especially worried when one girl took the water balloon.

"These aren't mine!" I cried. "They belong to somebody else."

All I could think of was, "If that water balloon breaks, with me holding this camera, I am going to start running!" At that point, I wasn't thinking clearly about where I would run, but I was worried about that camera getting wet!

Our school was a nice, intimate environment, but we were not insulated from current events. We all felt honored and proud when John F. Kennedy, a Catholic of Irish American descent, was inaugurated as President in 1961. We were scared and had practice drills during the Cuban missile crisis. During major events and crises like that, Papa often had to work late at the Pentagon, because the government wanted photographers to take pictures of major decision-making meetings. I am sure that I would have found details of what went on in those meetings interesting, but Papa would never give any information about what happened in the office, except to say that they were having big meetings in the war room. I'm sure that he was aware of the saying that "Loose lips sink ships." The country would be much safer if everybody had Papa's attitude toward work.

Nana proudly asserted that officers often asked for Papa when they needed pictures. I have reason to believe that what she said was true. I met at least one retired general who asked Papa to come to his house to take pictures of his garden and his tomato plants.

During the Cuban missile crisis, at school, we were asked to each bring a can of food to make a supply, in case we had to be stuck inside the school. During the drill, ironically, we took refuge in the library, among the books.

When I was growing up, the big fear discussed by the adults and us children was that Russia and the U.S. would get into a dispute and end up destroying the world with nuclear weapons. By God's grace and mercy, it didn't happen. I consequently feel more tranquil about the threats of our present day, such as Iran and radical Islamic terrorists. Ultimately, as demonstrated in Scripture, the only real safety is in the guiding Spirit of God and his merciful protection of us frail human beings.

We were in the middle of music class at school on November 22, 1963, when word came that the president had been shot. We tried to go on with our work, praying for him inside, but we sounded like a bunch of sour boards. We all cried and mourned together when the President died. The TV was on nonstop in our house for the days between the assassination and the funeral. It was one time when everything else seemed to stop and became irrelevant. It was hard to celebrate Thanksgiving that year.

We all were shocked and concerned as the civil rights movement revealed the abuses and injustices of segregation. When the news reports began to run stories involving the struggles of black people for equality, Papa finally decided that he had to tell me that some of my classmates were black. He did this, so that I would not inadvertently blurt out something that might hurt someone. To this day, I'm sorry that he ever had to tell me. It shouldn't have made any difference and I should not have needed to know that three of my best friends in my class were black. I love them, pray for them, and cherish my memories of them, even if we are no longer in touch with each other.

I wish that we could live in a world where all these meaningless distinctions and nonsense are seen as the irrelevance that they are. I wish that I never had to find out that people consider such trivial physical differences to be significant. I agree that everybody should be comfortable with who they are, and we should appreciate, be proud of, respect, and honor our own heritage, race, and culture and those of others, but for most purposes, I wish that the whole world could be color blind to the extent that we don't prejudge each other on the basis of physical differences or disabilities! If we embrace our differences and learn to accept, support, and affirm each other, we strengthen our bonds as a people and help to build the city of God!

Of course, we have the right to make some preliminary evaluations and assessments of each other, based on conduct, but the judgment of ultimate motives and responsibility by the individual is God's business, not ours! We need to affirm the value and dignity of every human being, including ourselves! After all, as the kids used to say, God made us, and He doesn't make junk!

As a sadder, but not necessarily wiser, grownup, I recognize that a color-blind society probably is an unattainable ideal, but we still should be working toward a society where we can share our identity, race, culture, and background experiences with each other in an atmosphere of mutual trust, respect, and acceptance. We aren't there yet, including for people with disabilities. In my own life, I have experienced what I suspected to be discriminatory treatment in work and social situations. I choose to forgive and get on with my life, rather than make an issue of it most of the time, because anger and frustration may do more damage to me than good in finding a solution. I still can readily identify with those civil rights advocates seeking to eliminate discrimination and racism and to promote mutual respect and acceptance among all of our people! [16] That is what I think is meant in a broad sense by "loving one's neighbor as oneself."

These adult later reflections aside, at Dunblane Hall, every year, we put on Christmas programs and spring programs in which the students performed plays or sang songs. During my first or second grade year, I was one of the little angels in the Christmas pageant. As described more fully in a later chapter, when I was in the eighth grade, all the classes got together from all eight grades to put on a little musical, called "The Keys to Christmas."

In the spring, we had a "spring festival," complete with raffles, grab bags, white elephant, used book sale, flower booth (at which my mother helped) buffet dinner, toss-a-ball in the fish bowl to win a fish, bake sales, and other things, all designed to have fun and raise a little money for the school. Both my parents got involved in the Fathers' and Mothers' groups, respectively. The sisters were glad to discover my father's photography skills, and Papa took pictures of many events, including my First Communion and Confirmation, as well as other breakfasts and occasions. He had a knack for catching people off guard in unexpected poses. For example, on one occasion, he took a picture of Sister Dorothy when she didn't expect it and caught her wearing an apron. She pretended to be annoyed about it, but then she laughed.

Concerning my exposure to other languages, when I was little, Papa tried to teach me some German words and phrases. He also used some German sayings around the house. In particular, if he thought that somebody should get off their backside and do something, he would say that they were standing there "cum ein ox on de barche" or something in German "like an ox on a hill." After I started learning French in school, Papa stopped trying to teach me any German, because he didn't want to confuse the languages for me, but I don't think I would have mixed them up. Even now, I still can say the words to the sign of the cross in both French and German.

---

[16] I also am aware that, for folks with disabilities and probably for people seeking to eliminate racial, religious, and ethnic discrimination, a certain amount of tension and conflict exists as to whether they identify as someone with a disability (or a member of a racial or ethnic group) or whether they see themselves as a person first and the other characteristic as secondary. I cannot speak for anyone else, but I personally don't identify myself as a blind person; I think of myself as a person who happens to be blind and hard of hearing. I also don't focus on my race, but I do identify with Mama's and Nana's Vermont and New England heritage and take pride in my German (tempered by shame at the Nazi connection) and Italian heritage. My ties to Pennsylvania are a bit more tenuous. My Catholic faith trumps everything, of course. Not everybody in my situation would make this type of identification. Everyone has to assess themselves and decide how they will approach their identity.

The French class was a particular problem for me, because I didn't understand the French, and Mme. Bernier tended not to use English. Eventually I spoke to her about it in front of the class, and after that, she tried to use more English. She was giving my parents French words in print with their translations, with a tape recording of the pronunciations, but nobody could connect the recordings with the words satisfactorily for me. It went better in the later grades, when we were given a formal textbook and records to which to listen. I continued my French studies during my high school years.

Every First Friday of the month, we all went down to the chapel in the building that housed the college and the high school for confession and Mass. The chapel was a nice, peaceful place, with a clock that chimed the quarter hours and struck on the hours, sounding like church bells. On one such occasion, Mama was there for some reason. We had to walk from the elementary school building to the building complex that housed the high school and the college. On these walks, I walked arm in arm with one of my classmates and sometimes with Mary Ann. We were discussing something about school and the teachers. Afterwards, Mama told me that it was a good thing that I didn't say anything bad or derogatory, because one of the sisters was walking three feet behind us. That experience impressed me with the necessity to always watch my words, because I would never know and could not look to see who might be around and within hearing range.

I was six going on seven in November when I entered first grade, and I really didn't want to wait until I was in second grade, the usual age, to receive Jesus in Holy Communion. How much I wanted to receive Him! Eventually, the teachers decided to put me in a special class with some other students with special situations, and I was able to receive First Holy Communion that year. My having been dangerously ill, as I described earlier, perhaps had something to do with why they made this arrangement for me.

My First Communion Day, May 24, 1959, was wonderful! I was dressed in my white communion dress and my veil. We were told to keep our veils as a special keepsake. My veil got lost, but I still have my dress. I don't remember who came for the occasion. I think that my Aunt Margaret came from Pittsburgh, along with cousin Jim and his new wife, Connie. I think that Aunt Maria came, too. At the Mass, the communicants were actually able to assist at Mass while inside the sanctuary railing, and we received the King of Kings and Lord of Lords! Catholics believe that Jesus is really present, under the appearances of bread and wine, and when we take Communion, we are receiving the Body of Jesus.

After the Mass and breakfast[17], we went to one of the parks in Washington, and we were able to feed the pigeons. I remember that my Aunt Margaret was terrified of them, and the birds especially seemed to like her, even landing on her arms and wrists. How much she wanted them to get away from her! I wanted them to come to me so much to let me touch them, but they were attracted to her!

Afterwards, Connie read me a story in the afternoon.

With the help of Sara and Mama, I learned Braille the way other students were learning the print. Sister Dorothy also tried to learn to understand a little Braille, so that she could grade my homework. During those first two years, I tried to write Braille with the slate and stylus.

During the summer between my second and third grades, Mama went up to Catholic University in Washington, DC; I think it was so that she could learn Braille, including how to write it on the Perkins Braille writer, to help me better. During those classes, Nana went with her so that she could look after me while Mama was busy in class. Nana and I even found a passing kitty cat to play with while we were waiting outside on a bench. During one of those weeks, one of the sisters took charge of me, and taught me how to write on the Perkins. After I learned that, I wanted nothing more to do with the slate and stylus, because I found the previous writing method slow and cumbersome, and I couldn't check my work as I went along. During my third grade, I did my homework in Braille on the Perkins. I think that my parents put print under the Braille, for the benefit of the teacher.

Papa foresaw that this situation couldn't last throughout my school years. He and Mama began to teach me to type on the portable, Royal, manual typewriter that Mama used to do the income tax forms.[18] They insisted that I practice half a page, then a whole page, every day. How much I hated it then, and how much I thank them for it now!

During the summer before my fourth grade school year, Nana and I went up to Massachusetts to visit the relatives for a couple of weeks. We flew up there on a propeller plane, my first flight, and that was an adventure! I took Linda, one of my favorite dollies, with me. For some reason, I got cold during the flight, and the stewardesses covered the doll and me up with a couple of blankets.

---

[17]  When I was little, we were required to fast from solid food for three hours before Communion, from liquids other than water for one hour, but were allowed to take water at any time. This practice was an improvement from the earlier rule that Mama remembered, which was to fast from midnight of the day. After the Vatican II Ecumenical Counsel, the rule was further relaxed to a one-hour fast from food and liquids other than water.

[18]  After the Remington that we bought to keep at home, we got a Smith Corona manual for home, and the Royal was for school. We never got an electric typewriter. I went from the manuals to the computer keyboards. I still prefer sharper touch, clicky keyboards to the softer ones that feel too much like marshmallows to me.

On that trip, Nana and I had a good time in MA. We stayed at night with Aunties Janie and Riri in Quincy, and during the daytime, we were at Uncle Joe's house. He also drove us to visit Uncle Bill and Aunt Catherine, and he took us to see the Abbiatti cousins and their mother, old Aunt Emily. During that particular visit, I remember how kind these cousins were to me. I grew tired and very sleepy. They didn't fuss, just put me in a big comfortable chair in a room by myself so that I could take a nap, and then join the company when I was wide awake.

All in all, during the week or two that we were in Massachusetts, I very much enjoyed being away from the typing practice! I enjoyed myself during the day, but I got tired and homesick and cried sometimes in the evenings. Back at the aunts' apartment, the four of us gals would sit around the kitchen table and eat toast and discuss all kinds of things before we went to bed.

Mama wrote me a letter or two in Braille while I was there. She particularly urged me to find postcards and to send them to family and friends from MA while I was away. To answer her letters, I had to use Cousin tom's typewriter, so I couldn't get away completely from the need to type.

Apparently, Mama and Papa enjoyed having Nana and me out of their hair when we were away for a while, especially not having to deal with Nana. When I got home, Mama said that she and Papa got along fine, even painting the house inside together. It was my first real inkling that I had of the sacrifice involved by my parents in having Nana live with us.

This plane trip aside, we usually took our family vacations and went to visit relatives by car. Mama, Papa, and I would drive the six hours necessary to go to Pittsburgh to visit Papa's relatives. I remember that this trip involved crossing mountains and driving through tunnels. I think that we once stayed at Aunt Margaret's big house, and I got to explore its many floors and to visit with the lady who rented a one-room apartment from my aunt. We usually stayed at Aunt Maria's house, but then Papa would take us driving to visit Aunt Margaret and Uncle Jim, as well as cousin Jim and Connie. We also went to visit Sister Hilda, as well as Sister Margaret James if she was stationed in Pittsburgh. We also visited some of the family friends who still lived nearby, and sometimes, we saw Gross-Mum at family gatherings. Occasionally, we visited the old house on Campania Avenue.

We usually stayed at Aunt Maria's house. We generally went to Pittsburgh around the fourth of July, because Aunt Maria had a big picnic on her patio and invited all the family to celebrate Independence Day. They set up a grill for the hot dogs and hamburgers. During our visits to her house, we enjoyed her good cooking and tasted the produce from her garden, where she grew tomatoes, kohlrabi, rutabagas, and other vegetables. She also made delicious tomato butter from those home-grown tomatoes. I don't remember if she had a grapevine that produced Concord grapes, but I know that it was Papa who taught me how to eat them, seeds and all.

Aunt Maria had a cuckoo clock on the wall of the staircase that went up to the second floor, where the bedrooms were. The clock struck the hours with cuckoos and played music, and it cuckooed once on the half-hours. As the years passed, the clock labored because it needed oiling and servicing, and eventually she stopped running the music. The clock was wound by pulling up weights with chains. Many years later, when Miss Frease went to Germany, she brought back a catalog. Papa ordered a smaller clock for us, but it didn't work well in our house, because it needed to be wound too often. Besides, the air conditioning from the window unit blowing on it interfered with its operation. I now have a cuckoo clock that runs on batteries and is more practical. Mine has little angels that go around when the music plays and is unusual in that respect. Within the last year or two, I found out that so-called eight-day cuckoo clocks only need to be wound twice a week. I bought one with bears that does not have music, because I didn't want the music to wear out before the clock like my aunt's. Now it is in the dining room, and the battery clock cuckoos from Nana's old room!

When we drove to Massachusetts, Nana would accompany us, and it took ten hours to get there by car. During long trips, Mama often brought a book, so that she could read to me on the journey. Sometimes, she tried to relieve Papa at the driving, but the way she handled the steering wheel to "feel the road," made Papa nervous. On one of these trips to Massachusetts, we visited Sister Margaret James, because she happened to be assigned to a school in Kingston, MA. Sometimes, we visited Aunt Irene's mother, Mrs. Cirilo, or some of the relatives on Grandpa's side of the family. When I was very little, Uncle Joe had a cuckoo clock at one time, but he didn't keep it as long as Aunt Maria had hers. On another trip to MA, Mama and I actually were allowed, with the permission of the people who owned it, to go through Nana's former house on Clarendon Street. I very much enjoyed actually visiting the place that I heard about so much in Mama's stories. I noticed that, even though this house was so much older than ours, its floors didn't seem to creak at all, which was a big contrast from my house.

For the most part, when I was younger, I didn't appreciate these vacations to visit relatives very much. My cousins, like most of the neighborhood children, were all older than I. They saw me as the little kid, the baby. To me, they seemed like grownup people with whom I didn't have any childhood things in common. Some of them, such as Tim Dean and Terry Nolan, took more time with me and paid me more attention. Gretchen Dean often wasn't around, because she was studying to become a nurse and later working as a nurse. After she graduated from nursing school, she worked in Washington, DC, for a while, and we saw more of her then. My cousin, Nancy Calabro, was like a big sister to me, until she started dating her future husband, Dick Pierce, and then she had no more time for me. The talk at these family gatherings was often of adult, grown-up things, about which I knew nothing as a child. Both my Aunt Maria and Uncle Ray smoked, which I didn't like at all. Even if they didn't smoke much in the house when we were there, the tobacco smell lingered. I think that Aunt Irene and maybe Uncle Joe, smoked, too. Uncle Sam smoked cigars, but I think that his sisters made him do it outside or in his room. As I said, the old great-aunties were much more understanding and sympathetic, because they liked fussing over me as a little girl. How much I missed being away from home! Also, in these places away from home, I had to learn my way around in strange surroundings. Sometimes, if a little girl lived near the relative with whom we were staying, she would come over to play, and that helped to relieve the boredom.

In retrospect, I am sure that both Mama and Papa each felt a little left out when visiting the other side of the family, but as a child, I was too self-absorbed to really understand this. Besides, as grownups, they seemed better at coping than I. When Sister Margaret James learned to drive, she began to side with Mama when Papa made derogatory remarks about women drivers.

In retrospect, I think that Papa had a little easier time than Mama, because he knew how to project a sociable, affable personality, and how to "make friends and influence people," to quote Dale Carnegie. Mama, on the other hand, with her easily bruised feelings and sensitivity, often felt left out when the Schneiders, Nolans, and Deans turned to family gossip or reminiscing about Campania Avenue. She also did not find funny some of the things that made Papa's relatives laugh.

When we went on trips, Nana often made lunch for us to take with us. Sometimes she made meat or cheese sandwiches and packed them to go, along with seedless grapes, apples, or pears. On other occasions, she would fry her delicious chicken, wrap each piece in paper towel, wrap together in sealed silver foil, and put the whole bundle inside a paper bag, with fruit, cookies, napkins and such. We took coffee and tea in thermos bottles and cold beverages in the ice chest. The chicken often was still hot when we stopped to eat and opened it.

When I was around eight or nine years old, I started taking piano lessons. Mama and Nana bought the upright piano for around $1,000, in part with all that money that they had stashed away in the savings account. I took lessons from Marian MacDonald, who taught out of her home, where she lived with her husband and her father. She was blind herself. She knew the Braille music, and she taught me. Like the written literary Braille, the music uses the six-dot cell to make symbols for the various notes and values of notes. Because you can't read Braille music and play at the same time with both hands, you have to memorize everything. I also couldn't hear and distinguish tones well enough to try playing by ear, and Mama wanted me to learn the right way by reading music. I think that Mama enjoyed the piano even more than I did. Although she had been away from a piano for years, she still was able to sit down at the instrument and make wonderful sounds, following the music. I knew that I would never be able to play spontaneously like that.

As I mentioned, Mama wanted me to do well with the piano, in part to make up for her failure to make a career of it herself. I did fairly well with the piano until after Mama died. I was getting little prizes for making the most progress, after the yearly recital that Mrs. MacDonald gave for all of her students. After Mama died, for the recital of 1966, I worked very hard to perfect the piece that I was playing. I kind of did it and put all that heart and effort into it for Mama.

A few years after she died, I just wasn't applying myself, and I stopped taking lessons. My heart went out of the music after I lost Mama, and I found that I didn't have the patience to pursue all that memory work, especially with the emotional turmoil and academic pressures of the High school years.

By the time that I was in fourth grade, I was doing my homework on the typewriter, mistakes and all, and it was much easier, except that I still needed Mama's help to correct the mistakes and typographical errors that I made, before turning in my papers. Nana bought me my first Perkins Braille writer. My parents set up my desk at first in their bedroom, so I could do my homework there. After the second floor was finished, my desk and work supplies were moved upstairs to the office in the areaway outside my bedroom. Mama borrowed another Braillewriter from the volunteer group, so I had one at school and one at home. After that machine broke and had to be returned, the Commission bought me another Braillewriter. My parents found and bought another manual typewriter, so I had one typewriter at school and one at home.

Because the Braille books were so bulky and took so many volumes for each print textbook, one of Papa's friends at work made me a little bookcase with compartments big enough for the Braille books. We kept this bookcase at school, and moved it from class to class, so that I would have a place to keep my books at school. The top of the bookcase was just big enough for me to keep my Braillewriter on it.

Volunteer Braillists did all of my books in the grade school years in Braille, and that resulted in our making new friends among these wonderful volunteers. I already mentioned the Stanulises. In addition, Wilma Hane was one of the volunteer Braillists, and she had particular expertise in

Nemeth Code, the form of Braille used for numbers and mathematics. She and Mama became good friends. Her husband, John, was a colonel in the Air Force. He and his wife were very kind to me. They showed me many of the wonderful things that they brought from faraway places. They had a nice Abyssinian Manx cat, named Fleabag. Their daughter, Pattie, was younger than I. She and I have become friends as adults. I called her parents Uncle Johnny and Aunt Murff. When I was in grade school, maybe around the fourth or fifth grade, Uncle Johnny was transferred, and the family moved away, and we missed them very much.

In addition to helping me with schoolwork and trying to keep up with the house (albeit with Nana's help,) Mama did a lot of logistical volunteering with the Braille groups. It was a good thing that Nana did the cooking and many household chores, because it freed Mama up to help the Braille volunteers and me. Mama also undertook to Braille music words and other text material if the Braillists couldn't keep up with the teachers. It was a busy time for her.

In addition to the out-of-town vacation trips, we took advantage of the summer school vacation time to visit Al Miller and family in Vienna, VA, and they sometimes stopped by our house. The three older children, Janice, Joanne, and Donald, were my contemporaries, and we played together sometimes. Julie was born after the rest of us were well grown-up. The Millers came to visit us whenever Aunt Naim came to visit Al from Pittsburgh, so that we could visit with her.

Papa tried to grow beans, tomatoes, mint, parsley, and Swiss chard with limited success, because the oak trees provided too much shade to let the garden get enough sun. The area where we lived used to be a brick-making place, and the soil had all that red clay in it, which wasn't helpful to the garden plants, either. Al, on the other hand, had better soil, more land, and more sunshine. He shared tomatoes, corn, potatoes and zucchini with us, as well as peaches from his miniature peach trees. We had two peach trees when I was little, but Papa decided to cut them down, because the squirrels were getting all the fruit. We did manage to grow a grapevine, and it produced Concord grapes in late August or September, but the squirrels, bees, and birds often beat us to the grapes. A few years ago, I finally lost the faithful old vine.

We did other fun things in the summertime. Occasionally, we went to one of the Chesapeake Bay beaches to spend a day, and sometimes Vickie went with us. In addition, Papa, Mama, and I sometimes went to Glen Echo Amusement Park. On one fun occasion, Papa, Mama, and I all rode on a fast-moving ride, called the Whip. Mama was screaming with excitement and maybe a little anxiety. I heard Papa ask her, "Well, Babe, do you want me to tell the man to stop it?" She said no, and I wasn't afraid. I felt very safe sitting between them, and I had a wonderful time!

We also often ended the summer fun season by going to the Gaithersburg Fair in MD. I enjoyed getting the opportunity to pat sheep, goats, and cows, and to learn new things about the animals. I especially liked the chicken house, with all the crowing roosters. Mama and I would have a good time trying to imitate the roosters! Papa and I also enjoyed riding on the Ferris wheel together. We bought home-harvested honey from beekeepers, too.

During the summers, I often had to do book reports about books that I was assigned to read during vacation from classes. I liked to read, and I particularly remember Little Women by Louisa May Alcott and the series of autobiographical stories by Laura Ingalls Wilder. In addition to supervising me and making sure that I did the summer assignments, Mama would be very busy trying to get the teachers to identify the texts that they were going to use when school started. The sooner we found out the title, author, and edition of the contemplated textbooks, the sooner we could start arranging to get a copy of the book in Braille or to have it Brailled if it had not been transcribed into Braille yet. As I progressed in learning to read Braille, I was able to get some Braille magazines and other Braille books from the National Library Service and the Library of Congress.

For all of the logistical reasons involved in my doing the work, my school work often took longer than other students, and I would often be up late at night doing homework, and needed to get up early in the morning for the long drive to school. Sometimes, I would forget to tell Mama about something that she needed to Braille or read for me. I would remember after I was in bed. I would bang on Nana's mattress and tell her about it.

"Shut your eyes, and go to sleep. I'll tell your mother in the morning," Nana would say.

She was the first to rise in the morning, followed by Mama and me and Papa. She called herself the dispatcher, because she got everybody going early in the morning.

Sadie Crawford led one Braillist group in Washington, DC. This group met in Temple Sinai, until they had to move to larger quarters. Mama didn't get formally certified by the Library of Congress to be a Braille transcriber for others besides me, but she helped out the group in any way she could, including dropping off print books to Braillists and finished multiple volumes to the Braille Room or end users. Jane McIver's mother started another group of volunteer Braillists in VA. These groups brought together people of good will of all faiths.

We also used Braillists in the Telephone Pioneers in New York, NY. One wonderful man, Richard Hannah, would take a knife and cut up books, to give them out to multiple volunteers, to get them done on time. This was especially necessary for geography books. Geography, by the way, was one of my favorite subjects. Mr. Hannah would tell Mama not to worry; they would find a way to get it done. Even when he had a heart attack, he asked for a Braillewriter to be brought to his hospital bedside, so that he could keep working on needed books. We all cried when Mr. Hannah died. Others in his organization did good work, too, but it just wasn't the same without him.

Somehow, with the help of faith, family, volunteers, and friends, I got through those elementary school years. Nana used to say that my school days would be the happiest days of my life. Looking back, I agree that they were a time of innocence and relative security with my immediate family, but they still were a struggle. It was especially difficult for me in the eighth grade, after Mama died.

# FAITH OF OUR FATHERS
# AND OUR MOTHERS

*A*s I mentioned already, I consider it Providential that I ended up in the Catholic educational system, beginning with elementary school, because my local parish would not have been able to provide me with so good a grounding in my faith. My parish, Our Lady of Lourdes, started originally in 1946 as a mission parish, with Mass being celebrated in parishioners' homes. Eventually, the basement structure was built which was meant to be the lower floor of the future, to be completed church. After a few years, the parish decided, instead, to build a separate new church on the parish's property, and Bishop Russell of the Diocese of Richmond dedicated the new church in 1963. Our parish was part of the Richmond diocese, until the Arlington Diocese was created and divided from the Richmond diocese, which didn't happen for a number of years, in the mid 1970's.

The parish owned at that time the whole block bounded by S. 23rd Street, Yves Street, S. 24th Street, and Hayes Street. In addition to this little church building, the property contained two houses that were used for the rectory and a residence for the parish housekeeper. After the new church was completed and dedicated, a new rectory was built for the priests. A second story was later added to the little basement building, turning it into the Lourdes Center, to be used for meetings, parish activities, CCD classes, Sunday brunches, dinners, dances, and bazaars.

The church was only three blocks or so away from my house. Sometimes I walked there with my parents, and sometimes we drove, especially if we were pressed for time or if the weather was bad.

The parish had previous pastors or priests that I don't remember. Papa mentioned Father Ryan and Father Batey, but I don't remember them very clearly. I may have met Father Ryan, and supposedly he was the one who did the official baptism ceremony for me when I was a baby. I remember what may have been my first visit to the church. I was given a prayer book to hold, even though it was a print book that I couldn't read. Even if I couldn't read books that were printed, I understood that they contained words, and I like the feel of them. I remember whispering meaningless words about God on that occasion. Eventually, as I said, Mama took me in her arms at home in the evening and taught me how to pray the rosary. I carried the rosary to Mass. Papa was very strict about making sure that I didn't "wiggle and jiggle" during Mass. I also learned that I must not bang the rosary against the pew and distract other people who were trying to pray. The Mass in those early, pre-Vatican II days was in Latin, and I didn't understand the words. However, once I began to learn Braille, Mama got me Braille prayer books and a children's Mass book. The children's Mass book she Brailled herself. Other books came from the Xavier Society for the Blind, in New York, NY, the organization that provides Braille, large print, and recorded Catholic periodicals, spiritual literature, and prayer books to blind and visually impaired users. Once I had the Braille prayer books and began to learn about the Mass at school in the religion classes, I could follow along with what was going on at Mass much better. After the changes resulting from Vatican II, I was very happy when the Mass was said in English, because that made it much easier for me to participate. Unlike some people, I had no desire for things to go back to "the good old days." I was relieved to hear that Pope Francis has gone back to restricting, subject to particular bishops' approval, the use of the all-Latin Mass. I'm also not comfortable with the use of parts of the Mass in Latin. The theory is that you can follow along with the English book, but it's hard to juggle the Braille Propers, with the changeable readings, and the basic Mass prayers, called the Ordinary of the Mass. I find the conflicts in languages personally distracting.

It's a good thing that my parents were good teachers and that I had the benefit of the teaching of the Sisters. I would not have learned my faith from my parish or my pastor's sermons. The first pastor that I remember was a Father Comaskey. He was born in Ireland, but he was assigned to our parish. He had a brogue that, to coin a phrase, you could cut with a knife. The Irish accent by itself made him hard to understand, especially with my hearing impairment, but the situation was aggravated by his tendency to raise and lower his voice during his sermons. Sometimes, he would talk very softly, and at other times, he would be shouting at the top of his voice. I got nothing out of his homilies. According to Papa, who understood him a little, the man was well educated, and sometimes what he had to say was well worth hearing, if one only could.

Unfortunately, Father Comaskey did not "have a way with people." He could be blunt and tactless. He was hard to get along with. To his credit, he helped to get the parish out of serious debt, and he was good and persistent at raising money from his parishioners and thrifty to a fault, but he put some folks off by his frugality. After Mass, when folks were barely finished with their prayers, he would walk through the church, turning off the lights, complaining that we were subsidizing Va. Electric Power Company. He was in the pastoral position in the parish by himself for years, because nobody could really get along with him and work with him. Father Warner lasted as an assistant pastor, or what we now call the parochial vicar, for a while during my high school years, but the situation really wasn't remedied until the pastor retired, although remaining in residence, and other pastors replaced him along with their parochial vicars. Father Comaskey lived in the Our Lady of Lourdes Rectory, until his health necessitated his getting more care than could be provided by his fellow active priests. First, he was moved to a nursing home. Then his remaining relatives in Ireland requested that he be sent back to them, and they took care of him. He died in Ireland, the place of his birth.

All of that was in the distant future when I was growing up. While he was with us, Father Comaskey was a real paradox. Surprisingly, he accepted the Vatican II changes in the Mass, stoutly maintaining that it was still the same Mass! He loved the Washington Redskins football team, and he sometimes said the Sioux Indian prayer after Mass. He always stood at the door to greet parishioners coming to Mass.

When he saw me, he would often squeeze my arm or shoulder or give me a strong handshake, and ask, "When are you coming in here with a big bouncing dog?" (He understood that dogs could be trained to guide. I agreed with him heartily about that. I wanted a bouncing dog, too.)

For all his brusqueness and "bull in a China shop" syndrome, he was a man of prayer and would often walk up and down the parking lot saying his rosary. I have vivid, pleasant, fond memories of his reciting the Stations of the Cross during the Fridays in Lent, especially because they were in English. When Mama was dying, he spoke gently and encouragingly to me on the telephone, referring to a woman who recovered from a serious brain injury highlighted in the news, and he told me not to give up hope.

While Father Comaskey was the only full-time priest in our parish, we needed visiting priests to say some of the Sunday Masses. We also had substitute priests during the two weeks or so that Father Comaskey spent in Ireland every summer. The visiting and substitute priests provided a welcome respite with their understandable, inspirational homilies. We frequently had members of the Oblates of Mary Immaculate, from Washington, DC, and members of the Order of St. Francis De Sales. One of the Oblate priests who came from time to time was Father Richard Hanley. One of the early homilies he gave concerned his experiences in growing up. The theme that he emphasized was, "Not much money, but a lot of fun." I guess that was a fair summary of part of my growing up experience. Mama and I complimented him afterwards, and he promised to remember us in his prayers, and he asked us to pray for him.

Nana went to church with us sometimes. With her increasing age and her trouble with her legs, she had some physical justification for not going all the time. However, as I was growing up, I came to understand that Nana, like Father Comaskey, was a paradox. As Mama explained to me, Nana always tried to make sure Mama and Uncle Joe did the right things and observed the faith when they were growing up, but she didn't practice what she tried to instill in her children and me. She had a fighting, angry relationship with God, just as she did sometimes with us, but I don't think that it was inconsistent with loving God.

In her quieter, more reflective moments, Nana would sometimes say, "When I ask for help and need help, God helps me." She also had a very straightforward, honest, direct approach to God in her prayer life. She said that at night, she would tell God. "Dear God, today I did the best that I could. If you like it, it's like that. And if you don't, it's still like that." A priest once told me that one must be a very secure person to pray like that. Sometimes, when she was in a more reflective mood, Nana also would quote her father as saying that, if everybody took their crosses to the common together and compared them, each person would go home with his own cross. That made logical sense to me. Light cross people would not trade with someone with a heavier one, and everybody could always find someone with a heavier burden than they had. In her later years, when people asked how Nana did so well, she would say, "Ask God!"

As Mama tried to explain to me, Nana had experienced so many difficulties and betrayals in her life that she questioned how all these circumstances fit with a loving God. As I grew older, Nana and I would have fierce debates about all of this, because I tried to convey to her the things that I was learning in school and was starting to experience in my own life. When these discussions were over, Nana would call me "the lady with the big faith." Nana had these wrestles and struggles with God and her faith all of her life. In his later years, Papa worried that Nana would not be accepted for burial through the church, because of her lack of observance. I told Papa that I didn't think it would be a problem, and it wasn't. By the time that Nana died at age 98, all the foibles and imperfections were put down to age and Alzheimer's disease. Her funeral was in our parish, and her burial was beside her husband in Quincy, MA, but I'll describe more about all of that later.

The teaching sisters at Dunblane Hall were a refreshing contrast to my parish. Sister Dorothy Raney was my first and second grade teacher. She had a soft voice, and sometimes she got laryngitis, which made her harder to hear. She would sometimes sit near me at such times, to make sure that

I could hear her. In some ways, she was another mother figure for me in the early years. She was a holy woman with deep faith, and she took her life with Jesus very seriously and tried to impart that to her students. During one religion class, she set up a table like an altar, and we acted out the Mass, so that we would learn its parts and what happens during Mass. This exercise was very useful to me, because I was able to feel how the tabernacle would be set up with its veil and the candles on either side, and the general layout. Even after I left her class, I remained friends with Sister Dorothy. The four main teachers rotated playground duty among themselves, so I still got to see her at lunchtime. She was assigned elsewhere after my sixth or seventh grade year. Her replacement the following year was Sister Thomas Marie. For a while, Sister Dorothy and I corresponded with tapes. I was able to see her years later, when she came to Washington for a meeting. I fell back into the old habit of holding hands with her, although I was a big lady by this time. Eventually, Sister Dorothy followed what she took to be the call of Jesus by leaving the Sisters of Providence and going into a much more secluded, contemplative order. When she did, she took the name of Sister Angela Marie. We stayed in touch for a long time, but eventually our correspondence petered out.

Sister Thomas Michael was teaching third and fourth grade when I came into third grade. [19]She reminded me a little of Father Comaskey, because she would raise her voice if she became excited or angry with what the students were doing. She was especially upset with girls who didn't complete their homework, because they were doing something fun or frivolous after school.

"You went out on a school night?" she would thunder incredulously and indignantly.

Her outbursts didn't bother me, because I lived in a house with parents who often yelled, but I sometimes wanted to hide under the desk when Sister was upset. I was very glad that I wasn't doing anything to merit her ire. In a way, though, it made me feel more secure, knowing that she cared enough to get after us.

Mama and Papa didn't have any problems with her, either, but I heard that some other parents did. Be all that as it may, she was assigned elsewhere at the end of the year.

When I entered fourth grade, the new teacher was a layperson, Miss Ruddy. She was nice enough, but she didn't know how to administer consistent discipline. The other students didn't like her, which I thought was unfair. She lasted only one year, and was replaced by Mrs. Delaney,

---

[19] After sisters began reverting to their baptismal names post-Vatican II, Sister Thomas Michael became known to me as Sister Mary Dempsey. I kept in touch with her for a while sometimes, but that was long after she left Dunblane Hall.

a calm, motherly lady who stayed at Dunblane Hall at least until I graduated from eighth grade. I never had Mrs. Delaney as a teacher, because by the time she came, I was in fifth grade.

Meanwhile, I joined the choir in my parish church, which was a good experience. Mrs. Jones tried to direct the choir of girls. We sang for one midnight Mass during one memorable Christmas. I remember that we sang the song "When Blossoms Flower Mid the Snows," about the Christmas Rose, in multiple parts. They sounded wonderful. Mama Brailled many of the hymns for me.

I should explain a little more about holiday celebrations. Mama liked holidays and entered into them wholeheartedly. Nana did somewhat, too, especially when I was little. When she no longer had to put on a brave front for my childhood innocence, however, Nana was often in a very bad mood during the holidays, because she missed so many people she had lost. Mama liked to decorate the house for Christmas. We usually had a cut live spruce tree, and Mama would put up the nativity set and the houses and other displays underneath it. We would go to a tree lot before Christmas to pick out a tree, and the trees all smelled so wonderful! Papa usually had "use or lose" leave at that time of the year, which meant that he was home more than usual at Christmastime. It was nice to have him around the house!

I remember coming into the living room in the morning one year, a few days before Christmas, and finding the tree already decorated. Nana said something to me about Santa Claus coming early to decorate it last night. It surprised me that it was early, but I just accepted it.

When she read the first edition of this book, Barbara Sheehan recalled an incident in which the grownups were getting ready for Christmas, and they put up chairs around what I wasn't supposed to find. According to Barbara, they told me that it was Santa's Workshop. It sounds like something they might have done, but I was too young to recall it.

I did hang up a stocking, and I would find goodies in it Christmas morning. One year, I received two ornamental balls made in Germany that opened up to reveal candies inside, along with a little wooden mouse. I really liked the mouse, and I still have him.

For Christmas cards, Papa would use a picture that he took during the year, usually of me, and have it made into a photo card to send to family and friends. As I grew older, I helped with writing Christmas notes and letters.

I don't remember exactly when and how it happened that I found out that Santa didn't come down chimneys after all. Except for the money, which came in Christmas or birthday cards, from the aunties, Aunt Maria, or the Abbiattis, the gifts under the tree were often presented to me as coming from one relative or another, or from Mama, Papa, or Nana. The year that the choir sang for midnight Mass, Mama and the Aunties gave me a two-volume set containing the lives of the saints. I still have these books.

About this time, Aunt Maria sent me a porcelain angel, with a tambourine in her hand and long flowing sleeves, with a musical movement underneath that played "Silent Night." Between this gift and Nana's music box, I started getting interested in collecting music boxes, and now I have a house full of music boxes.

I suppose that, at first, I thought that Santa delivered everything. However, I helped Mama wrap up packages to send to Aunt Maria and others, and she began to help me find gifts for some of my friends at school and for the teachers. I just gradually came to understand that, in exchanging gifts, we were Santa's helpers and were doing this to celebrate Jesus' birthday.

After the joyous celebration Christmas day, Mama and Papa made sure that I wrote thank-you notes to people who sent me gifts. They did the same thing for gifts on my birthday or other occasions. The instructions in the grammar books at school said that the thank-you letter should thank the person, name the gift, and say why you like it. I found it hard to fulfill the last requirement for gifts that I didn't like, need, or want.

At times, Papa tried to find things as gifts that Mama would like. I remember on one occasion going with him to shop for a pretty nightgown for me to give Mama for her birthday. However, Papa sometimes mixed humor and teasing with the Christmas gift giving. One year, he let Mama go all of Christmas day, thinking that he didn't have something for her. On the evening of Christmas day, she finally found the new electric frying pan hidden behind the screen in the unused fireplace. I don't think that she appreciated the joke. [20]

In our family, we would come home from midnight Mass, have bacon and eggs, and open one Christmas present before going back to bed until later Christmas morning. After we got up, we would open the rest of the packages.

For Thanksgiving dinner, as well as for Christmas, we usually had a roasted turkey, with Nana's delicious dressing (made without the giblets because Papa didn't like them,) sweet or white potatoes, whole cranberry sauce made from the recipe on the bag of fresh cranberries, Waldorf salad, nuts,

---

[20]  Our house had a working fireplace. We used it on a few occasions, but it tended to draw heat out of the house and wasn't very practical to use with the furnace. Also, it was difficult to clean out the ashes from the place into which they were swept down in the basement behind the furnace. As smaller furnaces replaced the old one over the years, this may no long have been a problem, but the use of the fireplace still wasn't very practical for me.

roasted chestnuts, vegetables, and pie and Nana's fruitcake (when she still made it) for dessert. I helped Nana with the dressing, and I also cracked nuts and took seeds out of the grapes for the fruit salad. A day or two after the holidays, Nana would make soup with noodles out of the leftover turkey and bones, and she, Mama, and I would eat the soup and the cooked neck, giblet, heart, and liver for lunch.

Nana often made her cutout butter cookies decorated with colored sugar beads for holidays. She had a whole bag of cookie cutters, with different shapes for different holidays: Christmas trees, turkeys, and stockings for Christmas, hearts for Valentine's day, bunnies, cross, and fish for Easter, and others for general use, including a big ginger bread man and a little dog with a little wooden handle. Unfortunately, we inadvertently threw away Nana's cutters. Over the years, I have collected some more, but my collection of cutters is small compared with hers.

On New Year's Eve, Mama observed a fun custom to express a wish for good luck and prosperity in the coming year. She would fill a pan with all the loose change that she could find, and she went through the house at midnight, calling out, "Happy New Year!" She went all over the house to the different rooms, including into the room where Nana and I usually were in bed. Often, we were too sound asleep and didn't hear her. Papa continued this custom after Mama died. We also enjoyed watching holiday favorite movies, such as *It's a Wonderful Life,* and *Amal and the Night Visitors,* (an English language opera telling the story of a poor crippled boy and his widowed mother who befriend the magi and their servant as they follow the Star on their way to Bethlehem). Papa Recorded it on reel-to-reel tape, which became impractical for easy listening with the passage of time and problem tape recorders, and I recently procured a treasured copy on CD.]

For Easter, we would dye Easter eggs on Holy Saturday evening. After Mama died, when Papa got involved in this activity, he started mixing colors or dipping eggs in more than one cup, to see how they would turn out. At Easter time, when I was little, we got out the fuzzy chicks, bunnies, and ducks, as well as little lambs and other toys that made noise or jumped around when they were wound up. When I grew older, Mama made Easter the occasion for some more serious gifts. On the last Easter before she died, she gave me a little bunny doll inside a plastic peanut shell that came apart to reveal the bunny.

In addition to singing for Christmas midnight Mass, the church girls' choir also sang the ceremonial Latin hymn when Bishop Russell, the Richmond Diocese bishop, came in 1962 to lay the cornerstone and in 1963 to dedicate the new church. They sang again when the auxiliary, Bishop Untercoefler, came in 1963 to confirm parishioners, including me.

The new church was a difficult change for some parishioners, who were used to what Papa called "busy" architecture of the old-style churches. Mama, for one, liked the style of the detailed statues and the more ornate decorations. The new church was more austere in style, with only two large statues hanging over the altars, one on each side. Mary and St. Bernadette were on one side, and St. Joseph and, if I remember correctly, Jesus on the other. The altar was in a corner, and the church had two naves: the main nave and the smaller side nave. The altar was constructed originally so that the priest would face away from the people, and the choir was situated behind the altar. After Vatican II, the choir eventually was moved to the front rows, and the priest celebrated Mass behind the altar, facing the main nave. The stained glass windows above the door, the smaller ones on the sides, and the larger vestibule were added much later. Eventually, many parishioners came to appreciate the simplicity and beauty of our church. My only complaint has been that the stone walls create echoes, which are aggravated by folks not using the sound system properly, and all of the acoustical difficulties make it very hard to hear for someone like myself with a hearing problem.

Sister David Clair was my fifth and sixth grade teacher. She replaced Sister Charles, who taught those two grades during my first four years at Dunblane Hall. Sister David Clair had an outgoing personality, creative and artistic talents, and a beautiful singing voice. She and Mama didn't get along very well, partly because Sister brought some of my behaviors to a head and had sit-down meetings with my parents. One thing that she was concerned about was my tendency to cry, more readily than she thought I ought. I cried when I made mistakes, because I knew Mama would be upset about them. I also had heard Mama say that "After the shower, the sun comes out," and I should vent my emotions. I had to learn over the years and through much of a lifetime that, while it is good to vent pent-up emotions in private or with family and close friends, a certain amount of emotional control in public is a sign of growing up and maturity and discipline. Sister also raised other issues that I don't clearly remember, concerning how I did my homework and organized my books and work. Mama complained to me privately that it was all very easy for nuns to talk, who weren't living in the real world, because they were isolated from reality.

If memory serves me correctly, about this time Papa was diagnosed with high blood pressure, and Dr. Williams put him on medication. It became a worry for all of us, because once you are on this type of medicine, you are supposed to help things along by limiting your sodium intake and refraining from alcoholic beverages. You also are supposed to watch your weight, and Papa needed to lose a few pounds. However, Papa liked some high-sodium foods, such as lunchmeats, frankfurters, half-smokes, and sauerkraut, and once in a while he had a beer. Mama also blamed tensions at Papa's work place for aggravating his condition.

I encountered other religious order sisters outside of school. During the year of 1963 or 1964, some of the members of Sister Margaret James's order, the Sisters of Divine Providence, came to Washington to study at Catholic University. Sister Margaret James referred them to us. On weekends, Mama, Papa, and I would go pick them up from their quarters at the university, and we went for many pleasant outings, touring historical monuments and churches. In one church, Papa had to lift me up to "see" by touch a large, life-size statue of Jesus. We had many pleasant discussions and visits during those rides and outings with the sisters. Mama formed a close friendship with one of the sisters, Sister Mary Agnes. I think that she was hoping that this sister might have been a friend and help to me if something happened to Mama. As discussed later, it didn't work out that way. I suspect that Mama was not very realistic in holding out this hope.

The churches and statues that we visited might have planted a seed for a wonderful dream that I had about Jesus. I don't remember exactly when it happened, but I dreamt of seeing Him above a table, in the middle of a ball of light, and that He told me that it was good that I had sympathy for Him in His passion. He also told me to pray the "Our Father." I felt very happy and peaceful after this dream. I still have a remembrance of it today. The light was very bright, but all around the light it was dark. I am reminded of St. John's gospel, saying that the Light shines in the darkness, and the darkness has no power over it.

The year of 1963 was noteworthy for public and family events that are fixed in my memory. That year, if I remember correctly, Pope John XXIII died. He didn't live long enough to see the completion of the work of Vatican II. He had a warm, friendly personality toward the flock of the faithful. Pope Paul VI, his successor, did great work for the church and is also known as a holy man, but we all missed Pope John. Both of these popes have now been declared to be saints. In November of that year, as I already mentioned, President Kennedy was assassinated.

The shadow of death visited our family that year, too. I think it was the year that Aunt Margaret Dean died from liver cancer. When she was diagnosed, Papa went to Pittsburgh to see her for a few days. After he came home, Mama went there by bus, too, to see her. My parents thus set a good example for me. While mourners can show respect and offer prayers for the dead in funeral Masses, it is essential to see loved ones while they are alive to give them comfort and support and to say good-bye when appropriate. Gretchen, too, went home from Washington to be with her mother.

When Aunt Margaret died, my parents went up to Pittsburgh for the funeral, and I stayed home with Nana. I think the reason was that it was during the school year.

When my parents came back, Mama said to me privately, "Papa cried last night. He'll be all right now." She was concerned that he didn't release his emotions readily enough in healing tears.

About three months later, Uncle Jim Dean died. This time, I think that I went with my parents to the funeral.

In the spring of that year, as I said, I began to get ready for my own confirmation. I decided to take the confirmation name, Monica, the mother of St. Augustine. I understand that she had to put up with a difficult husband and family situation, and I hoped that she might help me by her prayers and example to deal with my own home tensions. Aunt Maria wrote a letter that Mama read me, asking why I hadn't considered Walberga or some other German name. I didn't see myself as German. I saw myself as a Catholic U.S. citizen, and besides, I didn't know anything about that German saint. I found out afterwards that Papa's boyhood parish church in Pittsburgh on Campania Avenue was named after that saint.

Before receiving the sacrament, we took a short course of study, to make sure that we knew the most important elements of our faith. During this class and practice, I made friends with Rita Lorenzetti from my parish.

After the last practice by the choir before I was confirmed, Mama later told me about an incident. We all went to Confession. While we were waiting to go in, Mama saw two boys fighting. She told them to break it up.

"It's not me, it's my brother!" one of the fellows told her.

"Are you going to take your brother into the confessional with you, and tell the priest it's not you, it's he?" Mama retorted. Obviously, he wasn't going to do that, but Mama wanted him to think about it and what he was doing.

That incident sticks in my mind, and it teaches a profound lesson. We all go to receive the sacrament of Reconciliation, as it is now called, one at a time. We can only confess, acknowledge, or repent of what we are responsible for, and we must take responsibility for our own actions. We can't shift that responsibility onto anyone else. Likewise, each of us will go before God, one at a time, to receive his judgment, pardon, forgiveness, and mercy, based on our actions and state of mind, not anybody else's.

About this time, Mama and Nana bought me a beautiful China statue of Mary holding the little Boy Jesus on her lap, with Joseph standing by holding out an apple, with a basket of fruit on the base between them. Mama also bought me a beautiful blue crystal rosary for my Confirmation.

I don't know exactly how it happened, but Denise Bruner also ended up in my confirmation group at Our Lady of Lourdes. Our confirmation day was May 4, 1963, which was at that time the feast of St. Monica. The feast has now been moved to August 27, probably to be close to that of St. Monica's son, St. Augustine, on August 28. The day seemed to be cloudy and threatening rain, but later that afternoon, just in time, the sun came out. I was wearing a blue pastel dress. Bishop Untercoefler, the auxiliary bishop in the Richmond diocese, came to confirm us. I hurried to church and forgot my gloves. Denise's mother handed me a wrapped present for the occasion. She urged me to open it. Inside was a pair of white gloves that fit me, just what I needed. It was a wonderful, memorable day, but at first, I didn't feel any different as a result of receiving the sacrament. It has taken me years to internalize the working of the Holy Spirit inside me. After Mass, I was able to meet the bishop. Papa said jokingly that, with so many priests and bishops of Irish descent, it was refreshing to find a bishop with a German background.

As I said, learning to control my emotions was a long process for me. My entering sixth grade in the fall of 1963 was kind of a turning point. Papa read me the riot act before school started, and he told me in no uncertain terms that there was to be no more crying in the school.

"You are a big girl now," he said. "And big girls take it."

I will close this chapter by reprinting one of my poems from *The Ivory* Pyramid, my collection of poems. It is the best summary I can give of my spiritual journey over a lifetime. As the poem indicates, God has manifested His presence and consolations to me throughout my life from time to time. However, as I read in one spiritual writer's book, we tend to experience spiritual amnesia. In this autobiography, I will describe some of these high spiritual points in my life, but I am ashamed to say that I have forgotten many of the others.

# FACE TO FACE

Linda A. M. Schneider
2004

For St. Patrick
In a church named for him, I found the crucifix that inspired this poem.

*"Lift me up, Papa!*
I want to see Jesus Face to face,
So I can kiss Him.
The cross is too high, and I'm too little!"
"If only all of life were this simple,"
Her father probably was thinking.
"Here you go, Kiddo!" he said.
He swung her high up on his shoulders, so she could touch the feet,
And feel the mustache and the beard, and kiss him, Oh! so sweet!
She thought she was so very high, almost as though she could fly!

"Why can't I see Jesus?" She asked the Sisters.
"When He was with them, the people were so very lucky.
They got to walk and talk with Him and ask Him anything they wanted."
"Very soon, now," the teachers said. "When you receive First Holy Communion,
He'll come into your heart and be with you always!
You can't get any closer than that! He will be a part of you, and you of Him!"
First Communion Sunday was a wonderful day! She was so very happy
To receive Jesus the King!
To have Him with her always seemed such a marvelous thing!

With Confirmation, they said, the Holy Spirit would come,
And bring fortitude, peace, and strength,
And His many gifts and fruits of His great love.
She joyfully embraced the day, but at first felt no different,
But the temptations and tests remained.
Sometimes, inspirations and consolations came, but few and far between.
At times, she grew forgetful, and it seemed
As though they had never been!
"Lift me up, O Spirit!
I feel so lost and tempest-tossed!
I want to feel you're there, Lord! I thought things would get easier.
I know that, if You come, I'll have the strength
To get through the day, to persevere, to endure!"
It took her years to appreciate the subtleness of His reply:
"I stand at the door and knock. You have to let me enter,
Because I will not force the door!"

Childhood doesn't last forever with its tendency to trust.
Now, after Communion, she cries, from the growing pains of stretching faith,
"Lift me up, O Jesus, outside of myself, and help me keep perspective!
It's wonderful to have this time, when we're so close to touch!
I want to know You're really there, and I love You so much!
Sometimes, although it's wonderful, Your Real Presence doesn't seem enough!
Like Martha, I'm thinking of many things, distracted by so much stuff!"
The answer came, "Don't waste our time together. Let Me work out things!
If you really want to find Me, look up still:
You'll find me hanging on the cross, up ever so high!"

From the floor, she can barely touch the feet!
The woman stands, awe-struck, on a chair,
To reach the Hands of the impaled Jesus, high up on the Cross.

The statue is so life-like, the beams covered with tree bark.
It makes her feel small again, though she is not a child,
Filled with love and gratitude, but still perplexed.
"Lift me up, Abba! I want to understand!
I know He saved me by His death, but dying seems so hard!
Why did He have to do it? And why, in fact do I?
Sometimes I find the things He asks so difficult I want to run and hide!
I cannot do them by myself!"
He answered, "You don't have to! Let my Spirit be with and in you!
My grace is sufficient for you!"

The years have passed, each one a gift,
But bringing illusive possibilities and opportunities missed.
With each one gone; fewer remain.
Time goes on, inexorably as it will, and family and friends depart
For that great Eternity beyond, leaving emptiness in her heart.
Others have rejected her friendship, and injustice deals its blows.
Each grief has taken its toll, and the scars remain.
The toils seem so arduous; successes empty gain!
Even her hopes and dreams seem to be dying.
(Is there a resurrection for dreams, too?)
The self-will and desires all seem to end in vain!

"Lift me up, Papa! I feel alone and lost!
I need to know you're with me, and I am still too small!
I cannot seem to reach and touch you, Lord, no matter what I do!
However hard and long I stretch, His Cross is still too tall!
I want to surrender to your Will, no matter what it brings!
I still long for Jesus, for His love, Joy, and Peace.
To achieve that, I'm even willing my own self-will to release!"
It has taken much time and prayer to absorb His startling reply:

"Don't look up anymore; look across!
You'll never know how high you are!
You're higher than you know.
Only from your own cross, hanging up so high,
Can you really see Me face to face,
Because we're hanging side by side!"

# THE VALLEY OF THE SHADOW OF DEATH

$\mathcal{I}$n retrospect, my grade school years seemed to be building to the climactic crisis that was Mama's death. The memory gets sharper about some details when one understands after the fact that those events were the last—the last before... However, gaps remain with the passage of time, and I am piecing events together as well as I can.

Fifth grade was the time when my friends started going bananas over the Beatles. The girls thought that those singers out of England were really cute, and they loved the songs. It all sounded like a bunch of yelling with music to me, especially because I couldn't understand the words. I also missed words from my childhood records, too. As an adult, I have listened to some of those old records, and I am amazed at how much clearer they sound now with the better pairs of hearing aids.

Since I have so much difficulty with words, I like classical and other instrument music, including drums, country, folk, and popular songs when the singers speak clearly, and operas in English.

Because I couldn't share the rock 'n roll craze, I began to feel out of step with my classmates.

About this time, physically I started becoming a woman with the advent of the monthlies, although I was a long way from being a real "big lady." Another indication of my changing physical nature was that I developed acne, and, after consulting doctors, Mama and Nana were trying to help me combat it with soaps and various creams. On some occasions, as I got older, my parents started encouraging me to put on nylon stockings with little girdles or garter belts. At first, I really hated this, because I felt that I was being pushed to grow up sooner than I was ready. Mama also had to teach me to use a lady's razor under arms and on legs, and I also had to learn how to empty the razor to clean out the cut hairs.

In addition to learning to cope with the physical aspects of growing up, Mama began to talk to me about the "facts of life," as initiation into the sex act and sexuality was called. She told me as much as she thought I was ready to absorb. I only wish that she had been with me to help me cope with other aspects of becoming a woman and dealing with the opposite sex. On one occasion, however, I did ask Mama if it was OK to kiss a fellow.

"Sometimes, it's a good idea," Mama said. "It's the only way to find out for sure if you really want to kiss him."

On another occasion, we attended Eleanor Alley's wedding. She was marrying her sweetheart at age 18. I asked Mama if she thought that it was a good idea to get married that young, or should they have waited a while. Mama said that, if two people were seeing a great deal of each other, which they were, it probably was a good idea to get married. As far as I could tell, Mama was right. I think that Eleanor and her husband are still married. Eleanor ran a wonderful toy store, Gee Whillackers, before selling the business and taking a reduced part in it. I've ordered many fun and hard-to-find things to be sent to me from it.

When I was in sixth grade, the sixth, seventh, and eighth grades all joined to form a wonderful girls' choir to sing for the Latin High Mass for the graduation of the eighth graders in the class of 1964. After that, if I remember correctly, we began the transition to the English Masses, and we didn't do the same kind of liturgy for subsequent graduations.

Sixth grade also was a transition time for my girlfriend, Vickie. The public school system had gone to the division of the seventh through ninth grades into junior high, so sixth grade finished elementary school for her. I personally was glad to still be in grammar school, with the regular four years of high school ahead of me. After Vickie entered Junior High in seventh grade, she began to tell me details that did not make public Junior High sound very appealing to me.

Dickey seemed to be going through some kind of transition, too. A couple of years before Mama died, he stopped singing. Of course, canaries, like other birds, go through a molting period in which they lose their feathers before growing new ones. At such a time, they become lethargic. Dickey seemed to be in a prolonged molt from which he didn't recover like normal, and no matter how much Mama and I talked to him, and Mama whistled to him, he didn't sing. I don't know whether he was picking up on some of the tensions in the household, or was tired of being caged, or needed a rest, or had some premonition of what was about to happen.

Consistent with her no-nonsense personality, Nana tried a direct approach with Dickey. One day, she asked him bluntly why he didn't sing for us, and didn't he love us anymore. Dickey began to respond by tweeting assertively at her, but it didn't sound like his normal voice.

"If you have a cold, that's all right," Nana told him.

"Tweet, tweet, tweet!" retorted Dickey.

"That's all right, I said!" Nana insisted.

Dickey gave a couple more tweets by way of response before lapsing into quiet again. Maybe Dickey was trying to tell her that he just didn't feel like singing!

Mama, too, seemed to have some premonition that her time might be shorter than she would have liked. I don't recall exactly when, but I think that Jane McIver's mother, Tony McIver, became seriously ill and died in this time frame, and that might have put the subject of impending death in my mother's thoughts. On one occasion, when she was lying down with one of her headaches, she started talking about the fact that Nana might get along with Papa by herself better than Mama. I disagreed with her, fearing that they would fight. As it turned out, we both were right, but more about that later.

After President Kennedy's assassination, Lyndon Johnson was a stark contrast, especially from an auditory point of view. His slow, southern drawl was a far cry from President Kennedy's crisp speaking manner and flights of rhetorical zeal. However, President Johnson did seem to have a knack for getting civil rights, anti-poverty, and Great Society programs through Congress. He was nominated, with Hubert Horatio Humphrey as his vice-presidential candidate, to run for re-election. The Republicans, on the other hand, had a contested race for the nomination. 1964 was the first year that I recall paying close attention to politics, and I listened with interest to TV coverage of the Republican convention. I liked Governor William Scranton, the governor of Pennsylvania, and I was especially impressed by the way his wife vigorously endorsed and supported him in his campaign. However, he didn't get the nomination. Barry Goldwater did. Nana was a Vermont Republican from the old school, but she didn't care for Senator Barry Goldwater, especially when he voted against the new Medicare program for senior citizens.

"That son of a bitch took a plane to come back to Washington and vote against that bill!" Nana fumed.

I think that Mama started a new project during the summer between my sixth and seventh grades. Ellen's father, Mr. Reece, had been a carpenter in his younger years. When Mama and Papa acquired some mahogany boards, he put them together into a bookcase for Mama. She spent that summer, in her spare time, sanding and finishing that piece. I still have it in the bedroom that used to be Nana's, and I keep my keepsake books in it.

I think this also was the summer when Mama arranged to have me take swimming lessons. I went two or three days a week. During one of those lessons, I lost the topaz ring that Mama gave me in the pool. I didn't miss it until I came home. Mama went back to see if anybody found it. Fortunately, a very nice, honest, wonderful boy found the ring and returned it to Mama. Needless to say, it was the last time that I wore a ring in the swimming pool!

As far as the lessons were concerned, it was hard for the instructor to work with me, because my hearing aids come out if I'm in the water. For that reason, Mama arranged for one-on-one lessons for me. I learned to float on my back, but I couldn't seem to master swimming very well. I never made it across the pool. I would panic, and need to stand up and rest my feet on the bottom. It didn't help that the hearing aids have to come out in the water, and communicating with anybody trying to teach me is very difficult. For Mama's sake, it was a good thing that I never made it across the pool. The instructor teasingly told Mama that he would dunk her in the pool if I ever swam all the way across! On only one occasion did she think that she might have to start running!

When we went up to Pittsburgh that year, I was chagrinned to discover that, although Bill Scranton was from PA, Aunt Maria didn't think very much of him. She called him a "horse's tail," which was probably a sanitized version of what she thought for my young ears. She was very much influenced by Uncle Ray, who was a way-out conservative. I don't know whether it was on this trip or the one in 1965, but I was shocked to hear some of my uncle's views, including his denial of the happening of the massacre and extermination of the Jews and other minorities by Adolph Hitler.

When I mentioned it to Mama that evening upstairs, Mama's response was terse and to the point. "You have a mind of your own; make up your own mind," she told me firmly. In other words, don't believe what Uncle Ray says just because he says it if you know it isn't true! Saying something doesn't make it so!

In Massachusetts that summer, Nancy was dating Dick, and our easy comradeship from previous years was gone. It made me resolve that, if I ever fell in love with someone, I would try not to be so self-absorbed about it that I couldn't reach out to others and stopped paying attention to my other friends. I had the perhaps naïve notion that being "in love" would make you want to show even more kindness to others! Fortunately or unfortunately, depending on how you look at it, God didn't put me to this test.

Either on this trip or the year before, I had fun playing with a stuffed dog that Nancy had, made from lamb's wool. I liked it so much that Aunty Rene said that she would try to find me one. She sent me a similar dog for Christmas that year. I named the stuffed white dog Smokey, because he felt soft and fuzzy like Ellen Reece's dog by the same name.

Something else fortunately happened during that Massachusetts trip which helped to keep me from becoming a totally opinionated brat. My cousin, Tom Calabro, was home from college or his tour of duty in the Air Force, or whatever—I don't remember—and one evening he brought a friend, named Jim, home with him. Papa and Mama had gone somewhere with Uncle Joe and Aunty Rene, and Nana and I were in the house together. Tom's friend, Jim, started talking to me, and I launched into whatever intense opinion I had about politics or whatever was on my mind at that point.

"Do you know the difference between fact and opinion?" Jim asked.

I clearly did not. He went on to explain it to me. A fact is something that is or has occurred. i.e. "The mouse ran across the road, and a cat followed close behind." The opinion is how one interprets the facts. i.e., "The cat chased the mouse across the road." However, another interpretation could be that both the mouse and the cat were running away from the unseen dog that was crashing through the bushes. These are my examples, not Jim's, but I am trying to illustrate the idea. It was a useful distinction to learn. I haven't always remembered it, but it pays to recall this distinction from time to time. Nana was quite impressed with Tom's friend. Afterwards, she would refer to him as Professor Jim, when she reminded me to remember what he told me.

Aunt Irene wasn't the only one who tried to find things for me that I would like. Aunt Maria showed me her nice musical jewelry box with a twirling ballerina inside the lid in front of a mirror. I liked and admired it very much. For Christmas, she sent me a child-sized leatherette jewelry box with a ballerina.

I think it was in my sixth grade year that I went all out during Lent: keeping a three-hour vigil during Good Friday and saying prayers, and expressing my innocent willingness to "suffer for the Lord," and offer things up. People should be careful what they say that they will do, because sometimes God listens, and the results aren't easy.

Mama approved of my devotion to Jesus, but she did caution me to be careful about expressing these ideas too much in the wrong places. She pointed out that some folks do not understand and take it the wrong way. One's attempt at bearing witness and telling People about Jesus can instead put other people off and have the opposite effect from what one wants. As I recall another saint saying, sometimes (usually inadvertently) we prepare other people's minds to disagree with us. Besides, one often can say more by example than by verbal witness. I have subsequently confirmed, by experience, that people are not inclined to listen to fine speech if it isn't backed up by action. In fact, words without a living example are more likely to make folks go the other way and totally discredit the speaker, even if what he or she says is true.

I urged Mama to take frequent Communion, because I wanted to share my faith experience with her. Mama complained that whenever she tried to get close to Jesus, the Devil seemed to heap more troubles on her. Mama was right. The Devil likes to try to interfere with our attempts to find and stay close to God. The key is never to give up and to trust in Jesus and His love.

I think that either in this sixth grade or my seventh-grade year our class went on a tour of the Supreme Court. We were fortunate that Justice William O. Douglas came to talk to us after we finished the tour. I was very impressed with him, which might have influenced my later interest in studying law. I also about this time wrote an essay for a contest entitled "Uphold the Law: A Citizen's First Duty." I won second prize, which was a savings bond, if I remember correctly. In any event, I was interested enough in Justice Douglas that I wanted to read a copy of his autobiography, Men and Mountains. Uncle Bill's wife, Aunt Katherine, found a paperback copy of it, and Mama started reading it to me while I was in Seventh grade or during the following summer.

When I was entering the seventh grade, Papa found a small, portable reel-to-reel tape recorder in the Pentagon jewelry store. I used it during the last two years of grammar school and the first year or two of high school to tape classes for later reference and note taking. After that, I started using cassette recorders for this purpose during the rest of high school, college, and law school.

Sister Eileen Ann Kelly was my teacher for both the seventh and eighth grades. She replaced Sister Mary Ellen, who had a wonderful, upbeat personality and a great sense of humor. When

Sister Mary Ellen found out that I carried tea in my thermos bottle for lunch, she teasingly called me Grumpy Grandma.

I liked Sister Eileen Ann. She was from New England, and she had a bit of a New England accent. She was very encouraging and supportive of her students. She also could get angry, if she had a good reason and needed to protect girls who had done something wrong. For example, on one occasion two of the girls accidentally broke the glass on Sister's desk. They felt bad about it, and they arranged with a man to get a new piece of glass in exchange for some of their money and the old glass. They did this well-intended act of kindness on a lunch hour.

Sister Eileen Ann was furious, not so much about the original broken glass, but because she thought that the man had taken advantage of the girls.

"You tell him to come right back and bring me my glass back!" she told them. "It's thicker than this piece, and I could have it cut up for bookcases!" One of the girls might have said something about how the man liked our school. "He liked this place?" Sister retorted. "Sure, he liked this place! He was probably looking to see what else he could take!"

I never heard how the story ended.

I think that it was during the seventh grade that I participated in the spelling bee competition. I made it into the local eliminations, but I had to sit down on the word "chlorophyll." Needless to say, the correct spelling of that word is etched deeply on my memory.

For the most part, things seemed to be going OK in school. I don't know if it was resistance to growing up, hormonal changes, or suppression of emotions that I didn't understand, but in seventh grade, I began going through a very difficult emotional time. It manifested itself in anxiety with a queasy stomach, strange thoughts that were coursing through my mind, many of which I thought were evil, scruples as to whether I was resisting them enough or giving into them, and wanting so much to cry and relieve my feelings. Fortunately, the medicines that I was taking for allergies had the calming side effect of relieving the symptoms, but it was a bad time. It may have been some form of depression that wasn't recognized as such.

Mama wisely suspected that my emotional turmoil was a manifestation and cover for some underlying cause of distress that I didn't acknowledge or recognize. In terms of what might have made me unhappy, I only consciously knew that my family life, wonderful as it was, wasn't like the ideals in the stories. We didn't even always go to church together. Mama and I went to one Mass on Sunday, and Papa often went at another time. I wanted a family that was together, and would not be arguing so much. What I didn't understand was that the different schedules might have been necessitated by the difficult second job that Papa was doing, and I didn't realize at the time how important all this was for my welfare. Mama kept assuring me that they both loved me, and that I had made a big difference in their lives.

Mama helped me find priests other than our pastor to whom to confess, and they were very consoling and helpful, but they didn't come home with me when the emotional onslaughts kept coming.

Dunblane Hall was across the street from a parish church, St. Anne's. St. Anne's parish also had a school. Unlike Dunblane Hall, it was a parochial—supported by the parish and not just tuition—school. I think the same order of sisters taught at this school. In any event, Mama would drop me off at school, and then she would go across the street to St. Anne's church to pray for me before she went home, because she was worrying about what was going on with me.

Mama told me that, while she was at St. Anne's, she made the acquaintance of a beautiful lady with long, blond hair curled into a pageboy roll. She told me some details, which I have forgotten, about this lady, and I never met her. However, they became friends in need, so to speak. I'm glad that Mama had this consoling person in her life at this time.

I'm sure that Mama's prayers helped. It also was diverting to go to see some good movies with Mama and sometimes Vickie or Nana. We saw Ben Hurr, My Fair Lady, and Sound of Music. I eventually got the record albums for the two musicals, as well as *Mary Poppins,* which Mama and I saw later.

Of course, in seventh grade, the subject of high school would come up. I liked Dunblane Hall, and I guess that I cherished the hope or the wish to just go on to Immaculata High School. On one occasion, when I was talking about looking forward to high school or something in the future, Mama cut me short with the rejoinder and solemn advice, "Don't wish your life away. What if I'm not here?"

I learned a valuable lesson, reinforced by Mama's death. It's good to be positive and to have a forward-looking outlook, but the present needs to be cherished and fully lived each moment. We are given to each other for only a little while in the grand scheme of things.

Somehow, I got through that year. One other thing that I remember was that we were by ourselves driving home from school often, Mama and I. We would listen to WRC 980 A.M. on the way home. That year, one song that they played often was a song called Mama, sung by Vic Da Mone, about a son who is left to take care of his family after Mama died. For some reason, I thought that it was significant. It made me cry, but in a good way. I think that song was somehow prophetic.

After Mama died, although we didn't voice it, I think Papa and I thought it could have applied to him and me, instead of big brother and the other children named in the song.

> She said, "My son, I beg of you.
> I have a wish that must come true.
> The last thing you can do for Mama!
> Please promise me that you will stay
> And take my place while I'm away,
> And give the children love each day!"
> I had to cry! What could I say?
> How hard I tried to find words!
> I prayed she would not see me cry!
> So much to say that should be heard!
> But only time to say goodbye to Mama!

During the spring festival that year, I bought an alabaster statue, a bust of Jesus wearing his crown of thorns, mounted on a square marble base. I still have it on my bureau.

At the spring pageant that year, we put on a series of short plays, including one about the Country Mouse and the City Mouse. It was based in part on a play that I wrote as part of my creative writing assignments.

As the end of my seventh-grade school year approached, one of my friends in eighth grade, the grade ahead of me, was graduating. Mama and I went shopping for a gift for her. I think that we bought her a bumblebee pin; while shopping, I picked out a little jade pendant with a pearl on a chain for myself. It was one of Mama's last gifts to me. Before school ended, Sister Eileen Ann held a little auction for some surplus books. I acquired a copy of a book on church history.

If I remember correctly, Sister David Clair stayed at Dunblane Hall until I finished the seventh grade.

In the late spring or early summer, Mama and I went to see Mary Poppins. It turned out to be the last movie we saw together in the theater. Mama's interpretation of it was that the "medicine" is the pain of growing up, and Bert was trying to tell Mr. Banks to spend time with his children to help them through the growing up process.

The summer of 1965 was memorable and a little different from usual. I think that we went to Massachusetts first. I think this is when Nancy had acquired her little miniature dachshund, Hans, and I got to experience what it was like to have a dog in the house. He really loved Uncle Joe, and he really was his dog.

Nancy had broken up with Dick. She was hurt and angry, and she was even talking about trying to sell the friendship ring that he gave her. Mama said that, if Nancy really wanted to sell that ring, Mama would buy it from her. Nancy didn't sell it, as it turned out, but I think that Mama suspected (rightly) that this break-up was temporary and that Nancy would be very sorry later if she parted with the ring. I also think that this was the year that Mama and I were allowed to go through Nana's old house, as discussed in an earlier chapter.

After the Massachusetts trip, we did something different. Mama, Papa, and I went to Kutztown PA, for the Pennsylvania Dutch festival. We stayed at a Holiday Inn in Reading, PA. Aunt Maria took the bus from Pittsburgh, and she joined us there. It was so pleasant to be doing something other than visiting relatives as such, and Aunt Maria was so much more agreeable away from Uncle Ray! We had a wonderful time! An artisan at the fair, Luther Epler, sold us or gave me (not sure which) a sterling silver rooster pin that I still have. Mama told me to keep his card, and be sure to write him and thank him. Whether it was depression or a valid premonition, the awful thought went through my mind, "When you write this man, it will be to tell him your mother has died." That's what happened years later. I have no idea if he ever got the letter. He also made for us three little copper angels that Mama wanted to hang on the Christmas tree in memory of us triplets. I wished that we could have stayed on that trip forever!

As we were going home, as the maid, Tilly said in "Guess Who's Coming to Dinner", "All hell done broke loose now." We learned from Nana in a phone call that we had unexpected visitors! We arrived home to find that Aunty Rene, Nancy, and Nancy's latest boyfriend had come to call while we were away without notice. They were camped out in our living room. We might have enjoyed a surprise visit, but they stayed only a day or two after we got home. From Mama's point of view, they were treating our house like a hotel, spending the daytime sightseeing and coming back only to sleep, and not doing any quality visiting with us! She was especially disappointed, because they drove all the ten hours from MA to play tourist and neglect their relatives! Their heedless, thoughtless behavior hurt poor Mama's feelings. Papa told me later that she got on the telephone and cried to her aunties about it.

After all this, we made one last trip to Pittsburgh as a family. I was on the outside looking in, but from my point of view, it was, for the most part, a disaster! I think that we stayed, as usual, at Aunt Maria's. One night, the family all gathered at Aunt Margaret's house (which maybe hadn't been sold yet,) or maybe it was Jim and Connie's house, and Mama and I were left on the front porch, while the others were all visiting in the house. Mama, rightly or wrongly, felt snubbed or left out. Other things may have been going on that I didn't know. What I remember was later, upstairs at Aunt Maria's, Mama crying to me, and threatening to take the bus home without us the next day. I, the teenager, the 13-year-old girl, was there trying to calm down my own mother and plead with her not to do something that drastic, which she didn't. Part of me is still angry that I was put in that position, but like so many things in my life, I must forgive and let go. As the Scripture says, "Be angry, but sin not."

We had one relatively pleasant activity during this trip. We visited Papa's childhood friend, known as Babe (misnomer, because he was a big guy) Hess and his family. They were embarking on a new activity: raising pine trees for Christmas trees. I enjoyed feeling the different species. I decided that, apart from the spruce, I liked the Scotch pine trees the best of the long-needled trees. Perhaps that was why we chose that kind of cut tree for the Christmas of 1965. I'm sure all in all it was not a good summer for Mama. It was her last.

The end of August was coming. Mama made arrangements for Father Comaskey to say a Mass for Grandpa on the date of his death, August 26. On August 25, Wednesday, Mama woke up with one of her hands and arms not working right and bothering her. I have forgotten whether it was her right or left side. We had planned to go to the fair, and we went. Vickie came with us on this occasion. There was some kind of game of toss, and Mama won a pink French poodle stuffed dog. Papa took a picture of Mama, Vickie, and me with that poodle that one of us was holding. It turned out to be the last good picture that we have of Mama.

Thursday morning, I woke up early, and asked Nana if Mama and I weren't going to church for the early Mass for Grandpa. Nana said no, go back to sleep, because Mama was going to the doctor instead later that morning.

Mama went to see the family doctor that she and Papa consulted, Dr. Williams. I guess he did tests. When she came home, I asked her if they found out what was wrong.

"He says it's maybe a virus," Mama complained. "They always say that when they don't know what it is!"

On the way home, she had stopped at a store. She bought herself a circular pin, with an enamel flower and leaves. It was the last thing that she bought for herself. I still have it.

That evening, Mama rolled up my hair for what turned out to be the last time. I remember that she had a little difficulty doing it, on account of her arm and hand. I also remember a strange odor that I had never smelled before.

Friday morning, I think Ellen had come over to help Mama get her hair in order. She was going to go get Papa or drive him somewhere—don't remember what was planned—then her eye started to jump, and her face was strange. They feared that she was having a stroke. They took her to the hospital. As she was going down the basement steps, Mama started to cry and get emotional. She said, "Be a good girl, Lindy!"

Mama was in Alexandria Hospital for the next few days. Papa went to see her, and so did Miss Frease and I. I had her room telephone number, and Mama and I could talk sometimes. Papa took pictures of her in the hospital bed, but needless to say, we haven't framed those.

I didn't like the way that things were going. Mama didn't seem to be getting better, like she was going to come home. I was afraid, and didn't quite know of what, but probably of the unthinkable, losing Mama!

I reached out to my great-aunts. I already had reasons to think that they had feet of clay. Each sister blamed the other for the failure to move out of that stuffy little flat into a better place. On one visit to Massachusetts, I asked Aunt Janie to leave Aunt Riri, if she really was the problem, and come down and live with us. We set a deadline of November 19 of that year. Aunt Janie may have thought to humor a naïve little kid, but she never did me the courtesy of calling or writing me to say that she wasn't coming. I was serious, and I wasn't treated seriously.

However, Mama had always told me that I could trust my great-aunts, that they were "safe as banks." So, when I was worried about Mama, I wrote them a letter on the typewriter, and addressed the envelope. I'm pretty sure that someone mailed it. In the letter, I think that I asked them to come down to see us, and that we needed them. I don't clearly remember what I said, but it was a cry for help.

Later, Papa told me that Mama called them from the hospital. I think that he said that she was upset and crying.

On Wednesday, September 1, I woke up in the morning. I knew that school would start soon and summer was dwindling away. I turned on or was awakened by the radio. I remember there was some commercial about an additive for cars, that "guards and bars," and protected against deposits that slowed down modern cars. It was a little jingle that they were singing. I don't recall ever hearing it again, but the memory is burned into my mind as associated with that horrible day.

I think that I talked to Mama in the morning. I asked her if she felt better.

"To be honest with you, doll, no," she said.

I recall that Ellen went over in the afternoon to be with her. Papa must have taken leave from work, because he was around.

He had some kind of a problem with his bank or checking account, and he went to the bank after lunch to try to get it straightened out. In the middle of the afternoon, I answered the telephone. It was someone from the hospital. The woman asked for Papa. I told her that he wasn't there.

"Tell him that your mother wants him," was all that she said.

What apparently happened was that things began going very wrong with Mama. Ellen said that the last thing that she heard her say was, "I feel so sick, Ellen!"

The autopsy later revealed an infection in Mama's brain, which they thought, was an aneurism, almost impossible to diagnose at the time and difficult to have treated if they had. The result of its deadly progress was that Mama's lungs became paralyzed. The hospital was trying to reach Papa; without getting him, they had to do what they thought best, to put her on a respirator.

After Mama died, Papa withdrew his money from that bank; he didn't pull out my accounts, but he withdrew his. He held it against the bank that they delayed him over something stupid, and he wasn't there when all this happened, and he wasn't there in time to have said "no," to the respirator, which he might have done. Ten or fifteen years later, after the bank had changed hands, Papa proposed to open an account there.

"I thought that you didn't want to deal with that bank," I said.

"Why not?" Papa answered.

"If you don't remember now, there's no use in going into it," I told him.

The hospital finally reached Papa after he came home, or maybe before. Vickie's mother, Mrs. Virginia Reece, rode with Nana and me when we went to the hospital. Before we went, I found the crucifix that Mama said had been her father's, the one that he had with him when he died. She already had her rosary at the hospital. As I was looking for the cross, I kept thinking that Mama couldn't be dying, that God wouldn't be so cruel as to take her. As it turned out, it was time for Mama to go home to heaven, and that ultimately was good for her. It is the living people remaining behind who have to continue dealing with life after their loved ones depart.

On the way to the hospital, Nana kept saying, "She's going [to die]!"

Virginia kept saying, "No, I don't think so, Nana."

At the hospital, Papa and I were allowed into the ICU where Mama was. I gave her the crucifix, and her hand closed on it, like she was holding onto it for dear life. Papa took a safety pin, and he fastened her rosary to her hospital gown. Some people have said Mama's grasping the cross was only a reflex, but at that point I think that she knew what we gave her and that we were there.

I remember the horrible, mechanical, rasping sound that the respirator made. Intellectually, I understand that these devices can be used to prolong life and give a patient a chance to recover from a serious injury or illness, but in Mama's case, it only prolonged her dying. Part of me understands why Papa might have said "no" to the machine.

The next two days were horrible. Papa took me in to see Mama at least two more times, and she seemed less responsive than at first. As I said, I called Dr. Bregmann, and he went to comfort Papa. I think that I called others, including my teachers, but don't remember. Father Comaskey, as I said, tried to talk encouragingly to me and to hold out hopes that turned out to be vain. Somebody called the traitors from Massachusetts, along with the other relatives. Yes, I called them traitors, because that's how part of me felt about them. Friday evening, September 3, Mama died.

Papa hugged me and cried, openly and unabashedly. Mama probably was glad from heaven. Nana cried, too, and tears did not come easily to her, either.

At one point, I said something about "All the words left unsaid, and all the things left undone," a sentiment that Papa echoed.

Vickie came over. She tried to console me, and told me to wash my face. She started me realizing that I had to brace up somehow. Papa said I could cry, but finally I said that I could cry all night for Mama, but I had to stop somewhere.

Right about the time that Mama died, all the relatives showed up from Massachusetts. Of course, I understood that it was a long, ten-hour drive. Financial constraints or fears of flying probably kept folks from coming by plane. The great-aunts came, and I'm pretty sure that Uncle Joe and Aunty Rene came. Uncle Bill and Aunt Katherine came, and they drove the great-aunts (and I guess Uncle Sam,) down from Quincy. Everybody was very sad, but in the back of my mind was the rebuke, which I never expressed out loud, that they had all come too late. What good was it to come to bury a body when we would have benefited so much had someone come while she was alive? The aunties claimed that they never got my letter, but I'm not sure that I believe them. They certainly knew that Mama had reached out to them by phone!

Aunt Maria came from Pittsburgh.

September 3, when Mama died, ironically, was Aunt Riri's birthday. It also was, under the old church saints' calendar, which since has been revised, the feast of Pope St. Pius X. Mama especially liked him, and she gave me one of his medals to wear.

Before they closed the casket for Mama's funeral, the relatives said that I should put something that belonged to me in the casket with the body. Aunt Irene encouraged me to use a handkerchief with my name on it for this purpose. I was reluctant to do that, because it was unique and tactile, and I didn't think that I could get another one like it. I suppose that made it more appropriate, and I'm glad now that I did it. Mama, too, was unique, and I could never have another like her.

Labor Day that year was Monday, September 6, so the funeral Mass wasn't until Tuesday, September 7. Meanwhile, the body lay in repose in Everly-Wheatley's funeral home. They say that Mama was dressed in a beautiful blue dress. Papa asked Mrs. Mary Bruce, the lady who did Mama's hair, to come and do it right after she died. He was trying so hard to do the right thing.

Of course, friends and family came to the funeral home to pray and view the body. They signed the guest book, and many of them sent flowers.

One day, I returned home to find a vase of tea roses and baby's breath on our TV. It was from Mme. Bernier, our French teacher at school. Fortunately, Aunt Riri knew some French. Either she or someone else read the card to me. It said, "Votre mamman est toujours avec vous." Translation: "Your Mama is always with you." That is probably true, but I usually don't feel her presence so much as I would like. I really appreciated my teacher's thought, and that she wanted to send me flowers.

The neighbors were wonderfully helpful during this difficult time. The Pattersons and the Alleys brought over casseroles, other cooked dishes, and desserts. On the morning of the funeral, some of Papa's coworkers came over to help with household chores and anything else that had to be done. Nana was especially impressed with how Sergeant Ushima made the beds. She noticed that he made nice, neat, tight corners, and it reminded her of her brother, Gino.

When we weren't at the funeral home, the relatives and I sat around and commiserated. By God's grace I didn't say any of the sharp things that I have expressed here. I think that I was still in shock. The unthinkable had really happened.

Out of all those visiting family members, I especially remember Aunt Katherine. She pulled me into her lap at one point. I was too big to fit properly, but she still held me and tried to rock me back and forth.

"Aunt Katherine," I said. "How did you know I liked to be rocked?"

"Oh, all babies like to be rocked," she said.

I really appreciated what she did, but I was in an awkward position, and I knew I must be heavy for her. After a little bit, I stood up.

Sister Eileen Ann tried to offer words of encouragement, when she spoke to me over the telephone, telling me to be a brave girl, and that I could make a difference in that house by being brave. I didn't feel very brave, of course, but it did give me a purpose.

On September 7, we had the funeral Mass in Our Lady of Lourdes church. Father Comaskey celebrated the Mass. Many people came, including my entire seventh and eighth grades from Dunblane Hall, as well and friends and volunteers who had worked with Mama. Vickie didn't come, because she preferred to remember Mama alive. On this occasion, of all occasions, with the church full of people of diverse backgrounds and faiths, tactless Father Comaskey decided to preach a homily about how the Catholic church is the one true church! I did not hear or understand the sermon, but I heard about it afterwards from other upset people, most of them Catholics.

Father Hanley heard about it, too, from Papa, and he wrote a letter, saying that he almost got out of a sick bed (he suffered bouts with asthma). "He made me ashamed of my priesthood," Father Hanley said.

We buried Mama in Fairfax Memorial Park, which was then called Calvary Memorial Park, or something like that. Unlike the cemeteries in MA and much of New England, this cemetery was a flat expanse of open, grassy area. It used flat bronze markers, mounted on granite or some other firm surface, with the name and dates of the persons and other optional design features that mourners could choose. Papa and I chose a marker mounted on a granite base for Mama with her name and dates and a crucifix on one side and a rosary on the other.

Nana never liked this cemetery, because it was so different from the cemeteries she knew, with their vertical, carved stone headstones. When she was in one of her sad, bitter moods, she called it a cow pasture. We went to the cemetery on special days, like Mother's Day, Christmas, and Easter, to bring flowers. We put the flowers in a bronze vase that was inserted into a slot on the marker. When not in use, the vase fitted down inside the marker upside down, so that it would be flush with the rest of the marker. We often brought artificial flowers that would last longer, but in the spring Papa would bring real flowers cut from the azaleas or other spring blooms. The cemetery had some trees, but we weren't allowed to plant anything else. In Mount Walleston, by contrast, you could apparently plant something near a grave, if you wanted to, according to Nana.

After the funeral, as she was leaving to go back to Pittsburgh, Papa reminded me that he and Aunt Maria had lost their mother when Aunt Maria was about my age.

"She knows what it is like to be in this boat," Papa said.

Privately, I didn't see how she could understand what I was feeling, but I probably was wrong about that idea.

Ellen told me that Mama wanted me to have her watch and her jade bracelet. Mama also told me that she wanted me to keep her parrot pin. After the funeral, Papa helped me find those items among Mama's jewelry. I also kept Mama's yellow, pear-shaped topaz rosary beads with the detailed crucifix that she used to hang on her bedpost. We buried her brown beads with her. Papa had a similar set in black, and we later buried those with him.

In the weeks after the funeral, Nana and Ellen went through the rest of Mama's jewelry. I'm sorry to have to say that they needed to discard some of the costume pieces that were tacky, and Ellen probably kept some things that wouldn't have been suitable for me. I ended up sorting through what remained. I kept a pansy pin with matching earrings that I helped Mama pick out for her birthday one year. Ellen thought to keep them, but she gave them back to me when she realized that they were significant to me. I offered her another pin and earring set instead, but she declined them. Over the ensuing years, I have parted with some of Mama's treasures that didn't seem suitable for me, but I still have her watch that I attached to a lapel pin, her jade bracelet, her engagement diamond (set in a more secure setting as described later), the pansy pin and earring set, and other cherished keepsakes.

We had one small miracle in all that sorrow. Uncle Joe said that Dickey hopped around the cage all night after Mama died. A week or so after the funeral, he began to sing again. Papa accused Nana and Ellen of replacing the old bird, but they insisted that they had not.

I went back to school on Wednesday after the funeral. Aunty Rene stayed on for a couple of weeks, after other relatives left, but she and Nana were two strong-willed people, and they couldn't easily coexist for very long.

As Nana later said, "They all go, they all go, and only Nana stays."

# AFTER THE BALL

*T*he title of this chapter derives from a verse from an old song that Nana used to sing. The song was about a jilted sweetheart who found out that his love had chosen someone else after the ball:

> After the ball was over,
> After the break of dawn,
> After the stars were leaving,
> After the stars were gone!
> Many are the hearts that were broken,
> If we could see them all!
> Many are the hearts that were aching
> After the ball!

My mother's death was such a watershed moment. It left a vast emptiness in all of our lives, and some very broken hearts.

Nana was devastated, and she had to bear yet another loss. This blow was especially hard, because it defeated all reasonable expectations. A parent does not expect to bury a child, especially when there isn't any impending, aggravating, obvious circumstance, such as occurs when parents watch a son go off to war, knowing and evaluating the risk. When Mama died, Nana was going on seventy-six years old, and Mama would have been fifty-five that November. Mama's death also meant that, at her advanced age, Nana was assuming the mother role in the household, without Mama's abilities—to drive a car, transcribe Braille, help me with homework and correcting typographical errors, and comfortably discuss facts of life and issues of sexuality.

Papa had lost his wife, his helpmate, and the person on whom he could rely to do the things that Nana could not easily assume in raising me. As events revealed, he also had some concerns about my social and psychological development, and how he would help me to "grow up," without some of my mother's super sensitivities and emotional vulnerabilities. The circumstances also meant that he was now on his own in coping with some of Nana's difficult personality traits and hang-ups. Finally, he was burdened by a sense of "all the words left unsaid, and all the things left undone."

I lost my bosom friend, my confidante, the person I trusted more than any other human being this side of the Great Divide between this life and eternity. Mama's passing left a void that could never be completely filled in this life. I remember, after hearing that she died, having the sensation that I wanted to be alone, and then I wanted to go and talk to someone. With surprise, I realized that the someone was Mama, and she physically wasn't with me. I felt like the pope who wrote that, early in the morning, he woke up thinking that he should discuss something or other with the Pope. Then he remembered with shock, "No, I am the Pope." Although I didn't realize it until years later, part of me mourned Mama, and another part of me was very angry with her for dying and leaving me. It wasn't a rational reaction, but it was there. When I finally understood the existence of this feeling, I actively worked to forgive Mama and to let go, but at first much of this emotion was like a submarine inside me, where it caused a great deal of trouble.

Initially, some of the things that Papa did only seemed to make things harder for me and to sharpen the sense of loss. He became worried about Nana getting up early to see us all off, and he tried to discourage it, but Nana insisted that she normally got up early. Besides, as she said, even the birdies get up early, and it was a nice time to get up. As I said, after Aunt Irene left and we no longer needed the back bedroom for her, Papa did insist that Nana move downstairs, back to her old room on the first floor, which meant that I had to get used to getting up and ready on my own. Nana eased the transition by coming up to get me up and be with me and help me in the mornings for a while. At some point, Ellen started coming over to help with my bath and other things before bedtime. Looking back with the benefit of hindsight, it is a good thing that Papa made Nana move downstairs. When I was by myself caring for her (with the help of the live-in housekeeper, Patsy) and Nana was succumbing to a turbulent, irrational senility and increasing physical frailties, I could not have managed if Nana were still upstairs with me or refusing to be moved downstairs.

With the support of Ellen and Miss Frease, Papa insisted that I get my long hair cut short. He and the others thought that it would be better for me to manage a short haircut that didn't have to be curled. I'm sure that Mama's hairdresser, Mrs. Mary Bruce, and others gave me good hairdos, but it was a big change from the long hair in ringlets. They tried permanent waves with me, but the setting liquid made my head burn, and I didn't like the way my hair felt afterwards. Even ordinary hair sprays made my hair feel stiff (like straw) and unnatural to me. Over the years, I eventually learned to roll my own hair in soft rollers, either the foam type or the cloth rollers that twist shut.

However, the most painful thing that Papa did was to make me part with most of my dolls soon after Mama's funeral. Supposedly, he and Miss Frease had found a place or organization in Appalachia that would take my dolls "for the poor children out there." It didn't make me feel one bit better that they were going to poor children in Appalachia, although I probably would have preferred that to having them just thrown away. All I knew was that I had lost Mama, and now these cherished childhood companions were being torn away from me. Of course, they made exceptions for the stuffed white dog, Smokey, and for that darned French poodle. (I didn't have the heart to play with either of those very much.) Nana helped me to hide away a few favorites, including The Littlest Angel (a girl doll with brown braids and bendable knees and blue eyes), Sweet Sue, Betsy Wetsy, and the nurse doll that Nana bought me. However, in the rush to get them gone, Suzanne went with the bunch. Of all the dolls, I didn't want to part with her!

I have prayed about this, and I am trying to forgive Papa and to understand and be compassionate for what motivated him, but after all these years, it still hurts! If only he had given me more time to say good-bye, or if he had let my childhood passion for my dolls run its natural course, I probably, on my own, would have started parting with them, but he forced the issue. The result was, when I was old enough to make choices, I started collecting dolls again. I now have a house full of baby dolls, but I never could find a doll like Suzanne. Recently, I found a replica of a 1967 redheaded Barbie doll, and she is pretty, but it isn't the same. Eventually, a friend of mine helped me to find an old Barbie doll that goes back to the late fifty's early sixties. She's even closer than the replica; I think she will have to be the new Suzanne. She is as close as I probably will come, and I'm grateful to have her. It goes without saying that, in searching for a replacement for Suzanne, I have acquired a number of other unique Barbie dolls, including a couple of them with sleep eyes one of which has multiple wigs! As with so many things, I must keep praying and learning to let go.

Nana didn't make my situation easy after Mama died, either. She knew that Mama and Papa didn't get along smoothly much of the time, and she knew about the frictions between Mama and some of the Pittsburgh relatives. After she recovered enough to control her tears, her emotional turmoil manifested itself in anger. She often expressed this anger to me, sometimes blaming Papa for aggravating Mama's condition by creating tensions, sometimes asking me what happened in

Pittsburgh, and at other times vehemently asserting that, "He [Papa] didn't have to take her [Mama] to Pittsburgh and fight with her."

Although I knew full well that the last trip to Pittsburgh had been a real trial, I was afraid to tell Nana very much about the details. I didn't know what had happened in detail myself, and I was afraid that telling her very much would only confirm her anger and suspicions and make her worse.

The other long-term problem that I had with Nana was that I came to understand that she engaged in what I call "emotional blackmail." In other words, she knew how to try to make you feel bad or guilty if you didn't agree with her or do what she wanted. While this trait made it hard to deal with Nana, learning to recognize this kind of manipulation and deal with it appropriately has been useful to me in my life.

I should digress here to discuss the long-term relationship between Nana and Papa. Long after he died, Nana said something to indicate to me that maybe she wasn't happy initially about Papa marrying Mama. However, actions speak louder than words. In many ways, as events would reveal, Papa was a better son to Nana than my uncle, and Nana loved Papa. When she calmed down somewhat after Mama's death, she continued to emphasize Papa's good qualities. She would sometimes tell me that Mama was too sensitive about some of the things that Papa did and said, and that Mama took him too seriously. Nana would describe Papa as being like "those big German Shepherd dogs that go woof, woof, and are really big softies." She also appreciated how good and gentle Papa was in handling Dickey and in taking out splinters and cleaning out ears. She said that Papa would have made a good doctor, if he had the education and the opportunities. On that point, I agree with her.

Nana and I each had a detailed dream about Mama, but I don't remember exactly when they occurred. I will describe them here, because they seem to fit into this account of our mourning and recovery process.

Nana dreamed that a car was parked outside in front of our house that looked like the one that Mama's old boyfriend, Eddie, used to drive. Mama was standing in the living room, dressed in the blue dress in which she was buried.

"He brought me home," she told Nana.

Nana said that Mama also told her, "Don't leave Linda," and that she said something else that Nana wouldn't discuss with me. (I suspect it had something to do with Nana's poor mother, described in the earlier chapter.)

"Oh, Babe, why did you leave us?" Nana asked Mama in her dream, and then she woke up.

I dreamed that I was holding Mama, with my arms around her. She said to me, "Mama loves you very much, and she is with you every day."

Her voice didn't sound quite like Mama. Maybe someone else was speaking to me about Mama in the dream. In my dream, I sensed that I did not have much time, and that I could only ask one more thing. "Mama, what about Ellen?" I asked, because we were going through a bit of a tough relationship at that time, to be discussed later.

Mama didn't answer me, but she seemed to be evaporating from my arms. I tried to hold onto her, but she pulled me up off the bed and disappeared. When I woke, I thought that I was trying to climb back into bed. But when I was fully awake, I found myself lying in bed, with my left hand clenched around the sheet.

Another difficulty occurred in transitioning away from Ellen's help in the evenings. I eventually came to feel that I no longer wanted her help in getting ready for bed, but I felt that Ellen needed me, and I was reluctant to say so. I made the mistake of trying to tell Papa about how I felt, and Ellen overheard us. I didn't know that she still was in the house. That ordinarily quiet, soft-spoken person turned into a furious, hurt, and angry one! I much preferred Mama's fast and furious outbursts followed by quick contrition to the smoldering fury I glimpsed in Ellen that night.

The first couple of months after Mama's death were a time of upheaval and change for other reasons. We had to find a way to get me to and from Dunblane Hall for this last year. Papa drove me to school earlier, so that he could come back home and go to work. On some occasions when he couldn't drive me for some reason, Mr. Moore often took me to school. In the evenings, Dr. Bruner, Denise's father, would drive Denise and me back to Virginia. He would drop me off at my house first, and then he and Denise would drive the rest of the way home. I think that they lived in Arlington, not too far from my house.

I very much appreciated what Dr. Bruner did. On those trips, he would entertain us with recollections of his childhood, humorous accounts of his past and present dogs—he had a German shepherd, named Countess—and thoughts and philosophical reflections about humanity and world events. He liked to use the wild geese as an example. He noted that, if something happens to their leaders, the flock lands and regroups, selecting new leaders. If the geese could do that, he didn't understand why people couldn't conduct themselves better.

Dr. Bruner also liked to quote a saying, from what source I did not recall, which I often remember to remind myself to keep going despite difficulties.

The height that great men reached and kept
Was not attained by sudden flight.
But all the time while others slept
They were toiling through the night.

During the year after Mama's death, I saw less and less of Vickie, my childhood best friend. I think that she missed Mama, too, but I didn't understand why we were drifting apart. I made the mistake of confiding to Ellen that I thought that Vickie was growing away from me. It seems that Ellen said something to Vickie about what I said, because she came back to me with Vickie's supposed answer that she would not grow away from me. Ellen may have wanted to be a peacemaker, but I didn't think that it was right for her to break my confidence. I was concerned that Vickie may have taken what I said badly and that Ellen's intervention made things worse instead of better. The friendship between Vickie and me petered out, although I always consider my door open to her.

At school, I'm sure that my friends were sympathetic with me about losing Mama, but I didn't discuss my loss with most of them. I knew that at least one of my classmates had lost her mother years before, but I was a very private person, and I didn't talk about personal matters for fear of saying the wrong thing to hurt someone else. Denise, Deborah, and Gail, along with Mary Anne, were my closest friends. I identified with Deborah, because she, like me, had a grandmother living with her. Gail and I kept in touch after grammar school through much of high school, but I have lost touch now with all of my grade school friends.

In the next few years, I did vent some of my grief by writing poems and essays about Mama. I included one of these efforts, the Shakespearean sonnet, "Mama", in The Ivory Pyramid, my published poetry collection.

Sister Eileen Ann was very helpful and supportive. One day, I came into class to find a little China angel bell from her on my desk.

At home, Papa and Ellen tried to help me with homework during the first few weeks of that eighth grade year, but eventually Papa found someone who came in the evenings to work with me.

Her name was Candy, and she was a delightful young lady with a good sense of humor. I enjoyed working with her very much. I don't remember whether we paid her or she was a volunteer. [21]

Papa also read me the mail that came for several weeks from relatives and friends offering condolences, sympathy, and prayers at the loss of Mama. Many of them sent Mass cards, notices that they had arranged with a priest or monastery to offer prayers and Masses for the soul of the faithful departed and/or for the surviving family members. I appreciated these expressions of sympathy, but I liked the telephone calls and personal notes best. Sister David Clair sent a letter, saying that she was praying that God would bring joy to my heart once again. That letter made me cry, because its sentiments were in such contrast with the way I was feeling. At that point, I couldn't imagine how I would ever feel joyful again.

Sister Dorothy's response was more consoling. I think that she sent it on tape. She said that often Divine Love enters the heart through a fresh wound, and she prayed that it would be so for me.

As I said, folks were long on sympathy but often short on action. After the initial intense grieving passed, many of the folks didn't follow through in terms of friendship expressed in action and keeping in touch. Sister Mary Agnes, for one, did not keep in touch with me. She had her commitments as a Sister of Divine Providence, and her acquaintance with me was only peripheral. I also am sure that she didn't feel comfortable getting in the middle of our family situation. My teachers, even after they weren't my teachers any more, were better at maintaining correspondence and friendships with me.

I told Papa about the Vic Da Mone song, "Mama," that Mama and I heard on WRC on the way home from school during that last year. Papa found the record, and I still have it, but I don't play it very much.

Papa decided that, for the record so to speak, he and I should make a long detailed tape for Sister Margaret James about the events leading up to Mama's death. We did that, and Papa copied the song from the record onto the tape. He kept a copy of the tape for our reference. I think that I still have it, but I don't think that I can bear to listen to it again. Much of that old taped material had to be transferred to computer thumb drives for storage!

During these first few months, Papa hired a nice lady, Mrs. Thompson, to come two or three days a week to help with the housekeeping. She was a happy, upbeat person, and she owned a couple of cats, called Spotty and Sooky.

---

[21] Throughout my high school and college years and in law school, I needed the assistance of readers. At some point, I think that the VA Commission for the Blind started providing some funds to pay for readers. I no longer remember who was under what program. From this point, I will just talk about readers and not make the distinction, unless I clearly remember that they were volunteers.

My housekeeper, Patsy, used to quote a Jamaican saying that troubles sometimes come in bunches like bananas. I think something like that happened in the fall of 1965. Nana went to see Dr. Williams, and he found a benign ovarian tumor that needed to be surgically removed. Nana went into the hospital for the operation, and Uncle Joe and Great-Aunt Riri came down to our house to be there when she came out of the hospital. Meanwhile, I took only one part of a two-part influenza vaccine shot, and I became very sick. I don't know for sure that it was a reaction to the vaccine; it may have been one of my sinus infections. Dr. Lynden prescribed a strong antibiotic, which made my stomach nauseated and upset when I took it, but it eventually cured the problem. It was such a comfort to have Aunt Riri there while I was getting better!

Thanksgiving was approaching, and Papa decided that he and I should go to Aunt Maria's house in Pittsburgh for Thanksgiving, leaving Uncle Joe and Aunt Riri to hold down the fort at home. I didn't like the idea, but I obeyed Papa and went, against my better judgment and instincts. I was only fourteen, and maybe I didn't have that much choice.

Up in Pittsburgh, everything felt wrong. Papa probably thought that a change of scenery would be a good idea the first year, but I didn't find it beneficial. Aunt Maria cooked a very good dinner, and she even let me help her put butter on the turkey before she cooked it. Her methods were different from Nana's. Nana always stitched the turkey or chicken shut after she stuffed it; Aunt Maria used skewers or staples. It just wasn't the same as being at home with Nana's cooking, but she wouldn't have been cooking while in hospital or recuperating. To make matters worse, Sister Hilda sweetly said, "Now you and Papa will be real pals." We did become very close in the years after Mama's death, but at that particular moment, I didn't feel like being palsy-walsy with him.

In any event, I think that Nana came home from the hospital shortly before we arrived back home. I recall that at first, Nana had some trouble with the incision oozing or bleeding a little, but she recovered from that.

Uncle Joe stayed for a short time, and then he went back to Massachusetts. Aunt Riri stayed with us until late in the spring of 1966. Her presence made all the difference! She was as sweet, affable, and agreeable as Nana could be difficult. She was demonstrative and affectionate. She was able to help me with the homework, and she read aloud very well.

Aunt Riri also helped me to deal with my scruples and worries. She would reduce them to something funny, and her humor cut them down to size and diminished them greatly. For example, she would say jokingly, "You can't get arrested for thinking!" Laughter was the best medicine.

To cut me off from getting onto tangents and "making mountains out of molehills," as Mama used to say, both Nana and Aunt Riri sometimes would jokingly impose a penalty for bringing up a subject again. For example, they would say, "Whoever brings that up again has to put ten cents in the pot." I later sometimes used that tactic with Nana, if she wouldn't let go of a subject. As Father Kirwin, Father Hanley's successor as my spiritual adviser, put it, "Jump right off that merry-go-round!"

While Aunt Riri was with us, she and Nana sorted through some of Nana's things. Nana gave me her sterling silver rosary with the wonderfully detailed crucifix, and in return I gave her the rosary that Sister Mary Agnes gave Mama. Nana also gave me a stretchable band bracelet with a locket that had a picture of Aunt Riri when she was younger and her cat, Jacky. Nana gave Aunt Riri an old gold pin that had belonged to their mother. She gave me a necklace of off-white beads. I was distressed when the cord broke and the beads came unstrung. I tried to restring them, but Nana told me not to worry about them.

"The people who make beads need to eat, too," she told me. Throughout my life, I have found this perspective very helpful when I get too hung up over breakable possessions.

Aunt Riri and Ellen helped me through some of the difficulties that occurred when I encountered serious matters in the books that I was assigned to read at school. For example, I found the seduction of Little Emily in David Copperfield very upsetting, until they explained it to me and helped me understand that these encounters happen with human frailty.

I came away from the story with the distinct idea that it wasn't a good idea to have sex with your true love until you were married. The lesson was reinforced when I later heard of a friend's daughter, a girl two or three years older than I, who became pregnant as an unmarried teenager. The last that I heard about her was that she had a second child, and she was still living at home with her parents and the two children.

Papa's cynical comment about "affairs of the heart" was that often one loved in inverse ratio to the amount that one was loved. Judging from the many stories in literature of the tragic consequences of unbridled passions and unrequited love, not to mention the headlines in the news and the papers, I concluded that he was right too often. I decided that, if I fell in love with someone, I would try to do it right (with God's help, of course) or not at all.

Fortunately, some of the books that I needed or wanted to read such as David Copperfield and Moby Dick were available on records from the Library of Congress or the regional libraries like the one in Richmond. (Later the program for the blind was known as the National Library Service.)

Nana and I particularly enjoyed *Moby Dick*. She was able to listen while the records were playing. We especially laughed when one of the old captains, in exhorting his men to follow orders with more dispatch, called them "sons of bachelors." We appreciated that Melville was giving men equal time in using derogatory expressions!

To give me something to which to look forward, Papa showed me some rings and stones that he brought back from India. He had a tiger's eye ring, man's size, with two little zircons, one on each side. This ring was similar to a cat's eye ring with two little diamonds that Grandpa gave Mama and which she lost. Papa was going to have a ring made for her, but he never got around to it. In addition, he had another loose, unset green cat's eye stone, and a star sapphire set in another big ring. He decided that he would get the star sapphire set in a gold ring for me with the two zircons. He did this during my high school years. When I graduated from college, he substituted two little diamonds for the zircons.

At Christmas time in 1965, as mentioned in an earlier chapter, all eight grades of our school did the musical, "The Keys to Christmas," as their Christmas program. Papa recorded it, and I think that I still have that tape around somewhere. My friend, Gail, played the part of the airplane pilot. In the play, the plane has to make a crash landing, and the pilot and passengers end up spending the Christmas time in a cabin. While there, they reminisce about past Christmases, and they share what they regard as the keys to having a good Christmas.

At home, we decided to try a cut Scotch pine tree, instead of the spruce. It was my last live, cut tree. During the holiday, both Aunt Riri and I developed cold-like symptoms. We tried all the usual remedies, along with Aunt Riri's homemade vinegar candy, but our chest congestion and coughing persisted. In our house, we usually leave the tree up until the feast of the Epiphany, January 6, which coincided with the break between school semesters. When our symptoms persisted, we began to conclude that it was the tree that was bothering us. We took the tree down a few days early, and dismantled that tree in record time! After we put it outside on the porch, we immediately began to feel better. The next year, we had an artificial tree, but that's another story.

Even easygoing Aunt Riri had trouble dealing with Nana when she was in one of her temper moods, and Aunt Riri developed high blood pressure while she was with us, for which Dr. Williams prescribed medication. Aunt Riri missed Aunt Janie, and I'm sure that she was glad to get back to Quincy. However, those months that she was with us were a welcome respite, allowing me to ease into the loss of Mama and providing a good transition. Noting that Aunt Riri was only seven to ten years older than Papa and that they weren't biologically related, Sister Thomas Marie innocently asked me whether it was possible that Papa might marry Aunt Riri. Although we both knew that it wasn't at all likely, Nana and I had a quiet, private, "what if" laugh over that one.

To allow me to go shopping, on the weekends or holidays, Papa would take Ellen and me to a shopping center in the morning and leave us to shop and have lunch. He would pick us up later in the afternoon. Sometimes, Ellen and I took the bus to downtown Washington. Ellen didn't drive, but she knew her way around using buses, and she was very familiar with the bus schedule.

Before Aunt Riri left, I went shopping with Papa for gifts for her and Aunt Janie. I bought Aunt Riri a gold charm of a little girl's head with my initials to wear on her charm bracelet that the bank gave her when she retired. I bought a pearl pin for Aunt Janie.

After Aunt Riri left, Papa started trying to do some pleasure reading for me. When I wanted Papa to read to me, I would find him in his easy chair, and I would say teasingly, "I gave you back your glasses!"

We started working on that church history book, with Papa reading me a little each night, but we never managed to finish it. He also read some more of Men and Mountains to me, but we never managed to finish that one, either. At first, Papa didn't read so well as Mama, and I missed her terribly when he was reading to me. I never told him how I felt, and I'm very glad now that I didn't. Practice does make perfect. Toward the end of his life, after all the years of reading college and law school books to me, I noticed with pleasant surprise how much better Papa was reading.

Eighth grade was a bittersweet time for me. It was wonderful to be completing grammar school, but it was becoming clear to me that I would not be continuing on to Immaculata High School. The transportation issues from Arlington to DC were just too difficult. I was to start High School at St. Mary's Academy on Russell Road, in Alexandria, VA. [22]

For the spring program at Dunblane Hall, I think that we put on a medley of Stephen Foster songs, but we may also have sung the spiritual based on Ezekiel's vision of the great wheel:

---

[22] I graduated from St. Mary's in 1970; it was an all-girls school; the companion school, Bishop Ireton's, was all boys. Over twenty years later, they decided to close St. Mary's and merge it with Bishop Ireton's, making it co-ed.

Ezekiel saw the wheel!
Way up in the middle of the air.
Ezekiel saw the wheel
Way in the middle of the air!
And the little wheel flew by faith!
And the big wheel flew by the grace of God!
'Tis a wheel within a wheel!
Way in the middle of the air!

The verses of the song emphasized the three virtues of faith, hope and charity.

Our class was assigned to write a research paper for history, to get used to the kind of papers that we would have to start doing in high school and college. I remember that I wrote about the series of compromises that prevented the Civil War, but the war could not be avoided. In the end, Lincoln took the position that there could be no more compromising about extending slavery to the territories. He feared that further extensions would enshrine slavery, and that it ultimately needed to be eliminated. I felt a sense of accomplishment about that paper. I wanted to keep a copy, but we discovered that one of the carbon papers we used was put in wrong, and the page came out backwards. I don't know if I still have that paper among the things that are in the drawer filled with folders!

The close of the year saw the performance of the usual rites and traditions. Papa and I attended the father-daughter communion breakfast, and I received a ring rosary as a keepsake. I brought into class a small book, and I asked all of my classmates to write something in it. I still have the book. Papa took the class picture that was included in the back of our yearbook. We had our graduation Mass in the chapel at Immaculata, and Sister Eileen Ann gave each of us a crystal blue-beads rosary with a silver chain and a silver crucifix. Ellen gave me a book, An Angel Grows Up, which she autographed for me. She also read it to me during the summer.

After the graduation, I asked Papa to take a picture of me on the grand staircase that went up to the second floor of the school. I don't know if I still have it. As we lined up for the last time in the front hall at the end of the year, I heard the closing bell ring for the final time.

"This is my home, and I'm leaving it," I said sadly.

I don't remember whether Papa and I went to Pittsburgh that summer, but I know that we went to MA. Papa and Nana and I made the long ten-hour drive to Quincy. When we got there, Nana and

I were diverted off to the great-aunts' apartment, and Papa stayed with Uncle Joe an Aunt Irene. It hurt Nana's feelings. I think that she was expecting to be put up at her son's house. As she put it to me later, "We [she and I] were as welcome as snakes at a party!"

Looking back now, I suspect that Papa wanted some privacy and space to discuss family matters alone with his wife's brother and wife. He brought Mama's afghan with us in the box, and Aunty Rene put it together and sent it back to us later. We still use it, but the weight of the squares tends to pull the seams apart.

On that trip to MA, Nana brought Mama's mink hat to give it to Nancy. Fortunately, Nancy didn't want it. Aunt Janie couldn't believe that Nana wanted to give Mama's hat away.

"Don't give that hat away, Mal!" She told Nana and me. "It's made with real mink tails, and Linda can wear it."

The reason Nana wanted to part with it was that it was made with real fur. Nana was horrified at the idea of making fur clothing with the skins of little animals. I agree with her, to the extent that I won't buy a fur coat or cape or hat, except secondhand once at a church bazaar, but I did want Mama's hat.

On this trip, I brought a tape recording of my reading of a story I wrote. For some reason, Nancy was interested in hearing it, and took it up to her room. I found out later why. I was in her room to talk about the story and ask her how she liked it. Nancy took a telephone call while I was with her, and she said, "You remember Dick Pierce, don't you? (As though I could forget him!) He's on the phone." A little later, she went out. They were getting back together. She used listening to my story as a way to stay privately in her room to wait for his call! I was thus the first to find out about their reconciliation.

One very pleasant thing happened that summer. I came downstairs, after sleeping late one morning, to find Uncle Johnny in the dining room having coffee and toast with Nana. I was a little embarrassed, because I came down in a robe, but he soon put me at ease. He was traveling in the vicinity, and maybe came to Washington for some reason, but he stopped by unannounced.

He spoke with open emotion about Mama. "When Murff and I heard about Estelle, we sat together and cried and cried," he told us. "We just couldn't make sense of her dying so young. We kept asking 'why?' Finally, we dried our tears, and I told Murff, 'God doesn't promote the privates and the corporals. When he calls folks up to heaven, he wants the colonels and the generals.'"

His words helped us to feel better. We called Papa at the office, so Uncle Johnny could talk to him, too. He teased Papa about how he was going to elope with his daughter! We had a good visit.

As far as my overall emotional health was concerned, I temporarily got over what had been bothering me in the seventh grade. Now, it was OK to cry, and I had a specific reason, missing Mama, and I had many other challenges and changing circumstances to occupy me. However, many of these emotional issues resurfaced with a vengeance in my high school years.

I found my situation that year after Mama's death very confusing. Looking back, it seems to me that the adults in my life were sending me mixed signals. On the one hand, they treated me like a child, when it was convenient for their purposes, i.e., going to Pittsburgh for Thanksgiving, disposing of some of Mama's things, and assuming that I had no inkling of what was going on between Nancy and Dick. On the other hand, Papa was pushing me to "grow up," such as by getting rid of most of my dolls. Whichever way they were pushing or pulling, however, they all denied me the freedom or incentive to start exercising my say or right of choice.

From the advanced perspective of many years, it seems to me that parents need to encourage their children to grow up by giving them the freedom and space to start exercising choices in a safe environment.

# THE HIGH SCHOOL YEARS: SQUARE PEG IN A ROUND HOLE

*J*ustice Oliver Wendell Holmes, Jr., is quoted as saying "change is the law of life and the life of the law." My High School years definitely represented a change from Dunblane Hall, and they marked a time of other changes and developments in my life as well. These years were not particularly happy years for me, and I should say at the outset that, unlike many of my classmates and peers, I do not look back on these years as "the good old days at St. Mary's." Perhaps because it was a difficult time for me, memory has obscured many of the details about my high school experience. What follows is a reconstruction.

Like Dunblane Hall, St. Mary's Academy was run by a religious order of sisters, the Sisters of the Holy Cross, and all of its students were girls. The school was housed in a single building that had two floors and a lower level. The convent for the sisters was an old mansion located up the hill from the school. The sisters had a big German shepherd dog, named Cindy. In addition to the sisters who served as teachers and the principal, the school had lay teachers for many of its subjects. Students were assigned a homeroom, and then they moved around the building to different classrooms for different classes. I generally kept my bookcase with my Braille books, Braillewriter, and typewriter in the homeroom. If I needed the typewriter to take a quiz or for some other purpose in another room, I would wheel the little typing table into the exam room. I took the tape recorder with me to class if I were going to use it for notes. Now, Papa had to work with the teachers in trying to find out about books enough ahead of time for me to get them recorded on tape or to find a pre-recorded copy. We started using an organization, called originally Recording for the Blind and now Learning Ally, to get copies of or record books on reel-to-reel tape. [23] At the recommendation of

---

[23] This organization later changed its name to Recording for the Blind and Dyslexic, but it now goes by the name of Learning Ally. Most of its books are now produced on CD's.

this organization, we bought a Sony 105 tape recorder to play these tapes, because it was adapted to play tapes of the books that were recorded on four tracks, instead of the usual two. Eventually, when I went to college, we got a stereo reel-to-reel tape recorder to play the tapes at home, and I took the Sony to school and kept it there. The stereo tape recorder would play the four track tapes, because stereo channels corresponded to tracks one and three. To play a particular track, I moved the selector to play only one stereo channel. A few of the books from Learning Ally were still on small plastic records, which I could play on my Talking Book machine. However, these recordings were often inferior to the ones on tape, because the playing needle could easily scratch the records, especially if you tried to find a poetry selection or story in the middle of the record.

We had to use tape recordings or records for most of my books, because at this stage, the books were getting too long and the professors were jumping around too much to make Braille practical. Sometimes, for materials assigned on short notice, we used a local organization of volunteers to do recording of books and materials on a very short schedule.

The exceptions to the general pattern of recorded books were my language books. I took French and Latin during my High School years, and it was necessary to have these books in Braille, for obvious reasons. Even if one could learn pronunciation from a recording, it is also necessary to learn spelling and syntax and grammar, and having the written text is essential for this purpose. I started with second-year French, because I had French in grade school. It wasn't a complete equivalent to first-year French, so I had to do some hard work to catch up. As far as the Latin was concerned, I found it interesting, and I still remember the beginning of Julius Caesar's writing: "Gallia est divisa in tres partes." (Gaul is divided into three parts.) The rest has slipped out of memory, except that G's are pronounced like hard G's, and the C is a hard C and not pronounced like CH, which is different from Church Latin.

At home, Papa and Ellen continued to help me with extra reading. Sometimes, Barbara Sheehan would read to me, too. She recorded some of the things that I needed read, such as the Prologue to Chaucer's *Canterbury Tales*. While Barbara and I were reading, Nana would make us each a cup of hot chocolate with a marshmallow floating in it, and she would bring us the cups during our breaks. From these treats, I learned that I could get away with a little chocolate on an occasional basis.

Because the high school building was more complicated than my grade school, getting around the school by touch and feel would not work there. Over the years, the Virginia Commission for the Blind sent out a series of mobility instructors to teach me cane technique. I did well enough inside the building and found the cane useful. However, travel outside presented a different set of problems and challenges. As I mentioned, I do not balance very well on stairs without a railing. I learned eventually to go up outside stairs with the cane if I had to, but coming down was a real challenge that I never really mastered. Also, we had the difficulties caused by my inability to accurately tell the direction of traffic.

For practice, when Papa and I walked to church, Papa made me use the cane, instead of walking "sighted guide" with him and holding his arm. I didn't like having to do it, especially because I didn't see how I was ever going to do it alone with the issue of the street crossings. In addition to problems hearing the traffic, I also had a tendency to veer to one side or the other when trying to walk across the street, which could be very dangerous if I veered too close to traffic. My wrist became tired doing the arc of left to right with the cane, and I didn't feel relaxed and confident.

The freshman year at St. Mary's went well enough. Stephanie Shaw lived on Hayes Street next to the Williams' house, around the corner and up the street from me. She was my big Senior Sister, and she was able to drive. I think that she was my main transportation to and from school that year. My homeroom was with Miss Hengerer, who was my World History teacher. I liked her. I also made a few friends in my class, including Fran McGonagle, Kathy Smith, Renee Rolander, and Sharon Mangus, and some others that I haven't named here. Renee and Sharon often came to visit at my house. They also enjoyed the opportunity to meet Nana and Papa. For some reason that I have forgotten now, Nana and I started nicknaming Papa "The Governor." These two friends picked up on this nickname. One evening, when Papa came to pick me up at school, they saw us leaving, and they yelled out the windows of the Ladies room, "Bye, bye, Governor!"

It was good to have friends. However, I still found some things difficult at St. Mary's. The student body numbered around 400, and the freshman class was around a hundred students. Classes and halls were more crowded. The classes often involved interaction and discussion among students and the teacher, and I often found it impossible to hear my classmates. I compensated for my problem in hearing the teachers by sitting as close to the front of the room as possible.

Another difficulty I had was the change of perspective. I'm not saying that we were angels at Dunblane Hall, but the teachers encouraged and expected us to be serious and disciplined a good deal of the time. In High School, it seemed to me, discipline was much less rigorously enforced, which made it hard for the students who were serious about learning. The students seemed intent on challenging the authority of the school and the teachers, a trend that I tried very hard to resist. It began with the uniforms. The sisters set a rule about how short the skirts were to be. The students knew that the skirts would be hemmed that way, but they rolled the waistband to make the skirts shorter. I personally didn't like the idea that anybody might be able to see "all the way up to France," as Nana might have put it. Although I may have been mistaken (with the benefit of hindsight), at the time I didn't get the idea that most of the students in my class were taking their educational opportunity seriously at all.

In addition to a general rebellious atmosphere about authority, my post Vatican II High School years were a time of questions, doubts, and skepticism about matters of traditional faith. Some students and theologians were raising creative solutions to interpretative and factual questions about biblical happenings. In many ways, our religion and theology classes were interesting and stimulating, but they could be unsettling, too.

In our parish, as well as at St. Mary's, more changes came to the Mass. In addition to its being prayed in the vernacular instead of Latin, many new and folksier hymns were being sung. Guitars and later keyboards sometimes replaced the usual organ. Some hymns formerly associated with Protestant worship, such as "How Great Thou Art," were sung at Mass.

The main fund raising activity at St. Mary's was the students' selling of candy bars to raise money for the school. The chocolate smelled delicious, but it was off-limits for me to eat. Moreover, going up and down and trying to sell candy as not my strong suit. I sold a few bars to family and friends, and Papa sold a few bars to co-workers at the Pentagon, but I couldn't enter into all the fun and enthusiasm. We generally were excused from homework during the first kick-off day of the sale, but I went home and did my schoolwork, anyway. Despite what the principal said about excusing us, I had a feeling that the teachers would expect us to make up the work later.

The entire atmosphere of the place was much more secular than Dunblane Hall. In my grammar school, we often began the day with prayers, prayed the Angelus at lunchtime, and prayed at the end of the day. We said little short prayers between classes. At St. Mary's, the formal communal praying was considerably less. Even the textbooks seemed more secular to me. For example, I wasn't used to a World History book that took a dim, sometimes negative, view of the Catholic Church. Fortunately, Sister Eileen Ann remained at Dunblane Hall for the first year of my high school years, and I was able to go to visit her for an hour or two on some weekends to vent my sense of culture shock and adjustment difficulties. I found her wonderfully understanding and supportive.

At home I faced other difficulties. Despite his singing so consolingly for us after Mama died, Dickey began to fail. He stopped singing, and one day, he had a little fit or seizure in his cage. Ellen said that he probably wouldn't live very long. We went out for a walk, with me crying and feeling very sad. When we came back, Dickey was better. Nana went downstairs while we were gone and found a bottle of whiskey and added some to his water.

On another occasion, Nana also rescued Dickey when he hung upside down in his cage because his claws were too long. She took him into the kitchen and ran the faucet, dribbling water into his beak and down his throat.

"Just drink the water! You aren't dead yet," she told him.

After he revived, Nana patted him for a while before putting him back in his cage. Papa had to trim Dickey's nails so that it wouldn't happen again.

Nana, like Dr. Jackson, didn't believe in saying die until die was dead. She taught me about fighting optimism and positive thinking.

Ellen's tendency to have a negative outlook was not my only problem with her. I know that in her loneliness she probably felt a desire to be needed and to pour out her affection and attention on someone. In fulfilling this need, she tried to assume a mother role with me. The situation was aggravated by the fact that I did like, and in a way love, Ellen and needed her, but I couldn't admit her into the "mother" slot. My resistance to having that kind of a relationship with her was compounded by Nana's and my suspicions that Ellen was "setting her cap," for Papa and wanted to assume the mother role in name as well as fact! Nana felt that her suspicions in this regard were confirmed when, a year or two after Mama died, Ellen and her father returned to the Catholic faith. Ellen's father had married a non-Catholic, and he had neglected his faith for years. I was glad to have Ellen back in our church. She became an active member of the Women's Council (used to be called the Sodality,) and she was very helpful in setting up and working in bake sales, bazaars, and other activities. She often alerted me to goodies that I might like in white elephant sales and helped me look around at our church bazaars. At one of those sales, I bought a small, old-fashioned rubber baby doll with movable eyes, and I started rebuilding my doll collection.

When I was older, Papa and I talked candidly about his feelings for Ellen. I was relieved to learn that he did not have romantic feelings toward her. He didn't trivialize or treat her feelings lightly, but he told me, "I would want someone with a more upbeat personality and a sense of humor."

After her father died, I think before I began college, Ellen worked for many years as a teacher's aide in the nearby public school. She lived alone in the house until her death in the 1990's.

Meanwhile, another thing that I learned about Ellen was that she sometimes acted as an emotional catalyst. She would say or do something that would cause people to react emotionally in a way that often created conflict unnecessarily. (Her handling of my concerns about my friendship with Vickie is an example of this pattern of behavior.) I eventually learned not to rise to her bait or "let her get my goat," as Nana might have put it. Learning how to react to her somewhat negative or provocative comments helped us to get along better, and I found it useful to recognize this pattern of behavior in other people. Even though I tried to be calm and understanding of Ellen and her feelings, the tensions and conflicts in my emotions caused us to have a somewhat uneasy, seesaw relationship over the years, until after Papa's death.

Ellen sometimes liked to stir things up in regard to U.S. history, particularly the Civil War. The soft-spoken Virginia southerner and the feisty Vermont Yankee, Nana, fought the war all over again many times around our dining room table.

I instinctively realized that I needed someone to fill the role of a mother, but I wanted to choose who it would be. I chose Barbara Sheehan. She and her husband, Don, lived a block away from me on South 25th Street. Once I had my dogs, I could easily walk to her house. Before then, I saw her on Sundays, because Papa would sometimes stop to visit the Sheehans on the way home from church. Barbara also took Nana to the Podiatrist, and in the summertime I would go with them. After the doctor had treated Nana for her calluses, we would go to Lansburgh's department store to look around (and sometimes buy something) and then we went to the Hot Shop to have lunch.

For the second Christmas after Mama died, we had our first artificial tree. Nowadays, they are making the trees to look much more realistic and to be more convenient, but that first tree was a project. It had a pole that was supposed to stand upright in a stand that came with the tree, but the stand didn't work. Papa had to get another old stand from someone in the Pentagon and modify it to work with the pole. The stand that we used for our live trees was too large for the purpose. The branches were in bundles with numbers and color-coding, and they had to be stuck into holes in the pole. Between the branches, thick bushy green things, called pole covers, were supposed to fill in the bare spaces and make the tree look green. Papa fussed and complained all the time that he was putting it up, and he noted rightly that somebody, like a single woman alone and in an apartment, would have a hard time getting the thing together. To add insult to injury, the little bulb lights that we used successfully with live trees were too hot for this plastic material. We had to use some old bubble lights that we had that were shaped like candles and were much cooler. Because they didn't have clips to secure them, we had to tie them on the tree with strong thread. The following year, we bought little lights that were suitable for artificial trees and some newer bubble lights that had clips.

Eventually, in later years we bought the kind of tree that Papa Sheehan had: a spruce-like tree with hinged branches that unfolded from the trunk. These trees frequently can be found at Sears and Roebuck. I still use this kind of tree, although I have used live trees in dirt balls on two occasions when I was between artificial trees. The latest of these survives and is growing nicely in the front yard today. We used to put battery-powered light sets on it, but now it is getting just too big!

For that second Christmas after Mama died, Papa gave me a big jewelry box to house my treasures. I had my eye on the ones made by Bond Street that were sold at Woody's, but Papa found one for me at W. Bell and Company (the discount store) that was much nicer.

Sometime during the first year or two after Mama died, I began keeping a diary. Irony of ironies, I typed it! Why? Because the Braillewriter simply wouldn't go fast enough to suit me, especially when my emotions were running high and I was in a rush to pour my thoughts out onto paper. The result is — the joke's on me – that I can't now go back and refresh myself as to what I was thinking and feeling at the time. To compound the problem, out of some idea of privacy concern and maybe to use what I was learning, I wrote some entries in French! I will have to leave unscrambling those messy eggs to the post-mortem accuracy hounds!

I also sometimes hid the tape recorder in the dining room and turned it on to get "candid recordings" of Papa, Nana, and me, and some of the funny things that Papa did and said sometimes.

One pleasant memory of that first year was the retreat that we had at school around Easter time. We had the week as break after Easter, and we went back to school during the day for some talks and retreat by priests. It was a very nice occasion, and I enjoyed it, especially one particularly dynamic priest. His name was Father Dismas, and he made you feel good about flying and being with Jesus, instead of worrying about "Are you running with me Jesus," which was a popular book at the time.

I don't remember anything about the summer after my freshman year, but at some point Sister Eileen Ann left Dunblane Hall. Before she did, during the spring of my freshman year, we attended an Up with People Singers concert in the Immaculata gymnasium. These neatly dressed, polite young people, with their wonderful songs and high ideals, were a refreshing contrast to the Beatniks and the hippy culture. Among the songs that they sang, which also are on their record album, were "Freedom Isn't Free," "What Color Is God's Skin?" "You Can't Live Crooked and Think Straight," ballads about Joan of Arc, St. Patrick, and Paul Revere, and the "Up with People" theme song. Papa bought us each one of the record albums that the group was selling. I found this music very uplifting and inspiring, and I still have the record. I kept in touch with Sister Eileen Ann for many years, until I tried to call her at St. Mary of the Woods in IN, the Mother House of the order, and learned that she died. I miss her.

In late spring or early summer of 1967, Dickey died. We were sitting at the dining room table at dinner, when Nana saw him drop to the bottom of the cage.

"Don't cry too much," Papa told me. "He was suffering."

We think that he was having trouble with his legs. Even considering that he was the third bird, he had lived a number of years, and he brought us much joy. I missed him terribly, and the lovely song with which he often filled our house.

Dickey wasn't the only loved one to depart during my high school years. I don't remember when exactly it happened, but Uncle Bill's wife, Aunt Katherine, succumbed to uterine cancer during this period. I think that Nana's brother, Sam, also died in this time frame. The only specific thing that I remember was that he died on May 4, which was the same day on which I was confirmed.

Another recurring event during this time was that the VA Commission for the Blind continued to send home teachers to teach me independent living skills. A lady named Joy Gilpin came first, and later on a very nice gentleman, Gerry Arsenault, came. I tried to cooperate with these folks, but privately I resented that they needed to come to teach me things that other young folks seemed to learn on their own. What they mainly were trying to help me to learn was how to cook. I had to concede the necessity of my learning this from somebody, because I still had the fear of the gas flame. Moreover, Nana, although a good cook, was not a good cooking teacher for me, because she didn't know how to instruct in a hands-on manner.

I came to understand that the Commission might want me to go away in the summer for a few weeks to a rehabilitation place in Little Rock, Arkansas, and I really did not want to go.

The second year of high school was my sophomore year, the year of the wise fools, and it was filled with plusses and minuses. One definite plus was that I had an opportunity to start getting to know the Ambury girls. Mary was in the class ahead of me, and her younger sisters were like steps behind me. Mary and I became good friends, and we still are. I also got to know Fran and Angie, her two younger sisters; the oldest sister, Patricia, graduated ahead of us, and I never got to know her very well. The father of the Ambury girls was Dr. James Ambury, whose office was near their house. Mary always said to me to remember that, if we needed a doctor, to call her father and he would come. It turned out to be a significant remark.

As they grew older and started driving, the Amburies often helped to get me home from school. I don't remember all the details of how we arranged transportation during my High School years, except that Papa often took me to school in the morning, and we tried to make other arrangements to get me home, so that I would not have to stay too late.

On the minus side, I survived Algebra I in my freshman year, but I had to tackle Geometry, which I found a challenge with its drawings and the need to master shapes. Papa had to help me with protractors and tracing wheels. The math teacher was a Miss Girdley. I liked her, and she was very helpful and understanding with my struggles with the math. She or somebody meant to do me a kindness but inadvertently did me a disservice. She or somebody in authority at St. Mary's arranged for me to not have to take Algebra II. With all the difficulties I had with mathematics, I didn't argue over the point. Now, I wish that I had! When I later came to consider science as a major in college, I was told that I didn't have the necessary prerequisites. This example shows that not everything that makes life easier turns out to be a good thing.

Another plus was that I started getting to know Sister Antoinina, who watched over the students in the cafeteria. She was a warm, motherly soul, and we girls all enjoyed her. I still brought my lunch to school, but I often ate it in the cafeteria.

This probably was the year that our Latin class had our Roman banquet. We were instructed to make or improvise simple Roman togas for ourselves. We went to school that evening and ate bread and chicken on very low tables while sitting on cushions. It was interesting and fun, and fortunately the teacher didn't insist that we speak Latin during the banquet.

I recall my sophomore year as the time that Papa got the sapphire ring made up for me. Sharon had a star sapphire, too, but hers may have been manmade, instead of a natural stone.

I think that my sophomore year was the first year that Sister Ernestine was librarian at St. Mary's. Because of the schedule, I had study hall time, and I began spending it in the library. Early in the school's history, the chapel was large and the library was small. Eventually, religious zeal abated and the books needed more room, and the chapel was converted into a library. It had still the cold marble floor and the raised marble platform where the altar once stood. It had a cold, hushed feeling that seemed more appropriate for the chapel it once was than a library. Spending study hall there meant that I was exposed to periods of quiet when I was supposed to be studying. It also meant that I was under Sister's watchful eyes.

She seemed to be a pleasant, well-meaning lady, and I think that I also had her for an English literature class. During one of her classes, the subject of demonic possessions and exorcisms came up, which I found very upsetting. It seemed inconceivable to me that this kind of evil existed, and I found it very frightening to know that it was real. I think that the Devil used these fears to aggravate my scrupulosity and hang-ups.

Sister also took notice of the fact that I dressed and acted more conservatively than others in my class. Nana thought that she used the word "dowdy" to describe how I dressed. With the support of Papa and Ellen, she urged a shopping trip to find some suitable dress clothes for me. I went shopping and bought some things, but I ended up taking most of them back. They just weren't my style. My initially favorable feelings toward sister turned decidedly negative.

As with grade school, it took me longer than other students to do the work, and I didn't feel that I had much time for socializing and frivolous things. Papa remained concerned that I was putting book learning ahead of my social development, and he feared that I would succumb to an elitist, superior point of view.

He needn't have worried. God lets us trip over our own toes sometimes to make sure that we don't get too high an opinion of ourselves. On one occasion, I failed to study for a Latin quiz. Too late I remembered it. I had to take the typewriter into the room, and sit there during the quiz, unable to type anything on the paper, and knowing that by listening to my silence and failure to type all the other girls realized that I knew nothing. I wanted to go through the floor and disappear! Afterwards, the teacher said, "Next time, don't bother bringing the machine in here. Just tell me, 'Sister, I didn't study!'"

There wasn't a next time. Needless to say, the grade was a D or an F.

Instead of being angry, Papa laughed. "We're going to frame this paper!" he said. During the summer between my sophomore and junior years, I spent much time doing some of the household chores, including dusting and thoroughly polishing the furniture. As I will discuss in the chapter concerning my writing, these years also were the time during which I started really becoming interested in politics and writing some poetry. The fall of my junior year coincided with the Presidential campaign. Like so many in the nation, I was shocked and saddened by the assassination of both Dr. Martin Luther King (with the riots that followed) and Robert Kennedy. I wrote the poem "We're All on Strike," after the death of Dr. King. However, I came to feel that Hubert Humphrey should be elected as President instead of Richard Nixon, and I proudly wore an H.H.H. button on the lapel of my school blazer during the campaign.

When I came home from school on election day, Nana, the Vermont republican, greeting me with the comment, "I baked a pineapple upside down cake today, because Humphrey has to win."

Nana was good at forecasting election, but it was wishful thinking on all of our parts that day. I wasn't old enough to vote, but I went with Papa when he went to the polls and voted for Humphrey. We came home and had our dinner. We enjoyed the delicious cake for dessert and spent the evening listening to the results, and I was stunned that Richard Nixon actually won. I remember going into the bathroom, sitting on the commode, and crying.

"They are going to bite their nails!" I sobbed. "They are going to bite their nails and wish that they never elected this man! [Richard Nixon]."

As it turned out, almost six years later, in August of 1974, the night that President Nixon resigned in disgrace after the Watergate scandal, I finally felt vindicated. I went upstairs to get ready for bed and was walking around in a happy haze. I knocked my Aunt Maria's gift, the Christmas angel that played Silent Night, off the high chest and she broke. No part of the figurine remained in one piece except the head. I later found another one like it, but I will always associate that angel with the night I was proved right about Richard Nixon.

Meanwhile, emotionally my state of mind went downhill for me in the fall of 1968. On November 19, I went into an emotional tailspin, similar to what had happened during the seventh grade. It started in Sister Ernestine's study hall, in the dead silence of the library with nothing to beguile my senses and distract me. I suspect that a great number of emotions and fears, which were lurking like submarines in my subconscious, all came to the front and made their presence known. To name only a few, I still grieved for Mama, I was dealing with the tensions at home and the conflicting values discussed at school, and I hadn't come to terms with the evil realities in the spiritual realm and coping with sin and guilt. I also had the lurking dread of possibly being made to go away from home to the rehabilitation center. It was a painful way to learn a valuable lesson. Even if one does not want to feel a certain way, and even if you can't condone the feeling or let it rule your actions, one must acknowledge the emotions and find a way to constructively vent them. In other words, subconscious emotions cause a great deal of trouble!

After three or four nights of my not being able to sleep, Papa took me to a doctor recommended by Sister Ernestine. They hospitalized me to check for ulcers, since my stomach was queasy (as usual when I get emotionally upset.) No ulcers were found, and I was put on medicine to control symptoms and sent to a psychiatrist. I deliberately am not going into details here about the medications, because I am not against people seeking treatment for depression and other mental problems. Today, we know much more about effective treatments than they did in the late '60's. I do believe that some mistakes were made in my case. For one thing, someone I didn't like or trust recommended the doctors who treated me, and I had no real connection with them or reason to trust them. For another thing, both the doctor and the psychiatrist kept saying that I would be fine, and that I would be better soon. Their words were totally inconsistent with my state of mind and how I was feeling. Although positive thinking is good and often therapeutic, when it amounts to a lie, it isn't positive thinking at all. They didn't tell me the truth: that I was going through the valley of the shadow and that it had to be passed through and endured in order to come out the other side. Finally, the doctors paid too little attention to spiritual issues and they didn't make enough of an attempt to find the root cause of my problem or to teach me how to manage my scrupulosity and tendency to obsess.

All I knew was that it was a horrible time. Nothing that I believed seemed secure or solid anymore; everything I tried to focus on, including God and my faith, dissolved in negative thoughts, doubts, and scruples. The tranquilizers made me drowsy and dopey, and the other medicine made me not feel right. The psychiatrist was the kind that sat and listened and let me talk—talk myself into more holes—and he provided no answers. Needless to say, Thanksgiving was subdued that year. I eventually went back to school, but while I was out, Kathy Smith sent me a get-well wire—a box of chocolates. Although I couldn't eat the chocolates, the thought was worth more than a gross of candies that I could eat! She and I also shared a love of birds. The one bright spot in all this was that, for once, Papa and Nana were on the same side of the fence and weren't arguing. They shared their bewilderment, frustration, and helplessness at what was happening to me. The other positive aspect of this crisis, I reflected later, was that the thing I feared most of all was committing serious sin and offending the Lord. Jesus told us those are the only things of which we really ought to be afraid.

There came one horrible Sunday when I couldn't see any reason to go on living. Medicine or no, I wasn't feeling better and didn't seem to be getting better. I couldn't see any end or way out of the bottomless pit into which I seemed to be falling. I didn't know what to do, but I began to think about possibly ending it all. Fortunately, by the grace of God, Papa took me that day to see Father Hanley.

Father Hanley did what nobody else had done. He told me the truth. "I can't wave a magic wand and make this all go away," he told me. "I wish that I could, but I can't." On this and other occasion, he advised me to not let the psychiatrist get to me. He prayed with me. He made me see that I wasn't really at bottom, and that I could only go up. It was the beginning of my recovery.

Concerning Father Hanley, I think it was at the end of that year that he was assigned elsewhere and left the Oblate College in Washington, DC. When he left, he suggested that I start talking to a priest friend of his, Father George Kirwin. Father Kirwin continued to be most helpful to me. He taught me to use so-called reflex principles to combat scrupulosity, and that it was best to assess them quickly as scruples and dismiss them. I also gained some perspective on my situation when I learned that Martin Luther, who started the Protestant Reformation, came to his belief in the power of faith to save souls because he was so caught up in scruples. Years later, Papa would say to me, when he thought that I was getting off on a tangent, "Don't be like Martin Luther!"

As for Father Hanley, he eventually became the head of the Oblates. We kept in touch for a while over the years through correspondence. However, I heard finally that he left the priesthood and was getting married. I wrote him one last letter, wishing him well, and telling him that I understood if he did not want to answer. Although I let him go off into the sunset as he wished, I thank Jesus and the prayers of all the saints that he was a priest in the line of Melchisedek when I needed him to administer God's healing graces to me.

Slowly, I got better. We got another canary, and we named him Petey. I somehow finished my junior year. I learned that the goal was to get through the day without crying. I kept seeking spiritual guidance. Somehow, I managed to say enough of the right things to get out from under the treatment of the psychiatrist and to get off the medicine. As I improved, my sense of humor started to return. I came to a turning point when many things in life seemed very funny, and I would laugh explosively at the joke of life! I have found that laughter is indeed the best medicine, and the same reaction has indicated recovery from other later emotional crises.

It also helped that about this time I was reading *The Pickwick Papers*, Charles Dickens's lighthearted novel that chronicles the adventures of a lovable old gentleman and his friends, as well as his amusing valet, Sam Weller. I had to give a presentation to the class about the book. I enjoyed the book very much, and I tried to share that enthusiasm with the class. It gratified me that I was able to make them laugh, too.

The medicine that was prescribed for me may have helped control symptoms and let me sleep, but God cured me. I am thankful that I received Confirmation before I had these emotional trials, because I think the Holy Spirit gives graces for getting through difficult upheavals and suffering. I will defer until a later chapter the discussions of what else I have learned over the years about my emotions and how to control them.

Some books that I read years later helped me to resolve many of these issues. *A Bloodsmoor Romance,* by Joyce Carroll Oates, helped me to get comfortable with unseen spiritual realities, and *I Know My Love,* (I don't remember the author) dealt persuasively with the need to be in touch with one's emotions and to express them where appropriate. Another book, *The Chosen,* talked about a Jewish term for inane, meaningless discussion, which they called "bilple," or something to that effect. I found that term a good cue for when I'm engaging in meaningless mental bilple. These were novels, but they proved very therapeutic for me. One never knows the source from which God's graces and healing will come.

I don't have clear recollections about Pittsburgh trips, but Papa and I may have gone to Pittsburgh in the summer of 1969. This may have been the occasion when my Aunt Maria gave me a ten-carat gold cross pendant with a little pearl in the center and a ring with an opal. I don't know whether either of these items belonged at one time to my paternal grandmother, but I was glad to have these gifts. If the ring did belong to my other grandmother, then I have ended up with opal rings from both grandmothers, one of the little ironies of life. I think that it was during this trip that I found out how much Sister Hilda was in my corner. I was getting upset with my father and family affairs. Sister hugged me, while we were alone in the car together.

"Sh-sh! Don't cry. I'll talk to him [Papa]." She told me. She was one of my favorite aunts.

I also learned during this trip that Gretchen was dating Ted Johnson, an older man with a son who, like my Cousin Jim's son, Jeff, had Down's syndrome. Ted eventually married Gretchen.

Senior year at St. Mary's was much better, and, thank God, it was the last year for me at that school. I recall that we had a bomb scare, and I think that it was in the fall of that year. We evacuated the school when the fire alarm sounded, thinking that it was only a fire drill. After we were outside for a while, we learned that there was a bomb threat. We had to wait out in the cold for about an hour, while the police came with their canines and searched for the bomb. I don't think that they found one, and we were eventually allowed to go back into the school. We had gone out without our coats, but I had my plastic rain hat in my pocketbook, and I put it on while we were outside. I did not want to catch a cold!

That fall, I took the "College Boards," also known as the scholastic aptitude test. I think that it was one of those tests that you really can't study for, because it seeks to apply what you know. I don't remember if the test was put into Braille, or whether someone had to read me the questions. It may have been read, because some of these tests have to be filled in on their specific answer sheet to be machine-graded.

If I recall correctly, my birthday in 1969 was the occasion that I received my first portable cassette tape recorder. The era of reel-to-reel tapes for taking notes was on its way out. Sharon and Renee came over for my birthday that year.

Senior year was the occasion when we got our ten-carat gold class rings with the blue stone and the name of the school engraved around it, and Mary on one side and the Sacred Heart on the other. I think our initials were inside the band. When I called Papa at the office to tell him about the rings, Miss Frease answered the telephone. "That's right," she said laughingly, when she heard about the ring. "Find some more ways to spend your Daddy's money!"

In December of 1969, Nana celebrated her eightieth birthday. She said after that she would be going backwards. We told her to keep celebrating her birthdays, because she might as well celebrate getting younger instead of older!

During my high school years and, I think, extending into college, I started having my wisdom teeth taken out. The dentist removed three in his office, but the fourth was impacted, and an oral surgeon had to remove it.

During my high school senior year, Papa and I went to a drama club production of "You Can't Take It with You." The play was put on by a group composed of students from St. Mary's and from Bishop Ireton High School, the boys' high school run by the priests from the Order of St. Francis de Sales. We enjoyed it very much.

In the spring, we had a festival or bazaar with different arts and crafts and booths to raise money. We may have done it other years, but I do not recall very much about those bazaars, except walking around between the rooms looking at things and trying to find something to buy that might be practical. At the last bazaar, I recall buying a little pincushion and a figurine that looked like a cat's head.

Papa and I also attended a father-daughter get-together for the seniors. This time, the keepsake was a key ring with a cross and the word Shalom engraved on it.

Concerning my senior year at St. Mary's, I have one regret. Papa, Nana, and Aunt Betty tried to arrange for me to go to the prom with young Charlie. I didn't go through with it. Papa ended up escorting me. I am fairly sure that he did. I remember buying a dress and a white evening bag for the occasion. I wish now that I had gone with Charlie. It would have been a good opportunity for me to start to learn about the dating scene. How much I wish that Mama had survived to help me through this difficult transition to womanhood! Even so, I have to take responsibility for making a mistaken decision in this regard.

Finally, we were getting ready for graduation. Sister Dorothy Ann was my English teacher during my senior year, and she helped to get us ready by practice for the big day. I remember her telling us to keep our square caps on straight.

"Don't be lopsided, like Willie on the pickle wagon," she enjoined us.

She was an upbeat personality, with a wonderful sense of humor. The last that I heard of her, she was embarking on a second career as a nursing sister.

I kept in touch after graduation with the Amburies, especially Mary, as well as with Sharon and Renee and a few others. I've been back to St. Mary's for a couple of reunions, including the last big one for our class just before St. Mary's closed and was amalgamated with Bishop Ireton's High School.

I graduated with the class of 1970. I don't remember who among the relatives came for the ceremony, but among other now-forgotten gifts, Nana gave me a choker necklace of 14-carat gold beads. When I heard that she wanted to buy that necklace for me, I thought that it would be overwhelming, but after I felt the beads, I liked them. Because I find chokers too tight around my neck, I eventually had a 14-carat gold chain eight-inch extender added to them. Recently, I removed the extender and had the necklace restrung and lengthened by adding gold-hued pearls in between the beads. The necklace now goes very well with a gold bead and pearl bracelet that I bought separately.

Ellen gave me a little oval 14-carat gold pin with my initials on it. I don't remember what Papa gave me, but he did have the star sapphire ring made, and I considered myself well covered by that gift. Father Kirwin gave me a necklace with a cross with two loaves and two or three fish on it. The Alleys gave me a little stuffed Pekingese dog that resembled the little one that they had; they called their dog Peek. She was a feisty character who had no fear of automobiles.

Meanwhile, I had been applying to and looking at colleges. I seriously considered Sweet Briar College (in Virginia), Notre Dame (a college for women in Baltimore), and Trinity College, on Michigan Avenue in Washington, DC. After visiting all three, I chose Trinity. Nana came with Papa and me when we went to see Trinity. She liked the place, too, and she was very impressed with Sister Martha Julie, the sister who interviewed us.

I was glad to be getting out of St. Mary's, and I hoped for a much more mature set of classmates and for a better learning experience in college. As it turned out, I was not disappointed.

After graduation, I took a trip to MA on my own. This time, I flew on jet airplanes both ways. I stayed with the great aunts. Uncle Sam had died a few years before, on May 4, the same day that I was confirmed, and they were on their own in the little apartment. It was a very hot summer, and their place had no air conditioning. Their apartment was half of a duplex, but the other apartment was upstairs. A little girl was there and she cried a great deal. Uncle Bill was retired from the Quincy Fire Department by this time. He often came to take us out to smell the sea air in the evenings. He took us to the cemetery to visit Aunt Katherine's grave, as well as that of Uncle Sam. Their graves were in the Blue Hills cemetery, not the same one where Grandpa is buried. I think that he also took us to see Grandpa's grave.

On the evening before July 4, Uncle Bill drove us down to the beach, and we parked on a hill overlooking the water. Some young people were down on the beach shooting off firecrackers. That didn't bother Uncle Bill at first, because, as he put it, they had a nice, open, safe place to do it. However, when they started coming up the hill toward the place where we were parked, Uncle Bill said, "Let's get out of here!"

While I was in Quincy, I also toured the birthplaces of the two Adams presidents, John Adams and John Quincy Adams. Their old houses are very close to the place where my great-aunts lived, on Goddard Street. The aunties and I also walked downtown to the center of Quincy, and a barber there gave me a nice haircut.

Uncle Joe and Aunt Irene came to get me on July 4. We went to visit Aunt Irene's mother that day, and some of Aunt Irene's nieces and nephews were at her house, too. Uncle Joe had Hans, his little dog, with him. Hans got upset with all the activity and the noise of firecrackers, and he snapped and bit one of the little boys on the lip. Everybody panicked, and they had to take the child to the emergency room for stitches. Uncle Joe felt bad about it. He stayed behind while the others went to the hospital. All I could do was sit and hold his hand and try to console him. It was a bad day for Hans, too. Later that afternoon, he tried to hide under a chaise lounge in which I was sitting. I didn't know that he was there, and I let down my legs from a reclining position, and the chair hit the poor little dog on the head.

Aunt Irene fussed and complained to me about the incident with Hans and the child. She asserted very vehemently that Uncle Joe had spoiled Hans. After Uncle Joe died, she went to live with Nancy and Dick in San Antonio, TX. Ironically, Nancy and Dick had two little dogs, and she was crazy about them!

While in MA, I visited the Abbiattis. I think that Aunt Emily was gone by this time. They treated me with their usual courtesy, and they served me a dinner composed entirely of salads: potato salad, fruit Jello salad, bean salad, and chicken salad. It was a nice, cool meal to have on a hot day.

While I was in Quincy, Uncle Bill's granddaughter, Denise, went with us on our little trips, and it was nice to get to know her and spend some time with her. I think that she was a few years younger than I.

While I was with my aunts, I noticed how close they were to each other. They often fought and argued, but it didn't have quite the same intensity as disputes with Nana. They were like two sides of the same coin. As in previous visits, we had many pleasant discussions around the wooden kitchen table.

One of the subjects that came up was getting old. Aunt Janie resisted aging and didn't like it or the grey hair that typified it. I told the aunties that, when I got grey hair, I would be proud of it, because I considered that God had let me live to an honorable age. Now, people tell me that my brown hair has turned grey, and I still maintain my earlier opinion and point of view. Only, I wish that my hair had turned white, not just gray.

All in all, I had a very nice trip. I came home with a nice necklace of off-white summer beads and a sun hat as souvenirs. I put on a few pounds while I was away. Soon after I got home, I had dinner with the Amburies, and I mentioned it to Dr. Ambury.

"Maybe you were more relaxed while you were away," he suggested. I suspect that he was right.

At some point, pushed by the VA Department for the Blind, I did go away for a few days for some kind of orientation and vocational session. I don't remember exactly when, and, no, I didn't like it, but I did hear about some of the careers possibly open to blind people. A lawyer came and talked to us. It may have added to the foundation of my willingness to consider a career in law.

*W*e Trinity Alumnae have a little vignette that we like to quote that summarizes the Trinity experience. It goes something like this:

First speaker, "You mean that you went to an all-girls school?"

Second Speaker: "No, I graduated from a women's college."

The basic four-year women's college had all women students. During my four Trinity years, it was introducing its Master of Arts in teaching program, which I understand is co-ed now. It also has added a weekend college and a degree-completion program for women who have not previously achieved their B.A. degrees. I think they also added a nursing program in recent years. They built a fitness center and have a sports program, too. The whole complex now refers to itself as Trinity University, but Trinity College is still a major part of it.

Trinity College is a private college run by the Sisters of Notre Dame de Namur, (know hereafter as SND) an order originating out of Belgium. Following the changes begun by Vatican II, many of these sisters have gone back to using their Baptismal names, instead of the names that they received when they took their vows. These sisters no longer wear the long black habits and veils. They wear modest, every day clothes, and their heads are not covered indoors. For that reason, Nana noticed that Sister Martha Julie, who originally interviewed me in the spring of 1970, had snow-white hair like Nana's. Nana immediately identified with her for that reason, as well as her pleasant, welcoming personality. Like St. Mary's, Trinity College also had men and women lay teachers.

The SND order believes in developing the potential and education of their members to the fullest extent possible consistent with their community life and their progress in their spiritual walk with the Lord. They apply a similar philosophy to their students.

I understand that, since I graduated, many new things have been added to the campus, but I cannot address them. It has been many years since I have gone exploring on Trinity's campus.

I did go back with Joan Gahagen for my 45th class reunion in 2019, and I was amazed at the changes I noticed during that brief visit. I found the campus much more complex—we needed a little shuttle to get from place to place—with new buildings and programs. I was chagrinned to reflect that I might not have been able independently to navigate this new complex campus on my own with its many buildings and open spaces that vehicles can use, as I did in my college days. If I wanted to try, I certainly would need my guide dog, instead of the long mobility cane I used then. I hope to go back, God willing, for my fiftieth reunion in 2024, but I expect to need help getting around this new campus layout. For this account, I will confine my descriptions for the most part to the way that things were when I was there, around fifty years ago.

During my freshman year, in the fall of 1970, some of the seniors from the class of 1971 were assigned to be big sisters and mentors to incoming freshmen. Each senior had a group of freshmen, I think about six or ten. My big senior sister was Mary Evelyn (M.E.) Tucker, from Pelham, NY. She was a very tall young lady, about six feet, and we made quite a contrast if we stood together. She is a wonderful, caring person with a great sense of humor. We became good friends, and she was very helpful to me.

From some of the things that she and other older students told me, I gather that, in the years before I came, there was some push-pull between the faculty and some of the Trinity students. No, the Trinity women were not immune from some of the restless activism that affected students during the late 1960's. However, I received the distinct impression that everyone still respected each other and that, for the most part, the disagreements were conducted in a very civilized manner.

For the first two and a half years, I was a day student, returning home each evening after a day at college. I recall that, for my freshman year, I rode into school with Dr. Karin Kershenstein, one of the physic professors. Dr. Kershenstein, among other courses, taught the Household Physics class at Trinity, in which students received an education in the basics of physics by actually repairing broken toasters and other household appliances that students were encouraged to bring to class for the purpose. Dr. Kershenstein's husband, John, was also a physicist, but I have forgotten where he worked. He may have been in the Navy.

On the way to school, Dr. Kershenstein and I talked about many things, including cooking and food preferences. When I mentioned that I preferred poached eggs cooked soft, Dr. Kershenstein remarked that she liked poached eggs cooked firm, and her husband, John, liked them "if you just showed them a match," very soft. I told Nana this story, and she picked up on it right away. She knew that I tended to like my poached eggs soft, too.

After that, she would ask me in the mornings, "Do you want your eggs Karin-style, or John-style?"

I usually said in reply, "John Style."

"Two eggs, John-style, coming right up," Nana would answer.

If you didn't understand the inside joke, it would have sounded very strange to an outsider.

I drove home in the afternoons that first year with Haide McDonald, one of five nurses who covered the college infirmary. At that time, they covered the infirmary seven days a week, around the clock. The schedule later changed. Mrs. McDonald and her husband, Don, lived in one of the apartment buildings in Crystal City, not too far from my house. I became close friends with Haide, (pronounced Heidi) and eventually called her and her husband by their first names. She had a wonderful sense of humor, and we shared many pleasant conversations and laughs, as well as some serious discussions, on those trips.

Unlike Dunblane Hall and St. Mary's, in which school activities were primarily confined to one building, Trinity was a multi-building campus, with steps going up to Main Hall and Alumnae Hall, and sidewalks to traverse and driveways to cross between these two buildings and between Main Hall and the chapel and the library and the Science Building, as well as the other two dormitories, Couville and Kirby Halls. While I was at Trinity, at least one other student with a disability was there; she was a girl, named Pat, who was confined to a wheelchair. Fortunately for her, the campus had elevators in all the major buildings except the chapel and the Science Building and accessible entrances, too. For example, Main Hall had an entrance with a ramp on the lower level near the college bookstore.

During my first year, I took many prerequisite courses, and most of them were in Main Hall, but over the four years I had to learn my way to the Science Building for biology courses, to Alumnae Hall for the cafeteria and the infirmary, and to the chapel for some religious services but also for concerts and other activities. My yoga class met in a room in the basement below the chapel. I suspect that the mobility instructors probably were involved in teaching me, but I know that my fellow students participated a great deal in acclimating me to the campus. Sometimes, to avoid or shorten outdoor travel between buildings, especially in inclement weather, I used other entrances that were nearer my building of destination, as well as some connecting tunnels between some of the lower levels of buildings. I also relied on topographical clues outside, as well as landmark plants or trees. I wrote a poem, "Trinity Trees" about two bushy evergreen trees that I used to indicate the turnoff for the path to the Science Building.

As with St. Mary's, many of my books were on reel-to-reel tape, but I needed volunteer readers more than ever, because it was hard to find out what textbooks would be used early enough to get them recorded. Also, the professors often handed out copied material and extra assignments at the last minute. Most of my readers were fellow students. Since I would be on campus for an extended part of the day, I needed a way to study and work with my readers on campus. At home, Papa, Ellen, and Barbara Sheehan continued to help with extra reading.

In Main Hall, the auditorium and student lounge and offices were on the first floor; the second floor contained the classrooms, and the third and fourth floors contained student dorm rooms. The convent occupied a whole wing of this building on all of its floors. The little chapel for the sisters was on the second floor in Main Hall. Sometimes, students joined the sisters for noon Mass in this little chapel.

During my first two and a half years, I was given a room on the third floor of Main Hall, with a desk, chair, and still the little single bed, in which I could keep my tape recorders (both cassette and reel-to-reel,) typewriter, Braillewriter, and other supplies. My volunteers came to this room to work with me. Although the old building had an old-fashioned elevator, I often took the stairs up to this room or to the classroom level.

I found out very early that Trinity College holds its students to a high standard. I remember the first English paper that I wrote. I did it in a hurry and "on the fly." Needless to say, although I sometimes got away with this in dear old St. Mary's, the Trinity professor sent the paper back to me all marked up and with a lower grade than I expected. I would have to slow down and give more care and attention to making them right before I turned in future papers! Also, for major papers in college, as well as a few papers in high school, we sometimes had to pay someone to type a final good copy of my paper from my rough draft. We didn't have the luxury of WordPerfect, MS Word, and the other word processing programs that might have allowed me to correct my work on a computer. All of those nice developments were in the future, and the future, as they say, is now!

For the first two years, I concentrated on taking the required courses and some electives that I wanted to pursue. I decided early not to study any more languages in college, because I had studied both French and Latin in high school. Of course, literature was one of the prerequisites, and I encountered some old friends, including the Beowulf poem, the works of Chaucer, Greek tragedies, and Shakespeare. The Beowulf poem is one of my favorites. I also took a course specifically on Chaucer, and I was able to read other works besides the *Canterbury Tales*, including the tragic satire, *Troilus and Cressida*. I also focused on the works of Herman Melville, Walt Whitman, Carl Sandberg, and Emily Dickenson. In high school, I had done some extra reading about the War of 1812, and reading more works of Melville besides Moby Dick helped me to fill in my knowledge of naval concepts enough to finalize the story in *Slice of Life* "The Unsinkable Liberty M." I especially like Emily Dickenson and her poems, and I wrote a paper on one particular poem about the difficulty of coping with boring, inane details of daily life and the ways of coping with living day to day.

As with St. Mary's, theology classes encouraged students to explore their faith more deeply and to think about how Scriptures applied to daily life. During one class, we also took an ecumenical approach to exploring other faiths and their church services. We were asked to attend church with two or three other religions and to report to the class about our experiences. I remember going to the Methodist church with Barbara Sheehan, to the Baptist church with the Pattersons, and to high Episcopal Church with Mrs. Murdaugh. When I went with Mrs. Murdaugh, she invited me to take Communion with her. I did, and I'm glad. It helps to build bridges between faiths. Besides, many priests in the high Episcopal Church come directly from the line of ordained priests and bishops originating in the Catholic Church, and they also believe in the real presence of Jesus in the Eucharist.

At Trinity I made some friends in my class, including Jeanne Flatley and Liz McNulty, but I also had other friends in the classes ahead of and following me. Among them were M.E. Tucker, Mary Lou McGovern, Marian Miller, Joan Napier, Mary Ann Newhall, Jackie Hegerty, Pattie Mahoney, Sue and Mary Jo Blain, Joan Gahagen, Irene Harvey and Alberta Mikulka. Alberta graduated a year after I did and then joined me at Georgetown Law School the following year after I entered. While I was at Trinity, many of the students were serious about the business of pursuing their studies and education, growing up, learning all they could, progressing as Christians, and learning to assume their adult responsibilities. It was and probably still is the kind of place where you can always find someone with whom to have an interesting, intelligent conversation and where people go out of their way to help each other. It was also nice to be on a campus where you could go to Mass at noon in the little convent chapel if you had the time between classes. On holy days, such as the Feast of All Saints and the Feast of the Immaculate Conception, I think that they had Mass in the big campus chapel.

On November 1, 1970, my nineteenth birthday, I went back to my room with a friend who was one of my readers, thinking that we were going to do some homework and reading. To my surprise, when I unlocked the door, I found a number of my other friends already there. They were giving me a surprise birthday party! I still have one of the little beanbag frogs with the Trinity name on his back that they gave me as a gift.

I observed and became part of Trinity traditions. I learned to say the Trinity prayer, which I still say every day as part of my morning prayers:

> May the power of the Father govern and protect us!
> May the wisdom of the Son teach and enlighten us!
> May the love of the Holy Spirit renew and quicken us!
> May the blessing of the all-holy Trinity:
> The father, the Son, and the Holy Spirit,
> Be with us now and forever. Amen.

Also, just before the Christmas break, in the middle of the final exams, the faculty and students would have a Christmas party in the lounge, called Social Hall. Before the party, the students would have a "well sing." In Main Hall, a large atrium went all the way from the first floor to the ceiling above the fourth floor. We called it "the well." On the second, third, and fourth floors, banisters went around the well to keep people from falling down the hole. Each of the four classes would gather on a different floor to sing Christmas carols. Sometimes the classes would take turns with different parts of a song, such as the Twelve Days of Christmas. It was wonderful to hear the voices echo through the well. It was loads of fun!

At Trinity, the honor system was firmly in place. Some examinations were open-book, meaning that you took the test home or at school and could consult source materials. Some tests were given ahead of time, so that you could prepare an outline and then bring it to the examination room on test day to write the answers. Other exams were take home but not open book. Having this flexibility made it easier, because then I could get people to read me the questions and the sources for answers in the open book tests. Some exams were administered in a room on the day, and they had to be answered by memory. Someone still had to read me those questions, and I would type the answers. I sometimes needed extra time.

The freshman year went fairly well. I was able to get some of my poems published in Trinity publications. I was happier at Trinity than I ever was at St. Mary's.

In the late spring of 1971, troubles came to us in a bunch again. We were getting ready for the last push at college before the final exams. Friday night started as a crazy evening. One of his friends had given Papa a jump-start for our car. The jumper cable backfired, and blew out part of Mr. Fisher's battery. In addition, Papa wasn't feeling well.

Nana was worried about Papa. He insisted that she go to bed, so she put a bathrobe over her dress to keep him from knowing that she still was dressed when she went to check on him. She sat up in the chair all night. The next morning, he still wasn't feeling well, and Nana thought that he was running a fever. I was doing something upstairs when Nana called me. Papa had gone into the bathroom, and he was just sitting on the toilet, unable or unwilling to go back to bed.

We frantically called around, trying to figure out what to do. We called 911, and the rescue squad and ambulance came, but Papa wouldn't consent to go to the hospital. They helped him back to bed, but they said that, notwithstanding that he seemed delirious, they wouldn't take him to the hospital without his consent. They cautioned Nana not to try to lift him.

Nana walked up the steep steps to Ellen's house to try to find her (it's a mercy that she didn't fall.) Ellen wasn't there right at that moment. I couldn't get Dr. Williams. All I could remember was Mary Ambury saying to call her father, and he would come.

I was able to reach the Amburies, and Dr. Ambury came.

He arranged for the ambulance to take Papa to the hospital. As Nana was trying to help him get dressed to go, I heard her say, "Don't be ashamed, Carl! Let me help you! I couldn't love you more if you were my own son!"

Ellen came over shortly after that, and she said that she was going to go to the hospital. I said that I wasn't coming, because I didn't think that we could do anything at that point. They would have to do tests or whatnot.

Papa turned out to have pneumonitis, a respiratory infection. He was in the hospital several days. He became Dr. Ambury's patient for many years after that, until shortly before Papa died.

Meanwhile, I found the whole thing very upsetting, especially in light of what had happened to Mama. I had all kinds of conflicting feelings and emotions. Although I held together during the immediate crisis, I somewhat went to pieces afterwards. My condition was aggravated by Ellen's reaction. It confirmed Nana's and my idea that she had some kind of deep feelings for Papa. I felt guilty that I wasn't reacting with enough emotion or concern in reaching out to Papa. Barbara Sheehan came over at my request and did what I needed: just sat and held me.

I went to see Papa on Sunday, when he was more himself and feeling better. They put him on antibiotics. For some reason, I didn't want to go to see Papa after my first visit. Maybe I was afraid of confronting him sick after what happened to Mama. Also, I felt as though I was coming down with a cold, which may have been only psychosomatic, but I had no business seeing him if I was having real symptoms.

The last straw came Monday or Tuesday evening. I had come home from school and was trying to eat dinner. Ellen came over, as she often did, to sit with me during dinner, but that evening her presence felt particularly intrusive. Nana hit the ceiling, more or less telling her to leave and let me be and eat my dinner in peace. They got into an argument. Nana picked up a plate as though to throw it at Ellen. I grabbed hold of the plate, and Nana didn't throw it.

"I'll have you arrested!" Ellen said. She eventually left.

As I now know after studying Torts in law school, in contentious situations, a party in somebody else's house probably has a duty to retreat and not to trespass, but it upset me horribly that something like this could happen. I wanted very much to go and confront Ellen myself, but I was afraid of my emotions. I was right back in the stew again, queasy stomach and all! Dr. Ambury told me not to worry if I didn't feel much like eating, but to be sure and drink plenty of water. I was so afraid of the intensity of my feelings, and I didn't trust myself!

I took advantage of needing to study for exams to stay a couple of nights on campus at Trinity. My teachers and my classmates all helped me to get through the emotional crisis. The chaplain, Father Ed White, was very helpful and understanding. He brought up that maybe I should consider going away for a guide dog. After all, as he pointed out, with a means of being more independent and getting around, I would be out and about more, and I would have less time to get into mental and emotional tailspins or to feel sorry for myself.

I came home from Trinity, and Papa came home from the hospital. I got through final exams. Papa was better, but he had an allergic reaction to the penicillin, and it left him with a sore and sensitive mouth and hives. (Like father, like daughter?)

After life settled down a bit, we had me tested again for dog allergies. I surprisingly didn't seem to have them anymore. We started making plans for me to apply to two schools, Seeing Eye in Morristown, NJ, and Guiding Eyes for the Blind in Yorktown Heights, NY.

When I came home from Trinity, I found that Mary Ambury had taken the effort to learn some Braille, and she had written me a Braille letter! She was finishing her first year at Mary Washington College in Fredericksburg, VA.

I avoided a major conflict with Ellen, but I somehow again tried to specify that I couldn't be to her what she wanted. Fortunately, we patched things up between us.

A couple of weeks later, the second trouble came. Nana was already somewhat upset and anxious, because an unmarried lady, referred to us by a mutual friend or one of my cousins, made contact with us when she visited Washington on a trip. She seemed nice enough, and she came bearing gifts, ironically including a cameo pin and clip earring set for Nana! I was a little ambivalent about her. Papa really seemed to enjoy her company and went out with her on his own a few times. It was the closest that I came to knowing of Papa doing any kind of serious dating. He mentioned to me that he found Terry to be very nice. I don't think I said much of anything, and I am glad that I didn't. I am being sketchy on the details here, because my knowledge is imperfect and I am thinking of privacy. I'm not aware that this went anywhere after that.

In any event, no sooner had this incident receded over the horizon than something else happened to aggravate Nana. Gerry Arsenault, the home teacher from the VA Department for the Blind, was still coming to work with me. This day, he came to work on cooking. Nana, predictably, wasn't happy about someone invading her space in the kitchen. When Gerry came, he left his bag in the living room next to an end table near the door. Nana was, as she put it, angry and not paying attention. While we were in the kitchen, Gerry and I, she tripped on his bag and fell. She got up, but she hurt her arm. She didn't say anything to us about it. She waited until Papa came home from work and finished his dinner, and then she told him what happened and that she thought that she seriously hurt her arm.

We drove in the pouring rainstorm to the hospital emergency room. Nana had broken her left arm, a little below the shoulder. No, they didn't admit her. They put her arm in a sling, referred her to make an appointment with Dr. Swisher, the orthopedic doctor, and sent her home. Dr. Swisher put her left arm in a removable splint. After a couple of weeks, she had to remove the splint and started doing exercises. Ironically, Ellen was very patient and attentive and helpful to us at this time. She put hot compresses on Nana's arm. Mrs. Patterson also came over with casseroles. One of Papa's coworkers came over one evening to cook dinner for us. We moved a higher armchair into the living room, because Nana wouldn't be able to get up from lower chairs.

We had one amusing incident during that difficult period. In the living room, we had an easy chair that was a swivel chair that rocked. One day, around lunchtime, Nana called me.

"Help me, Lindy! I forgot and went and sat in this rocking chair, and how am I going to get up?" She rightly was worried that the chair would turn and maybe dump her onto the floor.

"You'll have to wait until Ellen comes back," I said.

"I can't wait until Ellen comes back. I have to go to the bathroom!" Nana cried.

I didn't know what to do. Finally, I said, "All right, Nana. I'll try and hold the chair still and you try to get up."

I got down on my knees and put my arms around the chair and tried to hold it still, while she got up. The chair tried to buck like a bronco, but we made it, with God's help. Needless to say, Nana didn't sit in that chair again until she was fully recovered! It was a long process, but she eventually regained the use of her arm.

Meanwhile, Papa and I went walking around the neighborhood, and Papa tried to help me learn to listen to the directions of traffic. Someone came out to interview me from Guiding Eyes for the Blind, and I got the feeling that they might have accepted me. After that, Papa drove me to the Seeing Eye school, and instructors interviewed me and took me for a test walk. They call these tests "Juno walks," because the student pretends to work an imaginary dog, called Juno, with the instructor at the other end of the harness. It is meant to test the student's tolerance for pace and pull and ability to give good commands and corrections. These Juno walks are essential to match students with the right dog.

Seeing Eye told me that they would not accept me, because I could not make enough independent safe decisions about street crossings. While the dogs are taught to intelligently disobey if the person makes a wrong decision occasionally, they feared that too many vetoes by the dog would put too much stress on the dog. I was devastated! All that I could think of was, "If I can't do it with a dog that has two good eyes and two good ears, how the heck do they expect me to have any independence with a cane on my own?"

Although Guiding Eyes had seemed more positive, I heard that Seeing Eye was the best (which I now know may not always be the case). I wasn't prepared to take second best. The truth of the matter probably was that I wasn't yet ready for a dog. Things were different six years later.

Meanwhile, at the time, Barbara Sheehan was quite consoling. "Something wonderful is probably around the corner for you," she told me. She was proved right when I got my first dog, Vincent, from Guiding eyes for the blind in the fall of 1977.

The first canary that we named Petey didn't live very long. When he died, I missed having a bird and wanted another one. Papa resisted, and he made me promise to do the cleaning and other things that the bird would need. In the late summer or early fall, we went shopping for birds. Ellen helped me pick out Petey II. That year at college, it turned out that I had no classes scheduled on Thursday. Thursday was my day to wash my hair and clean the bird's cage and change his sandpaper covers on the perches. Petey wasn't the best singer that I have ever heard, but he had a loud, clear voice, and he was outgoing and unafraid. He would peck my finger through the bars of the cage, something that none of the others ever did. If I put my hand inside the cage, he would walk along the perch in front of me and brush the back of my hand with his tail. By patience and persistence, I was eventually able to get Petey comfortable sitting on my arm, if I put my arm inside of the cage and took out some of the perches. Papa took a picture of Petey on my arm, and we used it for the Christmas card that year. The folks developing the picture could hardly believe that it was a canary on my arm!

My memories are vague about transportation arrangements during my subsequent years at Trinity. Dr. Kershenstein was pregnant during my freshman year, but she suffered a miscarriage. She became pregnant again, and she subsequently gave birth to a little boy. They named him John, after his father, but they called him Jay to avoid confusion. I think that she drove me for at least part of my sophomore year, and I think that Haide did, too. I think a lady named Gay Schneider helped with the driving during my second semester. I don't remember what we did for the first semester of my junior year, but I suspect that Papa had to do more of the driving.

I think it was at this time that Trinity had a program that encouraged students to teach courses in a subject they knew informally to other students. I tried to teach a course in Braille reading and writing with the Braille writer and an extra slate and stylus. I had a few takers, but only Sue Blain took it far enough to actually use the slate to write me something.

During the second semester of that year, I took an evening class, so I spent a couple of nights a week on campus. For my senior year, as described later, I was on campus five nights a week. Papa only had to bring me Sunday night and retrieve me Friday evening.

In my sophomore year, I again felt the need to seek help for my fragile emotions. This time, we did it right, and I was referred to Dr. Carlos Hecker, a psychiatrist, by one of my regular doctors. Also, after Papa's health crisis, I finally left Dr. Bregmann as a patient and became Dr. Ambury's patient, too.

Unlike the previous fellow, Dr. Hecker was able to respond as well as listen, and he helped me to understand many of my reactions and what was going on with my emotions. He also helped me to smooth out some of the rough edges in my relationship with Papa. I often decompressed from my sessions with Dr. Hecker by coming home that evening and watching the Heehaw show on TV. Eventually, I no longer needed to see Dr. Hecker on a regular basis. By my junior or senior years, I was able to derive emotional guidance from the guidance counselors at Trinity.

Meanwhile, at Trinity, I began to take biology courses as electives. The teachers I had for biology were Sister Marie Diamond and Sister Elizabeth Henry Bellmer. I became friends with both of them, Particularly Sister Elizabeth Henry. I took a genetics course with her. She took great pains to make sure that I understood the form of the DNA molecule. She made models with pipe cleaners and raised lines to illustrate for me the process of mitosis, cell division, and the process of meiosis, cell division to create gametes, i.e., female egg cells and male sperm.

No, I didn't dissect any frogs, and I wasn't able to work with fruit flies. However, the teachers helped me devise a way to conduct an experiment with flour beetles about which I wrote a report. Unlike fruit flies, flour beetles are large enough to handle, if you need to count their numbers.

I became good friends with Sister Elizabeth Henry, and I kept in touch with her long after I graduated, until she died from Metastasized breast cancer in 2008. I found her so helpful in getting to the crux of problems and succinctly summarizing the important aspects of a problem and coming to a well-reasoned, analytic solution. I very much miss her guidance and counsel, but I trust that she continues to pray for me in heaven, and I will always remember her.

We had a funny incident one Thanksgiving or Christmas that showed how well Nana had recovered from her accident. The turkey was cooking in the oven, but Papa had to go out for a while, maybe to the Pipe Place. He told Nana not to try to lift the turkey out of the oven, because he planned to be back in time to do it himself. The turkey was getting done, and he didn't come. I was still afraid of hot stoves, but I was trying to prepare myself to don oven mitts and try to get the bird out myself.

Nana felt that she couldn't wait. She placed the turkey platter on the top of the stove in the space between the burners. Then, taking a tea towel in each hand, she said, "Dear God, please don't let her legs break!" (She thought of the turkey as a hen turkey, but it may have been a Tom.) She picked up the turkey by her legs and plunked it into the platter. God must have been listening, because the legs didn't break. If they had, we would have had a big mess and a ruined dinner!

Although I eventually decided to major in English literature, especially emphasizing American authors and poets, I also took all the American history courses that I could cram into my schedule. One of my history teachers, Sister Mary Hayes, taught me more about writing than many of my English teachers. She also was an excellent lecturer, and she had a very soft voice. We had to get creative for me to hear her lectures. Papa put a microphone on his camera tripod, so that it would be closer to her mouth when she was talking and I could record and review her lectures. Sometimes, I used the earphones with the recorder while it was taping her, to listen better to the lecture in real time. The tape recorder acted like a big hearing aid when used that way!

I only had one economics class with Sister Martha Julie, but I distinctly remember her putting up on the blackboard (and reading aloud,) "Ain't no free lunch." I have found this principle useful to remember.

During my sophomore year, Papa was also busy trying to track down our relatives on his father's side in Germany, and he eventually found Dr. Walter Sterzinger, who gave us details about the rest of the German relatives. I summarized the general family tree in the introductory chapter of this book. The upshot of the correspondence with Walter was that Papa decided that we should go to Germany in late May-June of 1972, after school let out. I didn't face the fact that he really was serious and kept thinking that something might happen and he would change his mind, but he didn't. I didn't want to go, but by the time I realized that this trip was real, I was caught up in my fears and a dilemma. It was too late to back out, and even if I wanted to, I would be giving in to my fears, which might make them worse. Papa tried to have me learn some German before we went, but German is a complex language, and I just couldn't get into it. In retrospect, I suspect that part of me resented the fact that Papa wouldn't teach me while I was growing up, saying that I would confuse German with French, and now he was expecting me to learn a great deal in a few weeks!

We went to Germany, and I was under a mild tranquilizer for the trip. Although it was good for me to face down my fears, my frame of mind probably spoiled the trip for poor Papa! I'm truly sorry about that now, and I wish it hadn't taken me so long and so much travail to grow up!

We flew into Frankfurt on an overnight flight from Dulles Airport with a stopover in Gander, Newfoundland. We went first to Schweinfurt to visit Dr. Sterzinger and his family. Walter's wife was named Anneliese; they had three children. Harold and Rolf were teenagers, and Jutta was around five years old. They were very kind and hospitable to us. I had to get used to beds made up an entirely different way from ours. It seems that they don't tuck in sheets, but instead they rely on sheet-encased blankets or quilts for covering. I had to admit that the llama blankets that Anneliese used were very soft and velvety.

We toured churches and historical sites, and so much of what we experienced was visual! Also, Walter didn't speak much if any English, and poor Anneliese had to do the translating! We went sightseeing in Wertzberg, and Papa actually went up to the Bishop of Wertzberg and introduced himself. The relatives couldn't believe it! Apparently, they aren't so forward in Germany as we are with important personages. Anneliese and others also cautioned me that it is not good to discuss politics in company, because people often get into fights over politics. I remember being glad that it wasn't that way in the U.S. at that time, which makes me very sad that things have deteriorated so much now with animosity among people who disagree with each other!

Among the places we visited was Untersteinbach, where my grandfather, John Schneider, may have been born and grew up. We saw the old house, which was still standing. They say that it used to have grapevines growing up the side of it, but they were gone by the time we visited the place. Of course, Papa took pictures of it, as he did of many of the places that we visited. He sent the pictures around to relatives. One of those who saw the picture of the old homestead was Ethel Dean, Uncle Jim Dean's sister. She was an artist, and she painted a picture of the house, but she took artist's liberties and added the grapevines back in the picture, as they might have been. The painting came to us after she died.

Walter dropped us off in another little town to visit Elfriede, his half-cousin. Apparently, Walter's side of the family doesn't get along very well with the wing represented by Elfriede and her brother and sisters. She didn't speak to Walter, so he had to drop us off and go. Elfriede's daughter, Eva, was married to Manfred Begert, a banker who lived in Frankfurt. Elfriede's husband, Alfonse, was a dentist and a very kind, loving fellow. When I was homesick and cried, Alfonse just sat and held my hand. He was very comforting. He gave me a couple of little dental squares made of dental gold.

We visited Walter's direct cousin, Karl Kotzner and his wife, Paula, (both of them doctors) in Liebfling. It was Paula Kotzner who made me see how unhappy Papa was with my emotional upsets. I commented to her that Papa always seemed to be happy.

"No," Paula told me. "He pretends, but he isn't happy." She was very perceptive, and I'm sure, a wonderful doctor.

We spent the night in their house. It was out in the countryside. They had beautiful violets blooming in the grass with enormous flowers! The Kotzners gave us their room with its two side-by-side twin beds. I became good friends with their daughter, Gitti, especially because we could both speak in French. While there, we met Karl's sister, Maria Lechner, and her husband, Albert. Gitti and I corresponded with each other for many years. She is married now and has children. When Papa died, she sent me her own personal stuffed rabbit to comfort me. It was made from real rabbit fur. My first guide dog, Vincent, wouldn't let me bring it into the bedroom with us. I had to leave it in the office on a file cabinet. He probably knew it was real fur.

Anneliese's father also knew a little French, but he was very hard of hearing. I found myself shouting to him in French, trying to make myself understood.

We took the train to Munich and visited Maria Stadtler (Elfriede's sister) and her boyfriend Theo, as well as her brother, Carli. We never met Amanda, but we were told that she lived alone and had many cats.

While I was off in Tubingen, Papa visited Hilde's husband. He was then a widower; he was a butcher, named Fritz Ulein. He kept Great Dane dogs. I'm sorry I didn't get to meet him and his dogs. Papa said that he was a stereotypical jolly, plump butcher!

The high point of the trip for me was my visit to Tubingen. Jackie Hegerty, Trinity class of '73, was there studying for a year. I was amazed at the quaint town with its small streets and overwhelmed by the speeding, heavy traffic and the apparent disregard of drivers for pedestrians. I was able to stay in the dorm with Jackie for a few days, including Pentecost. With Jackie's help, I got to shop for souvenirs, and I enjoyed the opportunity to meet some of her friends. Being there for Fingsten (Pentecost) was rather special. We were out walking, and all of a sudden, this old gentleman came up to us. He asked me in German why I was carrying such a long cane. To my surprise, I understood him! I asked Jackie to translate for me, and I told him why I used the cane. He said, "Yah, Yah," and he put his hands on either side of my face. It reminded me of the light slap given by the bishop at confirmation. He made me so happy! It gave new meaning to the Scriptural reading about people hearing the Gospel in their own tongues, even though the apostles were only using one language. I think that God sent that old man to me!

We spent a few more days with Walter and Anneliese before leaving to fly home. I was relieved that the trip was over, and I enjoyed the flight. We reversed the route that we took to Germany, but we may have stopped somewhere other than Gander, probably London; I don't remember. Papa bought a new Leica camera in Germany, and he tried to test it by taking pictures through the plane glass window of the airplane as we were coming down to land.

Nana had a story for us when we came home. While we were gone, she said, one night the police came to the door. They asked her permission to look around our property. They told her that there was a robbery, and the police supposedly caught one or more of the burglars or robbers.

"We think that they threw the gun out of the car around here somewhere," they told her. "Can we look around for it?"

Nana told them it was fine with her and, by all means, do look around for it! We never heard any more about the outcome.

It was good to get back home to Petey, Nana, and a regular routine. Before I left for Germany, I started reading a good book, and I finished it after I returned. The book was *How to Stop Worrying and Start Living*, by Dale Carnegie. The book had many good ideas, but I found one especially useful in future stressful situations. "Live in day tight compartments." In other words, living through one day at a time is often the best way to get through difficult situations.

The last time she went to the podiatrist before we left, Nana found a pretty blue dress in Lansburgh's Department Store, but she did not buy it. Soon after that, Hurricane Agnes came that summer in June of 1972 and dumped loads of rain on us! It was such a relief to be able to get outside again afterwards! Papa and I went to Lansburgh's and bought Nana that pretty blue dress. I now have one something like it.

Mary Ambury planned to marry her childhood sweetheart, Peter, instead of finishing the last year of college to complete her degree. The wedding was September 2, a Saturday. She asked me to be one of her bride's maids. It was a wonderful honor. She invited Papa, too, but she told me to have him come just as a guest, and to not feel that he had to take pictures. They were hiring a photographer. Of course, Papa brought his camera and took pictures, anyway. It's a good thing, because the photographer's camera malfunctioned, and they ended up using some of Papa's pictures to fill in the gaps. It was a wonderful occasion. Papa took a good picture of me in my bride's maid dress standing next to Nana wearing the pretty blue dress that we bought for her. It's one of the better pictures that we have of her, and it is on the first page of this chapter.

After Mary and Peter came back from their honeymoon and moved into their house in Reston, VA, Papa gave them two azaleas to plant in their front yard. Peter and Mary are grandparents now, and all four daughters are married with children of their own. They have moved out to the Culpepper area, but they took cuttings of the original azalea bushes with them to their country home.

Changes were coming to Trinity. Haide retired from the infirmary. The school converted Alumnae Hall, except for the cafeteria, into a dorm for male foreign exchange students and Master of Arts in Teaching (MAT) students who were staying on campus.

I think that it was during my junior or senior year that I took a bioethics course at Trinity. Sister Marie Diamond taught the biology portion of the course, and Dr. Gostkowski covered the philosophical and ethical issues. In her presentation covering abortion procedures, Sister Marie factually and in a detached manner described them to us. The specifics and details were more effective than philosophical discussions in making me a lifelong believer in pro-life and anti-abortion principles.

I definitely decided to major in English literature. One problem that my teachers had was that I tended to do linear, one-track analysis of literature and poems, instead of quoting freelance from different parts of the work. They wanted to see more sophisticated analysis from me, and I understood their criticism. My problem was that it was much easier for me to follow the text closely in my analysis, because it was hard to tell readers working with me to jump around and find isolated passages.

I did try to get creative with my papers. For example, I wrote a paper comparing *Fibber McGee and Molly* episodes with *All in the Family*. I had recorded episodes from both shows that I used to form the basis of my comparison. It was fun writing that paper!

I don't remember when eighteen-year-olds were given the right to vote. If it was after 1972, I still wouldn't have been able to register in time to vote in the presidential election that year that I turned twenty-one years old, but I was sorry that Richard M. Nixon defeated George McGovern. It seemed that we were destined to have another four years of Nixon, but we fortunately were wrong in that assessment.

As I mentioned earlier, during my second semester of my junior year, I decided to take a sociology course that met in the evening. It didn't make sense to come home at 9:30 or ten P.M. and then get right up and go back again. The result was that I spent one or two nights on campus that semester. Once I decided to stay on campus, I moved into a room on the fourth floor, room 434.

We went shopping to find curtains for the window and a small rug for the floor. My friends were close by, including Patty, and the triplets (not sisters, but very close friends,) — Alberta, Joan, and Irene — who shared a room together.

One of the things that we had to deal with once I was staying on campus was the nighttime fire drills. I was afraid that I wouldn't hear the bell without my hearing aids, but my friends always came to get me. Staying on campus allowed me to experience the secure feeling of living in a real Christian community, where people cared about each other.

I recall that we got our class rings during my junior year, too. We had a choice of either a ten-carat gold signet ring with the Trinity seal or a ten-carat gold ring set with an amethyst stone that had the seal engraved on it. I chose the amethyst ring. I wrote a poem for that occasion, and this poem is included in *The Ivory Pyramid*.

Another highlight of the year was that I recall that I was admitted into Phi Beta Kappa that year. It was a nice recognition for all the hard work.

Petey seemed not to be feeling well. We were on some kind of day field trip in snowy weather, and I didn't get home in time to have him go to the vet. After he died, I got one more canary, and I named him Pretty Boy. He wasn't so easy to tame as Petey, and he was much more skittish. We nursed him through one illness in the summer of 1973, but he died in about a year. After that, the price of the birds went up to around $50, because they were quarantining the imported birds to try to eliminate a disease. I couldn't see paying $50 for a little bird that might die in the year, I was tired of the heartbreak of losing them, and I was beginning to question whether it was right to cage these birds of the air.

The Watergate Scandal began to unfold that summer, too. Nana and I were glued to the TV listening to the Watergate subcommittee Congressional hearings. We were shocked and dismayed to learn of President Nixon's Enemies List. We cheered when Senator Lowell Weicker of Connecticut strongly asserted that, "Republicans don't play games! Republicans don't 'cover up!' and God knows Republicans don't regard their fellow Americans as enemies, but as human beings to be loved and wanted."

I have already mentioned my relief in August of 1974 when President Nixon resigned. I should point out here that the disgraceful conduct in which he engaged, prompted by paranoia and a desire to retain office and power through conspiracy and illegal acts, caused me to reflect on the role of government employees in safeguarding the country. The much-derided government bureaucrats, the folks working day to day, 9-5:30, kept the government and the country running, despite the unbalanced actions of the leaders. Several courageous attorneys were fired, rather than engage in inappropriate conduct ordered by the President. When the budget gets debated, balanced budget folks have advocated cutting government back to bare-bones essentials. However, in my opinion, such actions intended to balance the budget may end up being misguided. I consider that good governments, like well-built highways, need expansion joints. They need to have sufficient people and flexibility to respond to emergencies and changing circumstances. We need to be careful not to cut back too far on our government lest we make it ineffective. My respect for the day-to-day work of ordinary federal employees probably contributed to my eventual decision to become one of them.

I think the summer of 1973 was when Jackie Hegerty married and became Jackie Newman. Papa and I went up to Connecticut for the wedding. It was wonderful to be going to pleasant New England without having to visit family! When we arrived at the hotel the day before the wedding, we discovered that Papa had forgotten his suit coat. We had to go shopping for a new suit coat for him, so that he would be properly dressed for the wedding! We had a good time. I think that, while we were in Connecticut, Papa took me to meet his old friend, Polly Pollard, and we began corresponding.

I don't remember whether Papa and I went to Pittsburgh during 1973. I know that we went at some point during my college years, and maybe during my law school years, too. We had some events to celebrate, including one of my Aunt Maria's big wedding anniversaries. I think that Papa went up for that one on his own. We also went for Sister Hilda's golden jubilee in the convent, and I know that I accompanied him for that occasion. On one of these trips, I heard all the derogatory comments of some family members about old Sister Hilda and her medical complaints. It made me realize that Mama and I weren't the only odd people out in this family situation. Papa, too, began to understand that I felt left out and an outsider with many of the members of the family.

For my senior year, I decided to stay on campus five nights a week, from Sunday night until Friday evening, only coming home on weekends. It gave me a chance to get more fully into campus life and to learn some real independence. I found that I enjoyed the food in the cafeteria and actually put on a few pounds during that last year.

Senior year at Trinity was bittersweet. It was the culmination of all of our work and efforts through the four years, and it was time to make plans for an uncertain future. At some point, I took the "Law Boards," the Law School Aptitude Test. I debated between continuing my studies in English literature, in which I was very interested, and pursuing a law career. I found the decision hard to make, but I knew that I enjoyed debates and analyzing issues, and I thought that a law career might give me a great scope for my talents. I also understood that a law degree would be a good foundation for other possible careers besides the practice of law.

I eventually decided to pursue a career in law, instead of going on for a graduate degree in English. I have wondered in the ensuing years whether I might have been happier teaching English than studying law and working as a lawyer. Unless I decide to get ambitious in retirement and change careers, it seems that I have taken the "Road not traveled by," to quote a phrase from Robert Frost.

In the fall of my senior year, we had Cap and Gown Sunday. We also planted our class tree on campus. The classes alternate colors among blue, gold, red, and green, not necessarily in that order. The class of 1974 was a green class, and that meant that we didn't have much trouble finding a suitable tree.

In the summer or fall of 1973, an artist lent a large oil painting that he had done of the Blessed Virgin to our parish church. He hoped that the parish might have or raise enough money to buy it before he would have to take it back. We didn't, but fortunately for us, one of the parishioners did buy it and donated it to the church. It shows Mary with a single tear on her face. What makes this painting special is that, according to the artist, when he was painting the picture, he went back to the work one day to find a drop of real water on her face. I eventually went with Papa for an evening visit to see the artist, and he told me the story. He could find no natural explanation for the tear, and he made it permanent with the paint. However, before I met the artist, I was sufficiently impressed that I decided to write a poem about the picture. See "The Madonna of the Tear," in *The Ivory Pyramid*. The poem was eventually published in our parish bulletin. When the artist saw the poem, he said that he wanted to meet me. Papa also took pictures of the painting, and for a while the picture was in our parish bulletin, too. He made a copy of the picture from his negative, and it hangs still in our dining room.

Much of the rest of my senior year was devoted to getting ready for comprehensives and the final paper and test in the major subject.

While I was on campus, I had to collect my mail from the college post office. A gentleman named Mr. Dickerson worked behind the counter. Many of the students thought that he was odd, because he didn't answer when they talked to him. I decided to keep trying. By the end of the year, he and I were good friends, and he seemed to be talking more to other people, too. Whenever I encounter someone who seems difficult, I try to remind myself to remember Mr. Dickerson and that people can come out of their shells if we give them a chance.

I applied to three law schools: Georgetown Law Center, George Washington Law School, and University of VA Law school. I chose Georgetown.

At our Trinity class dinner, hosted for us seniors by the class of '75, Sue Blain toasted all of us as, "A flock of Rare Birds!" It was a lovely expression to describe a bunch of unique people!

Finally, it was graduation day. As with Dunblane Hall, I hated to say good-bye, especially to all the wonderful teachers and friends. True to their characters, one of the sisters came to help Papa and me gather up my things from my room in Main Hall and get everything packed in the car. Trinity makes all of her women better for the experience.

I don't remember the particular family members and friends who came for the ceremony, but I received many wonderful gifts. They included, among others, a jade pendant from Sister Hilda, a double circle pin from Mrs. Murdaugh, a silver dogwood pin from Ellen, and the two diamonds for my sapphire ring from Papa.

Sue Blain gave me a sterling silver shamrock pendant on a chain. She also gave me a porcelain music box with a cardinal that plays, "Oh What a Beautiful Morning!" I still have the music box, and it became the first of a collection of music box birds!

Nana gave me a round gold medallion pendant with three little diamonds in a heart shape and a legend that said in French, "Je t'aime plus qu'hier, moins que demain." "I love you less than today, more than tomorrow." She had a personal inscription added to the back.

I still have Nana's gift, along with a box of keepsakes, my diploma, the friends with whom I kept in touch, and all the wonderful Trinity memories.

# THE "BIG LADY" BECOMES A LAWYER, PASSES THE VA BAR, AND GOES TO WORK AT THE SEC

When I graduated from Trinity College, I was twenty-two years old, an adult, and old enough to vote. I had fulfilled Nana's little regimen for becoming a "big lady." However, because I had the goal of becoming a lawyer, I wasn't finished with my education, and I would have three years of law school to complete. Before I could embark on this task, the VA Commission for the Blind, with Papa's consent, finally insisted that I complete six or eight weeks of rehabilitation. By this time, VA had its own rehabilitation center, on Azalea Avenue, in Richmond VA. It was a little bit like being told that I had to go back to the baby stroller for a while. Society said that I was an adult, and I had my Trinity diploma to prove that I could excel academically, but I still had to go off with other folks with disabilities to learn things that I supposedly needed to "get along and be independent." I suspect that my stubborn pride is getting in the way here as I try to recall this experience and sort out my conflicting emotions. Much of what I am saying springs from a perspective gained from hindsight and the intervening years, but I did not at the time clearly understand all of the elements that contributed to the emotional maelstrom caused by this experience.

The experience was unpleasant and difficult but it also had a mixed blessing and benefit aspect to it. I had to relearn something that Mama had always taught me and repeated, "You have to walk before you can run." As already discussed, I found it difficult to do that. I also had to try to interact with and encounter other rehab candidates, who had more difficult disabilities than I did. I didn't have the psychological preparation for recognizing what disabilities and problems others had and how I should react. Because I didn't always know what I was dealing with in the way of the problems that others had, I found out how some sighted people must feel in coping with a blind, hard-of-hearing person if they have no experience with how to react and interact. In that sense, it was good for me to be "on the other side of the desk," so to speak. Also, after I came out the other side of this experience, I had an even greater appreciation of how blessed I was. I am chagrinned and ashamed to have to acknowledge that I was not so loving (in the Christian sense) as I would like to have been in reaching out to others and sharing my strengths and compassion with those around me. I was then too preoccupied with my emotional turmoil that my time in Richmond precipitated.

One benefit from this trial was that I finally gained self-knowledge of how to deal with this type of emotional difficulty. As Sylvia, the counselor at the Center, told me, "You may not have your doctor around, and you may not have any medicine, but you always have your own head." I got through by coming home on weekends and crying and venting with Haide. I ultimately learned to cope, and this helped with other stresses that have come my way in life. Although I hate to admit it, spending time at the Center probably was the last necessary step in my growing up and really becoming an adult.

I won't elaborate any further in this book on the psychological details of my emotional difficulties in connection with those other later hard experiences and undertakings. However, below is the summary of what these repeated dives into emotional depths have taught me. I list these lessons at the end of this chapter in case others might find them useful.

Self-revelation and emotional maturity issues aside, I learned other things at the Center. Marge Owens, my Orientation and Mobility instructor, was excellent. She did the best that she could in this short time to help me improve my cane techniques and travel abilities. I also had a chance to practice mobility skills, because I needed to use the cane to get around the classroom building and to find my way back to my dorm. I also ended up doing some solo traveling, because I took the train from Alexandria, VA, back to Richmond on Sunday nights. A daughter of a family friend, who lived in the area, would collect me from the station and drive me back to the Center.

Marney was the home skill instructor, and she tried to teach me more about cooking and such rudimentary skills as sweeping up a floor, a skill I never really mastered. Some unpleasant things I simply found a way to avoid. We were expected to keep our rooms and bathroom clean, including cleaning the toilet by hand with a sponge. I quietly bought a Johnny mop and used it. I wasn't comfortable putting my hand down inside a commode!

Two relatively pleasant classes were the crafts class, where I started working seriously with kiln fire clay, and the sessions with Bobbie, in which she helped me to improve my signature. I very much enjoyed working with the kiln-fired clay, and I made a bird that I kept for many years. After I came home, Ellen brought me a piece of Williamsburg clay, and I made a dog with it.

In addition to the signature, Bobbie continued to work with me on the rest of the alphabet. I decided to use print for capitals and cursive letters for the small letters. I was getting too confused trying to keep four sets of letters straight!

While I was away in Richmond, Papa decided to retire from his job at the Pentagon. He thus had more time to help me when I started law school.

After Papa came to get me from the Center for the last time, we detoured on the way home to visit one of Papa's friends who had a home down in the Tidewater area of Virginia. For Mass that Sunday, we went to St. Mary's in Kilmarnock, VA. It was a small church, but it was filled with the Holy Spirit. The priest spoke in his sermon about the break-off of the Arlington diocese from Richmond, which was occurring about that time. St. Mary's would be part of the Arlington Diocese. The cathedral for the new Arlington diocese is St. Thomas Moore, in Arlington. We knew it as a church for so long that it seems strange to think of it as a cathedral.

I was so impressed with St. Mary's that I was able to offer some consolation to our assistant pastor, Father Grenelle, when he found out that he was leaving Our Lady of Lourdes to go to St. Mary's. I wrote him a letter, telling him how much I liked my brief experience in that tidewater VA parish. I told him that I hoped that he would have a good experience there, too. I never found out whether or not he did, but it may have influenced him for the glory of God. He ended up starting a healing ministry in our diocese, and he goes to different parishes during the year to offer special healing liturgy Masses. He may have retired from playing a regular, active part in this ministry.

After I came home from Richmond and before I started law school, I flew to Rhode Island to visit Sue Blain for a few days. It was wonderful to spend some relaxing time with her and her sisters in an out-of-school relaxed setting. I enjoyed meeting her parents. Her father was very hospitable, kind and thoughtful, and he baked some delicious Irish soda bread for us.

While I was in Rhode Island, Sue took me on a tour of some of the mansions owned by the old New England wealthy aristocracy. The mansions in Providence were grand places, but the so-called summer "cottages" near the sea were mansions in their own right. I was amazed at some of the luxurious features that they contained. Some of the bathrooms had three faucets in the bathtub: hot tap water, cold tap water, and seawater piped directly from the Ocean!

We only had a few weeks in August, after I got home, to get ready for my first year at Georgetown Law Center. Papa and I found time to go to the Gaithersburg Fair. We did most of the usual things, and we even tried riding the Ferris wheel. Both of us were surprised that we got dizzy and didn't enjoy it so much. Perhaps it was because we "lived dangerously" and rode on the double-wheeled Ferris wheel, or perhaps it was that we just weren't used to all that motion any more. I took the opportunity, while at the fair, to ask a beekeeper how they could tell whether a particular honey came from blueberries or lima beans. The lady said that the beekeepers keep track of when particular plants bloom and coordinate that information with when the bees deposit the honey in the removable racks that the bees fill with wax and honey. It was interesting.

Georgetown Law School was located on New Jersey Avenue, in Washington, D.C. Except for some clinical activities that took place off campus, the classes and school activities were confined to the one building. The school was by itself and not on the main Georgetown campus. No school housing was available to students. Everybody had to find lodging or an apartment outside the school, so my being at home and commuting was not out of place. I found it helpful that everything was confined to one building, especially because, at the time that I was in attendance, the neighborhood around the school was very bad. A liquor store was nearby, and I sometimes had to step carefully over bottles in the gutter as I was getting out of the car to go into the building. As with Trinity, many changes have taken place in the law school since I left. For example, I understand that the library may now have its own building, and I think other buildings house the legal clinics, but I have not kept up with the changes. I will confine my discussion to how I remember that things were when I was there.

The first floor contained classrooms. Downstairs on the lower level were the chapel and the place where you could buy deli sandwiches, including wonderful hot pastrami, and doughnuts for lunch. The Moot Court room was also accessed from this level. The library was on the second and third floors of the building. The fourth floor contained faculty offices. As an accommodation, they gave me a special key to operate the key elevator to get up to the library, so that I would not have to carry equipment and such up the stairs. I had a locked study carrel in the library, to be used, like my room at Trinity, to keep my tape recorders, typewriter, Braillewriter, and other supplies. I also worked with my readers in this little room.

In terms of getting textbooks on tape and needing to rely on readers and lectures recorded on cassette tapes, the coping methods were very similar to my Trinity years. In many ways, it was even harder, because the professors understandably wanted the latest, most up-to-date books in a fast-changing legal era, which meant that they often were slow to decide on a final textbook for their classes. They also tended to jump around in the books to suit their lesson plan and not to follow a chronological order at all. The local Volunteers for the Visually Handicapped, similar to Mr. Hannah of the Telephone Pioneers, had to cut one Constitutional law book up in order to record it for me as quickly as possible.

It was a good thing that Papa retired when he did, because he ended up reading a great deal to me to make up for material that we could not get in accessible format. He particularly had to read most of my contracts book, which we both enjoyed.

One thing that was different at Georgetown from Trinity was that our classes had men and women students. My readers were both men and women. It was the first time that I had an opportunity to interact with men students. Both men and women were volunteers who read to me and helped me with research and written assignments. I made friends with many of my readers, including Don Newman, a pharmacist and airplane pilot grandfather from Indiana who was at Georgetown to get his law degree. I am happy to say that we remained friends, until he died early in 2021, I think at the age of 97. I will miss getting his inspirational thoughts and reflections at Christmastime!

Among other readers who became my good friends were Judy Mroczka, whose husband, Ed, is very talented in remodeling houses and working creatively with wood, Emily Malek, whose husband, Harry, is a doctor, and Jo Ann Scott.

As you might imagine, I experienced some attractions to some of the gentlemen with whom I shared classes or who were my readers. None of these budding romances progressed into anything, but they added a little spice to my law school years. As discussed more fully in another chapter, most of my feelings were tentative and not serious. Those that I did consider of some consequence proved not to be reciprocated by the other party. Nana was my confidante about affairs of the heart. We had code names for the various people that only we two knew. For example, we called one fellow "the unreliable general," because he often changed his time to come or cancelled at the last minute.

In law school, they have some tried and true sayings. For example, they say that, "He who has himself for a lawyer has a fool for a client." Concerning law school, they say, "The first year they scare you to death; the second year they work you to death; and the third year, they bore you to death." That three-part saying was a pretty good summary of my three years

The first year, everything in law school is very different and new. I would not call it scary, but sometimes I found it a little daunting to learn the new legal concepts and the different research tools and methods for citing sources. Legal writing, too, is a little different from other research writing. During the first year, the large freshman class was divided into sections of about one hundred students, and each section tended to take the required courses together. The first year was mainly devoted to taking required courses. As I recall them, they included the following: Contracts, taught by Professor James Oldham; Property, taught by Professor John Steadman; Torts, taught by Professor Page; Civil Procedure, taught by Professor Frank Flegal; and Criminal Justice, taught by Professor Charles (Chuck) Ruff. It was a good thing that the building at the law school was accessible to people with disabilities, because Professor Ruff was confined to a wheelchair. He supervised the other required course, which was legal research and writing. However, second or third-year students did the "hands-on" teaching of that course. Each of these student teachers had a group of about twelve students. As part of this course, we had to draft a legal memorandum and a legal brief based on a fact pattern. Then each student had to do an oral argument based on the brief.

One truly sad incident marred the first year for our class. Some of the Georgetown Law School students were attending a party. Some men came in to rob the place and started shooting. David Collangelo, a member of our class, was shot and seriously injured. One of the students administered mouth-to-mouth resuscitation. David survived, but he was paralyzed from the neck down. He did complete the three years, and I think that he graduated with our class. The last that I heard about him, he went to work with the Department of Labor.

One diversion each year from all of our hard work and study was the Gilbert and Sullivan musical put on by a drama club composed of students and professors. The first year, Papa and I had tickets to

Iolanthe. We very much enjoyed watching the professors and some students playing the parts of the high lords and strutting around the stage. Some of the students and professors had good voices, too.

Unlike some of my classmates, I did not try to get a summer job in the summer of 1975. Instead, Papa, Nana, and I made a journey to New England. In the months before we went, we had been trying to get more information about the statues that my great-grandfather sculpted in Barre, Vermont. We managed to find Lelia Corti Commolli and her unmarried sister, Miss Corti, two surviving daughters of Elias Corti, Sam Novelli's friend and business partner. I corresponded with Mrs. Commolli for a few months, and we told her that we planned to come to New England in the summer. We made arrangements to come to see her in Barre. On this trip to New England, we all stayed initially at Uncle Joe's house for a few days. I think that he had moved into the first house that he owned in Norton, MA, by this time. We left Nana with Uncle Joe, and Papa and I drove north. We stopped overnight in Concord, to visit a family friend of Papa's. Leo Miller (no relation to my paternal grandmother that I knew of) was one of Papa's boyhood friends from Pittsburgh. He and his wife, Lynta, had lived in the Washington, DC area for a while. They may have gone back to Pittsburgh for a while, but later they moved to MA. We spent a very pleasant evening with them. Lynta painted pretty pictures. She gave us one of her oil paintings of apple blossoms. I still have it hanging in my house. The following morning, Papa and I went to the Lexington/Concord area and toured some of the historical sites. After all, we were coming up on the bicentennial in 1976, just a year away. In Concord, we found a big, old, wonderful climbing tree. Papa knew that I always wanted to know how to climb a tree, so he lifted me up into this tree and took a picture. I still have that framed picture hanging in my house, and it is a great conversation piece!

From Concord, we drove to Vermont. We met Mrs. Commolli and her sister that evening, and we spent the night in a hotel. Next day, we went to the square to see the statue of Robert Burns. Papa lifted me up to stand on the ledges around the pedestal, so that I could feel the engraved panels that Mr. Corti sculpted. The statue was way up high on top of the pedestal, and I was not able to feel it.

We went to the cemeteries to see other monuments on graves, including the Corti statue. As I mentioned in the introductory chapter of this book in footnote 4, the Corti daughters insisted that their mother's brothers did that life-sized statue. I was able to feel it, and it is wonderfully realistic and detailed, down to laces on shoes and buttons on clothing. It depicts the man sitting with his knees drawn up, as though thinking, with the implements of his sculpting trade around him. When we got back, we made the mistake of telling Nana what the Corti sister said about the statue, and she was, understandably, very upset. We only managed to calm her down by pointing out that the daughters were children at the time, and they would only know what their mother told them. Maybe the brothers did part of the work, such as the rough-cut implements. I wish that somehow I could verify whether my great-grandfather sculpted that detailed statue of his partner. When I was touching the statue, I noticed that the eyes are very distinct, with a circle cut into the eyeball to simulate the iris and the pupil. Maybe, if someone could check, they might find the eyes on the Burns statue are the same, which might arguably contribute to proving that the same sculptor did both statues.

From Barre, Papa and I meandered back to Massachusetts, spending a night in Rutland, Vermont, on the way. As we were driving along one of the hilly, twisting New England roads through the mountains, Papa noticed a sign that said, "Deer Crossing; Speed 15MPH!"

I said, "Oh, that's nice that they are looking out for the pretty deer!"

"Deer! Hell!" Papa retorted. "Do you have any idea what damage a deer can do to a car?"

I obviously didn't at the time. I found out years later, after Papa's death. My friend, Dorothy (Dottie) Hamilton Cornes, was driving somewhere with her mother when they collided with a running deer. From what she told me, the deer hit the car, bounced off the windshield, and ran away. The windshield was shattered, and there was glass in the front seat area. Fortunately, neither she nor her mother was hurt.

We passed through a woodworking town in Vermont, and we bought a couple of salad servers as souvenirs. They had some lovely salad bowl sets and cutting boards, but the prices were high.

We returned to Norton and spent a day or two more with Nana at Uncle Joe's. Before we three returned home, we paid a visit to Grandpa's relatives. Many surviving members of that side of the family all gathered in one place to see us. I quickly lost track of who was related to whom, but it was a wonderful, warm reception, and I enjoyed it. Grandpa's sister, Frances, who sent me a lovely Sacred Heart pin in an envelope a couple of years before Mama died, was there. She cried easily, which was typical of her personality. Her daughter, Marie Richards, kept in touch with me for many years until she died.

During this visit, we met one of the in-laws who was a handwriting expert. After we got home, Papa asked me to write some things down on paper for him in my imperfect handwriting. He sent them to the expert, without telling me, and the man did a report on my personality based on my handwriting. When it came, Papa asked me the questions in terms of how I would assess myself, and I gave him the answers. We both were amazed at the amount of agreement between my answers and his analysis based on my handwriting. I have to conclude that this type of analysis is a valid science.

It was a wonderful, memorable trip that summer to New England! I still have pictures that Papa took of me and the statues in one particular picture album.

The trip to New England finished off the grand, now old, Ford LTD. Before we traded it in for the Torino, I told Papa that I wanted the experience of getting behind the wheel of that car. Papa and I went down to the Pentagon parking lot on a Sunday afternoon, when no one else was around. He put the car in low gear, and then we switched places. He carefully guided me, as we slowly drove around the parking lot two or three times. Papa said that I would have been a good driver. It was high praise coming from him, especially in light of the way he joked about women drivers. The Ford LTD was a quiet, smooth-riding car, and I'm glad that I was able to have this limited driving experience with it by way of saying good-bye. When the time comes to retire my Toyota Prius, I hope that I can find someone to help me do something like that with it.

In the fall of 1975, I was presented with the Recording for the Blind Scholastic achievement award. Although it was awarded after my first year of law school, it was based on my schoolwork in college. It was a proud and memorable evening for Papa and probably Nana, too. Part of the award was a nice self-winding Braille watch, but I don't remember what else was in the award. I have to say that my Phi Beta Kappa key meant more to me.

True to the saying that I quoted earlier, the work seemed to intensify in the second year of law school. Students could start taking electives, but some courses still were considered useful for a broad general knowledge of the law. I took two semesters of corporate law with Professor Patricia King, and I also took one semester of tax law with Professor Gustafson. It was interesting to actually learn the general premise of the tax code, at least as it existed then, and why it contained some of its provisions. I also took an ethics course with Professor Mike Geltner.

In addition, we had an evidence course taught by two adjunct professors, Stiller and Schwartz. It was interesting to hear their reactions to some of the issues that were considered to be legally debatable in ethics class. On many of these issues, these adjunct professors who were in private practice took a much more conservative and definitive approach. These two lawyers admitted that they probably were not good teachers, but they tried very hard to instill in us that we should be respectful and courteous in listening to each other. On non-ethics issues, they argued frequently and took opposite sides openly in class. This exhibition of two-sided issues showed us students that the law could be seen in multiple ways and facets. The negative side was that the disagreements between the professors resulted in a problem with the grading of the exam at the end of the course. They gave a "true or false" question exam. However, I could tell from the questions and what I remembered of their lectures that the answers to many of the questions could be either true or false, depending on which side of the issue you took. I was using the typewriter to write my answers, and I took advantage of the fact to answer both ways on some of the questions with an explanation of each. The problem was aggravated by the fact that the professors divided the papers between them to grade. Someone (not I) complained to Professor Flegal, who was now dean of the law school, and he immediately understood the problem. I don't remember how they resolved it, but they had to take steps to make sure that the tests were graded fairly.

The courtesy that Professors Stiller and Schwartz tried to instill in us was in sharp contrast with the way Professor Roy Shotland conducted the class that he taught on legislation. He gave out long, verbose discussions as handouts of how he wanted his class to be a good learning experience and how his door was always open to the students. His positive words were belied by the way in which he conducted the course, in a very aggressively adversarial manner. In class, he often interrupted students when they tried to answer and came across as very contentious and argumentative. I remember on one occasion, he was interrupting someone to the point that the man couldn't get a word in edgewise. I raised my hand, and he called on me.

"I think what my colleague was trying to say," I began assertively.

He interrupted, countering with something derogatory, such as I was better than he if I could figure it out, or whatever. I didn't fully understand him, but I heard enough to think what he was saying was inappropriate.

"I beg your pardon!" I shot back.

He had the good grace not to repeat the remark, and I said what I intended. He made me angry, and I was darned if I was going to let him intimidate someone else or try to intimidate me. The result was that I learned to start developing a thick skin. I figured if Professor Shotland couldn't scare me, then I could handle whatever else someone might care to dump on me. This experience helped to confirm me in not being a respecter of persons. However, I still find this domineering, overbearing behavior hard to take from a friend. I don't like scenes, but I will endure them, if I must, to defend something in which I believe or that I think is right.

As I mentioned in the earlier chapter, Alberta Mikulka entered Georgetown Law Center a year behind me after she graduated from Trinity in 1975. We renewed our friendship, and we have kept in touch over the years. During her years in law school, Alberta met and began dating George Gilbert. They both graduated from Georgetown, and they married afterwards. They had a small law firm together for a while. George now works on Capitol Hill, and they now have three grown children, two boys, young George and Joseph, and their sister, Rosie.

This second year, if I recall correctly, was the time when I became involved in some extracurricular activities. I joined the staff of the Criminal Justice Law Review. Unfortunately, I didn't manage to find the time to write an article to get published in this journal, but I did take my turn for an hour a week covering the phone in the publication's office. I also participated in the Appellate Litigation Clinic under the direction of Professor Geltner. We worked on actual cases. My case involved an appeal by a man who had been convicted of selling illegal drugs. He sought to have his conviction overturned, on the grounds that he didn't get a speedy trial. I wrote the brief and the reply brief, and I was able to actually have an oral argument before the appellate court. The appeal was denied. I argued strenuously to Professor Geltner that we should try to go on and appeal to the Supreme Court. Professor Geltner heard me out, and then said no. He didn't think that we had a strong enough case to justify such a further appeal. I was very disappointed, even though it would have involved much more work had he said yes, but I had to accept his decisions. I thus learned an even more valuable lesson. Employees should have the opportunity to have their say and should give the boss the benefit of all their knowledge and judgment, but if the decision goes against their recommendations, it's the boss's judgment call. Absent some moral or ethical issue, they should accept the boss's decision. On the other hand, when you are the boss, you should hear your employees out and let them have their say, but in the end, it's your decision.

I became friends with Michael Geltner and his wife, Jane, who is a doctor. Mike later became my personal lawyer, until he retired. I very much value his advice and counsel and trust his judgment.

During this second year, I learned firsthand what it feels like to be the victim of a crime. Someone had come to read for me in my study carrel that morning, and then the man left. He said that he had a plane to catch to go home to Boston for the holidays that were approaching. I went to my desk to look for my cassette recorder to go down to my Corporations class. It wasn't there, and the other one was gone, too. The only thing that I could think was, "Couldn't they have left me one?"

After class, one of my fellow students, Frank, helped me to go to the office in the library and call in a police report. Officer Sevilla came out to interview me. He was very kind, but he couldn't offer much hope of getting my recorders back.

"It's Christmas time," He told me wryly. "Other people want to listen to music on cassette recorders, too."

He asked me if I had any particular suspicions of anyone. I briefly thought of the fellow going off to Boston, but I still said no. If I couldn't trust my readers and volunteers, I might as well give it up. I wasn't prepared to go there.

I never got the recorders back. When we heard that some stolen items had been recovered in a sting, Papa and I went to look, just to make sure, but my things weren't among the items. I hope other folks were more successful than I in recovering their belongings.

Between my second and third year of law school, in the summer of 1976, I worked as a law clerk with the Department of the Navy for six or eight weeks. Their offices were, at that time, conveniently close to my home, in the Crystal City apartment and office building complex off Route 1, near the border between Alexandria and Arlington.

The Navy also hired another law student, Carol Galbraith, to be my reader/assistant. When I was trying to figure out what to do, Carol would always remind me, "You're the boss." I wasn't used to being anybody's boss, and it was a new experience for me. Carol and I became friends, and we stayed in touch for many years afterwards.

I was working in the General Counsel's office, the section that dealt with contracts. I wish that I had asserted myself more to seek direction from my immediate supervisors about my assignments, because I might have gained more benefit from this work experience.

My overall supervisor and head of the section was a Robert Lieblich. At the end of the summer, he gave me a thorough evaluation and assessment. Although I mentally resisted his conclusions at the time, much of what he said proved to be an accurate judgment of my character. The thing that I most clearly remember was his opining that I would not make a good trial attorney, because I did not think in an adversarial mode. Mr. Lieblich said that I was more inclined to build up and bring points of view together than to tear down and get contentious. Although I was disappointed at the time, because I had Perry Mason in the back of my mind and thought that I might like to try cases, I now agree with Mr. Lieblich's assessment of me and believe it to be true.

Papa and I set out at the end of that summer in 1976 to go to the Gaithersburg fair again. I didn't get away for a vacation that year, and I wanted to do something. We didn't make it. On the way, we had to pull over, because Papa thought that he had a flat tire. He did, but the reason that the tire went flat was that a piece of the car's muffler started breaking and punctured the tire. Papa was in a quandary. He could change the tire, but he needed a way to hold up the muffler tailpipe, or the same thing would happen again. Fortunately, a man stopped to help us. He was a musician, and he was traveling with his guitar. He gave Papa some old guitar strings to tie up the muffler. They were made of wire, and the heat from the car wouldn't melt them. God was watching out for us that day!

Apart from my law studies and my beginning legal career, life went on and other things happened. At some point during my college or law school years, Papa took a trip to Las Vegas to visit Gretchen. He brought me back a little bank replica of a slot machine, along with some interesting red sandstone rocks from Red Rock Canyon. He also gave us a wonderful description of the "city that never sleeps." One thing that he particularly enjoyed was hearing and seeing Sammy Davis Jr. in a show.

Uncle Ray Nolan, Aunt Maria's husband, died in 1976, but I don't remember exactly when. If Papa went to Pittsburgh for the funeral, I'm pretty sure that I did not go with him.

Nana had another bad fall. I think that this accident happened in the summer of 1976, although it may have happened the previous year after our return from New England. As she told us later, she was bothered by the trash from the fish that she had cooked, and she went downstairs to put the trash into the barrel at the bottom of the stairs. As she turned to go upstairs, she tried to catch a cantaloupe to keep it from falling. She fell in the basement and hurt her leg. Papa had to help her back herself upstairs on her buttocks. We helped her into bed. By the next morning, she still couldn't put any weight on the leg, and she had to go to the hospital. This time, they admitted her for a few weeks. She had broken a bone in her knee, and they put the leg in a cast. Eventually, she began doing therapy. She had more therapy and exercises to do when she came home. I think that a physical therapist came to our house to work with her a few times a week.

It was another difficult, trying time. The Alleys helped us to get a borrowed wheelchair through their church for Nana to use when she came home from the hospital. Papa played guinea pig with me, putting me in the wheelchair to see if he could get me up the hill through the yard to the back door. It was too rough a ride. I think that he ended up taking Nana up Ellen's driveway, and then around to the back door. I don't remember quite how we managed it. It is a testimony to Nana's indomitable spirit and determination that she was able to come back from this injury. After that, she used a straight or four-footed cane for the rest of her life, but sometimes she cheated in the house and used the furniture for support she needed. I remember coming home from work or school or whatever was going on at that time, and trying to help Nana with her exercises.

When we weren't engrossed in other matters, we enjoyed watching the bicentennial celebrations on TV. I'm glad that I was around for these big celebrations. I'd like to be here for the 250-year mark in 2026, but only God knows whether the country or I will be around then.

I'm sure that I voted in November of 1976 in the presidential election. I probably voted for Jimmy Carter in that election, and I probably voted for him again in 1980. He was the last Democratic president to be against abortion. I've tried to be vigilant about voting in elections. In my opinion, folks who don't vote, however difficult the choice may be, don't have a right to complain afterwards about the results of the voting. In this country in our elections, abstentions don't count.

I can't say that I was bored during my third year of law school, but the focus subtly shifted. Students continued to pursue their academic course interests, but everybody had a weather eye on what was to come next, such as job interviews, passing the bar exam, and finding a full-time legal job. I took two semesters of Securities law with Professor King. In addition to taking a Constitutional Law course with Professor Geltner, I also took Federal Courts and the Federal System, with Professor Lacovara, one of the lawyers fired by President Nixon rather than dismiss Archibald Cox. I enjoyed all of these courses.

I interviewed with a few law firms, but I began to hear horror stories about how much after hours and intense work is expected of law firm lawyers. I knew the difficulties that I had working at the same pace as other people, considering all the adaptations I had to use and how much I relied on the assistance of others with reading and research. I began to think that I would be better suited to working in the government.

It may have been over the Christmas break or in the spring of 1977, before my law school graduation, but at some point Papa took a trip back to Germany, this time with Aunt Maria. Considering that I had dampened his enjoyment of the first trip, I was glad that he was able to go again.

I seem to remember that Papa got sick and went into the hospital for a short time just before my graduation. I don't have a clear recollection, but I remember that some of my readers came over to the house to help out with some things during this time frame.

My graduation from Georgetown Law School was a pretty momentous occasion. Gretchen came with her son, Eric, who was then around six years old. I recall that he solemnly told me to be sure and make just laws. I think that Sister Margaret James came, along with Aunt Maria. Jim, Connie, and Molly came, too. Molly took a nice picture of Nana with her Polaroid camera, sitting in a rocking chair on the front porch. On the back, she inscribed it as "to one of my favorite people." I kept that framed picture on my desk at work until I retired in September of 2014.

Concerning my graduation gifts, the relatives pooled their funds, and they bought me a leather attaché case. For his gift, that spring, Papa waited for the diamond experts to come to Woody's, and he had Mama's diamond taken out of its gold four-prong setting and reset in another gold ring in a six-prong cocktail setting. He thought that the diamond would be more secure that way. I kept the original ring, and I eventually had the green cat's eye stone set in it. We used up all the stones Papa brought back from India, one way or another, except that I lost the little tiny star sapphire that was in the original box.

Along with the other students, I received my diploma. In addition, the law school presented Papa with an award, in recognition of all the help that he gave me in completing my studies. Many of my classmates didn't realize that Papa wasn't a lawyer. He always was dressed in trousers and jacket when he dropped me off at school. After seeing me safely inside, he would sometimes get himself a doughnut or sandwich downstairs, and then he would go to the Martin Luther King library to read the Wall street Journal. Needless to say, it was an especially proud occasion for me when Papa received his award.

Concerning the diploma, unlike Papa's award, it was in Latin. Papa and I were annoyed that it was such an elitist document and not comprehensible to someone reading it. However, when we reviewed the paper translation, we were glad that it was in Latin, because it had language that appeared to gloat over the knowledge of lawyers compared with the rest of the ignorant population. If it hasn't already been rectified, I think that the language and tone needs to be changed for future diplomas!

After graduation, I took a bar review course to get ready to take the Virginia bar examination in July. The examination was in two parts: a general multi-state examination that most if not all states use and a part specifically related to Virginia law. At the advice of one of my classmates, I took the bar review course offered by an older Virginia lawyer.

Meanwhile, I kept exploring government agencies as possible employers. I had a couple of interviews with the Federal Aviation Administration, but they didn't hire me. I checked out the Food and Drug Administration, particularly the Bureau of Medical Devices, but no opportunities seemed to be readily available there. I kept checking with Nancy Wolynetz about possible openings at the Securities and Exchange Commission, the SEC. She was the attorney recruitment coordinator and the selective placement officer. Ultimately, I interviewed with Dan Pillaro of what was then called Market Regulation, now called Trading and Markets, and with the Office of General Counsel. I received offers from both. I decided to accept the Office of the General Counsel offer.

In July, Papa and I drove down to Roanoke for the Bar Examination. It was administered in the Hotel Roanoke, a grand, old, spacious, somewhat luxurious place. We understood that the hotel went back to the days of the railroad tycoons. Papa and I joked that the old railroaders knew how to live! We stayed at the hotel. It had large, well-furnished parlors with pianos, grand open spaces, comfortable rooms, and a delicious but expensive restaurant. The restaurant did offer a nice, convenient, reasonably priced buffet in the morning to help the budding lawyers to get ready for their days of examinations.

I was allowed to bring someone to read the questions for me and fill in the blanks on the multi-state test. I typed my Virginia essay question answers. Unfortunately, although I passed the multi-state part of the test, I did not pass the Virginia portion of the test.

I think that it was in the late summer of 1977 that Manfred Begert decided to pay us a visit, before I received Vincent. He was on a pleasure trip to the United States, and he planned to come through Washington. Papa was very happy to return Manfred's hospitality. He made sure that the house looked its best, and he got out the best glassware to serve beverages. I think that we took Manfred out to dinner. Afterwards, we spent a very pleasant evening with Manfred, whose English was excellent. We discussed the animosity between Elfriede's side of the family and Walter's. All of the family history and conflicts seemed to be news to Manfred. The next day, we took him to the train station. Even after Papa's death, I kept in touch with Manfred for many years.

I had to take the bar review course again in the fall to get ready for the February examination. This time, I went with the more established bar review program. How hard it was to stay awake during those evening lectures!

In February, Papa and I went down to Richmond for me to take the VA section of the examination again, and this time, I passed. I was admitted to the Virginia Bar in 1978. At some point, in later years, I was able to meet the qualifications to get a certificate of membership in the bar of the Supreme Court and eligibility to practice before the Supreme Court, but so far I've had no occasion to use this privilege.

Meanwhile, after the trip to Roanoke and before I started work at the SEC in late September, Papa and I made another trip to Pittsburgh. We drove up there in our new, 1976 Ford Grenada. Papa liked this car, because it was built higher than some of the low-slung models. It gave him more headroom and space for his legs. Neither Papa nor I was sorry to turn in the Ford Torino. I don't remember for certain, but I think that this trip to Pittsburgh may have been my last trip there with Papa. After all, I was now an adult, and I could start making more independent decisions about my relationships with family members. I think the occasion for this trip was Tim Dean's wedding to Doreen. I remember Tim's being kind to me as a little girl, and we all were happy that he was getting married. It was a fun wedding. I think that this was the first time I had "pigs in a blanket." These were cabbages stuffed with meat and cooked, I think, in tomato sauce.

Papa and I were coming to a meeting of the minds and a better understanding of my relationships with the family. On the one hand, I was gaining some new perspective as I matured. I came to understand that Papa had long-standing relationships with his nieces and nephews who were older than I was. He knew them as children, long before he met and married Mama or I was born. I needed to respect these relationships and not feel neglected or displaced by Papa's affections for these cousins. On the other hand, Papa realized that I did not share many interests with these relatives and that some of them did not accept my disabilities and me very well.

We stayed with Aunt Maria as usual. I think that she was alone in the house at this point. We made the usual visits, but I think that we went to visit Paul's house. He and Pat were married by this time. Diane was the oldest daughter, but the twin girls were just little babies.

We also made one final visit to the house on Campania Avenue. Gross-Mum had died by this time. Emma and Paul were there alone; they had no children. Paul had recently recovered from a stroke.

Emma gave Papa a set of pins awarded to my grandfather representing his landmark years of service with Westinghouse: 25, 50, 75, and so forth. She also gave me a ring that Gross-mum had made with his Diamond Jubilee diamond and, I guess, her engagement diamond. I later put the diamond circle on a charm bracelet, and I had the pins made into a large pin that I wear sometimes. It's quite a conversation piece. Papa also told Emma that, if something happened to them and they had to sell the house, he would like the Man. We never heard what happened to the statue of the knight in shining armor. I know nothing more about the Stasiaks or what happened to them. After the publication of the first edition of this book, a lady tried to contact me on a social media site to ask me if I knew anything else. I don't do social media, and I had no way of answering her. Anyone with questions for me should send a message or letter to Author House, and they can get in touch with me and maybe relay an answer.

On the way home from Pittsburgh, Papa took me briefly to Seven Springs, PA, where he and Mama spent their honeymoon.

I began work at the Securities and Exchange Commission (hereinafter called the SEC or the Commission) on or about September 26, 1977. I will summarize here my legal work during thirty-seven years at the SEC, but I provide some details in a later chapter about events leading up to my retirement in 2014. Although I probably am not giving enough details to satisfy the curious, I am my father's daughter. I know that loose lips sink ships. Moreover, this book is about my personal life, not my adventures at the SEC. I will describe coping mechanisms and other details about my work life, to the extent that they are part of my personal story, including friends that I made at work.

From September 1977 until 1979, I worked with the Office of the General Counsel. While there, I worked on legislative drafting, FOIA requests, and reviewing tapes and transcripts of witness testimony in investigations, as well as drafting legal memoranda and letters. In 1979, I went to work with the Office of Consumer Affairs, now called the Office of Investor Education and Advocacy. While there, I responded to complaints and inquiries from the public. From 1984 to 1985, I performed similar duties at the Commission's local regional office, at that time called the Washington Regional Office in Arlington, VA. When the functions of this office were consolidated in the Philadelphia Regional Office and the local office closed, I went back to headquarters, to work in the Office of Chief Counsel of the Division of Investment Management, where I was working at the time I retired. I responded to public inquiries and requests for legal interpretations or no-action positions under the Investment Advisers Act of 1940 and the Investment Company Act of 1940.

The Commission hired a legal assistant to help me with reading and research. Until 1983, Darlene Dunn, then married to a gentleman surnamed Khalatbari, was my assistant. Her husband was from Iran. From her, I learned many interesting things about Iranian culture and the disagreement of many intellectuals with the government of the radicals who deposed the Shah. Darlene had a large Irish setter, called Sport. We also enjoyed exchanging dog stories, especially after I came home from Guiding Eyes with Vincent.

Dottie Hamilton Cornes was my assistant while I was in the Washington regional Office and for a short time after I came back to headquarters. James Waeldner was my assistant after I came back to headquarters, from about 1985 until 1995. My last full-time, designated assistant, Judy Gechter, was hired after he took another position in the Commission in 1995.

When I first went to work at the SEC, the agency was located at 500 N. Capitol Street. The VA Commission for the Blind sent a mobility instructor to help me learn how to get around the building with a cane. We encountered obstacles and difficulties. It was a more complex building than any of my schools, swinging doors in some places could open into my path if my coworkers were not paying attention, and elevator doors often closed quickly. The instructor and I began to think that I would get around better and more safely with a guide dog. I did much better in getting around the building and gained more overall independence after I began traveling with a guide dog, to be described in the next chapter.

# LESSONS FOR LIVING

1.  Some events and situations normally and appropriately will cause sadness, i.e. the betrayal or hurtful actions or words by a friend, death or serious illness of a loved one, or horrific events in the country or the world. It's OK to cry over them or even to hide for a while in a cocoon, but, as the chaplain at Georgetown, Father Malley, told me, "You can't stay in there."

2.  Whether it's grief or an emotional slump caused by a stressful situation, you have to recognize that you are going through difficult time, that it should be temporary, and that a certain amount of plain old endurance is needed to come out the other side.

3.  Live in day tight compartments. "Yesterday is history; tomorrow is a mystery; today is a gift, which is why they call it the present." So goes the old saying that I have read somewhere. You only have to get through one day at a time, one hour at a time, and even, if it's really hard, one minute at a time.

4.  If your mind starts to stew, use reflex principles to recognize the junk and dismiss it. If it doesn't go away completely despite your best efforts, understand that you may not be able to turn it off but you don't have to let it rule you. As one of my friends, Peggy Clark, told me, (possibly paraphrasing Martin Luther), "You can't stop the birds from flying over your head, but you don't have to let them build a nest in your hair!" I agree with this analogy, but I have to admit that sometimes it takes time and effort to clean up the mess they leave behind when they do fly away!

5.  Garbage in, garbage out. What you put in your brain has a lot to do with your state of mind. Recently, an expert in brain health said that we should avoid "automatic negative thoughts," which he labeled ANTS. He also said we should avoid hanging around too much with other people with ANTS, or our ANTS would mate with their ANTS and we would have super-ANTS! Instead, as St. Paul said, "reflect on what is pure, honorable, and good." We make fun of Peter Pan for saying, "Think lovely thoughts," but it doesn't hurt, and it often helps. It's also useful to rehearse

pleasant music in your brain to help lift your mood. When I was in Richmond, for example, they played a song on the radio that had a refrain about seeing the hopes of a new tomorrow build back up again, and I latched onto it. Being positive isn't being Pollyanna; it just means that, while we recognize the existence of evil, with God's help, we refuse to be mastered by it!

6. Act against your feelings and try to do something nice for folks and stay positive and upbeat, even if you feel rotten.

7. If you don't feel like eating for a few days, drink plenty of water! The flip side of that injunction is to not use your bad mood as an excuse to abuse drugs or alcohol, to pig out on sweets and overeat, or to go on a shopping spree that you can't afford. The substance abuse inflicts its own punishment in health consequences, withdrawals and hangovers, the extra pounds accumulate and cause more grief, and the bills from the store eventually come in the mail and accumulate interest if they aren't paid on time.

8. 8. Vent your emotions constructively by private crying (especially applicable to us women,) punching pillows or a convenient beanbag, beating a drum or playing other vigorous music, active exercise, or discreet confidences with a trusted friend.

9. Find a diverting hobby or read a good book. It's OK to escape harmlessly for a while, especially if you come back to reality renewed and refreshed.

10. Hold on tight to the Lord! He provides grace and strength, directly and through other people, more than we can possibly have on our own! He is always there, and He never lets us down. He will help us if we give permission, but we have to ask and give Him and His grace space to act in our lives. Although God sometimes does something drastic to get somebody's attention, as he did when he knocked Saul off his horse, He never forces our doors.

11. Anger, after a period of emotional doldrums, can be a sign that emotions are trying to achieve equilibrium. Although anger needs to be controlled and constructively harnessed to reach solutions to problems, it can be a step toward recovery.

12. A sense of humor and laughter often are the best medicines and a good sign of recovery.

13. If, when the stress is removed and grief starts to abate, you still don't seem to be rebounding after a reasonable time, seek the help of a priest, counselor, psychologist, psychiatrist, or trusted friend. Don't wait until you are a basket case to yell "Uncle!"

# FIRST DOG, FIRST LOVE

When I first began work at the SEC, the agency hadn't yet hired my assistant. It was hard to get work done without a designated staff person to help me. I did bring one of my Braillewriters to work, and initially, I may have brought a typewriter, too. Eventually, the SEC provided me with a nice, Olivetti manual typewriter, and I could keep both of my typewriters at home.

Some members of the staff of the Office of General Counsel volunteered to help me when their time and workload allowed, including Dianna Barry. She worked as the secretary to James Ferber, the solicitor for the SEC. We became good friends. Sometimes, Diana and I would take an extra hour or two of leave to go shopping or run errands in the downtown stores, especially after I got Vincent. We also sometimes met downtown on a Saturday to do this, and we enjoyed ourselves very much.

Another person who volunteered was Chris Gregory. She was excellent at helping me, but she, too, was new at the Commission, and she hadn't been employed with the agency long enough to apply for the position as my assistant. We stayed friends, even after Chris left the Commission. Through Chris, I came to know Doreen Hitchcock, who later helped me with Nana after Papa died, and Dottie Hamilton Cornes. As mentioned in the previous chapter, the Commission hired Darlene Dunn Khalatbari to be my assistant, and she came to work a month or six weeks after I began work.

As far as my methods for doing work, in many ways they were similar to what I did in college and law school. Darlene would read memoranda and other legal documents to me, and she conducted research through the SEC's library, federal securities laws and SEC rules, and databases to find documents to support my findings and legal writings. I would type my rough drafts, and she would proofread them, go over them with me orally to make sure that we had them right, and then use the word processor to produce a final copy to give to my supervisor. As discussed in later chapters, many things changed once computers were equipped with software and speech synthesizers that allowed me to produce much more perfect, finalized drafts on my own.

As mentioned in the earlier chapter, Gary Deschain was my orientation and mobility instructor from the VA Commission for the Blind. He attempted to work with me on cane travel inside the building at the SEC, as well as some outdoors work. However, he became concerned about the difficulties posed by my hearing situation in dealing with traffic and about the problems posed by hurrying coworkers, swinging doors, and a complicated building structure. He encouraged me to consider again applying to a guide dog school.

At bottom, I never completely gave up on the idea of having a guide dog. As I already said in earlier chapters, I liked dogs and believed in their intelligence. I always wanted one, and having a dog to increase my independence seemed an added bonus. I knew that my friend, Jane McIver, had guide dogs, and I had already met her first dog, a German Shepherd called Bambi, from the Seeing Eye. Janie and other blind people had told me a little about the programs at the guide dog schools, but some things you have to experience to fully understand them.

Because of Seeing Eye's earlier rejection of me, I did not reapply to that school. Instead, I reapplied to Guiding Eyes for the Blind, located in Yorktown Heights, NY. That school accepted me for the class beginning on Saturday, November 19, 1977. The SEC gave me leave from my new job to go away for the four-week program. I hadn't accumulated much annual and sick leave, and I would have preferred to take leave without pay to save what leave I did have. Through an administrative error, or someone trying to do me a favor, or a failure of communications, I ended up using all of my accumulated annual and sick leave.

Papa drove me up to Yorktown Heights. We arrived late Saturday afternoon. Papa stayed for that evening and for Sunday morning. I guess he must have spent the night in a hotel. He took some pictures and got to see part of the introductory orientation. The first thing that they wanted me to do was to hang up my cane and try to learn to get around the building without it. I would have to fall back on the general orientation skills that I used as a child. The reason was that we generally would not be using our canes when we got our dogs, and we still needed to be able to orient ourselves so that we could direct our dogs where to go. I'm sure that they also took me out on a so-called Juno walk, in which the student holds the harness handle and the instructor takes the lead, like the dog, and evaluates the student's preferred pace and pull. This test is very important in matching the student with the right dog.

After the preliminaries on Sunday morning, the school required all outsiders to leave. The instructors gave us our dogs on Sunday afternoon. It was one of the few Sundays that I ever missed Mass for a reason other than illness.[24]

I must confess that, deep down, I really wanted a German shepherd. Mama read me the book, *First Lady in the Seeing Eye*, by Morris Frank, the first man to have a guide dog in this country and one of the founders of The Seeing Eye. His wonderful dog was a German shepherd female that he renamed Buddy. (The dog's original name was Kiss.) I also remembered all Nana's stories about Leelo, the German shepherd that they had when she was a child. However, I heard from the people who interviewed me from the guide dog schools and some of the instructors that most of the dogs these days were Labrador Retrievers. I heard some instructors say that German Shepherds were higher in energy level and harder to control, and that they probably would not be suitable for me. I wasn't surprised when I was given a yellow Labrador retriever, named Vincent (August 22, 1976-December 14, 1990).

By way of setting the scene, I should point out that we had twelve students in our class, divided equally between men and women. When I was there, two students shared a room. Each room had a door that came into the room from the inside hall and a second door that led out onto a curb, with the parking lot beyond. We went out this door to curb or "park" our dogs on leash: take them on leash and encourage them to circle around and sniff on the parking lot cement and do their liquid and solid elimination business. Inside the room, each of us had a sink, with a drain and second faucet below it to fill the water dish if we wanted, a place under the sink to hook our dogs on tie-down, and a button to use to summon an instructor. Each two-person room had a bathroom. As it turned out in our class,

[24] On Sundays during the program, volunteers came to take us to church, but we had to leave our dogs in our rooms on tie-down while we were gone.

two gentlemen received German shepherd females, three other gentlemen received black labs, and the sixth gentleman received the only golden retriever. Of the six women, four received black labs, including my roommate, and one other woman and I received yellow labs. The only other student in the original group with a hearing impairment was Frank, who originally received the Golden Retriever.

Two instructors were primarily responsible for the class. The lead instructor was Dave Pietrantonio, (hope that I spelled it right) and the other instructor was Mike. I don't remember Mike's last name. Dave gave my roommate and me our dogs on leashes and sent us back to our room to pet them and get acquainted. It was rather discouraging for us at first, because neither of our dogs wanted anything to do with us. Vincent stood by the door listening for Dave; my roommate's dog, Radar, whined and cried with a high-pitched sound. He lived up to his name in that respect.

That first evening, at dinner (and for most other meals,) we were expected to put the dogs in a down position next to us at the table but facing outward.[25] We all had a terribly difficult time positioning our dogs and making them behave and stay lying down. Dave made us all feel wonderful (I'm being sarcastic) by saying that we were doing great! The last class upset the table on the first night! My tension and frustration were aggravated by the fact that Dave tried to impose a rule that we were not to discuss dog matters at the table. Yet we were expected to pay attention to our dogs at all times and make them obey us, and correct them if they didn't, and not let them get away with anything! It all seemed pretty impossible!

The next day, I went for my first walk with Vincent: just a short walk around the block, with the instructor close behind me. Vincent still didn't want anything to do with me, but with the instructor close behind us, he did take me around that block. I was told to keep talking to him and to tell him what a good boy he was! Moreover, because he was under stress and I was new to him, Vincent pulled strongly against the harness and my handle. I felt as though my arm was being pulled out of the socket! Fortunately for me, his normal pace was much slower and he generally had a light, even pull, and he worked calmly and steadily, generally ignoring other people (unless he knew them) and with minimal animal distractions. He did like to sniff, and they kept telling me to correct him in class. It seemed to me that I was correcting him all the time, and both of us were getting very frustrated. By the providence of God, Steve Orcutt was around. He wasn't one of our regular instructors, but he

---

[25] For a few meals during the program, we left our dogs in our rooms to get them used to being calm and well-behaved during our absence. However much I want my dog with me at all times, on some occasions it's better to leave my canine buddy at home for a period of time during the day.

was there to help students who needed a second objective view of what might be going on with them and their dogs. I told Steve that I was having problems with Vincent and sniffing. Steve watched what we were doing. He told me that I should stop and correct him if he stopped, but the main thing was to keep him going, even if he was sniffing somewhat, so long as he had his mind on business.

I found out all Vincent's wonderful qualities later, after we were home, used to each other, and much calmer! During class, I didn't see how I was going to be able to trust this stranger at the end of my leash and handle.

We students spent the next four weeks practicing working our dogs in various circumstances, ranging from quiet residential streets, to "country walking" without a sidewalk, to busy White Plains, as well as New York City and its subway. We rose early to "water and park" our dogs, fed them twice a day, learned to groom and brush them, and had to park them for the last time at 11 P.M.

I found the program very intense and difficult and emotionally draining. Vincent resisted all of my commands, it seemed, and I was constantly correcting him. I found out, later, that this resistance was indicative of a stubborn, independent streak that, coupled with intelligence, resulted in a guide able to think and make intelligent decisions concerning my safety, even if it meant disobeying my commands. Once he decided to work for me, these qualities meant that he was loyal to me and not easily swayed by others. During class, however, this contest of wills was pure frustration. When we were sitting in the lounge waiting to go out, we were supposed to position our dogs under or next to our chairs. I constantly had to slide this 70-pound dog back into position when he crawled out to look around or not to be under something. I wondered if I would ever be able to relax again!

Dave compounded the problem by taking a sardonic, somewhat cynical attitude toward us students and our dogs. When he handed me Vincent the first day, I said, "Oh, he's lovely!"

Instead of saying something positive, such as, "I'm glad that you like him," Dave's answer was, "That's what they all say." If he didn't believe in the poetry, potential, or value of the program, why the heck was he involved in it? He didn't seem to believe in the intelligence of his dogs, and he kept downplaying our expectations. At one point, he said to me, "You don't have Rin Tin Tin or Lassie." What he didn't understand was that I didn't want Rin Tin Tin or Lassie: dogs that did things by rote. I wanted smart, intelligent Vincent, and I wanted him to be the best that he could be. I realize now that Dave was trying to keep students from having unrealistic expectations from their dogs. The school properly emphasized that we needed to focus initially on our dogs being trained to stop for curbs and stairs, navigate safely around uneven terrain and obstacles, and protect from oncoming traffic, even if it means intelligently disobeying. Other abilities sometimes emerge depending on the dog and the interaction with the master.

I know that I'm biased, but not every student was fortunate enough to end up with a Vincent, and Vincent and I turned out to be well matched, which isn't always the case. As I can verify from my experiences with six dogs, each dog is different, and you only get from the relationship what you are willing to put into it in terms of work, love and discipline, to help it develop to the best of its potential. However, what discouraged me about Dave's attitude was that he still took this cynical reaction, even though I was working my backside off to try to make it work.

I never could figure Dave out, except that he got along much better with the dogs that he was training or "educating" than he did with the people students. I've also learned through subsequent experiences in my life that, once you understand the social order on which dogs operate, it is much easier sometimes to relate to dogs than to complex human beings. If you find a dog instructor/ trainer who is good with both dogs and people, they are to be praised highly!

The stress of the training program was taking its toll on me, and I was beginning to wonder if I would get through the program. Two of my friends saved me by coming to visit me on the weekends when we were allowed to have visitors. M.E. Tucker came to see me from New York. She was the first one to tell me that I indeed had a beautiful dog. Yellow labs can range from beige to a cream to an almost white to white. Vincent was almost white, with a big black nose and soulful brown eyes, but nobody ever told me that before M.E. While I realize that the most important thing is to have a dog that does well at the guiding work, the way that she described Vincent made him sound very special, which he proved to be. M.E. also encouraged me to continue working with Vincent, and she reassured me that he would understand that I was trying to respect him and develop his full potential.

Emily Malek and her doctor husband, Harry, came to visit me one weekend. They made me feel that I was doing something right in working with Vincent, because they said that other students' dogs were jumping around and getting excited in company, but Vincent was staying calm. I confided my emotional distress to Emily and Harry. I had some of those mild tranquilizers with me, but I didn't want to have to use them. Harry reassured me that they were safe and wouldn't impair my judgment, and he helped me to see that it was better to use them and get through the program than to come apart emotionally. My friends gave me the confidence that I could get through this difficult situation successfully. I'm glad to say that occasion was the last time that I had to resort to those pills!

We students all suffered a psychological jolt when Frank, the fellow with the two hearing aids, was sent home without his dog as not working out. In the last two weeks, two retrains came to join us. One was a woman who brought her dog back to correct excessive barking. The second was a man back for a second dog after his either retired or died. This man, Jimmy, was given the Golden Retriever, Lock, that originally was assigned to Frank. My roommate wondered aloud, when we were alone, whether Frank was sent home to make Lock available for Jimmy. We liked Jimmy and didn't blame him, but we were wondering what was going on. Frank's leaving hit me especially hard, because now I was the only student with a hearing impairment, and I worried that I would be the next one to be sent away. Our suspicions were heightened when Jimmy kept saying how wonderfully well Lock worked! Frank certainly hadn't done anything to ruin Lock while he was working with him. From the benefit of hindsight, Frank may not have been ready for a dog, just as I wasn't ready in 1971, or Lock may not have been the right match for Frank. He certainly seemed to be well suited for Jimmy.

Finally, it was time for us to take our pictures with our dogs, individually and as a class. We were given new harnesses and silver medals for the dogs' collars with the name of the school on them. I was very relieved when I graduated and was able to fly home with Vincent. By this time, he seemed to be listening to me better.

Papa met us at the airport. He took one look at Vincent and said, "Hello, George!"

By way of explanation, Papa and his nephews, especially Cousin Jim, had an inside joke between them that they called each other George, or Bill, or Axle, or other odd names. Papa did the same with Vincent. It didn't matter. Whatever Papa called him, Vincent understood when Papa was talking to him. Sometimes, I called Vincent "Pal" or "Eyes." He seemed to understand that these were my names for him, too.

At the school, when we went out, we were in vans with our dogs sitting in front of us, and we weren't supposed to let our dogs onto the furniture. In coming home from the airport, we had to break the furniture rule, at least when we rode in the car. The only place that this good-sized dog would fit was on the back seat of the car.

Before I got Vincent, Papa made protestations that dogs didn't like him, or maybe he didn't like dogs, but very soon it was clear that he fell in love with Vincent. Vincent was unquestionably my dog, especially in a work context, but he also loved Papa. If Vincent didn't feel well, or started limping, or had diarrhea, Papa was quick to suggest a trip to the vet. They had a special relationship.

Soon after we came home, Papa noticed that Vincent was having trouble on our basement stairs, because the wooden stairs were not backed and were open. Papa got boards and put backs on the stairs, closing them. We eventually got a piece of carpet that was left over from an old rug and put it on the basement stairs. Nana joked that we had to get a dog before the stairs were fixed!

Nana, like Papa, was surprised at how big Vincent was, but she loved him, too. He liked her. It was obvious to me that Nana was very at home with dogs. She picked up on the expression to "park the dog" as meaning to let them do their business. One day, she said to me, "Excuse me. I have to go park." We laughed.

After keeping Vincent on leash a day or two per the school's instruction, he had the run of the house. Unlike my later dogs, Vincent never ended up on the furniture. He wasn't tempted to sleep with me on my bed, because, I think, he was allergic to my acrylic blankets. If his nose was too close to them, Vincent sneezed. He did put his front paws and upper body on my bed in the mornings to wake me, encouraging me to hug him and pat him to help me get going. Sometimes, he pulled the covers off me. Mikki and Remus did that sometimes, too. Remus also knew how to put her front paws on my shoulders and shake me!

Vincent, like my other dogs, enjoyed some cooked meat and vegetables added to his dog food, but we tried to be careful what we gave him. He also liked a piece of banana, orange, or apple. He also enjoyed an occasional poached egg and a piece of toast. A few months after we came home, we had some severe diarrhea episodes, but we eventually had to treat Vincent for whip worms. We also had a problem with ear infections, until I discovered that Vitamin C helps to keep these infections away. After I put him on 500 milligrams a day, we did much better.

Vincent generally was good about not chewing up my things, and he learned to love chewing on cooked soup bones from which the marrow had been removed. Papa and I ate the marrow on crackers, and we enjoyed it very much.

It soon became clear that Vincent was our "Great Communicator." He was very verbally aware, and he conversely found a way to make himself understood. He knew that it did no good to look at the door to indicate to me that he wanted to go out. He would take me by the skirt or the sleeve and show me the door (go out) the sink (check the water dish,) the bed (time to go to sleep,) the stove (water boiling,) and once, the cherry pie on the kitchen table, (how about cutting us both a piece.) He communicated well with others besides me. One day, Nana came to find me and asked, "The dog is lying in the bathroom. Do you think that he needs to go out?"

Even when I was trying to walk "sighted guide" by holding someone by the arm, heeling Vincent on leash, he still insisted on keeping my skirt in his teeth. He wanted a piece of the guiding action. In fact, he saved me a couple of times from tripping or falling when the person who was supposed to be guiding me didn't stop for steps! This kind of behavior wasn't taught by the instructor folks at Guiding Eyes; it came from Vincent's inherent understanding of what his job was and that I needed his guiding and protection from hazards.

Years later, Texas Mary was trying to show me some things about the roof of the house. We had gone out my front bedroom window onto the porch roof. Vincent came out with us. At first, he happily walked up the house roof, and he enjoyed looking around at the neighborhood and talking to dogs across the street. However, when Mary started showing me how to position my body near the edge of the roof without falling, all the games ended for Vincent. He came over to us, and he lay down with his body between me and the edge of the room.

He seemed to be saying, "I'll fall off this roof if I have to, but I'm not letting you get too close to the edge!" Mary and I thought that he was wonderful!

At home and while working, Vincent rarely barked. Sometimes, at home, he would let out a frustrated "woof" if a ball or toy went under a piece of furniture and he couldn't get it. When he was working, he held his tail high and slightly curved and was generally serious. He would respond enthusiastically if friends came to visit, but he learned to ignore people that he didn't know.

I also was able to teach Vincent to help me in other ways, such as by alerting me if water was boiling unattended on the stove. He also learned to help me to find dropped objects by walking over to them and putting his head down to show me where they were.

We didn't have a fence around the yard in those early days. When we started letting him out the back door off leash, Papa usually kept a close eye on him. Once in a while, Vincent would disappear out of the back of our yard. A little while later, we would see him walking up the sidewalk to come in the front door. He must have mapped out a little excursion for himself. Naturally, we did everything we could to discourage these AWOL incidents. Eventually, we put up a three or four-foot parallel bar fence around the backyard, with three gates. After we had the fence, we only had to make sure that the gates weren't left or blown open.

When I first came home, Papa noticed that my ankles were swelling, especially the left one. We checked this out with the doctors, and I have done so repeatedly over the years. The swelling seems to be caused by a circulatory situation and fluid retention, about which nothing can be done, except to wear good support hose and keep the legs elevated whenever possible. It may be more pronounced on the left side, because that is the side on which I work the dog. It might be related to arthritis, but that wasn't clear. In recent years, I had a venogram done, to see if they found anything specific in the circulation from the groin area through the legs, but nothing showed up that could be remedied.

When I discovered that I was getting unusually short of breath after walking around our hilly block with Vincent, I began to think that my allergies were flaring up again. After Mama died, I eventually stopped taking the injections, especially when I seemed to be free of symptoms. After I had Vincent, I consulted Dr. Yuill Black, and I went back on injections again. Fortunately, I was able to get the injections at the Health Unit at work.

Guiding Eyes sent me home with the general rule to listen carefully to traffic and trust the dog on quiet intersections but to seek help in crossing busy streets. Because the crossings between my house and Our Lady of Lourdes church were generally manageable, it meant that I would be able to walk to church on my own, but I usually went with Papa. It also meant that I could walk to Barbara and Don Sheehan's house by myself, too, once Vincent learned to turn off the sidewalk at their entrance. It was very nice to have this added independence.

At work, Vincent was popular, too. Darlene, Dianna, and Dianna's friend, Elaine Funk, all liked Vincent, and they helped me to get him across the street at lunchtime to park in the grassy strip on the other side of North Capitol Street.

At work, I found another friend, Elizabeth Tsai. She is from the Philippines. She and her Chinese-American husband, Tom Tsai, have two children. They are good Christians. Elizabeth and I had lunch together in one of our offices, and we would share our faith and the news of our families. She liked Vincent, too. She told me many interesting things about life in the Philippines. Papa and I went to visit at her house for special occasions, such as birthdays or holiday parties.

During one of Elizabeth's parties, she served little pastry turnovers filled with meat and vegetables, similar to (but better than) quesadillas. She gave us some leftovers to take home, advising us to freeze them, and then heat up as many as we wanted another day.

By this time, we had a nice toaster oven in which I was comfortable warming foods and cooking others. One Sunday night, I heated up a few of those little meat pies, and decided to add a couple more. I found that I had too many on my plate. I had to answer the telephone or was called away for some other purpose. When I came back, I found that Vincent had relieved me of two of the little, tasty pies! What I had left was just enough! He really was a gentleman. Some dogs would have eaten all of them.

By this time, Father Comaskey was no longer pastor at Our Lady of Lourdes, but he still was in residence. He thus lived to see me come into church with "a big, bouncing dog." The pastor for the first two or three years after I received Vincent, if I remember correctly, was Father O'Connell. We teasingly called him "Santa Claus," because he looked the part physically. He also had an easy-going disposition and an upbeat personality. In 1979, Father Gerloff replaced him. That pastor ran up so much debt that the bishop told him to find a way to pay it off. The result was that the parish offered 120 $500 notes to parishioners to raise the $60,000. The notes were to be paid off, on a rotating, lottery basis, without interest. Papa and I together bought five of these notes.

I made one friend during my training at Guiding Eyes, Elsome Templin. Her black lab was named Vernon. Because both of our dogs had names beginning with V, we thought that they might have come from the same litter. We corresponded for many years, comparing notes about our home lives and our dogs.

I also learned that Richard Chaise, who then worked at the SEC in another division, had a wife, Kay, who had a German shepherd. Her dog was named Marcy, and she came from Seeing Eye. We had some pleasant visits together with our dogs.

Through my dog, I found another wonderful friend and spiritual counselor. Someone told me, when I was trying to work out a problem or issue with Vincent, that I ought to compare notes with Father Seamus Kuebler. He traveled with a guide dog from Seeing Eye. At the time, he was located in the Washington, DC area, and we spoke by telephone. We didn't meet at that point, but we enjoyed comparing notes about our dogs. I don't remember the exact sequence of events, but eventually, Father Seamus went home to be near his mother; when she died, he stayed on to look after his father for a while. I will later describe the monastery he founded.

I still kept in touch with other friends, too. Mary Spellerberg was living in their house in Reston, and she and Peter had four little girls. When we went to visit them, Vincent let the little ones hold onto his back as they walked around the house.

Alberta Mikulka married George Gilbert, a friend from her law school days. I think that their oldest child, George, was born somewhere between 1980 and 1982.

Charlotte Frease retired and moved into a mobile home on her wheat farm in Kansas. Eventually, she ended up with four companion dogs.

To see how much more independent I really could be with Vincent, Gary, the Mobility instructor, started working with me to practice the subway route to and from work. Once Gary thought that we were ready, Papa would drop me off at Crystal City, and I would take the Blue line into Washington, to Metro Center. At Metro Center, we would change trains and go to Union Station, which was the closest stop to my office. To go home, we would reverse the route.

Although we had some adventures (such as getting into a returning train instead of the elevator up to the Red Line level or taking a wrong turn inside the station and ending up at the wrong escalator or elevator,) Vincent learned the route inside the subway system very well. He was also very good at cutting in front of me as we approached the edge of a platform, to let me know that we had open tracks ahead of us, and we should turn either left or right. On a few occasions, I thought the door that was opening was my train, but Vincent wouldn't move. It turned out to be the train on the other side of the tracks that was going the other way!

The tricky part was that we had to cross some busy intersections between the Union Station Metro stop and my work building. I tried to follow procedures as instructed by the school and sought help of other pedestrians. I had only limited success in getting such help and a few scary incidents. On one memorable occasion, for example, I thought that I was walking across the street "sighted guide" with someone. He dropped me in the middle of the intersection and went another way, leaving me groping for my dog's harness handle and praying! After that, I never dropped my dog's handle again with a stranger. These difficulties made me think that Vincent, if at all possible, needed to learn more in order to help me cross streets safely.

Another problem that we had was that Guiding Eyes at that time did not teach their dogs to use escalators. However, because the elevators in the Metro system sometimes were not working, we needed to learn to use escalators. Papa undertook successfully to teach Vincent to use escalators. I heard that Pilot Dogs, in Columbus, OH, was already teaching their dogs to use escalators, and we were fairly sure that it could be done. The problem that made the schools generally avoid escalators was the danger of dogs hurting their paws or catching their toenails. The danger point is the place where the moving part of the stairs encounters the stationary surface at the top and bottom. Vincent was aware of this problem and would jump off at the end. Our biggest challenge was to teach him to wait just long enough to jump so that he would not pull me. A few times, I had to let go of him if he jumped too soon. He would turn around and joyfully greet me when I came off.

When I would tell Papa that he was jumping too soon, Papa would say to Vincent, "Do we have to go back to school, boy?" and he would work with him some more. Eventually, both Seeing Eye and Guiding Eyes decided to teach their dogs to use escalators, with care.

Vincent liked to play ball, and he would retrieve a tennis ball enthusiastically and run to get it when it was thrown again. We tried to encourage him to give it back to me in my hand, but he would often drop it close to the person with whom he was playing. Sometimes, he would stand at the top of the hill in the backyard, roll the ball down the hill to me, and then bark at me to pick it up. If the ball did not land near my feet, I wouldn't be able to find it, and I would try to have him give it to me. He was better at getting vigorous exercise with this game when playing with a sighted person. Papa, for one, could throw balls far back up the hill in the yard and give Vincent a real run for his money. With the help of a friend who held the ball to encourage Vincent to get into this pose, Papa took a wonderful picture of Vincent, standing alert and poised with his ears thrust forward and his tail out and up, as he looked at and waited for the ball. The picture hangs in a frame in my bedroom.

In addition to playing ball with Vincent, Papa would take Vincent for leash walks around the neighborhood in the evenings. If Papa was watching his favorite football games on Sunday, Vincent waited patiently for Papa to walk or play with him. We couldn't get over how he seemed to know when the commercials came on or it was half time!

Vincent also loved the snow. When snow first began to fall, he would be climbing up on the back door every hour, asking to go outside and get his fur full of snow. He would come inside and warm up, and then he would want to go back outside again for more. I think that it was the winter of 1978-79, but we had a huge snowstorm and two or three feet of snow. Vincent and the dogs across the street got to visit each other, because no cars could drive. Vincent had a wonderful time running, or kind of swimming, through that deep snow. We tied a red ribbon on his neck, so that the white dog would still be visible against the white snow. Afterwards, when he came inside, Nana had to wash off the red dye that bled from the ribbon onto his fur. We teased him about having a "ring around the collar!" as in the commercial for Whisk detergent.

Sometimes Vincent would tease me. He knew that I couldn't see him. If I called him to come to me, I would hear his tags on his collar jingle as he danced around me, just out of reach. He knew that I couldn't find where he was if I didn't touch him. He seemed to be saying, "You can't find me!" and enjoying it. However, if I told him to come get harnessed, or got the harness out, the game would be over immediately. He was always serious about his work.

When Papa came to meet us in the Crystal City metro station, Vincent would see him, and then, wagging his tail vigorously, he would run with me to greet him. He would make a deep bow and then jump up, once, and put his paws on Papa's chest. Papa would grab Vincent's paws one in each hand, and shake him a little bit.

"I'm stronger than you are, boy!" Papa would tell him, holding him up on his hind legs as he held Vincent's paws. "I'm stronger than you are. I'm not going to let you get down!"

Vincent would make little response noises, enjoying it all the while, and Papa would eventually put his paws down on the ground. Consequently, he generally did not jump up this way on anybody except Papa. It was their thing between them.

In the late fall of (I think) 1978, I went to NY to pay a visit to M. E. and her husband, John Grim. They were living in an apartment in the city. Vincent and I traveled to New York on the AMTRAK train, and I very much enjoy train travel. Vincent was good on the trip. M. E. met us at the station. John had a pet retriever mix female, named Mindy. Once the dogs established that Mindy was top canine (but not pack leader) in her own house, the two dogs got along fine. I was recovering from a cold, but M.E. pampered me with hot tea and honey during that rainy weekend. John was a prince, and he walked and brushed both dogs. We had a wonderful visit. I recall that I went back a year or two later. This time, we had better weather. M.E. and I went shopping in the NY stores, and I bought several items, including a pair of patio style Daniel Green slippers. She and John told me about their careers as professors of theology and comparative religions. John, in particular, studied Native American culture and particularly that of the Sioux. He has done sun dances with the Sioux. M.E. spent time in Japan after graduating from Trinity. They had so much to share.

Although Papa, Nana, and I were all enthralled with Vincent in those years, other events received our attention. At work, Mr. Ferber, solicitor for the Commission and Diana's boss, retired, and Diana eventually did, too. She finished her Bachelor of Arts degree from, I think, the University of Maryland. Papa and I were invited to a family gathering to celebrate Grandma's graduation, and Papa took pictures. It was wonderful!

As I said, I left the Office of General Counsel and went to the Office of Consumer Affairs on a detail in 1979. The detail became permanent when the job seemed to be a good fit. Darlene accompanied me to the new office. However, at this time, that office was in a different building, at 1100 L Street NW. The building had nice, spacious halls and offices, and it had a wonderful, reasonably priced government cafeteria on the first floor. I enjoyed their hot sandwiches and sometimes their entrees at lunchtime.

The difficulty was that this building wasn't close enough to Metro Center to allow me to go into the office by subway and walk to the building on my own. Papa began driving me to and from work. Oh, how much he hated the traffic and lane changes on the bridges into the city! I finally realized fully that I was an adult one morning, when I was running late getting ready for work. That morning, Papa said, "Let me know when you are ready to go. If you are late, it's up to you. I'm not going to bother about rushing you anymore." Ironically, that was more of a spur for me to hurry than constant nagging. It was, as he said, my responsibility!

If I had to take the subway to work for some reason, Papa would drop me off at Crystal City, and I would meet up with a colleague traveling by subway to work and walk to the building. Going home, I would walk with a friend to Metro Center, and then I would take the blue line back to Crystal City.

In September of 1981, Aunt Janie became ill. It was obvious when we talked to her on the telephone that she didn't feel well. The last time that I spoke to her, on a Sunday, she abruptly ended the conversation, saying that she had to go, and get off her legs. It sounded as though her legs were bothering her.

Aunt Irene confirmed that Aunt Janie wasn't well; Aunt Irene suspected breast cancer, but she said that Aunt Janie wouldn't go to the doctor. That night, in bed, I cried and said the rosary on Mama's yellow, topaz-colored beads. I prayed that Aunt Janie might get better, but if she could not, I prayed that the shock wouldn't kill Aunt Riri, too. I knew that they were very close. As I was praying, the rosary broke in two places, with one bead separating from the rest. Although I don't consider myself superstitious and don't put much stock in this kind of thing ordinarily, I felt somehow that my prayers had been answered.

Monday, I kept praying, of course. Tuesday evening, September 15, Papa came to get me at work. We were driving home through the rain. A man lost control of his car (possibly going too fast,) and he hit us. He had a nice, new car, and it was all smashed in the front. Our car only sustained minor damage. When Papa stopped suddenly trying to avoid the collision, Vincent fell off the back seat and bumped his nose on the back of the front seat. A policeman helped us, confirming that nobody was hurt. He made sure that both drivers exchanged insurance information and names and addresses. As it later turned out, we had to use a little Toyota loaner car while ours was repaired.

When we got home that evening, we got the news that Aunt Janie had died. That morning, Aunt Riri found her dead, sitting on the floor beside the bed. She may have had a heart attack. For her sake, if she could not get better, I was glad that she went home to the Lord quickly. The night that I heard of Aunt Janie's death, for probably the only time in my life, I wanted to open one of Papa's wine bottles and get numbingly drunk. As Nana might have put it, I wanted something stronger than tea in my radiator! I'm glad to say that I didn't do it. It was a fitting tribute to Aunt Janie that I restrained myself. The family story goes that she was allergic to alcohol.

I'm sure that they had a dickens of a time sorting through all the stuff in that little apartment where the aunties lived. The dining room was used as a storeroom, and it was so packed with stuff that Uncle Joe called it "the warehouse." I was sorry not to be invited up for the great sorting. I asked Aunt Riri to keep me in mind, and I told her that I would like a keepsake, but nobody ever sent me anything at the time. Years later, Uncle Bill's granddaughter, Denise, sent me a pin that may have belonged to Aunt Riri.

My prayers about Aunt Riri were answered. She lived on for many years after her sister's death and survived Nana. At first, she moved in with Uncle Bill, but she later entered a nursing home. As mentioned in a later chapter, she and Uncle Bill died after Nana.

I still miss Aunt Janie, Aunt Riri, and Uncle Bill. With Aunt Janie's death, Nana had only two siblings left, Aunt Riri and Uncle Bill. Somehow I feel that Aunt Janie was praying for us that we didn't get seriously hurt in that accident.

Nana was slowing down. She seemed able to do less of the housekeeping and the cooking. We hired a wonderful lady, Pearl Bowles, to come once a week to do the heavy, thorough cleaning. Pearl was very diligent at her task. She was allergic to dust, and she considered it her enemy. Fortunately, she came to clean the day before the evening that Manfred Begert from Frankfurt came to visit us, as described earlier.

Papa and I began taking over more and more housekeeping chores, cooking, and kitchen work. Papa would fuss about the cooking, and he would complain that he didn't understand how this little bit of dinner took so much work and produced so many dirty dishes. (No, we didn't have a dishwasher at that time.) I didn't have the heart to tell him that part of the problem was that he didn't clean up dishes as he went along. Instead, he would leave them until the end of the meal. Nana kept telling Papa that she thought that he was doing very well with the cooking. It was high praise coming from her!

On the way home from the subway or from the SEC, if Papa came into town to get me, we would go by the park near my house and have a good ball game with Vincent. Papa was still on the lookout for things that I could touch or feel. On one occasion when he was playing with Vincent, he met a couple of young boys. They had found two little snakes, called decays, because they lived under fallen logs and fed on the insects that thrived in the decomposing vegetable matter. The boys planned to take them home as pets. (I couldn't help wondering how their mothers would feel about that.) Papa asked them if I could feel these little harmless snakes. I really enjoyed touching them. They were like little live rope pastas, and they coiled around my finger. I could understand from this experience why some people like snakes. They are so incredibly flexible and limber! Apart from other motivations, I suspect that some people like them, because they admire their incredible ability. I'm sure many a dancer wishes that he or she could move like that and be graceful.

As the years went along and Nana did less and less cooking. Papa and I often would go to the Hot Shop Cafeteria in Crystal City for dinner. We knew that Nana could still get something for herself, and it was a change and a break for both of us. I especially liked their roast beef and their delicious pies, especially the lemon merengue, coconut custard, and coconut cream pies!

Sometimes, too many children on tours and class trips would be in the restaurant for us to have a quiet, pleasant dinner. When Papa saw from the parking lot that the restaurant was too busy, he would drive back out without having to pay. He would tell the parking attendant by way of explanation, "Too many kids!" He asked the man to teach us how to say it in Spanish, too. We laughed. When this happened, if we didn't go home to eat, we sometimes stopped at Roy Rogers, The Howard Johnson Hotel, or (rarely) the Hyatt Hotel in Crystal City restaurant.

I used up my leave when I went away to Guiding Eyes for Vincent, and I had to wait for my annual and sick leave to build back up again. Eventually, Papa and I were able to take trips. As I mentioned in the previous chapter, we went to Richmond in February of 1978 for me to take the VA State part of the Bar Examination a second time. On this occasion, I think that we left Vincent with Barbara and Don Sheehan. I think that Vincent went with us when I went back to Richmond with Papa to be admitted into the VA bar.

We left Vincent for the last time with Barbara and Don in the fall of 1978, when we went to Ocean City for a few days. It was wonderful to be on a trip with Papa and not be visiting relatives or doing anything serious. By a happy coincidence, we ended up coming right at the time that kite fliers were having a meeting or convention there. We bought a kite, and I had the fun experience of flying it on the beach. I also liked walking on the beach and listening to the water and shopping for souvenirs in the goody stores.

While we were gone, Don and Barbara enjoyed Vincent, too. When we came to get him, after we came back, Don said, "Linda, I'll buy you a pony if you'll let me have Vincent!" We all laughed, because, of course, the answer was "no!"

When we didn't go on long trips, we went to day activities, like the Labor Day picnic at Old St. Mary's church in Fairfax, VA. After an 11 A.M. Mass and blessing of fire trucks and other tools, they have a wonderful chicken picnic, with crafts, music, and white elephant sales.

Papa and I functioned as a team. He helped me balance my checkbook and pay bills. Whoever had the money paid for whatever had to be paid. He would call me at work, and we would plan the dinner menu and evening activities.

We also began making decisions together about household furniture. We bought a new wing chair for the living room. We also decided to get new chairs for the dining room. In my dining room, I have the original buffet, china cabinet, and table, all made of pecan. Mama had bought originally six maple chairs to go with the table. Maybe they couldn't afford pecan chairs, or maybe Mama liked the style. Neither Papa nor I thought that the maple chairs were comfortable. We went to Hecht's Department Store when they were having a furniture sale, and Mr. Alexander, the salesman who regularly waited on us in the Ballston store, showed us four pecan chairs, with upholstered seats and tall, straight cane backs. Not only would they match the rest of the dining room set, but also they were much more comfortable. In addition, one of the four had arms, which would allow Nana to use it to get up more easily.

As things have turned out, I'm sure that Mama and Papa are having a good laugh in heaven. I still have the pecan chairs, and I have recovered the seats and probably will have to do so again. Eventually, the cane will need replacing or repair. What's really funny is that they haven't held up so well as the little maple chairs! The seats began to work loose from the rest of the chair, except for the armchair. I had to have hickory wood braces with screws put on the straight chairs to hold them together. I bought two tall-backed oak chairs to make the six for the dining room. I also eventually bought another armchair at a church bazaar for the dining room, so we have two armchairs at opposite ends of the table. As for the maple chairs, one has fallen apart and probably been discarded. The other five are still hanging around the house; two are in the basement; and one is in the front bedroom. Two are in the kitchen as spare chairs!

When I was in law school, I began having mammograms; eventually, I chose a female gynecologist. For my primary doctor, I also chose a woman, Dr. Nancy Falk, whose office was in Washington, DC. I suppose that I was thinking that it might be good to have a doctor accessible from work. In November of 1978, I began having respiratory symptoms, along with a fever that went up and down. I lost my voice and my appetite, and all that I felt like eating at lunch and dinner was Progresso soups. Dr. Falk didn't prescribe antibiotics at first, saying that it was a viral infection. She waited a week or ten days before ordering a chest X-Ray. It showed an infection in the left lung, which did respond to the antibiotics that she eventually prescribed. Papa was angry that she let me suffer so long without being more pro-active. (Yes, he came a long way from the guy who downplayed the necessity for these medicines when I was a kid.) Although I understood the rationale for not prescribing antibiotics immediately, I also felt that she should have been more pro-active. The situation was aggravated because I felt too bad to talk for myself or to bring up my history of allergies, asthma-like symptoms, and sinus infections that often migrated to the chest.

It was such a relief to get my appetite back after being sick that fall, and I remember being so happy to be able to venture out to church and the Christmas bazaar at Our Lady of Lourdes!

After a reasonable interval, I found Dr. Peter Morrissey in VA, and I requested that my records be transferred to him. I truthfully gave my reason as wanting to have someone as my doctor whose office was closer to my home in VA. I was very happy with Dr. Morrissey's thorough, compassionate approach for many years, until he retired. I then have Dr. Christine Baselga as my primary doctor. When she moved to Falls Church, I transferred to Dr. Janine Chu, in Arlington.

If I got sick, and then came downstairs feeling better, Vincent would always want to snuggle and love me. "Hey, kissing won't make her better!" Nana would say, laughing. Maybe not according to conventional wisdom, but it surely helped!

Vincent did another thing for me that was quite comforting. Sometimes, if my lower back bothered me, he would lie quite still on the floor and let me sit with my back up against his soft, warm back. It was much better than a heating pad!

Whenever Vincent did something unique or wonderful, Nana would ask, "What else does he have to do for you: dress you?"

In the fall of 1979, Papa and I went to Rehobeth Beach, and this time we took Vincent. We took the ferry across the Bay to Cape May. I liked this beach better than Ocean City, because it seemed quieter and more family oriented. I bought a beautiful heart-shaped scrimshaw pendant on this trip. Papa arranged to have someone hold the camera and snap a picture of him and me with Vincent. The resulting photograph is of Vincent, him, and me. It is on the first page of this chapter. Papa bought me little angel figurines on both beach trips.

We all were engrossed and fascinated when Pope John Paul II came to the United States on a visit. The young people loved him, chanting, "We want you, John Paul II." The Pope answered, "John

Paul II wants you!" Through his friends in the Pentagon, Papa was able to get a picture of the Pope with President Jimmy Carter, which I still have. He also got a picture of the Pope by himself.

Sister Hilda became ill. Papa went up to Pittsburgh, hoping to see her one more time, and he stayed for the funeral after she died. He took the picture of the Pope with him to give her. Since she died, he gave it to the Mother Superior of the convent instead.

Papa and I didn't go back to a beach again until the summer of 1981, which turned out to be our last good trip together. This time, we went to VA Beach. It was much hotter than the northern beaches, especially because it was summer instead of fall. I didn't like the heat. We also had the unpleasant experience of being refused at two restaurants, because they didn't realize that they had to let Vincent come into the restaurant. By law, guide dogs are supposed to have access to public places with their masters. We eventually got it straightened out, with the help of the Chamber of Commerce, and we were served by both places before we went home. We also took a day trip from VA Beach to Bush Gardens. Vincent was very good, even riding on the gondola between the sections of the park.

On this VA Beach trip, I made a good friend. Papa wasn't comfortable in the water, and he tried to find someone to help me go wading. One young lady was vacationing there with her friends, named Cindy Swigert. Papa asked her to help me go wading. We traded addresses, and we have kept in touch since then. Cindy is now married to Douglas Goble.

In the fall of 1981, if I remember correctly, Sister Margaret James and Aunt Maria came to visit for a few days. I don't remember whether it was a particular occasion, or maybe a "just because" visit. We enjoyed having them, but now Papa was in charge of the kitchen. He now understood the reason that both of these ladies were overweight and plump, because he was trying to satisfy their big appetites. He privately complained to me that they were like eating machines. However, one day my aunt and cousin did the cooking. They treated us to a tasty dish of meat wrapped in cabbage leaves. They called it "pigs in a blanket." I think I had it when we went to Tim's wedding, too.

Papa and I still saw movies together once in a while. We went to see the first Star Wars film together. It turned out to be the last film that we saw together in a theater. From that beginning, I acquired a love for the Star Wars series. I own the first three on video, and I have subsequently acquired the whole series of nine movies and the two sidebars on DVD. The earlier three original films, in my opinion, excel the later ones, although it's nice to satisfy one's curiosity about the background of Dark Vader and the other characters. The subsequent three round out the outcome for Luke and his protégé. The two side ones about Hans and the events leading up to the capture of the princess are interesting, but not really necessary for the basic story.

I don't remember when we did this, but Vincent did get an opportunity to go into the water. Papa and I went to visit Rita Lorenzetti (yes, my confirmation friend) and her father at their beach house on the Chesapeake Bay. Vincent had a wonderful time, playing with sticks that were thrown into the water. Meanwhile, Rita and I went wading a good distance out. Vincent finally decided that he needed to go and find me. He swam out to where we were. Once he found us, and he satisfied himself that we were all right, he started swimming back. Papa didn't want him to get tired, so Mr. Lorenzetti waded out to intercept him halfway. He let Vincent rest his rear paws on the bottom for a few minutes, with his front paws on Mr. Lorenzetti's chest. Then Vincent swam the rest of the way back to the beach.

Soon after we came home from Guiding Eyes, the school helped me to get in touch with Vincent's puppy raiser. He was a boy named Tim Holtz. We corresponded for a while. I learned many good to know things from the puppy raiser family, such as the fact that Vincent always tucked one leg sideways when he sat, which I also noticed. They also told us that they had to work with him to not be "grabby" when taking things from your hand, and he learned the word "gentle." When Tim and his family came to Washington, we got to meet each other and visit together. I felt a little sorry for Tim, because Vincent didn't make over him very much. At one point, he backed up next to me and sat down, clearly indicating that I was his master now. Tim understood. Later, when we were alone upstairs, Vincent went over to Mrs. Holtz and kissed her on the face. After all, I'm sure that she was home with him a great deal while Tim was at school, and he did remember Tim's Mama.

About this time, Mama's cousin, Jeanne Rhode, Uncle Gino's daughter in California, started corresponding with me. It was wonderful to make a new family contact. One of her sons, Ken, had a black lab, too.

Uncle Johnny and Aunt Murff still kept in touch. Uncle Johnny had retired from the Air Force, and they had settled in a house in Shalimar, FA, near Clearwater and Fort Walton Beach. Uncle Johnny embarked on making specialty candles. He made two for us, with pictures of my high school and college graduations on the sides. He still came to visit us sometimes when he was in town, telling us all about his nice house not too far from the beach, and his Japanese style bathtub. We always enjoyed his visits.

Fun and games aside, I was also trying to push the envelope in terms of what Vincent could do to help me with street crossings. I heard about a school in Palm Springs, CA, Guide Dogs of the Desert, which had trained a deaf-blind lady with a guide dog. I corresponded in Braille with this lady and met her once when she came to Washington. I contacted Guiding Eyes, to ask them to consider taking us back for additional training and work on street crossings, but they declined. I finally found a lady dog trainer, Karen Melenberg (eventually she married Bob Maida and became Karen Maida) who worked with us for a while. She did everything that she could to strengthen Vincent's traffic awareness and to help me understand what he might be trying to signal me, such as situations when he was unhappy with the traffic and the crossing. It's very important for the guide dog user to be able to "read" the dog. Through this process, I learned a great deal of useful information about the way dogs think and about the strengths and weaknesses of my particular dog. It was one of the most challenging and stimulating endeavors in which I have engaged. We did as much as we could to develop Vincent's potential and abilities, but we eventually brushed up against limitations. Guiding Eyes sent someone out to review what we were doing, but they declined to go any further. Because I pushed the envelope this way in working with Vincent, they informed me that the school would not take me again for another dog. When I inquired in 2002 about reapplying to Guiding Eyes when I was retiring Remus, they found no record of this refusal in my file. Sometimes, time does remedy difficult situations and render problems moot.

In 1980, a new friend came into my life. I went to a young adults' group outing from our church. We went to dinner at the Chesapeake Bay Fish House. I met Mary Le Sueur that evening, and we became friends. Mary was working as a physicist with the department of the Navy. She originally came from Texas, and for that reason, to keep from confusing her with Mary Ambury Spellerberg, Nana called her "Texas Mary." Mary also liked to play ball with Vincent, and she could throw balls so far that she hit the metal utility shed in the back of the yard with a great clang.

Mary also contributed to my education about what drivers of vehicles can and cannot see. When I told her that Vincent didn't like walking in front of trucks when we were doing street crossings, she said that he was smart. To demonstrate what she meant, she took me around to show me different kinds of trucks. She helped me to understand that, in some trucks, the driver's vision is blocked by the front of the truck, and the driver might not see Vincent and me crossing the street.

In 1981, Mary was transferred to Pittsburgh, and we began keeping in touch by tape. I still saw her sometimes, when she came back to the Washington area.

I felt as though my 30th birthday in November of 1981, was a landmark that should be celebrated. My childhood friend, Vickie, was working at Basco's, a discount store, in the jewelry department. She helped Papa and me to select a nice, ten-carat gold ring set with a six-millimeter pearl and a little diamond on each side of the pearl. Papa presented it to me on my birthday, once it was back from being sized. I don't remember what Nana gave me, but Barbara and Don gave me a little music box that played, "I Love You Truly," the song that Mama used to sing to me.

About this time, I also made a new friend at work. Bonita Kelly worked in opinions and review. We started bringing our lunches (if we didn't buy them) to the cafeteria in the L Street building and spending pleasant lunchtime together. Bonita shared with me some fun reminiscences of her childhood.

As Vincent grew older, to combat possible pancreatitis and to keep his weight in check, the vets put him on Hills Reducing Diet, because it was higher in fiber and lower in fat. I started using egg separators to separate the white, and I only gave him the egg white. I ate the extra yoke.

Except for losing Aunt Janie and Sister Hilda, Nana's gradual decline, and some difficult situations at work not pertinent to be discussed here, these five years were among the happiest in my life after Mama died. Papa and I were really becoming close, and Sister Hilda was right that we really would be pals eventually, although the relationship was different from the one I had with Mama. We even reminisced about her. From me, Papas found out some things that I knew that Mama never bothered to tell him, such as that she found it very aggravating when he pulled into the garage so far to the left that she had no room to get into the car on the driver's side. She had to enter through the passenger door, crawling over me to do so. Fortunately the cars then still had the straight bench seats which allowed her to do so.

To top it all off, I had achieved my goal of becoming a lawyer and had a good job, and I had a wonderful guide dog and friend, Vincent. It was the beginning of a pattern that I have mentioned to my friends many times. I may never win a money lottery, but it's enough for me to keep winning the puppy lottery and ending up with good dogs!

# "YOU ARE THE LAST OF THE WEINMUNDING LINE"

In the fall of 1981, my life began heading toward another one of those decisive points, the death of my father. As with Mama's last year, some warnings manifested themselves, but we could not clearly read them until afterwards. As with Mama's situation, God provided some timely help and support.

For one thing, I once again felt the need for emotional counseling. This time, if I remember correctly, I began seeing a lady named Sheri Halfish, and I found her very helpful. Papa was very supportive and assisted me in finding her.

I once again am having trouble reconstructing events, but I think what prompted this need for psychological counseling was an episode at work. I met a man when taking Vincent to park, who expressed some interest in me. However, I didn't know him from Adam, literally, and I didn't appreciate his assertive courting on short acquaintance. His compliments and flattery were all very fine, but I resisted and was put off by his idea that we were destined to be together. I did a great deal of praying and much soul searching and consultation with friends to make sure that I wasn't yielding to exaggerated or unwarranted fears. Carol Galbraith and I went to Calvert Cliffs in MD for a Sunday outing, which was a good place to talk and get one's thoughts together. A winding trail meanders through the woods down to the beach, crossing a little stream several times on footbridges as it goes. Down on the shore, one can see the cliffs that one has gradually descended along this path. The wind and tide have worn away the rocks, revealing fossils embedded in the cliffs. Visitors are not allowed to touch the cliffs or dig fossils out of them, but you can gather things up from the beach or the water.

Vincent jumped into the water, and he was having a great time jumping and playing in the waves. The lifeguard lady saw him, and she told us to get him out, because he was supposed to be on leash. She gave me a shark's tooth, one of the nice fossils and other neat things to be found there. I also kept a piece of composite rock that feels as though it has shells embedded in it.

I eventually decided that I wasn't comfortable making further acquaintance with this fellow, and I told him I wasn't interested, and to not call me anymore. In this time of emotional turmoil and self-doubt, I found Barbara and Don very helpful and supportive. As Barbara said about the fellow, "I sure would tell him to slow down!"

I'm pretty sure that all this happened before Papa died, but I don't remember discussing it with Papa. I know he worried about my maturing as a woman, and that he wanted me not to be afraid of life and possible relationships. He read me a poem about a timid little lassie who built up a tower and wall around herself, and when an opportunity for love came, she was afraid to take it. As the last line of the poem noted, she was cheated of heaven by its own stars. I think Papa feared that something like that would happen to me.

If I wasn't going to be courted by strangers, it made me realize that I needed to acknowledge my feelings for someone. One gentleman in law school had aroused deep feelings in me. We kept in touch by casual correspondence after we both graduated, but I finally decided that I needed to write him a letter, telling him that I had some feelings for him, and asking how he felt about exploring this further on a mutual basis. He fortunately was as honest with me as I had been with him. He thanked me, and told me that he was already involved in a relationship to which he was committed.

Although I was disappointed, it was good to know where I stood. I now understood what Papa meant when he quoted a saying from somewhere that he didn't know to the effect that, "One [sometimes] loves in inverse ratio to the amount that one is loved." My great aunts Janie and Riri said something similar when I asked them why they never married. "The right person never asked us," they said.

For another positive thing, I think it was that fall that I renewed my interest with clay. I took an adult-education course in cleaning and glazing green ware, which are unfired ceramic pieces. I didn't make these pieces, but pouring liquid slip, liquefied clay, into molds, produced them. The course was held at Thomas Jefferson High School, which was used as a community center in the evenings for these courses. Papa would bring me and come back for me, or maybe he waited in the area. I don't remember. Vincent was good, and he was a hit with everybody. I enjoyed very much cleaning – removing the seams left from the mold – the various pieces on which I worked. I made in this way a ceramic ornamental Christmas tree, into the holes of which little reflective lights are inserted. The tree is lit by a bulb and socket in the base that plug into an electric outlet. I also made a couple of angels, into which I later had music box movements inserted, some Christmas ornaments, and various other little trinket boxes and such. I kept a few things, including the tree, and I gave many other things away that year as Christmas gifts. I needed help with under glazes, which varied in color, and over glazes, too. Ellen and Papa were very helpful with the glazes. Ellen, in particular, was very good about applying the under glazes to the tiny surfaces of some of the little Christmas ornaments shaped like cathedral windows. It was a great outlet, and it started the development of my interest in pottery and clay-modeling courses, which I took after Papa died.

At work, we were looking forward to the Commission's consolidating its staff in a new building. Nancy Wolynetz had set up an advisory committee of employees with disabilities. Now, they sought volunteers for a special committee to consult about features of the new building and make sure that they were compatible with the needs of employees with disabilities. These features ranged from the emergency evacuation plan to elevators with Braille numbering to Braille and raised letter signs to hypoallergenic and fireproof carpeting. I was one of the members of this committee.

Nana was becoming increasingly paranoid. She was always a little suspicious and expectant of the worst in unfamiliar situations, but now she began obsessing with lost objects and alleging out loud that someone stole them. A description of one particular incident will illustrate this point. Among her treasures, Nana had a pie-taker, a silver-plated frame with two handles into which a Pyrex pie-baking pan could be inserted. We knew where the pie pan was, but Nana one day couldn't find the silver pie-taker frame. The significance it had for her was that one of Grandpa's brothers had given the pie-taker and dish to her. This brother, whose name I don't know, was nicknamed Houdini by the family, because he said that he was going to "come back" after he died.

Nana fussed and complained that someone "stole my pie-taker." Our previous employees were unquestionably honest, and I don't know whether anybody was working for us at this point. Nana's tirades really got under Papa's fur.

"Who wants her old pie-taker, anyhow?" Papa wanted to know. Late in the evening, after she went to bed, we found the silver frame in a drawer or on top of the china cabinet. "I'm going to take care of her really good!" Papa said. "I'm going to polish up this thing, put it with the baking dish, wrap it up with the matching pie knife, and give it back to her for Christmas! I'll tell her that Houdini brought it back!"

Fortunately, unlike her later years, Nana still had enough self-knowledge and sense of humor to appreciate that the joke was on her.

Papa wasn't exactly paranoid, but he kept goading me to exercise initiative and independence. When I would ask his advice or help with something, or just in passing, he would say to me, "What would you do if I weren't here?" or "Do what you would do if I weren't here!" It bugged me no end. I couldn't really put myself in the posture of not having him. I didn't know what I would do. We wasted so much quality time that we might have had together, because he kept bringing up these emotional issues about something that I didn't see how I could anticipate!

Meanwhile, Papa was having trouble with his shoulder. Dr. Ambury prescribed pills for the condition. They helped somewhat, but Papa didn't want to have to keep taking them. He also had flare-ups of gout.

The 24-hour intestinal virus made the rounds that year at Christmastime. Fortunately short in duration, it was extremely intense and uncomfortable. All three of us got sick, within three days of each other! That Christmas, I had to be content with Mass on TV, a new experience for me. Papa and I commiserated with Aunt Maria by telephone about how bad it was. The darn germ came to Pittsburgh, too!

["Linda] asked me 'Am I dying, Papa?'" Papa told Aunt Maria.

It really made me feel so bad, and I still remember how awful it was. Even Nana got it, which was very unusual for her. After Papa and I were recovered enough to go out, we came home to find that Nana had sprayed our chairs and the phones with disinfectant! Papa complained that it was enough to make us sick again. Over the next few weeks, Papa had some vomiting episodes, but he and I thought it was a relapse from the virus. I did notice that he seemed to be hoarse and to have a frog in his throat, but I put it down to allergies.

On January 13, 1982, on one snowy evening, Papa called me at work and said, "I'm not about to fight with that traffic tonight in the snow. You'd better come home on the subway."

I took the subway back to Crystal City, where Papa met me and Vincent. He didn't drive there in the snow, and we three "mushed" home in the snow. When we got home and turned on the news, we found out about the Air Florida crash that had knocked cars off the Fourteenth Street Bridge, the one he probably would have taken. We also heard about the crash in the metro near the Federal Triangle station. People were killed in both incidents. It gave us all the shakes, after the fact! Through the intervention of Divine Providence, Papa wasn't on the bridge, and I wasn't near Federal Triangle!

The next day, we walked over to Barbara and Don's house to discuss the close call we had. It was a sobering experience for all of us!

By God's grace, I made both Papa and Nana Valentine's day cards that year. I wrote them each a note, thanking them for what they had done and asking forgiveness for some of the things I did. Nana laughed at hers, but she still appreciated it. We found Papa's among his papers.

Similar to what I had done with Diana, Papa took me to meet Bonita Kelly in Crystal City for some shopping before Easter. I bought a pair of earrings (clips, can't use pierced,) and a gold-plated butterfly necklace with enamel on the butterfly on a short chain. Papa suggested that I let Nana give the butterfly to me for Easter, since she couldn't get out to find something. Nana went along, happily telling me to hold onto that gold butterfly. It grieved me that she no longer knew the difference between the fine jewelry and the costume jewelry, but I was glad to go along with it and make her happy.

I think that Papa sensed that something was seriously wrong with him physically. At one point, he said to me, in passing, "I'll keep going as long as I can for you."

As the spring arrived, it became increasingly obvious to me that Papa wasn't well. As I said, it started a little while before then with hoarseness and a cracked voice that didn't go away. At first we put it down to allergies, but it became apparent that he just wasn't himself. He also seemed to know that something was very amiss. Often, when I came home after work, I would ask him how his day was, and he said that he was going through pictures. I didn't think anything of it, because he needed to sort out his things. I knew from visiting him at the office in the Pentagon that he kept an untidy desk at work, and I suspected his pictures and papers at home were in the same state.

At some point, Papa decided to replace his Rolex watch. He bought a nice, battery-powered Seiko calendar watch. He sold the Rolex, but he kept an old watch for use in situations that he didn't want to take the Seiko.

I was seeing the nurses in the SEC Health Unit for allergy injections. The nurse there at that time was very sympathetic and helpful. Her name was Brenda Tejada, and I was grateful that God put her in my orbit at this time. I began to worry that I was seeing the unraveling of someone I cared about, just as I had with Mama. Part of me feared the worst, but I still tried to hope for the best.

I had wanted to go away for a little mini-vacation, but Papa resisted. In the spring, he asked me if I wanted to go. I told him, "No, let's wait until you are feeling better." I didn't want to make him go if he didn't feel well. Had we known then what we later found out, we might have gone. Even if we didn't we would have decided with our eyes open. After he died, I had to wrestle with the added grief and feeling of being cheated of one last trip together. However, I console myself by reflecting that, at least, I made my decision with his best interest at heart. At least, I didn't have to reproach myself on that regard. We aimed for less ambitious outings instead of a long vacation. We bought tickets for the Pete Seeger concert in the DC area in mid-July.

In the spring, in May or early June, we had the house painted on the outside trim and the wooden windows and frames. It meant that the windows were open. One night, I went to get ready for bed, and I put my foot in my bedroom slipper. Something stung my toe.

"Papa, owe! My toe!" I screamed. I didn't know Papa could get upstairs so fast. I felt bad about making him come, but I didn't know what bit me!

Papa caught the wasp and put it in a glass with some sugar water overnight. The insect came in through the open window and was attracted to the fragrant powder that I put in my slippers. I'm sure that he didn't like my big toe thrusting in there to squish him.

Meanwhile, I spent a miserable night with my sore toe. Next day, Brenda removed the stinger. "And you were worried about his heart!" she said, when I told her how fast Papa came upstairs. When I came home from work, Papa looked up the critter in the dictionary. Then we took him outside and let him go.

During that spring, I also remember getting a little virus or cold myself. I enjoyed being able to rest and pamper myself. On either this or another similar occasion, I came downstairs when I was recuperating and ended up lying on the couch with Papa and watching a made for TV movie, "Shootout in a One-Dog Town." We both enjoyed it very much. In 2020, I bought a video copy of it to play for memory's sake from time to time. I also took advantage of the recuperating time to read *The Wizard of Oz* for the first time.

In late May or early June, our broker at Paine Webber, John Deane, had a Labrador female that had puppies. He asked Papa to come and take pictures of them. I went with Papa to take the pictures. Papa put one puppy in my lap, which was fine with me, and then he floored me by putting a second one in my lap. He took a picture of me with the two puppies and this "How could you do that to me?" expression on my face. I think that this set of pictures was the last that he took. I kept them in the album with my guide dog pictures.

June also meant that we were coming up to convention time. Two big organizations try to look out for the interests of blind people. They are the National Federation of the Blind (which tends to emphasize can-do and independence at all costs) and the American Counsel of the Blind. I was a member of two ACB affiliates, Guide Dog Users Inc. and American Blind Lawyers Association (think it has since changed its name.) The conventions of these affiliates that year in 1982 were in

Atlanta in early July. I signed up to go, but I had learned from previous years that it was better for me to have someone with me. Papa had gone with me to these conventions when they were held in Grand Rapids, Michigan, I think in 1978, after I had Vincent.

Papa's appetite began to fail. He decided to get a second opinion from his previous doctor, Dr. Williams. I went with him for the appointment. The physical exam revealed what Dr. Williams thought was an aneurism in the aorta that goes down into the abdomen. Dr. Williams told Papa that he would need to go into the hospital for tests, and that he should try to eat more, because he was losing too much weight.

It became increasingly obvious to me that Papa wouldn't be able to go with me. I found someone else to accompany me, Norma Villani. Her husband was a friend of Papa's, and he had been a member of our church. He died from kidney disease, but Norma was also our friend, and she agreed to go with me.

The Friday before we were to leave, Papa and I went to the Hot Shop for dinner, and then we came home. Vincent wanted to play.

"Not tonight, George. I just don't feel like it," Papa told him.

A little while later, Nana came to find me. "Do you know where Vincent is?" she asked rhetorically. "He's lying on the floor at the bottom of Papa's bed."

Faithful loyal Vincent! It didn't need any translation. "It's OK if you don't want to play with me. I know you don't feel good, and I'll stay with you."

We were to leave July 4, Sunday. As I was getting ready to leave, Nana said, "Don't go."

"I can always come back," I told her.

I wondered if I should go, too, and I raised my dilemma with Don Sheehan, who took us to the airport. "Maybe if you go," Don told me. "He will realize that he has to go and get this taken care of."

Norma and I flew to Atlanta on Piedmont Airlines. We made a couple of stopovers en route, and we took Vincent to relieve himself on one of them. Poor Vincent didn't like the flying. We worried that he might not get back on the plane, but he did.

We enjoyed ourselves for the Sunday evening. The program on Monday was interesting. I don't clearly remember what it was about. In the afternoon, we came back to my room to check messages. It was Papa on the telephone.

"Please come home. I need you to come home. I have to go into the hospital." Of course, I said that I would come. Inside, all that I could think was, "Couldn't he have given me one more day?" I was supposed to go home Wednesday. I frankly was enjoying myself, and deep down, I suspected that I was walking into deep trouble that I would have to face in going home. I'm sorry to have to admit this, but a selfish part of me wanted to put off facing the trouble as long as possible.

However, I knew that, if Papa needed me to come, it must be serious, and he probably was worried and scared.

Practical, wise Norma suggested that we have a nice dinner and try to make the best of the evening. The next day, we went to the airport and changed our flight to a direct flight back to National Airport, on a different airline maybe. It cost more money, but it didn't make sense to put Vincent and us through the stopovers.

"Thank God for money," Norma told me. "And that we can use it to help ourselves!" If only everything else in life could be solved this easily!

I arrived home Tuesday to find that Aunt Maria had come from Pittsburgh on the bus. Nana put her up in my parents' room, and not upstairs with me. Of course, had Papa come home from the hospital, we would have needed a different arrangement, but Nana rightly figured in the meantime that I needed my privacy. Nana was not on comfortable terms with Aunt Maria.

We saw Papa in Alexandria Hospital that afternoon, and they were taking tests. He thanked Aunt Maria for coming and being there with him. He asked me to buy him a new pair of pajamas. I found two good pairs for him.

By the foresight of Divine Providence, before I went to Atlanta, Darlene, my assistant at the Commission, brought me some Red Zinger loose tea that she bought at a farmer's market. I tried some, and I found that it was very soothing and made me drowsy, so I was only drinking it at night. When I got home from Atlanta and realized that Nana did not get along well with Aunt Maria, I liberally dosed Nana with that tea, encouraging her to drink it. I drank it myself, because I also needed its soothing effects. I hoped and prayed that the tea would keep Nana calm, and that we wouldn't have any big, explosive arguments! By God's grace, we didn't. As usual, Ellen was the unpredictable wild card in the emotional mix. I never found out what was in that tea; it had some kind of spice of whatever in it that had much stronger effects than anything that Sleepy Time puts out. I gave the jar back to Darlene when it was empty; I never had any more of it ever again. It was there when we needed it.

During those tense, anxious days, Vincent did what he could to run interference for me. If Ellen or someone else seemed to be getting on my nerves, he would come over to them and ask to go out. The person, suspecting nothing, would happily go to the back door to let him out, and eventually they would go to let him back inside. He thus created a minute or two of space for me to get myself together. I didn't dare praise him out loud, but I think he knew that I was happy with what he was doing.

In the next few days, the following events happened, although I don't clearly remember the order. The tests, particularly the CT scan, revealed that Papa had inoperable, terminal lung cancer. The doctors discussed the treatments with me, but they decided to do some mild chemotherapy to try to control symptoms. Obviously, dealing with the abdominal aorta was now a lower priority, given the severity of the diagnosis. They moved Papa into pulmonary intensive care.

When the diagnosis came, I remember sitting at the dining room table and crying. Ellen tried to console me, telling me that it was "all right."

"Nothing is ever going to be all right again," I said. I couldn't help reflecting that, in the face of this terrible sorrow, all of our disputes and arguments seemed so petty and meaningless!

Nana's prayer was that somehow Papa could come home. "We'll take care of everything," she said. "He can just sit and direct traffic."

When Papa first told me, I said, "Oh no! I want you to rock my babies!"

Papa wasn't kidding himself. He knew that he was dying. He asked me to take one of the pairs of pajamas back. I was sufficiently in denial that I couldn't bring myself to do that. It almost seemed to me that, if I did, I would be conceding the inevitable, and I wasn't ready to do it.

Papa told me to sell the car (which I decided not to do as it turned out.) When I said something to him about things at work, he said, "Put some water on your back and keep on going!"

He asked me to tell the parish church that they could keep the proceeds of one of the $500 notes that he gave them to pay parish debts, if they would say Masses for him perpetually. After Papa's death, I approached our parish with Papa's proposal, but the pastor told me that they couldn't do that. They repaid all five notes when our turn came. After Father Seamus established his Augustinian monastery, to be discussed in a later chapter, I donated that money and some extra to the monastery, requesting that they say Masses for my parents and my little siblings.

Papa tried to make me promise that I would never use a machine, like a respirator, on him. I couldn't do it. I did discuss the use of such a device with the doctors, but it didn't seem indicated, anyway, and it became a moot point.

A little incident one Sunday will indicate the tense dynamic in my house. Aunt Maria and Ellen were going to be driven to church. I said that was fine, but I preferred to walk with Vincent. They insisted that I drive with them. Mike Geltner understood.

"They are trying to treat you like a little kid," he said.

The Amburies, law school Judy, the Spellerbergs, Texas Mary, and my other friends were very supportive. Father Seamus sent me a very consoling message on cassette tape. He said that he was praying for us, and he spoke of how a loving Jesus wanted to heal Papa. As it turned out, the way that He chose to heal him was to call him Home to Heaven.

Because we didn't know how long we had, at some point Aunt Maria decided to go back to Pittsburgh. Strange as it might sound, I was glad to be on my own with this problem. Nana and I had already gone through the unthinkable in losing Mama; we would have to face this time together, too.

At some point early in the second week, Cousin Jim came for a visit with Papa. I think that I was perhaps at work when Jim came to see Papa. They had a visit, and Jim took notes of what they discussed, which I will describe later in the next chapter.

Sue Blain came to stay with me for a few days. She could drive, and she was able to drive Papa's car, so I could get around with more independence. Sue was in the process of entering the SND's, but I don't remember whether she was a postulant or a novice. As things later turned out, the last that I heard, she did not enter the order. However, at the time Nana was quite upset at the idea of Sue becoming a nun.

"I hope that some nice, young man comes and keeps you out of that convent!" Nana told her.

I was embarrassed at Nana's bluntness, but Sue took it in stride and laughed.

"Nana rattles your cage to get you riled up, and she's laughing at you. Don't you know that she has a Yankee sense of humor?" Sue insisted. She helped me appreciate Nana and understand her better.

I started to look for a nurse/assistant type of person to come and help us if Papa did come home from the hospital, however temporarily. I interviewed one nice lady who might have fit the bill. We never got to find out whether it would have worked with her or not.

Wednesday or Thursday of the second week, the doctors decided that they needed to do a procedure on Papa. Fluid was building up around his heart. They opened his chest and inserted a drain. Before he went into surgery, Papa asked to see a priest.

Sue and I went to Our Lady of Lourdes rectory. We found Father Gerloff there, and we asked him to come. He said no, he could not; he needed to go and say the weekday noon Mass. Sue and I left.

In the car, we mutually expressed our shock, disappointment, and frustration. We thought that he should have put a note on the church door, saying that he was called away to a sick bed, and asking people to pray until he got back. I've waited in many a doctor's waiting room, because somebody else had a greater need than I.

"And they say that they won't ordain women!" Sue exclaimed. I think that the facts here speak for themselves! Yes, the hospital chaplains were available, and I'm sure that Papa was given Last Rites at some point before he died, but at that point, he was asking for his community pastor.

Papa came through the procedure all right, but now they moved him into cardiac intensive care. I liked the nurses in this unit much better. They didn't talk down to him, as though he was a little kid. Ellen came with us to the hospital on at least one occasion. He now was under oxygen. The facemask made it hard for me to understand him.

Vincent came with Sue and me to see Papa on one visit. He walked over and put his head on the bed, and then he lay down next to the bed. I am glad that he and Papa saw each other one last time. The nurses in the unit liked Vincent, too, and were impressed with him. They told me that I could bring him back again, but I wanted to be careful. I didn't want anybody to raise objections. Those wise ladies knew what was important. When it may not be possible to prolong or save earthly life, other things, such as being with loved ones, human and canine, become more important.

On Saturday, July 17, Sue and I went to see Papa in the morning. I was having trouble understanding him with the mask, and I asked if he could use the nasal oxygen while I was there. We almost got into an argument about it. I'm so glad that I didn't, but told him to do whatever worked for him. I have read since then that sometimes, as part of the self-protective mechanism in cases of pending death, people get into arguments to ease the pain of separation. I'm so glad that, by God's grace, I didn't fall into this trap.

Sue and I went home. For some reason, I just sat, even though I had things in mind that I needed to do. Finally, I called Mary Spellerberg. I was on the phone with her when the operator interrupted the call. It was the hospital. Papa had taken a turn for the worse, and I had to come back.

When we got there, Papa was still sitting up in the chair, but now he had the oxygen mask on his face. He was having such horrible trouble breathing and was gasping for breath. I told him that I loved him. He said, "I love you, too, Honey." It was the last full sentence that I heard him speak.

From then on, all he could do was say, "Help, help." I told him not to worry, that all of our time together was worthwhile, not to feel bad about anything. I told him that Jesus, crucified on the cross, couldn't breathe either.

I told Sue that I wished that some Pentecostals were around to pray for him and us. She said, in effect, that we could do what they did. I took Papa's rosary and gave him mine. Sue and I prayed the rosary aloud. We said the Regina Caeli between rosaries. This prayer speaks to Mary, the Queen of

Heaven, about Jesus' resurrection, and it asks God through her intercession to bring us to the joys of eternal life. We got about two and a half times around the rosary.

The nurse came through. She said that he seemed a little better. "Just keep doing what you are doing," she encouraged us.

I still wanted him to get better, but part of me knew that he could not. All that I could think was, "Suppose we win this round? Will we have to go through this all again?"

Sue brought me a wet face towel for my face. I didn't feel like I deserved anything. We were with him, but we didn't quite know what to do for him. A little later, Papa said, "Sponge off my thighs!"

The nurses came, and they asked us to step outside so that they could put him back in bed. When they let us back into the room, they told us that the end was very near. I think I just said, "No."

Sue and I and the nurse were patting and holding him. Then, everything slowed down and stopped. He was conscious up to the last second.

The last thing that I said to him was, "I'll be the big lady that you always wanted. I promise I'll make you proud of me!"

The nurse told me that he was gone. I put my hand on his wrist, and his body felt empty to me. All that I was holding was an empty shell. I knew that Papa's soul had left his body. To people who doubt the existence of life after death, I can only respond that I saw my father go, and he went somewhere else.

When I first got Vincent, Papa used to say that he didn't understand what all the ladies saw in Vincent, that they wanted to pat him. On one occasion, he said, "I wish that I was a dog, so that all the ladies would pat me, too!" On his deathbed, he got what he wanted. He died, like a king, with Sue and the nurse and me all holding him and patting him. He died with us praying for him. Mama and St. Joseph must have been praying for him, because he had a "happy death," in the Christian sense of the word.

When they said he was gone, I wanted to cry, but then I stopped, because I could only think that he was still watching me. My next thought was, "I can't throw balls far enough for my pal. How am I going to tell Nana?"

Later, when the nurses washed Papa's body, they found the old watch still on his wrist, and they gave it back to me later. I had the movement taken out of its case and put into a pendant case. Since I was not to have Nana's watch, for the reasons explained in the next chapter, I wanted a pendant watch that was part of family history, too. That particular movement had numbers that were raised enough to feel.

After it was over, we walked outside into the July heat, and I was amazed at how hot it was outside. I felt as though I had been far, far away.

When Sue and I walked into the house, Nana didn't need to be told. Maybe she read my face, but somehow she knew.

"Did Papa die?" she asked.

I said yes. Aunt Maria, later on the telephone, said that she was just grateful that he wasn't alone and that I was with him.

In the days that followed, Nana expressed how hard Papa's death hit her. "Dear God, why didn't you take me?" she asked the Lord. "I was old, but Linda needed her father!" We knew it hit her hard because she would never admit before that she was old. Part of me agreed with what Nana said on an emotional level, especially as Nana's mental and psychological condition deteriorated, but I also realized that God has his reasons and his times. As events turned out, it was providential that Nana remained with us a few more years, especially for her sake.

During the following days, it was my turn to have to make decisions about the funeral and the rites for the dead. However, the first decision that I had to make was whether to have an autopsy. I said yes, because, like Papa in the hospital, I wanted answers. The autopsy, as explained to me by Harry Malek later, showed that my father died from the effects of lung cancer, but the cancer was all over his body. The disconcerting thing that it also showed was that the lung cancer, which spread throughout the body, wasn't the original source of the cancer, but they could not find the primary source.

Fortunately, Everly-Wheatley, the funeral home, still had records of the arrangements that were made for Mama. I did things similarly for Papa. I ordered a blanket of roses to cover the casket. For some reason, I felt best when I was sitting beside his casket during the viewing.

Sue Blain helped me to select the readings for the Requiem Mass, including the Gospel reading about the raising of Lazarus from the dead and the hymn, "I Am the Bread of Life." I was very grateful to have her with me.

So many people, including Father O'Connell, came up to me at the viewing and said that Papa called them while I was in Atlanta. He must have spent his last days at home while I was away on the phone, trying to reach out to people for himself and to help me. Father O'Connell said that Papa kept saying, "See to Linda." I regret to have to say that so many of those people never followed up with me afterwards! Papa, and Mama, too, reached out to people in their dying days, and it turned out to be in vain. Part of me is still angry on their behalf when I remember how hard they tried for me and how little support they got from other people they cared for and had befriended. Still, I know I need to forgive and let go, with God's help. As I read or heard someone say at some point, sooner or later, we all have to forgive one another for not being God. In other words, our expectations of others often are unrealistic. In the end, it didn't matter that so many people didn't follow up with me, because God directly and through my friends and volunteers saw me through this loss and the other crises in my life.

Some of the loving acts of my friends were truly memorable. Sister Elizabeth Henry was in England when Papa died, or during the following year. She was either doing research or shepherding the Trinity sophomores who were spending a year studying abroad. M. E. had participated in this program in the late '60's. Anyway, Sister Elizabeth Henry, remembering that I was looking for a lamb for my Easter displays, sent me a beautiful stuffed lamb, with long fuzzy ears and felt paws. I still have it.

Nana understood right away. "Oh, isn't that nice! She sent you a little lamb to comfort you!" Nana exclaimed.

As far as the viewing and the funeral were concerned, of course, Aunt Maria and Cousin Jim and Connie came. So did many of my friends, including, I think General Williams. He knew Papa because he was in the Judge Advocate Corps in the army, and they met at the Pentagon. He and I also became friends, especially when he learned that I was becoming a lawyer. We kept in touch after Papa's death, until General Williams died.

The Director of Consumer Affairs at work, Robert Wolf, came to the viewing, too. As He said, "it is a hard blow." I don't remember if Cousin Tom, who was working in the area for Woody's at some point, came. I really didn't keep close track mentally of who was and wasn't there in terms of my long-term memory.

I found out that Gretchen was fighting her own battle with a serious lung condition about the time of Papa's illness and death. She was diagnosed with a fungal infection, aspergillosis, and one of her lungs had to be removed in surgery. She was in the ICU herself when Papa died. After her recovery, she did her best to keep in touch with me after Papa's death.

During the viewing, Father Gerloff was going to come to lead the rosary one evening during the viewing. I asked Father Hurley of Germantown, MD, to come, too. He and I together served on the advisory board for the Metropolitan Washington Ear, a close-circuit radio reading service for the blind and others prevented from reading printed material. He met Papa when Papa drove me to the board meetings. I wanted someone who really knew Papa to be involved. Unfortunately, Father Gerloff, for whatever reason, was praying so fast when he led the prayers (they alternated leading the decades of the rosary) that I felt that it was inappropriate. Father Hurley assured me in an undertone that he would slow things down. When it was his turn to lead the prayers, he spoke as slowly, distinctly, and reverently as Father Gerloff was fast and hurried. Inwardly I smiled, despite the sad occasion. I don't think that anybody else noticed what was happening they probably thought that it was just different styles of praying.

Connie suggested that I put something into the casket with Papa. I put a crucifix that Father Comaskey had brought back from Ireland many years before for Papa. We had it hanging in Nana's room, because other rooms already had wall crosses. We placed it on Papa's chest.

At the bank, the wonderful lady was very kind. She put off official notification of death (with the consequent freezing of accounts) long enough for me to write some necessary checks on the account. I had a durable power of attorney, and I was Papa's executor and sole legatee, but other things would have to wait until the will was filed in court.

The funeral Mass was at Our Lady of Lourdes Church, with burial beside Mama at Fairfax Memorial Park. At the conclusion of the prayer at the cemetery, I stood up.

"Papa was a veteran and did his part," I said. "I want to sing Taps." I knew that I couldn't carry a tune, but I sang it anyway.

> Day is done!
> Gone the sun
> From the hills, from the plains,
> From the sky!
> All is well!
> Safely Rest!
> God is nigh!

After I came home from the cemetery, I felt exhausted and drained. Suddenly, I remembered the Pete Seeger tickets. One of my friends said that she would go with me, if I still wanted to go. I knew that Papa in heaven wouldn't mind if I went, because we both enjoyed Pete's specials on TV, especially his song about growing old and another one about the problems with garbage. However, I didn't have the energy or the heart to go. I said that I would catch Pete Seeger another time.

It was not to be. I became engrossed in other matters, and the opportunity never came my way again that I recall. Dear old wonderful Pete now is gone, too. I'm grateful that I still have many of his record albums, as well as a CD and DVD from a WETA TV PBS special.

Sue stayed with me a few more days after the funeral to help me get adjusted. During that time, we had to take Vincent to the vet for one of his ear infections. They gave us medicine to put in his ears that had to be kept in the refrigerator. Sue at first wasn't comfortable with dogs, but she tried to help me take care of poor Vincent with his inflamed ears.

On one occasion, she said to him, "Poor old Vincent! For all you know, we could be putting ketchup in your ears!"

He heard the sympathy in her voice and put his paws up on her legs and kissed her and tickled her legs. She became a fan of his after that.

Alberta, (who was married to George Gilbert by this time,) Jo Ann Scott, and law school Judy were also very helpful and supportive. They said that they would help me transition to find ways of getting things done in the way of checks, bills, and paperwork, now that Papa wasn't physically with me anymore. They were as good as their word.

The title of this chapter is taken from Beowulf's last words to Wiglaf, the only comrade who stood with him in fighting the dragon. Beowulf had no children. He told Wiglaf, in effect, that he was his heir, that he was the last of the Weinmunding line. I was in a similar position. Everything that Papa had was mine, but I would have given anything to be only Papa's daughter again.

# "YOU ARE THE CAPTAIN ..."

What follows is a reconstruction of events in the five years between Papa's death and the end of 1987. So much happened in a relatively short period of time that I am finding it hard to put these events in the proper order.

As I mentioned in the earlier chapter, it probably was a good thing that I began seeing a counselor before Papa's death, and I continued to see Dr. Halfish for a while after he died, because it gave me a forum for trying to deal with some of the emotional feelings and conflicts occasioned by his death and aggravated by situations at work. On the one hand, I was relieved that Papa wasn't hurting anymore and that I didn't have to worry about him. I was glad that I could be with him at the end, however difficult that was. On the other hand, another big piece of my world, support structure, and security was gone. I also had to wrestle with my feelings of being cheated out of the opportunity for one more last good trip together, which I have already mentioned in the last chapter.

Things were difficult and in transition at work, too. At some point during this period, God again provided me with some comfort and consolation. One night, I was lying in bed, and I was confronting the fact that I didn't want to go back into that office again the next day!

"Mama, I don't want to go in there tomorrow!" I cried in anguish.

I can only say that I experienced a sensation of overwhelming comfort and love. At the time, I associated it with Mama, but it may have been from God directly! I won't try to make that determination.

Nana was both a comfort and a burden. She mourned for Papa, of course. She tried to give me a vote of supreme confidence. When I wanted to cry or became discouraged, Nana would say, "Now, you are the Captain, and Vincent and I are the crew. If the captain falls down, what will happen to the rest of us?"

I appreciated very much her confidence in me, but it also restricted my freedom to mourn and vent very real emotions. Moreover, I wasn't used to being the boss, or the captain, or whatever you wanted to call it, except that I had learned to be "pack leader" of the guide dog user/dog team made up of Vincent and me.

When I was a young girl, I didn't understand how Mama could argue or speak sharply to her mother, Nana. After Mama died, I often wished that Papa and Nana could get along better than they did. Now that both of my parents were gone, I had to deal directly with Nana and all the aspects of her personality, including her temper, strong will, stubbornness, and deterioration from old age. I have learned from this turn of events that people should be very careful not to judge others in their approach to their problems and crosses.

It was as though God were saying to me, "All right. If you think you can do better, here is the same hand of cards they had. See what you make of it or how well you do." I'm not sure that I did much better than my parents did. Only He knows how well I succeeded or where I failed!

Vincent, too, mourned for Papa in his own way. If anything, he became even more loyal and supportive of me. Also, if I cried before Papa's death, Vincent would come over to me and try to comfort me and have me stop. After Papa died, he didn't do that anymore. I think it was because he knew why I was crying, and maybe he wanted to cry, too. One day, I went looking for him, and I found him in my parents' room, (which was still unoccupied, as we had no live-in employees yet). Vincent was lying on the floor near the bottom of the bed, where he waited for Papa that last Friday evening. I went and sat on the floor next to him and hugged him.

I couldn't resist quoting Shakespeare's Macbeth to Vincent. "'Wake Duncan with thy knocking; I would thou couldst.'"

However, I didn't have too much time to mourn and brood. I now had to deal with the entire household situation, find ways to get things done that Papa used to do, work on getting Papa's will through probate with Mike Geltner's help, and make decisions about markers for my parents' graves. In addition, the SEC was preparing to move most of its employees, including the Office of Consumer Affairs, out of their three Washington, DC buildings and into the new building at 450 5th Street, NW, in late August or early September of 1982.

I think that I must have taken a week or two of annual leave right after Papa's death, but the memory is quite fuzzy in my mind. However it was, it soon became clear to me that I was going to need at least part-time help. Nana was no longer capable of maintaining the housekeeping or cleaning. I had made progress in the cooking endeavor, but it still took me longer than the average Jill. I didn't think that I would be able to come from a long day at work and put together a decent dinner from scratch at a reasonable hour.

One person who was very supportive after Papa died was Al Miller's wife, Sigrid. She often came to check on us on Sunday afternoons, and I think that she may also have helped to keep flowers on the graves in the cemetery when I wasn't able to get there. Nana, too, recognized that we probably would have to hire someone. One summer Sunday afternoon, when Sigrid came, Nana asked for her help in solving something that was on her mind. She knew that alcoholic beverages could be an irresistible temptation to some folks. She gathered together all the alcoholic beverages in the house that she could find.

"Sigrid, Al likes this kind of thing, doesn't he?" Nana said. "Please take all of this stuff out of here. It's downstairs in a bag. I'll go down and open the garage door for you, and you can take it out to your car."

"All right, Nana," Sigrid told her in her pleasant, German accented voice. "I'll take it all away, and then you won't have to worry about it anymore."

Although it's out of chronological order, I think that I had better relate the sequel to this story. Years after this, Sigrid died, and I lost track of the Millers. A few years ago, I decided to try to find Al, just to say "Hi." If we weren't going to keep in touch, I didn't want the fault to be mine. I tracked down what I thought was his number and left a message. He called me back a week or so later.

In case I hadn't done so before, I mentioned that I heard that Sigrid had died, and I expressed my condolences and said that we missed her. Al had since remarried, but he and I spoke with loving remembrance of Sigrid. In the course of the conversation, I mentioned to him how helpful she was to us after Papa died, and that she had checked frequently on how we were doing. I even told him how she had helped Nana get rid of the alcoholic beverages, including the partly used wine and whiskey bottles and the leftover beers.

"Oh," said Al. "So that's where the sour beer came from? She never said where it came from. You know, beer goes sour, too, if it stays around too long after it's opened." We laughed. It was the last contact I had with Al.

In the months after Papa's death, Barbara and Don were still quite helpful and supportive. Barbara took me to do errands and to get my hair done. One day, when she took me to the bank, I was finding the delays and complications of dealing with bills and paperwork especially frustrating.

"The devil is tempting me to get upset now," I told Barbara.

"Oh, no! Tell him 'shoo! Shoo!'" Barbara said, like you would for a fly or other bothersome insect. "We don't have time for him! Shoo!"

Her remark made me laugh and defused the tensions. I also had occasion to reflect that this is the power and confidence of a good Christian person, who is well-grounded in the Lord! People like this know very well how to put the devil in his place; he definitely doesn't like wholesome laughter and not being taken seriously, and with God's grace behind us, his power is really minimized.

In a later meditation, I asked the Lord why, if the Devil is in hell, he still can get out and tempt us. I knew that Misery loves company, and Hell is a state not a place, but I thought that something else was involved. I seemed to hear God's answer, "Because people let him out!" I guess they do, whether from weakness, carelessness, or for their own purposes, thinking wrongly and foolishly that they can control him once they do. Now, often when I am tempted I remember Barbara's words and picture myself throwing the Devil's key into the next county!

At the recommendation of General Williams, I consulted a wonderful agency, Mothers Indeed. They sent me a couple of temporary people, but we eventually found Margie Locke. She worked for the Department of Recreation in Washington, DC, but her hours were such that she was able to come to my house between 10 A.M. and 2 or 3 P.M. Sometimes, her schedule was such that she could come early and get me into work in the morning. She did the cleaning, cooking, and the laundry, and she prepared dinner in advance so that I only had to heat it when I came home. Margie worked for me this way until the summer of 1983. After that, she helped out on weekends with Nana. She drove me to do errands and, while she worked for me during the week, sometimes to medical appointments.

When Margie was little and growing up, her mother was blind, and Margie was comfortable working and being with a blind person. Although she was originally from one of the Carolinas, Margie had worked with the Job Corps program in Maine. She learned to appreciate the fun of snow and to drive in it. We both enjoyed snowy times. Margie also sometimes would pose my dolls in funny positions on my bed, to make me laugh when I found them with their legs up in the air in kicking positions! I remained friends with Margie and kept in touch with her, until she died in 2019 at the age of 82.

Having Margie working for me solved the problem of the inside housekeeping for a time, but I also had to find companies or people to take care of the trees, trim the azaleas and what roses we had left, and mow the lawn and pick up the yard after Vincent and eventually Mikki. I won't go into the details of who did what, except to say that it has been a struggle over the years to find competent, reliable help in this area that doesn't believe in fertilizers and other chemicals that could be harmful to the environment or the dogs.

As I mentioned in the last chapter, I didn't sell the Grenada, but title had to be transferred to me. I had to add my employees with drivers' licenses to my auto insurance policy so that they would be covered while driving my car. Although at first blush it might seem strange that a blind lady would want a car, the reality is that taxis and even services like Uber and Lift are very expensive if used regularly, Para transit, though less expensive, cannot be relied upon to get anywhere on time, and for someone like me with a hearing loss getting around by public transportation with the resulting necessity to cross streets isn't very practical. The cars are getting quieter, and drivers are becoming more distracted, aggressive, and reckless. Moreover, my employees who had their own cars were not always willing to transport me with my dog, which meant getting hair and muddy paws in their cars, and the situation is aggravated if the dog is having a medical problem or is aging and has unreliable body functions.

In addition to the requirement to add my employees to my auto insurance policy, I also had to start doing the quarterly federal filings for withholding social security taxes and income taxes, the parallel state filing, and the unemployment insurance state filing. For a while, I tried to do these filings with the help of volunteers, but eventually they had to be added to my accountant's work, along with my state and federal income tax filings.

Although Mike Geltner was responsible for the court filings in connection with probating Papa's will and for preparing the final accounting that had to be filed in court, I still had to marshal all Papa's assets and get title to the house and car, and I had to have his securities transferred to me. I also had to make the necessary reporting filings on the securities that I now owned at work. Employees at the SEC are subject to restrictions on holding some securities, minimal holding periods for others that we are allowed to hold, and requirements to report what we have to the SEC. As a member of my household, Papa's securities had to be reported along with mine, even when he was alive. However, he did not want me to know about or deal with his personal business in this regard, which was fine with me. As an accommodation, the SEC allowed Papa to file separate holding reports directly with them, as though he were an employee, to satisfy my reporting requirements. After he died, however, I became responsible for everything as long as I was employed there until I retired.

In addition to dealing with the complexities of Papa's securities holdings and general financial matters, the bills now also were all mine. I found out in concrete terms just how inflexible and inelastic money is: you either have it in the necessary amount for whatever you need or want to buy, or you don't. Experience is the best teacher about this reality.

Another matter that I had to consider involved the notes left by Cousin Jim of his last conversation with Papa. According to Jim's notes, Papa expressed a wish to try to get to the bottom of his situation and how he came to be so sick. He remembered that he had a reaction to the antibiotics that made his mouth sore in 1971, and he associated it with the soreness that the chemotherapy was causing. He implied that maybe this condition began back in 1971. I could understand his making the connection in his mind, but I knew that this possibility wasn't likely. From experiences that Billie Long had, to be discussed later, and from what Harry Malek told me after reviewing Papa's autopsy, lung cancer can be very hard to diagnose early enough to be successfully treated. Papa's shoulder pain may have been an unrecognized early warning, but the diagnosis wasn't made in time. In addition, I knew about the work that Papa did in burning film to get ashes from which silver could be refined. As discussed in the earlier chapter, I'm sure that Papa was exposed to a great deal of noxious and toxic substances in this work, and they probably contributed to his developing cancer.

The second matter that Jim's notes covered was harder to resolve. Papa asked Jim if there was anything he would like. Jim said that he always admired Papa's snake ring with the diamond, and that he would like to have it. Papa told him that the ring was lost. He then said, according to Jim's notes, that he had a tiger's eye ring. I agonized over whether I was required to give Jim Papa's ring. If Papa wanted it done, I would have to honor it. I finally took advantage of the fact that the notes didn't add, "And you can have it." Instead, I sent Jim Papa's Seiko watch, with a letter of explanation. I told Jim that I wanted to keep Papa's ring, because I could at least wear it on a chain as a pendant. The watch would do me no good. I also sent Aunt Maria penknives for her sons, and I sent a rosary to Gretchen. I gave Aunt Maria the flag that Papa was entitled to have on his coffin as a veteran. I didn't need another flag, because we already had one that was flown over the Capitol, and that one had tactile stars, which made it more meaningful to me. I knew that the flag that Papa received as a veteran would be very meaningful to Aunt Maria.

I confirmed that Papa already bought one extra plot in the cemetery where my parents were buried, presumably for me. It was on the other side of Mama's grave. I bought a fourth plot in case I married, so that my husband could be buried next to Papa. In passing, I once made the remark that, at least, we also would have a place to put Nana if something came up.

"Do you want to start a war?" Ellen asked me. She knew how much the relatives would have fussed if Nana's body wasn't taken back to MA. She also probably thought that Nana would care, too.

I'm not sure that Nana would have cared if her body were buried closer to my parents, because she once said that she would have preferred to be cremated but Grandpa made her promise to be buried beside him. However, I tried to explain that the reason I had in mind was some kind of physical inability to get her back to MA, or some practical national catastrophe, like a war.

Concerning my parents' grave, Papa was a veteran and entitled to a marker on his grave. I decided to have the marker placed at the foot of his grave, and to have Mama's marker moved to the foot of hers. At the head of their two graves, I ordered a joint larger marker, with their names and dates and a mention of my brothers and my little sister. As the inscription on the marker, I used two lines from a translation of Chaucer's Troilus and Cressida:

Together forever, forever so at rest.
The counsels of the heart are always best.

These lines were taken from a passage in which poor Troilus is trying to persuade his sweetheart that they should run away to stay together, rather than have her go to dwell with the Greeks.

Ellen was still next-door, and she did her best to be helpful. I had another friend on the other side. After the Marcies sold the house on the corner of S. 26th and Hayes Streets, Clifford and Anne Peterson bought it. The house was rented out frequently, because Clifford's job took him abroad for long periods of time. I don't remember exactly when, but Paul and Judy Childs rented the house for about three years. They still had two or three children at home, but most were grown and away. Judy was very helpful to me, taking me shopping and to do errands, and very positive and supportive. She was a good antidote to Ellen's tendency to sometimes take a negative point of view.

We had fun being silly sometimes. On one occasion, we went to look at nightgowns, one of which I bought.

As we were making our way to the cash register to complete the purchase, we were passing all the fuzzy flannel gowns.

"Vincent likes those nice soft materials, doesn't he?" Judy observed. (He did, too!)

I started to laugh. "Judy, do you realize what anybody behind us thinks you are talking about referring to somebody called Vincent in the nightgown aisle?" I asked her.

"Oh, we could have a lot of fun with that!" Judy agreed.

Walking next door to visit Judy and her family provided an illustration of Vincent's ability to make decisions. I came down the front steps with him, turned right on the sidewalk, crossed my driveway, and then gave him a suggestive right turn command, (right right,) meaning that Vincent should find the steps and walkway to their house. He took me up some steps and along a walkway, and brought me to the door. I had no idea where I was going, and I just trusted and followed him.

"Oh, he brought you around to the back!" Judy said, when she opened the door.

Vincent knew where we wanted to go, but he correctly judged that the back steps and walkway were easier than the front!

I still had to deal with the drawbacks of Nana's losing her hearing. As she got older, Nana became more paranoid about locking doors. One evening, I came home from work to find the outside screen door locked. At that time, I didn't have a key to this lock. I began to knock and rattle the door, trying to get Nana's attention. Vincent stood quietly beside me and didn't say anything, but the other dogs on the block heard us and began to bark. Their barking got Nana's attention, and she let us into the house.

Once we were inside, I turned around and told the neighborhood dogs, "All right, we're inside now." Everything was quiet.

Afterwards, Nana joked that, of course, the others would bark, because Vincent, the King, was locked out of the house!

As I mentioned in the previous chapter, Alberta, Jo Ann, and Law School Judy undertook to help me as volunteers during this initial period. They were wonderfully supportive with all the paperwork and check writing, as well as with my emotional struggles. We also found time to do some fun things. Judy and I sometimes went to concerts at the Library of Congress, or we went shopping for goodies and fun things in old town Alexandria; Jo Ann and I went to concerts, too, as well as Masses at Georgetown, and Alberta came to visit with George and little George (after he was born.) On my first birthday after Papa's death, she came over and helped Nana to bake for me a lemon sponge pie (one of my favorites) according to Nana's recipe. Mary and Peter and the rest of the Amburies were also friends and support. Mary and Peter often came to visit with their little girls, but Peter couldn't linger too long inside on account of his dog allergies.

It eventually became necessary for us to resume the friends' relationship with the three main volunteers, without the burden of the perennial paperwork. Chris Gregory recommended Dottie Hamilton Cornes, and she came at least once a week to work with me on bills, paperwork, and mail.

As far as Nana's medical needs were concerned, we were fortunate that Dr. Ambury was often able and willing to come to our house. Eventually her podiatrists, too, began to see her at home. Before that happened, Margie often took Nana to get her feet taken care of. Nana sometimes asked the doctors to also take care of Margie, because Margie, too, had foot troubles.

Eventually, the priests and the Eucharistic ministers began coming to the house to give Nana Communion. She liked "the Irish priest," as she called our new pastor, Father Burk. Unfortunately, the protocols call for just saying the prayers, administering the sacrament, and leaving. How I wish they would allow more leeway for these seniors like Nana. Nana needed a person to represent Jesus in an interactive, personal way. It might have made a difference for her.

As far as my own life with the parish was concerned, I volunteered to be a lector after Papa died. I've been doing that ever since, until it became too difficult for me to get regularly to church, as discussed in a later chapter. The parish used to have to give me the lector notes ahead of time so that I could put them into Braille. Now, they e-mail the notes to all the lectors, and I would copy them ahead of the Mass at which I was scheduled to read. It made it much easier. I already get the Sunday readings in the Braille Propers of the Mass that Xavier Society for the Blind sends me.

We had a funny episode during the late evening Mass on one Christmas Eve. One of our parishioners, Mr. McDonough, had driven me to church, because I didn't like to walk at night in the dark for safety reasons. I was lectoring as usual, from a podium on the right side of the altar, with a chair behind me to allow me to sit when not reading. I was sitting there during the Offertory of the Mass, with my second guide dog, Mikki, lying beside me. Through a lapse on my part, I didn't have my foot on her leash. Suddenly, she stood up and walked away from me. At the same time, our Pastor, Father Burke, (who was celebrating Mass,) announced, "This isn't part of the ceremony."

Someone presently brought Mikki back to me. During the Communion time, one of our ushers, Steve O'Neill, came to me and said, "The cat bit John McDonough; I will take you home."

What happened was that a cat that lived across the street from the church followed someone into the sanctuary. At the Offertory time, the cat started walking down the aisle toward the nativity scene. I suppose that the cat assumed that, if a famous feline could visit a queen, he could go to see the baby Jesus. Mikki got up and walked after the cat. Someone caught easygoing Mikki and brought her back to me, but others made the mistake of trying to catch the cat, instead of leaving it to find its own way out of church. The cat bit poor Mr. McDonough, and he had to go to the emergency room for stitches! Needless to say, the incident was talked and laughed about by parishioners for weeks thereafter!

When I reported back to work after Papa died, it was to get ready for and to move offices into the new building at 450 5th Street NW. I'm pretty sure that the VA Commission for the Blind sent a mobility instructor to help with my adjustment to the new place, but I don't have a clear recollection about it.

Once I was settled in the new building, I resumed my allergy injection schedule. Unfortunately, I made the same mistake that I did before. I eventually stopped going back to Dr. Black to get new serum, when life became too hectic. I had to resume injections again later in the late 1990's, with Dr. Botansky. I now see another allergist in VA. I know now that I possibly will need to stay on these injections for the rest of my life. [26]

The new SEC building straddled the block between fifth and sixth streets; the "front door" was on the fifth street side, and the entrance was level with the sidewalk; the "back door" was on the sixth street side, with steps going down to the sidewalk. Both of these doors entered the main lobby, and they had both straight doors and revolving doors. Although these revolving doors were bigger than others to accommodate wheelchairs, and Vincent and I used them once in a while to keep him in practice, we generally went in and out through the regular doors. E Street bounded one side of the building, and the other side abutted against other buildings that filled the remainder of the block to D Street. Much as we all wanted to be in one place, some of the IT people and the personnel staff remained in satellite offices in Alexandria, so the shuttles between buildings were still needed.

The new building was fairly close to the Judiciary Square Metro stop on the Red Line. I only had to cross both 5th Street and E Street to get to the side of E Street that intersected the walkway that led through the square to the escalators down to the Metro. Before this location was turned into the Police Memorial, we had grass near the walkway in which Vincent could park before we went down to the subway. We had to change trains at Metro Center, and then go to Crystal City. The S & L at which I banked was in the Crystal City arcade, and I could go by the bank to deposit my paycheck on Friday and then walk up to the entrance of Crystal City from which someone could get me or I could take a taxi.

Once the yellow line was completed and running a few years later, we also had the option of walking, with someone's assistance, to the archives station and taking the yellow line directly home to Crystal City.

Another thing that I did on my own, before Hecht's closed the old store, was to walk over there at lunch hour. If I went out the back door of my building, I would cross both 6th Street and E Street. Then, I would walk up E Street toward 7th Street and go in the back door of Hecht's. We would walk

---

[26] In 2023, I had more tests which don't show the same allergies as before, and I paused the injections at that time.

through the store to the little coffee shop on the F Street side, and I would order either a tuna fish or chicken salad sandwich. I often bought honey-glazed doughnuts to take home, because I knew that Nana liked them, too. I was sorry when Hecht's moved, because the location of its new building was no longer readily accessible to me, and that store didn't have either a coffee shop or a restaurant.

Sometimes Darlene or other friends would go with me to Woody's, but that was further away than old Hecht's, but nearer than new Hecht's.

We also had restaurants within walking distance of the new building. General Williams began to meet me for lunch on various occasions. He would come to my building and meet me in the lobby, and then he, Vincent, and I would walk to a restaurant to have lunch.

I still saw Bonita for a while, and she, too, was shocked and saddened by Papa's death. At some point, and I still don't know why, she abruptly broke off with me. I had no idea why or what I could possibly have done to offend her. I agonized over this for a while, but I finally wrote her a letter, sending it to the SEC, which was the only address I had, apologizing if I inadvertently offended her, and thanking her for her friendship. A few years before I retired in 2014, I heard that she died. I never had an answer to what this was all about, but I'm glad she was my friend when she was.

God meanwhile sent me a couple of new friends. Billie Long and her housemate, Frances Cisna, were in the Navy together. After getting out of the Navy, they worked as accountants. Billie worked with the SEC, but I don't remember where Frances worked as an accountant before she retired. Both of these ladies loved cats; when I first knew them, they had four, including a brash, talkative Siamese. They both fell in love with Vincent. Billie would often come to take Vincent for long, recreational walks, since Papa wasn't around to give him the pleasure of just being walked like a dog without being responsible for me. We also got together to go to dinner at our favorite Chinese restaurants.

Before I knew her, Billie had been diagnosed with lung cancer. I think that she had surgery to remove one lung. She received radiation and chemotherapy, and when I first knew her, she was considered cancer free. Frances died from cancer a few years later, and after that Billie was eventually diagnosed with lung cancer in the other lung. That time, she did not survive. The only reason she was diagnosed in time to have the extra years of life that allowed us to be friends was that she was seeing a rheumatologist, Dr. Shainker, who believed in turning over stones and thinking outside the box. She originally went to see him on account of shoulder pain. Dr. Shainker ruled out other causes, and he finally decided to check for possible lung cancer.

After what happened to Papa and Billie's experience, I again became concerned about finding out more about what was making my ankles swell. Billie recommended that I consult Dr. Shainker, in what was then called the Washington Clinic in Friendship Heights, MD. He did a very thorough examination of me, and thought that arthritis might be involved, especially since x-rays showed some arthritis in my neck. He tried a fairly expensive medicine, but it didn't really seem to affect the situation, and we stopped it eventually. On the evenings that I had the appointments with him, Billie would pick us up from work and take me for the appointment, and then we would go to dinner afterwards. Years later, I eventually started seeing Dr. Lawson, another rheumatologist. He put me on Bextra, a medicine that seemed to help. I used it when I went to the Seeing Eye for my fourth guide dog, Gemma, in 2002, going up from one to two a day for the period of the training. However, when Bextra was taken off the market, I used what I had left on an occasional basis until they were all gone. I have declined to go on anything else since then except Tylenol arthritis up to twice a day, on account of various possible side effects. I found other natural remedies, which seemed to be helpful.

In addition to the conflicting and turbulent emotions caused by Papa's death, I also had to deal with the discrepancy between my aspirations and ideals and the underlying reality of my work situation. I became a lawyer hoping to make a difference in the country somehow. I also aspired to have a job that I really liked doing. During my first four years at the SEC, I had become somewhat reconciled to the attitude that, as Papa put it, every other week is payday. (He said Tuesday, but with the direct deposits, it's Friday.) The work in the Office of Consumer affairs had the advantage that it was directed toward helping ordinary customers, and I tried to develop my skills in handling telephone calls from complainants unhappy with their brokers or the companies in which they had invested. However, the amount of work often seemed overwhelming, and the pace could get fairly hectic at times. I ended up discussing these emotional conflicts about the work situation with my counselor.

In trying to sort all of this out, I turned to the Lord one night in prayer. I asked Him if He really wanted me to keep doing all of this boring stuff.

"I mean, I'll do it for You, not for anybody else," I said.

It's hard to describe what happened next. I felt as though I had been jolted by a kind of electricity. I felt very happy. It seemed that I was being answered. I eventually became aware that this divine-induced high could not last, and I wanted to cry, because I didn't want it to go away. I felt that I had been answered.

In the fall of 1982, Jeanne Rhode came to visit from Jamul, (a suburb of San Diego,) California. I took leave, and we spent a very pleasant time together. Margie was glad to meet her, and she saw the family resemblance with Nana. I was glad that Nana, too, was able to see Jeanne while she was still mentally alert enough to know what was happening. While Jeanne was with me, we played tourist. Jeanne drove the Grenada to a parking place, and then we took public transportation and/or tour busses into town to see the memorials and historic sites. It was wonderful to have this time together and to have the opportunity to get to know Jeanne in person. I still have a little pewter replica of the Lincoln Memorial as a reminder of that pleasant time.

The period after Papa's death was an opportunity for me to start exercising decisions and putting my own stamp on the house. Before he died and after I got Vincent, we started minimizing the use of glass or breakable ornaments on the Christmas tree for safety reasons, and we began using more and more felt ornaments from the church bazaar at Barbara's Calvary Methodist Church and other handmade ornaments. At some point after Papa's death, I decided to retire Mama's nativity set (which I eventually gave away) and I began acquiring durable figures made by Fontanini. These figures depicted shepherds and other folks doing various things, and they were considerably larger than Mama's set. For a while, the set included a leather camel that Anne Peterson, the lady who owned the house next door, brought us from Egypt, but my second guide dog, Mikki, chewed it up. As a Christmas gift, Mary Spellerberg's husband, Peter, made for me a wooden stable large enough to house the new, taller nativity figures. He mounted in the loft a musical wind-up movement that played "Joy to the World."

I also eventually bought a second new wing chair and matching ottoman for the living room. A few years later, I replaced the couch and club chair that went back to Mama's time with a new couch and, eventually, a new recliner rocker. Before any of the old furniture went out of the house, I had someone come and check it with a metal detector, just to make sure that Papa's ring wasn't inside the furniture somewhere, but we never found it.

At some point during this period, I had the house painted inside. Apart from the expense, it was a major undertaking, which necessitated moving the furniture around from it accustomed places, and Nana found the experience disruptive and disorienting.

"Please wait until after I'm dead before you do this again!" she pleaded.

I could understand why she found the temporary changes difficult and overwhelming, but it hurt me to reflect that her request probably would end up being granted for reasons beyond our control.

Although part of me enjoyed being able to arrange the house and furniture to suit me, another part of me often felt like the little girl who became tired of "playing house." After a day of such play, such a child just wants to go back to the real house and let Mama tuck her into bed at night.

Unfortunately for me, the house that I was arranging wasn't a playhouse, and I didn't have any safe, responsibility-free zone to which to retreat. Even if I didn't feel like one all the time, I was an adult, a "big lady," and the responsibilities were unavoidably mine.

Sometime during the first year after Papa's death, Aunt Maria and Sister Margaret James came to stay with us for about a week. Their goal was to go through Papa's pictures and keep only the best to be later put into albums. We threw away boxes and boxes of pictures! Those we kept amounted to about two or three cartons full of loose pictures! It hurt me to see so much of Papa's art, which his pictures represented to me, go into the trash, but it couldn't be helped. I had to trust their judgment, because there was no way they could have described all those pictures to me. We were just too many years early for the pictures to be digitized on thumb drives or other storage media. As it was, those pictures that remained sat around for a few years in their boxes, until one of my later housekeepers put them into albums. I keep them, because I know how much skill and care Papa put into them, but I have no idea what most of them are. As relatives depart for the great beyond, fewer and fewer people remain who may be able to tell me what they are or to label them. I hate to think of what will happen to them after I'm gone, but, as with so many things, I must trust in God for the solution.

I don't remember exactly when, but work intensified in 1983 when Bob Wolfe left, and Jonathan Katz became Director of the Office of Consumer Affairs. He put a big emphasis on wanting "quick and dirty" research to get the work out quickly. It put more pressure on me. However, I still felt the need to be as complete and thorough as possible, even if the assignments took longer.

I don't remember which director was involved with this incident, but it illustrates the point.

Someone wrote us a letter asking about a brokerage issue. Because it wasn't my area of expertise, I consulted an attorney in the Division of Market Regulation, now called Trading and Markets, which is responsible for brokers, dealers, and securities exchanges. He helped me to draft an answer to the letter. It went out under my signature, as imperfect as my signature might be. The inquirer didn't like the substance of the response or the clarity of the signature, so he wrote again, this time to the chairman's office. The chairman's office assigned the letter to Market Regulation, and they sent us a copy of the man's letter with my response that he had marked up. The attorney who helped me to answer the original letter was assigned the response to the second one. He answered the letter, referring back to my reply, and backing me up. He was more supportive than my boss

He found me later and told me about it. "He complained about the signature," the attorney said. "We'll give him a signature! I'll get my dog to sign it."

Some people have asked me whether I want to get an automatic signer, so that I won't have to labor of that signature. I don't think that it's a good idea. Handwritten, my signature would be pretty hard to forge, but if someone got hold of the automatic template, it could be a recipe for disaster! Besides, I had to work darn hard to learn to make that signature!

In addition to Dottie, Chris also referred me to Doreen Hitchcock. She and Margie began covering Nana and me on alternating weekends. In the spring of 1983, Doreen noticed blood on one of Nana's undershirts. Dr. Ambury came to the house. He confirmed that it was a tumor on one of her breast, probably malignant. A surgeon would have to remove the tumor, and, as it turned out, the entire breast. Adversity focuses the mind. Nana told me calmly where things were and seemed to be mentally together when she went into the hospital. Part of me wished that she could have passed on to the Lord, while she was alert and somewhat the Nana that I knew, but it was not to be.

Uncle Joe came to stay with me during the time of Nana's operation. She seemed settled in her hospital room, and she had a nice Chinese lady as a roommate who did not speak English.

The day of the surgery, Uncle Joe, Vincent, and I went to the hospital to be with her before they took her down for surgery. Someone came and told us that Vincent couldn't stay in the room. I wanted to make an issue about it, because service dogs should be allowed in hospitals unless there is a health reason to keep them out of a particular patient's room, such as allergies or an open wound. However, I knew that fighting Nana would have got up out of that hospital bed if she had realized what was going on! Fortunately, they let us stay long enough for us to tell Nana that Vincent had to go out, to explain why we were leaving with him.

Later, Uncle Joe told me that he had asked Nana to come back to MA with him after the surgery. He said that Nana told him that she would never leave me, that she would "go home in a box." That was what happened in the end.

Nana came through the surgery all right. We asked the doctor afterwards if they got all the cancer. They removed her breast; the tumor was apparently attached to the chest wall. The doctor's answer was that "We got all of it that is ever going to bother her." Nana was going on 94 years old. Apparently, tumors at this age grow more slowly. He didn't seem to think that we would have any consequences from it; something else would end her life.

After Nana came home from the hospital, she told us about a couple of things that happened while she was there. We never knew how true her stories were, but here they are.

Nana said that, when she was recovering from the anesthetic, they heard her say that she couldn't leave Linda and Vincent. They asked her who we were, and she told them.

She also said that, while she was in the hospital, she thought she heard some other patients in other rooms getting delirious. It bothered her, and she wanted the door closed, but she didn't feel strong enough to get up and do it. She said that she told the lady next to her with gestures that she wanted the door closed and her legs weren't strong enough for her to get up and do it. The lady must have understood her sign language, because she got up and closed the door. The nurses came, and they wanted to know why they shut the door and what they were doing in there!

Nana recovered physically from the surgery and the loss of her breast. I think it was the one on her right side. She declined a prosthesis, but she was disappointed at losing the throwing ability in her right arm. One evening she tried to toss a package of toilet paper upstairs to me on the landing. Normally, it would have found the mark. It went wide, and she was so unhappy about it!

While Uncle Joe was with us, one day when we were sitting around the table, I heard him ask Nana for her pendant watch that grandpa gave her. I distinctly heard her say, "All right, Joe, you can have the watch."

She didn't sound happy about it, because she wanted it to be left to me. In her will, she did leave me the watch, along with half of her estate and her wedding ring. However, I heard her tell him that he could have it, and I felt that I needed to honor that statement. I kept thinking of how I would feel if Mama told me I could have something and then did something else in her will. After Nana died, I gave Uncle Joe her watch. We agreed that I would keep her wedding ring, and he would get the watch. I only asked that the watch not go to Tom. Tom had Grandpa's watch, and that was enough. I understand that Uncle Joe passed the watch to my cousin, Nancy.

After Nana's surgery, it seemed clear to me that part-time help would not be enough. Ethel Stanulis had referred me to Lou Ella Lee and Ruthe Parker. Ethel's husband, Ed, had died, but Ethel's mother, whom they affectionately called Pop-Pop, was still living with her afterwards. Lou Ella had helped her with Pop-Pop.

Lou Ella and Ruthe worked together as a team. They were a study in opposite personalities, but they were both excellent. Lou Ella was calm and deliberate, and she could drive, but she was always late. Ruthe was bouncy, a little nervous, and excitable and sensitive. She couldn't drive and relied on public transportation. Even with the sometimes-erratic bus schedules, she always managed to arrive on time and even sometimes early. Each lady waited until the other arrived before leaving.

These two nurses covered me around the clock for a few months in the summer, until Patsy was able to come to work for me.

During this interim period, I found out how important it was to communicate necessary information to my employees and Nana's caregivers. I went to Trinity for a few days over a weekend to visit Sister Elizabeth Henry. I thought that I had told Lou Ella where I was going. I found out that she didn't get it, or maybe I didn't say and give enough information. However it happened, one morning while I was gone, the two ladies found it hard to arouse Nana from a very sound sleep. I think that they were afraid that her breathing had stopped. She eventually awoke, but it was a close call. They were very worried that she might die, and then how would they get in touch with me? It was a scary incident, and it taught me a very important lesson about making sure that the right hand knows what the left is doing!

Lou Ella and Ruthe were the ones who referred me to Leleet Edwards, also known as Patsy. Patsy was from Jamaica; she had gone to England to work and make a better life for her family. Eventually her husband and four children joined her there; at some point, Patsy and her husband divorced, I think after the children were grown. Patsy came to America and worked for many years as a live-in with Mrs. Bortnick, a lady with two sons. The boys were grown up and Mrs. Bortnick wanted to move to Virginia Beach. Patsy didn't want to go there, and she was looking for another live-in position.

I interviewed Patsy, and she came well recommended by Lou Ella and Ruthe. Nana liked her, too. She started working for me in September of 1983. Doreen and Margie covered us on alternating weekends.

Patsy was an excellent cook, a steady reliable, honest lady, and very straightforward and plainspoken. She abounded in down-to-earth wisdom and common sense. She said wise, true things, such as "Nobody knows God's Business." "Man writes, and God wipes out;" and "Circumstances alter cases; donkeys wear two braces."

As I mentioned earlier, Patsy was a talented seamstress and dressmaker, and she knew well how to use a sewing machine. She was wonderful at helping me to run errands and to repair my knitting mistakes. She was one of the few people I knew who could go into a store or thrift shop and buy a dress for Nana or me and have it fit. She also made me some lovely dresses. In terms of shopping for Nana, it was getting to the point that I had to try on things myself and judge whether they would work for Nana by how well they fit me.

Patsy covered us during the week, but sometimes she would stay on an occasional Saturday if we had something to do, or she might stay over the weekend if I was away on vacation. At least once a year, Patsy would use her two weeks of accrued vacation to go home to Jamaica. Sometimes, Lou Ella and Ruthe covered while she was away. On one such occasion, Ruthe patiently helped me to soak Vincent's sore paw in Epsom salts until the infection came out of his toe. She helped me to cover a music box with shells, and she baked good cookies that even Nana liked. Ruthe and I also shared a love of doll collecting, and she gave me a beautiful older feminine figure doll.

On one occasion while Nana was still alive, one of Margie's friends, a lady named Jackie, covered for Patsy while she was away. Patsy appreciated very much that Jackie left the house very neat, tidy, and clean. Unfortunately, the second time that Jackie came as a substitute, after Nana died, was not so successful, but more about that in another chapter.

All of these ladies who worked for me while Nana was alive deserved big gold stars for being so kind and patient in dealing with Nana. As she got older, Nana was getting more and more difficult. Her temper and paranoia were her enemies. She also felt cold most of the time, and she would bundle up to sleep in her chair during the day. At night when she was supposed to go to bed, we put a heater in her bedroom to get it toasty and warm, hoping that she would get comfortable and sleep the night away, but she would often get up and wander the house. We put deadeye bolt locks on the cellar door and eventually the kitchen door, to keep her from hurting herself during these nightly walks.

Fortunately, Patsy felt a great deal of identification with Nana, and she did everything that she could to help me. She calmly answered, "I don't know," to anything that Nana wanted to know that might upset her, such as details about my planned day outings. I had to be the "bad news bear" most of the time. Patsy and I told Nana that all the meats on the menu were chicken, because Nana said that she wouldn't eat beef or lamb. For the first few years, when we said that it was chicken, she happily ate Patsy's delicious cooking. Ellen and Doreen chuckled a little at this benign deception, but it broke my heart that we had to resort to these strategies. I was losing my Nana by inches, and I could do nothing to stop the process!

Nana found it harder and harder to get up and down from the commode, so we put the shell of a bedside commode over the toilet to make it higher and easier for her. I didn't trust the extenders that supposedly clip to the toilet, and they didn't fit our toilet right. The commode frame with its legs seemed sturdier; the problem was that it leaked urine, because Nana didn't position herself properly on it. When the time came for me to modernize the bathroom fixtures after Nana's death, I learned from her difficulties and bought higher commodes for both bathrooms, as well as a deeper tub for the bathroom upstairs.

Nana also became incontinent in her bladder, and we had to put a waterproof cover over the mattress, put a plastic mat used for office swivel chairs under the bedside commode near her bed, and put protective plastic-lined pads under her.

Nana began to fall occasionally. Her guardian angel and the care of the Lord protected her, so that she didn't break any more bones. The first time that she fell, she scooted into the living room, hoping to pull herself up by the stable, immovable piano. This time, and on other occasions, I was able to put my arms under her and lift her either to her feet or onto the couch or a chair.

If she fell like this, she would panic and start to cry, saying, "How am I going to get up?" On one of these occasions, Vincent came over to her, nudging her with his nose on the backside, as though to try to help her get up. Vincent's actions made her laugh, which made her relaxed and easier to lift. In fact, Vincent became very solicitous of me as a result of all this, and he was uncomfortable if I tried to lie on the floor to do exercise routines.

The last time that I picked Nana up, she was dead weight. It told me that she was no longer strong enough to help me lift her by partly fusing her legs to get up. The situation was getting more and more difficult.

At night, I would sit with her, playing her music box, praying as I knelt beside her bed, asking the Lord silently to let her go to sleep quietly and go Home some night, in her own house and her own bed. I knew that finding a body in the morning would be a shock, but I thought that I could bear that, instead of what seemed to be coming. As Nana's condition deteriorated and the dementia got worse, I saw NURSING HOME written in larger and larger letters, and everything inside me fought against it. Nana had taken such good care of me, when I was little and vulnerable, and now it was my turn to do that for her. I didn't blame God for what was happening, but it didn't seem fair to me that we couldn't have a happy, peaceful ending to such a loving life. I didn't want to have to turn her over to possibly uncaring or unreliable strangers.

I kept checking different things with the doctors, hoping and praying that they would find something treatable or to give us some hope as to a cause of what was happening to Nana, but they all kept coming up with Alzheimer's disease. It was all very discouraging and depressing.

I went to a couple of meetings of the Alzheimer's Association, but I didn't find that particular chapter helpful. We seemed to be doing all that we could physically do for Nana. As for the support groups that invited people to share, I didn't feel comfortable talking to strangers about the very personal pain that I was enduring on behalf of Nana and to some degree inflicted by Nana and the things that she did and said. I felt that these folks couldn't know anything about my Nana, and I didn't want her case dissected in some impersonal way. This kind of group might have worked for others, but it didn't work for me.

Nana's situation was aggravated by the fact that she was losing her hearing. I did everything that I could to try to compensate, including having my hearing aid service people come to the house to fit her with a hearing aid or fix the one that she had. The problem was that Nana would only wear a within-the-ear-mold hearing aid, which wasn't powerful enough and was pretty useless. I also tried using a small battery-powered amplifier in lieu of a hearing aid with an earplug. It helped some, but it was hard to get it all together. I strongly advise anyone with a senior citizen relative who is losing their hearing, or who is in this boat themselves, to forget about vanity and use the necessary equipment to keep in the conversational loop as long as possible. With hearing loss comes loss of human interaction, which can increase isolation and failure to communicate. Without the stimulus of human contact and interaction, paranoia and frustration by the senior will be aggravated and the downhill slide will increase.

Also, in her anger and paranoia, Nana could say some very hateful things, including some with racial overtones, and it was almost impossible not to take them personally, or to remember that she didn't know what she was doing. She also suffered from insecurity and a fear of dying, particularly because she didn't want to die and leave me vulnerable. At night, as Patsy was helping her to get settled in bed, Nana would repeatedly ask her, "Are you going to stay with us?"

"Yes, Nana," Patsy would answer several times. Finally, to end the conversation, in response to the last question, Patsy would say, "Good Night, Nana."

Like a little child, Nana would get furious when Patsy left on the weekends, because she felt abandoned.

"She flies the coop on Friday!" she would say indignantly about Patsy to the next person to come on duty and to me. Doreen took it with a grain of salt and laughed at it a little, but neither Margie nor I thought that it was funny.

Nana was getting increasingly upset when I went out on excursions with Judy or away for the weekend. "The Brooklyn Bridge is still on sale!" Nana would say, when she heard the telephone ring. She thought that it would be a solicitor trying to sell something. This was before the days of the "Do not call" list. Now we still have the problem with all the spam telephone calls! The current state of affairs would have justified all Nana's fears and driven her crazy! Nana worried that someone would try to and succeed in taking advantage of me, or that I would be too naïve and gullible.

My goal was to help Nana to be as happy as possible. At some point, my cousin, Tom Calabro, moved to MD and went to work for Woodward and Lothrop's, and at one point he was a manager in the downtown store. He came to visit us, and both Nana and I were glad to see him. I hoped that it might be the beginning of more regular visits, but it didn't turn out that way. I tried to invite him over and make times for us to get together, but something always seemed to come up; he was very busy.

Around 1984, Anne and Cliff Peterson sold the house next door to Susan and Walter Graham. On one of Nana's birthdays, I decided to have a little party with cake and ice cream, and Walter came over. I really appreciated his coming; it helped to make a happy day for Nana.

At times, we still saw rare, fleeting glimpses of the Nana I used to know. On one evening, I was out in the kitchen preparing to cook a rib-eye steak in a little electric broiler. Nana came out to the kitchen to see what I was doing. Ellen was visiting in the living room or the dining room.

"What are you trying to do here?" Nana asked. I said something to the effect that I was trying to cook the steak.

"Get out of here! I'll do it!" Nana told me. She got the frying pan, and the butter (probably margarine.) She proceeded to cook the steak the old-fashioned way, on the burner on top of the stove.

Ellen was aghast and could only see the negative. "The pan is going all over the burner, and the fire is high!" she told me.

I didn't say anything, but inside I was thinking that Ellen should leave her alone. Sometimes, one has to do what one can, even if it isn't perfect. It was important to Nana and to me.

I went into the dining room, and Nana finished cooking the steak, and she brought it to me on a plate with a fork. It was delicious, and I enjoyed every bite of it! I also cried, while I was eating it, because I knew in my bones what turned out to be true. It was the last time that Nana cooked anything for me like that.

On another occasion, Nana saw me sitting glumly on the couch, feeling discouraged.

"What's the matter?" she asked. "I'm coming, Lindy! I'm coming!"

She came over to the couch and sat down beside me and cuddled me. She wanted so much to make me feel better!

Nana wasn't the only one with health concerns. At some point during this period, Vincent's liver enzymes began testing too high, and they feared, after some tests, that he had cirrhosis of the liver. They put him on prednisone. It made him super hungry, and he had to go out to urinate more frequently.

We found out how difficult it was for Vincent one morning, when I was eating breakfast. By way of explanation, before the kitchen was remodeled, the wooden kitchen table was against the wall between the kitchen door and the back door. We had a set of enclosed shelves above the kitchen table where the electric outlets were. The toaster sat on one of these shelves, plugged into an electric outlet, and we used it up there without bringing it down to the table.

I was getting ready to drink my tea, when I heard Patsy say, "I know I put two slices of bread in the toaster!"

"Yes, Patsy," I answered. "I'm sure you did!"

"I know I put two slices of bread in the toaster!" Patsy insisted.

I hid in my tea cup; I choked, and I gagged. I did everything that I could to avoid laughing out loud. Patsy would not have appreciated it at the time! I could imagine what happened! Vincent somehow got up there, and he took a piece of toast out of the toaster, all without knocking down the toaster or burning himself! It was a miracle!

I didn't say anything to reprimand him. I figured that, if he was so hungry and motivated to do something like that, which wasn't typical behavior for him, I should pretend that I knew nothing about it.

However, I didn't dare feed him more, because I didn't want him to gain too much weight, but I divided his food in thirds and began taking a lunch for him to work. When we went out to dinner, Billie and I began surreptitiously feeding him bread under the table. I think that God intervened to heal Vincent. General Williams went on a trip that also included Fatima in Portugal, where Our Lady is said to have appeared to three children in the early 20th century. He said that he would pray for us there. About that time, I was walking back to my building from lunch.

Someone was walking with me, but I have forgotten who it was. At one point, I felt Vincent pause, and through the handle, it felt to me as though something bumped up against him, but my companion couldn't see anything. Vincent was just looking intently down the driveway or alley to his left. Not too long afterwards, the enzyme levels dropped back to normal, and we were able to take him off the medicine.

After I hired Patsy and could arrange for Nana to be covered on weekends, Billie and Frances began inviting Vincent and Me to their beach house in Avalon, NJ. We would leave work Friday evening and come back Sunday night. They owned the house, which they had winterized for year-round use. To use it as a tax benefit, they rented it for the summer months. While I was there, I met their friend, Mary Zook, called Zookie, who lived nearby year-round. She had a cat, named Felix. He was a cat that Billie had rescued from being mistreated. Billie's mother also had a cat, named Morris, that was found wandering around lost. He was a special breed, a Scottish fold. The name comes from the fact that this breed of cat has ears that fold down, instead of standing up straight like most other cats.

Vincent loved the beach, and he very much enjoyed playing ball with us. He also got along well with Billie's cats when he encountered them. All the cats ran and hid, except for feisty Ching, the Siamese!

I think that it was in 1983 that I finally wrapped up the probate and accounting on Papa's estate. We had a funny incident when it came time to sign the final papers that listed all the assets. We needed a notary. Mike Geltner said that he knew of one close to my building, and he came to meet me at work with the papers. We walked down 5th Street past my building to one of the buildings next door. We went inside. All kinds of confusion and yelling and talking were going on. I found out later that it was a bail bondsman's office, and the bondsman was a notary. The old man took one look at a blind lady going to sign a bunch of papers, and he decided that he needed to make darn sure that I knew what I was signing.

"Do you know what you are signing?" he demanded.

I tried to tell him yes, but he wasn't satisfied. He proceeded to read me the entire document. Only then would he let me sign it and notarize my signature. It probably didn't hurt for me to refresh my recollection about what was in the filing!

After we left and were walking back to my office, Mike said something about it being a new experience for me. Then he added, "You'd better be good, or I'll take you back to the bail bondsman's office!"

In the late summer of that year, I paid another visit to M.E. and John. By this time, they were living in a house. They had a fenced in yard, and Vincent was able to run around and enjoy himself. Mindy had died and was buried on the property. M. E. noticed that Vincent went to check out Mindy's grave.

In addition to these trips, I continued to go on outings with Judy on the weekends. I must confess that during this time, I became an avid collector of music boxes, porcelain dolls, bricbracks, and jewelry. It was all part of an escape mechanism. Unfortunately, it taught me to associate all these things with positive feelings, and I now have to watch that these tendencies don't become like an addiction.

God also provided me with some spiritual consolations. In either 1983 or 1984, Texas Mary signed me up for an Encounter with Christ on a Cursillo weekend. Although I did not become a follow-up member of the movement afterwards, it was a wonderful time to hear the inspirational talks of the speakers and to encounter Jesus in them and in the other members of my group. The particular discussion group that I was part of during that weekend chose the name, Travelers to Emmaus. During the weekend, the house was decorated with roosters, because they are considered the birds of the resurrection that crowed early on Easter morning. Often the roosters had tails with many colors. The motto of the group is, "Des Colores," a phrase that summarizes how the Body of Christ is composed of many diverse, unique people. Together, like the many and varied colors in the decorative roosters' tails, they contribute to the beauty and sanctity of the whole in their great variety and diversity. In the closing ceremony, each of us was given a wooden cross with special symbols on it. I was pleasantly surprised to find one of the sisters that I knew from Trinity among the members attending our closing ceremony!

In the spring of 1984, my life was turned upside down for a few months. On the evening of the first Friday during Lent of that year, I was sitting at the dining room table, trying to decompress after a busy week, when the telephone rang. It was Elsome Templin, my old friend from my class at Guiding Eyes. She had gone to the Rehabilitation Center in Richmond. There she had met Wayne Barber, a partially sighted rehabilitation candidate like her who was a few years younger than she was. They thought that they were in love and serious about each other. Before their allotted time at the Center was up, they had boarded a bus, and they were in Washington, DC. She was calling me for help!

For the next two months or so, Dottie and I had our hands full. Patsy made it clear to me that she would not continue to work for me, if I had either of them staying with me for more than a night or two. It was probably good that she took this stand, because I was already in deeper than I wanted to be. We put them up for a few days in a hotel, and then we had to find a place for them, together or separately, while they tried to work things out. During that period of time, my work performance suffered, and I found out more about social agencies than I ever wanted to know and was afraid to ask. Eventually, the kind pastor at Our Lady Queen of Peace parish put Wayne up in a residence that they had for men looking for work, and Elsome decided to go home to her mother for a while.

By Easter, they were separated, at least temporarily, and I heaved a sigh of relief. I didn't have long to enjoy it, because soon after that, I became ill with a cold and respiratory infection. Dear Dr. Morrissey didn't bother having me come into the office, because this germ was apparently making the rounds. He called prescriptions for cough medicine and antibiotics into the drugstore. I had a few days of lying around, reading, and listening to "All Things Considered," on PBS. Nana sang some old Italian songs to me, but the problem was that I had laryngitis with this illness, and I couldn't make Nana understand me. Patsy declined to be interpreter between us, and it was a frustrating time.

When Elsome and Wayne met again, they talked things over. Wayne told her that he, for one, wasn't ready to get married, and they went their separate ways. Elsome eventually married someone else, and I lost touch with her. Perhaps she blamed me that she ended up breaking up with Wayne, or maybe her life just took a different path. Wayne went on to complete college, after overcoming various circumstances and obstacles, including epilepsy and his low vision caused by albinism. He is a very intelligent man with a great interest in science. In the meantime, he sometimes came over to help us with projects on the weekend, such as repairing the sockets in the dining room light fixtures. The last that I heard of him, he was working for the Environmental Protection Agency.

In the summer of 1984, Vincent and I went to visit Jeanne and Bill in Jamul, CA. They showed us wonderful hospitality, and they took us around San Diego and other interesting places. One of my favorite things was the jewelry store in old town San Diego, where I bought a strand of amber beads. Pat and Mike Young had a similar type of place in Old Town, Alexandria that was one of Law School Judy's and my favorite places. During this visit to California, Bill eagerly shared with me figs from his fig tree. I agreed with him that they were delicious. Fruit picked fresh off the tree is a thousand times better than the package!

In the fall of 1984, I accepted a position in what was called the Washington Regional Office of the SEC, which was located in a building in Ballston Common, in Arlington, VA. Darlene remained in the Office of Consumer Affairs and did not accompany me to the new position. I thought that someone had accepted the position as my assistant in the new place, but it didn't work out. The lady incorrectly assumed that a promotion was part of the position. The misunderstanding caused us to conclude that it wasn't appropriate for her to take this position, especially because she stood me up on the first day. Hoping that it might work out, I proposed Dottie for the position. Eventually, the SEC hired her.

That November, Dottie and Doreen gave me a memorable birthday, and took me out to dinner for a surprise. They gave me a seahorse pendant on a chain as a gift.

I will only say of the Washington Regional Office at the SEC that it was the best of times and it was the worst of times. Many of the people there were very nice and helpful, and the atmosphere was more relaxed than headquarters. My new dentist turned out to have an office on the first floor of the building where I was working, and it was nice to be on the VA side of the bridge. We had some fun times, including a wildly funny Used Gift Exchange at the Christmas party. One of the division heads at the office, Herbert Brooks, a fellow GULC alumnus, asked me to come to his daughter's kindergarten class with Vincent to talk about guide dogs.

However, it gradually became clear that Dottie was not sufficiently organized and focused in her work habits to be a good match for me as my assistant. In the spring of 1985, the SEC decided to close the Arlington office and to consolidate the regional functions in the Philadelphia Branch Office, making it the Philadelphia Regional office. Employees in the WRO had a choice of going back to headquarters to work or moving to Philadelphia.

Dottie and I ended up back in headquarters, in the Division of Investment Management. I started out there by taking responsibility for responding to all the telephone inquiries about the Investment Advisers Act of 1940 and the regulation of investment advisers registered with the SEC. Eventually, everybody mutually agreed that I needed a different assistant. Jim Waeldner came to work with me in either the summer or the fall of 1985. I continued to see and be friends with Dottie, and she was still of great help to me with my personal affairs.

When I returned to headquarters at the SEC, I joined an ecumenical group of employees who got together once a week for Bible study. The group met off the premises in a room provided to us by the Salvation Army, whose building was on the other side of Fifth Street, and across E Street from our block. I found these occasions for serious Scripture study and prayer very spiritually nourishing and supportive. We took turns preparing the presentation or leading the discussion on particular scripture passages. The guiding leadership and mainstay of the group came from Daniel Savitsky. We tried to keep the group going after he died from cancer, but eventually the press of hectic schedules and time conflicts caused our group to disband. It was Dan who first told me, guided by the Holy Spirit, that God was giving me my wonderful dogs to remind me how much He loved me. I visited Dan in the hospital when I knew that he was dying. I told him that my brothers didn't survive, but I wouldn't have wished for a better brother than he.

In the summer or fall of 1985, I began to notice that Vincent's behavior was changing. When we were in the subway, he no longer cut in front of me on the platforms, but he would walk straight up toward the edge and stop. I knew my dog fairly well and trusted that he wouldn't change his behavior without a reason. I took him to George Washington Speech and Hearing Center to be tested for possible hearing loss. I had been tested at this place and they helped to fit me with appropriate hearing aids, but I trusted that they could creatively come up with a way to test Vincent, because they also worked with other non-verbal people, like babies. They didn't disappoint me, but as far as we could tell his hearing was very good.

We next consulted Dr. Kotch, a canine ophthalmologist. He found what he thought was deterioration in the retina of one of Vincent's eyes, and he said that I should retire him immediately.

Billie encouraged me to seek a second opinion. I think that it was she who suggested the University of PA Veterinary Hospital, and their ophthalmologist, Dr. Ruben. We kept praying. Billie, Vincent, and I took the train to Philadelphia for the appointment and came back either that evening or the next day. When he examined Vincent, this doctor said that he found only a cataract in the left eye.

We had at least a year, maybe more depending on how fast it progressed, before I would have to retire Vincent.

As I told Dr. Ruben, either Dr. Kotch made a really big mistake when he examined my dog, or God intervened to heal him. However, now I understood why Vincent wouldn't cut in front of me anymore. He realized that he wasn't seeing out of that eye, and he wouldn't turn a blind eye toward the tracks and the trains!

I think that it was about this time in 1985 that I began to carpool with Mike Kigin. He worked in the Office of the Chief Accountant at the SEC. He agreed to take me both ways, in exchange for a fixed sum that I would pay, so much a trip one way, to cover gas. We continued this arrangement until Mike retired, I think around 2006.

# THE LITTLE MOOSE

*D*uring 1985 and 1986, my big quest was to find a way to have a good successor to Vincent. Because Seeing Eye had rejected me, I did not want to reapply there, and it seemed that Guiding Eyes would not take me again. I checked out the various other guide dog schools, but they were either too far away to provide the follow-up that I thought I would need, or they did not seem inclined to take me or to deal with the hearing situation. Fidelco in MA did train with German shepherds, but it sounded as though their dogs were too high energy for me. I consulted Steve Koten, who used to be with Guiding Eyes. He expressed a willingness to possibly provide me with a dog that he had privately trained.

Because I thought that private training might be a good idea, I felt led to check out other breeds for the kind of judgmental qualities and situational awareness that I considered that I needed in my next guide. With Billie's help, I went to visit two breeders of Irish water spaniels. I concluded that the breed had potential, but it would have to be the right dog. I almost settled on a six-month old female puppy, named Mia.

Meanwhile, I heard about Moose. He was a large yellow Labrador retriever that his owner was trying to find a new home for, because he persisted in going across a busy highway to visit the kennel across the road that raised Doberman Pincers and Shar Peis I thought that maybe he had learned some street wisdom from these escapades, which could be useful in traffic work.

I consulted with Karin Maida, and we checked out Moose. I was either very foolish or very gutsy, but I put a harness on Moose, a green dog, and walked with him for several blocks to see how responsive he might be. Karin was following a few feet behind me. When we got to curbs, she would yell, "Curb!" so I would know it was coming and wouldn't sprain an ankle but could correct Moose. It was a wild trip!

We decided to take Moose, and we donated him to Guide dogs of the Desert. Steve was going to work there, but before he did, he brought me Sugar, the yellow lab he had trained. If I didn't accept her, he had another student in line for her.

I tried to work with Sugar under Steve's guidance for two or three days. She seemed to be a good dog, but the one problem I had with her made her unacceptable to me. She "crabbed," meaning that she tended to walk toward the right, which meant that I was putting constant leftward pressure on her to be able to walk straight. I didn't feel physically comfortable walking with her.

Meanwhile, Nana was continuing her downhill slide. I began to hear some of the old stories with strange, improbable twists, and some new things that didn't seem connected with prior reality at all. She began to perceive things as totally different from what they were. For example, I felt bad that Nana never had a diamond. I bought her a one-carat cubic zirconium pendant with a 14-carat gold setting. She thought it was a little penguin set with a diamond, and she proceeded to give it back to me. In another instance, a little gold-plated ring with a diamond chip came in the mail. She started wearing it with her wedding ring. I didn't like the idea that it was only gold-plated and turning color. I bought her a small diamond ring instead, and we managed to switch it with the other one without her knowing. She may not have known the difference, but it was important to me that she had the right thing.

In 1986, I was accepted for training at Guide Dogs of the Desert. At some point, Steve Koten left the school. Alvin Whitehead took over the training of Miki, the dog that he thought was appropriate for me. Meanwhile, they decided to reject Moose for their program. In the late summer or fall of that year, I went back to Jeanne's house in Jamul for a visit. We did some more fun things in CA, including visiting Redwood Forest in the Redwood National Park and Mendocino on the coast. I was able to share a few more figs with Bill. They were planning to sell the house and move to Redwood Valley near Ukiah later that year.

Jeanne and Bill took me to Palm Springs, to Guide Dogs of the Desert. Alvin gave me a test walk with Mikki, a yellow Labrador retriever a little smaller than Vincent. I told them that I had a home for Moose, and we took him back to Jamul with us. What I didn't tell them was that I personally wanted to see what Moose was capable of as a guide for me.

I flew home with Vincent in the passenger cabin with me, and Moose was in the kennel crate in the pressurized section of the baggage compartment. Once home, I tried for four hectic weeks to work Moose. The first time that I walked with him to church, he ran a curb—that is, didn't stop for it – and I sprained an ankle. However, I had to keep walking on that sore ankle, because I had to work him to find out what he was able to do. Fortunately, Moose and Vincent coexisted, but I had to make sure that Moose didn't get too rough in trying to play with Vincent.

Moose had potential. He went up and down stairs slowly and carefully, which I loved. He also blocked my driveway when Mike Kigin dropped us off at the house until Mike pulled away, telling me that he was alert for a moving vehicle. However, he had a stubborn and independent streak that didn't respond to my attempts to make him listen to me and work for me. The problem was especially bad if someone else was around and Moose thought that someone else could do his job for him. At home, he was a playful, mischievous clown, who chewed up one of my bedroom slippers, flipped around the pages of my discarded Braille magazines to enjoy the noise they made, and carried one of my big life-sized vinyl baby dolls from one end of the house to the other by the diaper. He wore me out!

Out of desperation, I took Moose up to Guide Dog Foundation in Smithtown, Long Island, for a couple of days of evaluation. The school's instructor who worked with me, named John, confirmed what my gut instincts had guessed: Moose was more suitable for a man, or at least for someone with a drill-sergeant, no-nonsense regular personality like Texas Mary. Even if he could be made to work, I was not a good match for him. I cried with Moose trying to comfort me, but I accepted the verdict.

Texas Mary took Moose off my hands. With her assertive, no-nonsense personality, she was a well-matched mistress for Moose. The first thing that she had to do was to nurse him, with vet-prescribed antibiotics, through the case of kennel cough that he picked up at the guide dog school. She kept him as a companion dog. She even took him wind surfing. As it turned out, Moose would not have been able to work as a guide dog. We later found out that the reason that he was so careful on steps was that he was in pain. He had arthritis in his shoulders, and it would not have been good for him to work in a harness.

Mary married Kevin Miller a year or two later. Unfortunately, the marriage didn't last. I lost touch with Mary, but the last I heard from her on the telephone, Moose lived on to at least age sixteen.

Meanwhile, Vincent went willingly back into service as my guide for a little while longer. Dr. Morrissey eventually took precautionary X-rays of the sprained ankle, to make sure that I had no bone chips in it, but it wasn't broken. It was a couple of months before it totally stopped hurting.

Other things were happening with my friends. After his mother and father died, Father Seamus felt called to a more cloistered monastic life. With the consent of the bishop, he founded a monastery, the Monks of St. Augustine of the Primitive Observance. After trying one location in Maine that was too cold and damp for Father's arthritis, they relocated to Peaks Island, in Maine.

Uncle Johnny developed brain cancer, which eventually killed him. I was sorry not to have visited him in his house in Florida while he was still alive.

In this period, God sent me two other influential friends. A member of my parish, Pam Cleary, befriended me. We got together to read spiritual articles, including descriptions of Marian apparitions, and we discussed engrossing, important subjects, such as the relationship between deliberate sin, man's free will, and heaven and hell. As one of the articles that Pam found said, if human beings are to merit heaven, they must also run the risk of choosing hell. Pam was also a fervent believer in the sanctity of life, and she often cried when thinking about or discussing the plight of unborn children killed by abortions.

I should digress here to elaborate on my pro-life convictions. God is the ultimate source of all life, but human beings through the exercise of their free will have an impact on their lives and those of others. They participate with the Divine Creation in begetting new life. Although society rightly protects the choice of people as to whether to conceive children, once a life begins at conception, it deserves the protection of law. In answer to the argument that some folks try to make that children with disabilities or birth defects should be aborted in the womb, I think that my own life is an ultimate refutation of that notion. Also, we Catholics believe that our sufferings, through union with Jesus, can be offered up for our good and the good of others. Although we don't pretend to have the ultimate answer to the mystery of suffering, we do know that God often works through the difficulties we and others have in life to bring about ultimate good. Moreover, disrespecting the lives of the fragile unborn inexorably leads to disrespecting and trivializing the lives of the elderly, seriously ill people, and people with disabilities. These convictions have led to my membership in the pro-life committee of my parish and participation in the annual march for life and other similar activities until I became physically unable to do so.

Pam and I also did some fun things together, such as going to a doll show in the Washington DC Convention Center, where I found a doll similar to the one Mama had as a child.

Dottie and I also concluded that it was all we could do to efficiently use our time to concentrate on paying bills and important paperwork. I sought volunteers to help with fun reading and less weighty matters, such as going through catalogs. One of these volunteers was Karin Goodlatte. She and her husband, Ray, originally lived in Vermont, and she was familiar with some of the places that Nana talked about. When she came, I introduced her to Nana as "our friend from Vermont." Among other fun books, Karin read me *The Hobbit*, the book that gives the background for the Lord of the Rings trilogy.

During these years, I also grew close to my Aunt Maria. We started calling each other, to catch up on family news. We became much better acquainted as telephone buddies. Among the other things that we shared was that both of us, in a way, were lone survivors. Aunt Maria was the last of Papa's siblings; I was Papa's only surviving child.

I still kept in touch with Uncle Joe and Aunt Irene, and I tried to remember to call the Abbiattis sometimes. Sister Margaret James and Gretchen, too, were very supportive and tried to keep in touch with me. I heard much less frequently from Jim or Tim.

Once Vincent retired, my life was going to change yet again. In mid-April, 1987, I went for training for my second guide dog with Guide Dogs of the Desert, located near Palm Springs, CA. Because I was a first-time student in that school, I had to stay the whole four weeks of the program. It was the last class before the school stopped training students for the terrifically hot, dry days of summer. Even as it was, the daytime temperatures went over 100 degrees Fahrenheit, but it was more tolerable than similar temperatures in Washington, DC would have been with the high humidity. Also, although I engaged in strenuous physical activity while there, I found that I was not stiff or sore as I expected to be. I have reason to think that the dryer climate agrees with me.

The school was much smaller than Guiding Eyes. We had two instructors with our class, plus the housekeeping staff. The instructors were Alvin Whitehead, who originally came from VA, and another instructor, named Mike. I don't remember Mike's last name. We had six students in the class: four ladies, three of whom received Labradors and one of whom received a golden retriever, and two gentlemen, one of whom received a German shepherd and the other one who received a golden retriever. The school had a much tighter budget than Guiding Eyes, so we did not have the sumptuous cuisine that Jose produced in Yorktown Heights.

Inge, my roommate, received a golden retriever, named Brenda. Elizabeth and Donna Hawkins shared a room, and each of them had a black Lab, Billy and Wilma respectively. Marvin had the shepherd, Prince. I forgot the name of Gene's dog. I received, as originally planned, a yellow Lab, Mikki (June 22, 1985-March 5, 1999.) A picture of her and me is at the beginning of this chapter. Sometimes people confuse pictures of Vincent and her, because both dogs are considered yellow Labradors. To clarify the confusion, I tell them that Vincent was almost white with a black nose; Mikki was a little darker, but her nose matched the rest of her body.

As at Guiding Eyes, we spent some time getting our dogs used to parking on the cement driveway or road near the school. Unlike Guiding Eyes, we were allowed to turn our dogs loose together in a communal run for part of the last two weeks. We also were taught what to do in the event of an earthquake: namely to evacuate the building with coat or bathrobe and shoes, especially if it happened at night. I slept with my clothes on a chair, just in case. I later learned from Judy who worked for me and was also from San Diego, CA, that the better protocol is to get into a doorway or under something, like a heavy piece of furniture until it is over. Going outside may not be a good idea, because debris from buildings can fall on you. The school in Palm Springs was out in an open place, so if you got away from the buildings, you might be OK.

Like the program at Guiding Eyes, we were taken out to work our dogs in a variety of settings; we went to Palm Springs for city work; to Banning for residential work with funny streets and irregular sidewalks; and to Los Angeles for one day of big city work. One particular route, I don't remember where, had very bad, broken-up sidewalks. I personally dubbed it "nightmare street." I fell down while walking this route and skinned one of my knees. The one positive thing that I remember about incredibly noisy, busy Los Angeles was that I received more unsolicited offers of assistance for crossing the street than I ever received in Washington.

In class, I made a friend of Donna, and we kept in touch by letter for a while after I came home.

Marvin was the most interesting member of our class. He used to be a canine trainer in a police department. The vision problem for which he needed the help of a dog was caused by astigmatism, which sometimes also affected his balance. We discovered that he had a severe allergy to flea dip, and we all had to spend one hot day washing off all of our dipped dogs, because he broke out if he came into contact with them. Marvin had divorced his first wife, and now he was married again and this second wife was expecting a baby. Although we weren't supposed to leave the premises overnight until the end of the program, when he heard that his wife had delivered the baby or was in labor, he went AWOL, with the instructors' tacit understanding, to see his wife and new baby. He came back after a few days.

On account of our particular needs, Mikki and Prince were the only two dogs in the class to receive escalator training. That meant that Mikki and Prince were friends, which worked out well on one occasion. We were sitting around waiting for our turn to go out, and Marvin dozed off. Fortunately, Prince came to me. I grabbed the end of his leash and held onto it. When I heard Marvin stirring, I just said, "Here's your dog," and gave Prince back to him. The instructors would not have appreciated it if they found out what happened.

Because of his positive, upbeat personality, Marvin was a boost to the morale of all of us. He knew as much or more than the instructors about dogs and their psychology.

On one occasion, I had gone with Mikki to the utility building that served as the laundry room with the washing machines and dryers. I was trying to get her to go down. She wouldn't listen to me when I did what Alvin had told me. Marvin came along, and I told him my problem. He took the leash near the clips on Mikki's collar and had Mikki down on the walk in two seconds, without making much of a fuss about it. I learned almost as much from him as from the instructors.

At Guide Dogs of the Desert, we received a bonus in having the opportunity to have our dogs learn to remain calm and focused with a cat around. The school had a resident feline. Alvin called the cat Alice, but it may have been a male; perhaps the name should have been Alex. Alex had to be either inside the school building or in the kennel at night, because he would have been a tempting morsel for coyotes. My roommate, Inge, was distressed to find Alex in her clothes closet in our room. If our dogs were acting odd, it may well have been Alex; you never knew where he was going to turn up. One day, we had to return prematurely from a planned trip, because we had forgotten something. Alvin saw Alex under a telephone repair truck. He called him back into the premises. Some of us wished that Alex had been allowed to go adventuring elsewhere!

As with Guiding Eyes, I found this program difficult. The weather was very hot during the day, but it cooled off at night. Sometimes the wind blew strongly and made a whistling sound when somebody opened the outside door, and it reminded me of Pentecost. The daytime heat meant that we lived in short-sleeved tops and shorts, with liberal sun block applied all over the body. We even took the class pictures in this attire on account of the heat!

I fell down during one of the training routes over difficult pavement. At night, the desert was incredibly still. I never heard coyotes howl, although others did. I guess they did so when I was asleep without my hearing aids!

In this course, we had only the two instructors, and we didn't have a person like Steve Orcutt to whom to take our problems. Some members of the school's board did come out to the school on one occasion, when the instructors weren't around, and we did get to vent with them, but they weren't in a position to evaluate how we worked with our dogs.

Concerning the instructors, Mike was easygoing and affable. Alvin could be brusque, demanding, and unsympathetic. My upset psychological state was aggravated by the fact that I was mourning the loss of Vincent as a partner. I knew that I was going home to him as a home buddy, but however good Mikki turned out to be, she would never be a guide like Vincent. Alvin complained that the turnover to Mikki wasn't happening fast enough. As with Dave at Guiding Eyes, he wasn't very good at dealing with the psychology of the situation. Neither Alvin nor Mike seemed to have any good ideas about dealing with street crossings with a hearing loss, other than the same injunctions that I had been given at Guiding Eyes. Unlike the instructors at Guiding Eyes, Alvin seemed genuinely glad that I had someone like Karin Maida with whom to work once I came home. When we weren't working our dogs, I found consolation in listening to a cassette recording of St. John's Gospel.

One of Papa's nicknames for Vincent was "the big ox." I started calling Mikki "Little Moose," because she reminded me of the original Moose. We heard that, like big Moose, she and her sister had been donated to the school when they were about six months old. Like that larger Lab, she was more squared-off in her conformation than Vincent, probably because she had a convex curvature to her back in the middle. Unlike Vincent and Moose, her nose was beige or brown, matching the rest of her coloring, instead of being black. Fortunately for me, Mikki was much easier to control than big Moose!

The turnover with Mikki eventually happened when I became protective of her and she began to realize that I was in her corner. We caught Mikki chewing on a furniture leg, and Alvin corrected her so sharply that she cried. I knew why he did it, because you can't have working dogs chewing on furniture, but it seemed unfair in that the dogs in the school's kennel (before they came indoors with us) had wooden platforms on which to lie. Of course, out of boredom the dogs would develop the habit of chewing on wood if left that way unsupervised! We had to overcome this problem with the help of bitter apple and close supervision after I got home, as discussed later, but we eventually succeeded. Meanwhile, Mikki became adept at finding the Ladies' room in department stores, because it was one place that she and I could go that Alvin couldn't follow! I ended up making a funny poem about Mikki:

> I love my little moose!
> I don't know what I'd do
> Without my little moose!
> I'd be a very sad, unhappy silly goose
> If I didn't have my crazy little moose!

I was able to receive some consolation when I managed to hook up with volunteers to get to Mass on some of the Sundays. It was a very nice church, and the folks were wonderful. At the parish gift shop, I bought a beautiful, detailed wall crucifix. It still hangs in my bedroom above my bed.

As with Guiding Eyes, I had some problems with Mikki during the training. Unlike Vincent, she really didn't try hard to argue with me, but she pulled out strongly when working, too strongly for my comfort. I tried not to draw conclusions during class, because it tends to be a high stress setting for people and dogs. I concluded that I would have to take Mikki home and "see what evolved," as Sister Elizabeth Henry might have put it.

After I came home in mid-May, the hard pulling persisted, especially in unfamiliar places. I did finally get Mikki to relax and pull more lightly on a well-traveled route, such as the walk to church. However, she still pulled like the dickens or otherwise got upset when she didn't know where she was, or if she thought that we were going to test her with traffic. For these reasons and the way that she turned her head to look around when she was working, we began to wonder if poor Mikki had tunnel vision. She seemed to understand very well what we wanted of her, but she had trouble carrying it out.

However, she tried her best to take care of me. On one occasion, I was lying on the couch with my feet on, partly under, or against Mikki. She shifted her body in such a way that she covered my feet. She didn't want them to get cold.

Mikki had a whacky sense of humor. She would bark at me, causing me to get up to see if she needed to go outside, and then she would jump into the chair in which I was sitting. She would push against me with her paws, as though to say, "Ha, ha, I got your chair!"

Mikki looked so cute curled up in the big reclining rocking chair that I did a little bronze statue of her in the chair.

However, Mikki seemed to know that I couldn't see and needed verbal communication. If she came upstairs to join me after I was in bed, she would bark. I finally figured out that she was announcing her presence. I guess that she didn't want to sneak up on me if I was in bed.

When she was working, Mikki tended to wag her tail if she saw people or just in general. She was a social butterfly in canine disguise, and I found her apparent lack of seriousness a distinct contrast with Vincent. Although she refrained from barking while working, at home she would bark for the mailman, people passing by, or others coming to the door. However, she would stand on the couch with her paws on the back of it, wagging her tail at the mailman.

As it turned out, Karin Maida didn't seem to be available too much when I came home with Mikki, so I started looking for someone else. I found Janice Morton, whose business was called Academy Dog Obedience training. She had worked with private clients, and she also gave obedience classes for the city of Falls Church and Fairfax County. She was very helpful to me in trying to work out these problems with Mikki. We formed the relationship that led to her training Remus for me, to be discussed in another chapter.

My working problems with Mikki were the occasion for my finding another friend at work. I don't remember exactly when Billie retired, but I think that she was still working at the SEC when I brought Mikki home. Katie Nix began going out with Mikki and me at lunchtime to take care of the parking chores, and she observed us working. She had dogs at home, and we became acquainted at first to share our dog stories. It turned into a lifelong friendship. I often spent Thanksgiving with Katie and her extended family.

Another problem that I had to work out with Mikki came from her Labrador and "bird dog" genes.

Mikki came from the desert region near Palm Springs, and she wasn't used to the flying birds that one often sees on the east coast. The problem was aggravated by the fact that it was the year for the seventeen-year cicadas. The birds and the cicadas were a big distraction for Mikki. With the advice of Janice Morton, I began using a pinch collar as a teaching tool to get us past this problem.

We fortunately progressed to the point that I no longer needed the pinch collar, and we could go back to using the choke collar.

We also had problems with Mikki expressing her stress by chewing up throw pillows, pulling the hair off one of my musical porcelain dolls (on my birthday, no less) and otherwise being destructive if I wasn't paying attention to her. She bent the shafts of thumbtacks parallel to their heads and mangled the silver shamrock pendant that Sue gave me. Fortunately the jewelers could repair the shamrock, and I got the thumbtacks away from her before she swallowed them or hurt herself. I couldn't even trust her with the solid, crystallized glass Christmas ornaments that Vincent ignored, because she treated them like bones and tried to chew on them. She also rendered some of the nativity lambs lame by biting off one of their legs. Mikki ironically could be left loose in the house with Vincent on the rare occasions that I went somewhere without her, and then she tore up nothing. We finally concluded that she was trying to get my attention by acting up if I was in the house and ignoring her, and then we were able to solve the problem. I did not find her to be the independent thinker and good assessor of streets that Vincent had been.

Mikki got along well with Vincent. Unlike Moose, she didn't try to jump on him and to play rough with him, but sometimes she would lie on her back on the floor, rolling around and making whining or crying noises. Vincent would come to me and politely suggest that I put them outside. After they were outside a while, they both came in much calmer. When Jim Waeldner at work heard about this behavior, he laughed and said, "They're keeping house!"

I laughed. "I wanted you to like Vincent," I told Mikki. "But I had no idea he was your sweetheart."

The feeling seemed to be mutual. On one occasion, Mikki had chewed up a throw pillow; I put it back on the couch and hooked her to the piano on tie-down. When I went back to get her, I found that Vincent had left the beat-up pillow beside her as a consolation prize. On another occasion, I thought that I caught Vincent messing with the kitchen trash, a rare occurrence for him. In annoyance, I tried to pull him over to the piano to hook him up on tie-down. Mikki lay down between me and Vincent and the tie-down. "Hook me up; I did it!" She seemed to be saying.

I had to give in and just laugh! "You'd better be nice to Mikki," I told Vincent. "Look what she did for you!"

Finally, one Sunday, we were eating dinner in the dining room during a thunderstorm. I reached under the table to find Mikki lying close to Vincent, with her head resting on him.

"Who's comforting whom here?" I asked them.

Even with all the working problems that I was having with Mikki, I still found her to be a wonderful, loving companion and a real comfort. She was almost a therapy dog for me. I started letting her lie on the couch and my bed at first, because I found out that she would relax there and go to sleep without getting into trouble. Then I realized how comforting it was to have her snuggled up against me on the couch or in bed. Having her lie beside me so close reminded me of Mama's lying down with me. I still don't know how we managed at first to do this on a single, twin bed, before I combined the two twins into a larger king-sized bed. We woke up wrapped around each other in some very odd positions. No, I don't let my dogs sleep on the mattress under the covers. They lie on the top blanket or coverlet. That minimizes dog hairs on the sleeping surface and is a layer of protection against any fleas or ticks that my preventatives miss.

Sometimes, Mikki would bark at me. I would get out of bed thinking that she wanted to go out. She would get onto the other side of the bed instead. I would have to get into bed beside her on the other side. She was trying to tell me that she wanted to change places!

Mikki also used her tail to communicate. If I called her name, she would bang her tail on the floor to make a drumming sound and tell me where she was. We said that Mikki had a drummer tail!

Nana at first had trouble learning Mikki's name, a clear sign of her deteriorating memory. "Is the name Mickey, like Mickey mouse?" she kept asking.

I spelled the name with a feminine form, and I sometimes called her Mikki-San, because someone said that her eyes looked Japanese. I couldn't see the point of trying to explain all of that to Nana about Mikki's name, so I just said yes when Nana compared her to Mickey Mouse. Inside I was thinking, "Mouse she ain't."

Nana's nickname for Mikki was the Jumping Jack, because Mikki had a habit of jumping straight up in the air, up and down, to greet people or when she was excited. Friends told me that she would jump up five or six feet to see out the front door through the pane of glass on the inside door if she saw someone coming. Our front door inside has only three little glass windows in it, and they are in odd locations and not adjacent to each other.

Nana also picked up on the fact that Mikki didn't have the judgment that Vincent did. She would say, "Vincent has more sense in one of his little toes than Mikki has in her head!"

Heaven help me, but sometimes I privately agreed with her, but I didn't think that it was a good idea to say so.

I was still amazed by Vincent's intelligence and ability to understand. Before I started using a talking programmable thermostat, we used to have a thermostat with raised markings to allow me to adjust it, but it wasn't programmable or automatic. Before we went to bed, I would lower the temperature a couple of degrees, to keep the house cooler while we slept.

One evening, I told the dogs, "I'm going to put you out once more, and then I will fix the furnace, and we will go to bed."

After they came back into the house, I started to go upstairs. Vincent stood at the bottom of the stairs blocking my path. I wondered why, and then I remembered that I hadn't adjusted the thermostat. I turned around and went into the hall to do it, and Vincent went upstairs. He clearly heard what I said, and he didn't want to be hot at night with all that fluffy, thick white fur!

When I told Billie the story, she said, "You'd better be careful what you say to him!" We laughed.

My experience with the last good picture taken of Mama at the fair and Papa's good picture of Vincent made me realize the value of having at least a few good pictures of my dogs. I hired a photographer to take a set of pictures of me with Mikki and Vincent, some with each dog and some with the two together. I have a framed picture of the three of us hanging upstairs across from my office.

While I was at work, Vincent turned out to be Nana's pal and comfort in retirement. When she sat in her chair, wearing her glasses and all bundled up in Afghans and throws, Vincent would sit next to her chair, and Nana would put her arm tightly around him. Eventually, Nana's arm would relax, and Vincent would lie down on the floor next to the chair, and they would both be asleep. I made a little bronze statue of Nana sitting in that chair, hugging Vincent.

Sometimes, to give Mikki more work experiences, Janice and I would go on weekend outings to shopping malls and goody stores. I also visited her at her house with Mikki and sometimes with Vincent, too. Janice had two dogs: a large German shepherd male, called Sheppy, and a black with some white Lab mix female, called Kelly.

Janice also had a wonderful black cat with a white undercoat, Fred. Fred was the kind of cat that would meow at you when you came into the house. Translation: "Go find somewhere to sit so I can get in your lap and you can hold and pat me!" I loved doing it. He got along with the dogs, too. He had extra toes with non-retractable claws on his front paws; I heard all kinds of good stories about Fred and his escapades when he was younger. He used those extra claws like fingers to open doors and cupboards to find goodies for himself and his special canine buddy, a previous German shepherd, named Prince. I cried a few years later when I heard that Fred died. If I ever got a cat, I'd like to have one like him.

The summer of 1987 was very hot and humid. Because I didn't feel so confident of Mikki as Vincent and to escape the heat, I spent much time on the weekends reading, including the three books of the Lord of the Rings Saga. I also began dictating the story onto cassette about Princes Gertrude and King Gideon that became my first long novel, *The Unbroken Circle.*

During my spare time in 1986 and in the fall of 1987, I took a couple of adult education courses at Thomas Jefferson High School that involved learning to work with stoneware clay and have things fired. I really enjoyed these courses, and they provided me an outlet for some of my stress and frustrations. One problem I had with the clay was that it was very messy and made a lot of dust, and I wasn't sure that was good for my allergies. The other difficulty with working with clay is that unfired, dried pieces, called green ware, often break before they are fired. They can be repaired at that stage, but sometimes they break again when they are being fired.

During one of these classes, I made at home a stoneware crucifix by hand. I worked on it for several days, and while I was working on it, I had to keep it covered up to keep the clay moist. Working on it that way reminded me of Jesus' body wrapped in a shroud before burial. It was a very spiritual experience working on that piece. I thanked Him for "sitting for me" while I was making it. It broke in the box when I took it to the school to have it fired, and I had to take it home and repair it, after I finished crying when I found it broken. Eventually, I managed to get it fired. It broke again several years later, and I repaired it. Eventually, I augmented it with wax, and I sent it to Wegner Metal Arts to have two bronze casts made from it. I kept one, and I sent the other to father Seamus, so that he could hang it in his monastery. As discussed later, they had moved to Florida by this time.

Alvin Whitehead came to see Mikki and me for one follow-up visit when he came back east to visit relatives in VA. He didn't seem to have any problems with how we were doing, although he did inquire whether Mikki was excessively destructive in the house. That problem forced her sister to muster out of service as a guide dog. Because we were beginning to overcome our problems, I said no.

As I mentioned, Vincent got along well with Mikki, but he had his own ideas about what was appropriate. Especially if Patsy was away or I was alone in the house with Nana on the weekend, Vincent would go out into the backyard by himself and come inside. Then Mikki would go out. If I went with them, both of them would go. Vincent also still made sure that he got my friends to take him for walks sometimes. He would act like they needed to go outside, and Mikki would go out. Vincent would make a U-turn and double back inside the house and invite Judy or other friends to take him for a walk. He also would sometimes drop his bone on the floor so Mikki would go and grab it. When she was busy, he would come and ask me to pat him.

Unfortunately, Mikki never learned to like retrieving balls. She would bring a ball back once or twice, but then she would take the ball and go to the back door. "OK, I have my ball; can I take it into the house now?" If Vincent was trying to play, she might stay in the game longer, but she was young and faster than he, and he couldn't compete with her.

Mikki did have one shining hour as a guide. I decided to go to the bazaar at Barbara's church, Calvary Methodist Church, one Saturday in November. Barbara's church was only a block or two away from our church, but we had to cross some streets. People had given me some general directions, which I tried to follow. What I didn't know was that, in deciding to walk on this particular side of the street, I would be walking down a block with a huge tree growing in the middle of it, almost blocking the walkway. By the grace and protection of God, Mikki somehow guided me around that tree without my getting seriously hurt. She did an excellent job that day. Needless to say, I had someone assist me in going home on the other side of the street with my purchases.

At work, things were changing with the way we used computers. Attorneys were issued Word Perfect word-processing software on their desktop SEC computers, and they were expected to do more of their own drafting, instead of giving the work to support staff. E-mail was coming, too, and it would soon replace telephone as the informal means of communication within the SEC. Fortunately, through speech synthesizers and screen-reading software, it was beginning to be possible for me to have access to these technologies, too. It was more to learn and more adjustments to make to a technological age. The frustration is that the adaptive technology necessary for people with disabilities to access this new computer technology is always two steps behind the latest new innovation. We still too often feel left behind and neglected. I especially resented it when, a few years later, Windows largely replaced MS-DOS, which was easier to adapt because it was text-based. I don't care how much money Bill Gates has made and is willing to give away! He flew high on the wings of the technological raven at the expense of the very little people that he so eloquently claims to champion! I wish that Uncle Sam had broken up Microsoft instead of AT&T!

Things were happening with Aunt Maria, too. She was in a very serious accident. She and some other parishioners were standing outside of church one Sunday. Someone lost control of their car and hit two or three of the bystanders, including my aunt. She had a long recovery from this accident. Somewhere in this time frame, she also went on a serious diet and lost a good number of pounds.

I heard that she was looking well. God protected her for a reason. Her oldest son, Cousin Paul, had worked with the steel mills in Pittsburgh, but many of those jobs were going away. He decided to take a job in Indiana, but his wife, Pat, didn't want to move until the girls were done with the school year. Aunt Maria went to Indiana with Paul to help him get settled, until the family joined him later.

As the year of 1987 was drawing to a close, I had inklings that I would soon be confronting the crisis of Nana's advancing Alzheimer's disease, along with the need to adjust to a less than ideal canine partner.

# THE HOUR OF LEAD

*B*y the fall of 1987, it was becoming increasingly clear that we probably would have no happy endings with Nana. At some point, I consulted an expert in elder care. I no longer remember her name, but we began to discuss ways and means to help the situation to work better at home. One result was that I hired another lady to provide some assistance to Nana on a part-time basis to supplement what Patsy was able to do. Another thing that I had to consider was the possibility that Nana would have to go to a nursing home. I was still resisting that course of action. However, at some point I started visiting various nursing centers. The adviser lady was trying to help me narrow the choice down to the better ones.

Billie came over to help me celebrate my birthday in 1987. Vincent wasn't feeling well; his ears seemed to be bothering him, and it made him not want to eat. He kept looking to us to solve the problem. It scared me sometimes how much my dogs trusted me and expected me to solve their problems. We did get Vincent feeling better eventually, but it reminded me again of the fragility of life.

On another level, the way my dogs trusted me reminded me of how I should react to God. As I told one of my spiritual advisers paraphrasing Cardinal Woolsey, "Would that I could trust my God half so well as my dogs trust me."

At Christmas time at work, we had our usual holiday party. Many members of the staff brought homemade dishes, including the main meats. I do not know if it was a form of food poisoning, or if it was merely the intestinal virus in an extremely severe form, but I became very sick before the holidays for a day or two. I was freezing and sick to my stomach, with diarrhea. Mikki was lying on top of me on the bed, but I still couldn't get warm. Patsy tried to feed the dogs. Vincent went downstairs and ate his dinner, but Mikki wouldn't leave me. My bathrobe was lying on top of the covers. Mikki externalized her stress and worry by chewing holes in the bathrobe.

I called Dr. Ambury, and he told me how to take the Pepto-Bismol in such a way as to minimize the diarrhea. Meanwhile, it was the night to pay bills and do paperwork. Dottie came over, and she managed to persuade Mikki to go downstairs and eat her dinner. Dottie got the necessary checks together and I signed them. After that, she put both dogs out and saw me settled for the night, with Mikki back on the bed with me.

The next thing that I knew, Patsy was calling me on the intercom. "It's almost 11 o'clock, [in the morning], and maybe you'd better come down. This dog [Mikki] hasn't been out!"

Needless to say, I didn't go to work that day. It took me a day or two to recover. It was one of the few times that I remember being sick when Nana wasn't involved in my recovery or overtly expressing concern about me.

I should digress here to explain how things turned out with Dr. Ambury. He eventually retired from the regular practice of medicine, and he became a deacon in our parish. I don't remember whether this happened before Nana died, but I think that it was afterwards. In any event, he was somewhat involved in her medical treatment until shortly before she went into the nursing home. Mrs. Ambury, Dr. Ambury's wife, became seriously ill, and her husband nursed her with tender loving care. She died at home in his arms. In 2005, Dr. Ambury did not appear for morning Mass, and parishioners checked on him. They found him unconscious in his house. He seems to have suffered a heart attack. He was hospitalized, but he died a few days later. We all miss him.

Meanwhile, in 1987, Nana's situation was showing signs of further deterioration. She was beginning to imagine that my brothers, particularly Johnny, were around and that she was talking to them. She seemed to be more violently agitated and upset at times. It was becoming much more difficult to cope.

As I recall, I signed up for another course to work with clay during the period of late 1987 or early 1988. I still found working with that clay a good vent for frustration. Not surprisingly, I began making some crucifixes.

In February, I accepted Aunt Murff's invitation to visit her in Florida. I flew to Fort Walton Beach with Mikki. The plane was delayed and we sat and sat on the stopover. Once I arrived in Shalimar, the town near Clearwater where Aunt Murff lives, Pattie commiserated with me, sharing stories from when she worked as a stewardess.

I had a wonderful time in Florida. The light seemed so much stronger and brighter there, even though it was February. I got to see the nice house and the one bathroom of the two that had the Japanese-style tub that Uncle Johnny had described to us. Unfortunately for my desire to experience what it was like, Aunt Murff was no longer using this tub, because it was lined with tile, and it was difficult to keep the grout between the squares clean and mold-free. I noticed that Aunt Murff had a beautiful ceramic tile floor in her kitchen. She told me how durable and practical it was, and I later decided to put a similar floor in my kitchen when I had it renovated in 1995.

While I was visiting Aunt Murff, I went with Pattie to the Shore Mall and bought a beautiful heart-shaped pendant with a pearl and a diamond from Bailey, Banks, and Biddles. Aunt Murff and Pattie also took me to various places of interest, including Fort Eglin Air Force Base. I was told that the golf course on this base is one of the few places where you might encounter both alligators in the swamp and bears in the woods! I also went shopping in a wonderful store that sold religious articles. Among other things, I bought a hanging plaque with the words to "Footprints" on it, as well as a Fontanini crucifix from which I took impressions to try to duplicate it in stoneware clay and porcelain.

We also went to the beach one afternoon. It wasn't hot enough to go wading, but I enjoyed walking on the beach and listening to the water. Of course, I bought a rubber alligator for a souvenir.

Mikki proved to be a good, easygoing traveling companion. She also got along well with Murff's cat, named Pootsie.

In addition to getting to know Pattie as an adult and meeting her nice husband, Ron Ward, I was introduced to many of Aunt Murff's friends. She had different friends as guests on the various evenings. Aunt Murff and her guests reminisced about their military experiences in various locations, including Aunt Murff's stay in Japan to be near Uncle Johnny when he was there after World War II. I told Aunt Murff that she ought to write a book! Before I left, Aunt Murff gave me a crucifix that she had. The cross was lined with mother-of-pearl, but the corpus of Jesus on the cross was made of plastic. After I got home, I found out that the plastic material glowed in the dark. Like Sister Elizabeth Henry, I didn't think that it was appropriate to make it that way, but, as discussed a little later, it came to a good use in the end!

Patsy apparently had a very hard time with Nana while I was gone. "Don't leave me alone with her ever again!" she told me. Coming from capable, resilient Patsy, this was bad news indeed. It confirmed that things were indeed getting worse.

Another circumstance confirmed that Nana was losing her grip on reality. While I was gone, Margie came to visit Nana. She brought a friend with her, Seldin French. Seldin was from New York; because his parents came from the West Indies, he had a very British-sounding accent. Nana knew him and had seen him before, but on this occasion, she thought that he was an old Scottish friend from Vermont, even though this gentleman, who happens to be black, doesn't look at all like a typical Scotchman.

"How did you know that I was in trouble?" she asked Sel.

God bless him, but Seldin played along. He sang with her, "You take the high road, and I'll take the low road ..." I've heard him sing it before, and he sounded wonderful! I'm grateful that he could give her some happiness.

After I came home, Nana fell again. This last time, she hit her head. We decided to take her to the emergency room. They checked her out and decided to release her. How I wish that they had kept her overnight! I needed a little space to think and regroup, but I didn't have any. The wonderful vacation in Florida seemed a distant memory!

The adviser lady and I narrowed the nursing home choices down to three, and I visited them all. They all seemed quite good, but I thought that the atmosphere at Mount Vernon Nursing Center seemed more informal. For a week or so, I had 24-hour coverage through the nurses supplied by the Private Duty Nurses Association. One of them, in particular, seemed quite good. My dilemma was that we did not know how long Nana had to live. If I had known for certain that we only had another month or two, as things turned out to be, I would have damned the estate, spent all her money on the nurses, and let her die at home, which would have been what she wanted. However, I couldn't see the future. If the money had run out, then I would be limited to nursing homes that accepted Medicare/Medicaid patients ad initio. According to the adviser, the better nursing homes probably would keep her and transfer her to the Medicare/Medicaid status if she came into the facility at first as a paying patient. The adviser also cautioned me not to feel guilty if Nana did not live long once she entered the nursing home. Many families, like me, waited as long as possible to put relatives in nursing facilities, and often their condition was close to the end when they went into the place.

An opening became available, and we chose Mount Vernon. Our hope was that Nana might have more interaction with other patients and the staff than I could provide her at home. If so, and she could make the adjustment, it might be better for her there for a little while.

The meals that the place served patients were excellent, as confirmed by Patsy when she visited during the weekdays, and they served a variety of things to Nana to try to tempt her appetite. I think that the staff at the facility took reasonably good care of Nana, but they did confine her to her chair, and I think that they resorted to sedation more than I would like. However, I could understand their dilemma. They didn't want her throwing things in a fit of temper or walking around unsteadily and falling and hurting herself.

Nana went into the nursing home in March. I went to see her as often as possible in the evenings, and Patsy went during the day. We tried to encourage her to eat. At first, Nana thought that she was in a hospital. How I wish that they had played along with that idea. We might have eased the adjustment for Nana by a little benign deception. As Nana said, she wasn't afraid to be in a hospital, but I knew that she wouldn't accept never going home to my house. No, the folks at the nursing home told her and wanted me to tell her that the place was her new home now! They didn't get it. When someone is losing it like Nana, you have to tell the person whatever you can that is close to the truth to get acceptance of and coping with the reality. As I mentioned already, we told Nana for years that the beef, lamb, and other dishes that Patsy served were all "chicken," because for some reason all she wanted to eat was chicken. That inaccurate statement may have allowed her to live longer than had we told her the unvarnished truth! Likewise, had they let her think that it was a hospital, and that she had a chance to get better and go home, she might have accepted it better and tried more to cooperate. The thing that concerned us most was that her appetite was now going way down.

In retrospect, I think that I wasn't given the best medical advice. We probably should have considered putting in a feeding tube, but for some reason it didn't occur to me. It seemed as though we should encourage her to keep eating, but it all seemed so hopeless, as though we were prolonging the life of a shell that wasn't the Nana I knew. Also, Dr. Ambury wasn't the doctor checking her in the nursing home. I probably should have tried to find someone he recommended to continue her care or participate in the decision to put her in the nursing home.

I brought Mikki with me when I went to see Nana. Sometimes, I brought Vincent, too. For some reason, most of the patients and staff were drawn to Vincent. One resident said that Vincent reminded her of her white German shepherd that helped her take care of all the other dogs and cats that she had.

One of the residents, a little soft-spoken lady, was very good at coming to see Nana and trying to talk to her. After Nana died, I inquired about this lady, and I was very happy to learn that she was able to go home.

On Easter Sunday, Law School Judy and I went to see Nana. She seemed to know us. She was either drowsy or sedated, but she sat in her room in the chair we had brought from the house when she moved there, and she seemed fairly peaceful for once. I couldn't help wishing that she could quietly pass to the Lord then and there, while we were with her, but God knew best.

During the following week, I went to see her a few times. One evening she seemed to know who I was and that Mikki was lying on the floor. I noticed that something that used to be on her nightstand wasn't there. I had reason to think that she had started to throw some things. The orderly or aide or male nurse – whatever he was – confirmed that she wasn't doing very well. I appreciated his honesty.

Aware that she wasn't doing well, Uncle Joe decided to come down to see her. I think that he went Friday and also confirmed that she wasn't doing well. On Saturday, April 16, he went to the nursing home, and I waited at the house. I remember that I was pressing clay into the mold that I made for the crucifixes.

They called to tell me that they finally decided that Nana needed to go to the hospital, because she was going in and out of consciousness. How I wish that they had decided to do something a little sooner! Perhaps I should have been more pro-active, but what held me back was that I didn't seem able to do much better when I had her at home, either, and her downward spiral had the feel of inevitability.

I went to Fairfax Hospital soon after they admitted Nana. They told me that she was, as they put it, very fragile. They had her on IV fluids, and they were going to see if they could build her back up. The doctor asked me if I wanted to sign a do not resuscitate order. I told her no. If her heart stopped, they should try to restart it; if it did restart and would keep going on its own, fine, but I didn't want her put on a machine. I didn't say this to the doctor, but I considered that any kind of mechanical respirator would be extraordinary care in these circumstances.

"Well, that will do for now," the doctor said, and then she added. "We all have to get out of this world one way or another."

Father Bill Chaps came to give Nana the last rites. She may not have been conscious enough to take Communion, but he administered the sacrament of The Anointing of the Sick. I tried to pray the responses. It was a beautiful, moving prayerful time. I thought that I felt Nana shift position during the prayers.

"She knows that I bug her," Father Chaps said. Apparently, he was the one who came to visit Catholic residents at the nursing home. "I tell her that she's a tough weed," he continued.

"Did she laugh at that?" I asked him.

"She smiled a little," he said.

He was a wonderful, kind, caring priest, the kind that I wished that we had in our home parish. Perhaps that was why Nana had to live to enter the nursing home: so that she would get in contact with a priest who could reach her.

On Sunday, Uncle Joe and I went to the hospital. I brought my Braille volume for that section of the New Testament, and I read Romans, chapter 8, verse 28, to the end of the chapter, aloud to Nana. I don't know if she heard or understood, but if so, I wanted her to hear the passage.

The next few days were an anxious time. Of course, we went to the hospital, and at night before I went to sleep, I would call the nurses and check on Nana. I told them to tell her that I loved her. At this point, I pretty much had decided that, if Nana got better, she wasn't going back into the nursing home. I privately spoke to Dr. Morrissey, and he said that he would help me if he could to make that happen. I think he knew that taking care of Nana was part of my well-being, and it was consistent with his being my doctor to help me. I didn't care if I had to mortgage the house or what I had to do: she would come home. The problem was that I knew Uncle Joe wouldn't have held still for that. During Nana's last days at home, he and my aunt were encouraging me to go with the nursing home as a solution.

The doctors didn't think that Nana was very conscious, but how would they know? I needed to talk to her when my Uncle wasn't around.

Wednesday of that week, Dottie came to get me at work. She brought me to the hospital by myself. I sat beside Nana, called her name, and tried to get her attention. She moaned, and tried to open one eye. I think that she knew that I was there. I told her that she would come home, but she had to try for me. I told her to hang on until Uncle Joe went home. I also read her a passage from Scripture. I think that it was First Corinthians, chapter 9, verse 13 and following, about the value of love. I didn't know how much she could hear me, but I had to try to get through to her!

The doctors asked if I wanted to have them feed her by a tube through her nose into her stomach. I said yes. I wasn't going to let her starve or thirst to death. She was on the IV, but at some point they needed to get more nutrition into her. It seemed ironic that the same procedure that was used to save my life as a baby was being attempted on Nana at the end of her life. On Thursday or Friday, they tried to put the tube in, but they weren't successful. They were going to try another day.

By Friday evening, Uncle Joe had decided that, if nothing changed, he was going home. When we visited Nana in the hospital, we told her that he would be leaving.

Friday night, I thought of calling, as usual, to check on Nana, but I decided not to do it. I'm sorry now that I didn't, but I had just seen her in the hospital. I also thought that we might be in for a long period of recovery or illness, and I decided to pace myself.

Saturday morning, April 23, I was awakened by the telephone. It was one of the doctors from the hospital. Early that morning, Nana's heart stopped. They followed my directions and tried to resuscitate her. They could not get her heart beating on its own, and, since I didn't want the machine, they had to let her go. For her sake, I'm glad that this last period of nursing home and illness was only about six weeks long. I also was relieved that Uncle Joe hadn't gone home yet. It would have been hard on him – he was around seventy-three years old – to turn around and come back.

Patsy, Uncle Joe, and I went to the hospital. Nana's body was still lying in bed under the covers. She still felt warm. We touched her and cried a little. It seemed impossible that she wouldn't just wake up and start talking to us, but I knew that she was gone. Unlike Papa, who went willingly, I suspect that Nana resisted to the end. I will never know for sure, but maybe my not calling Friday evening, along with her understanding that Uncle Joe was leaving to go home, allowed Nana to let go.

As with Papa, I needed to decide about an autopsy. I would have preferred to have a full autopsy, as was done on both of my parents. However, the medical examiner doctor that was to do the autopsy was pregnant and wouldn't have been able to do a full body autopsy for a couple of weeks. If I only wanted her brain examined it could be removed from the body and examined in due time. If it had been only up to me, I would have waited on the full autopsy. In consideration for Uncle Joe and the rest of the family, I decided on only the partial examination of Nana's brain. I felt that I needed answers about her mental deterioration. At that time, Alzheimer's disease could only be conclusively established by such an autopsy. Like the ancient Egyptian kings and queens, Nana would be buried without her brain. However, I figured that, if God planned, (as Scripture says,) to resurrect the dead from the earth and the sea, after bacteria, elements, and animals have done their work on the bodies, He could resurrect Nana, even if her brain was somewhere else.

The autopsy report that I reviewed later mentioned that they found plaques and tangles in Nana's brain, consistent with Alzheimer's disease that often comes with advancing age.

As Sue had done for me when Papa died, Pam Cleary helped me to select the readings and the hymns for Nana's funeral Mass. Pam also dictated the readings to me, so I could copy them. I decided that I would lector for Nana's Mass. Pam also kept reminding me of the Scripture passage that quotes the Lord as saying, "Be still and know that I am God." It was and still is a consoling thought.

Nana's body lay in state at Everly-Wheatley funeral home. I decided to use the crucifix that Aunt Murff had given me for the inside of the lid of the casket during the viewing. Nana always said that she hated the dark. I knew that, when the lights were turned off during the night, the corpus of that cross would glow. It was my last little secret between Nana and me. After the funeral, I took that corpus off the cross and replaced it with one of my stoneware impressions. The strange plastic corpus did its work.

Cousin Tom came for the viewing. How much I wanted to reproach him for not paying Nana more attention during her life, but I bit my tongue and held my peace. Nana was at peace with the Lord. Picking a fight with family members over her dead body wouldn't bring her back. Whatever they did or didn't do for her was and is between them and God, and yes, I still have to forgive and let go, but how hard it is, even now! I did tell Tom that I wanted very badly to scream, which was true, and that I didn't know of any woods deep enough for me to use for the purpose, which still is true.

I decided that I didn't want one of the church cantors, who didn't know or care about Nana, to sing at the funeral Mass. I asked Pam, Dottie, and Karin Goodlatte if they would lead the congregation in singing the hymns, and they agreed. We tried also to encourage the congregation to join in the hymns. I very much appreciated the help of these three friends.

As discussed in a later chapter, I have lost touch with Karen, and Dottie moved back to Atlanta. Pam Cleary was diagnosed with breast cancer a few years later and died. During our last conversation, she asked me to pray for her.

As planned, I did the announcements, prayers of the faithful, and the first and second readings for Nana's requiem Mass. (The priest or deacon always proclaims the Gospel.) At the end of Mass, I gave a eulogy for Nana.

> What do you say about a ninety-eight-year-old lady who died?
> That she was strong-willed and fearless,
> Picking up bees without getting stung,
> That she was determined and confident,
> Telling Germs that, "I'm not going to catch it."
> That she could carry a tune into old age
> And sing "The Star Spangled Banner" correctly …
> As the bad cigarette commercials said,
> "It's not how long you make it—
> It's <u>how</u> you make it long!"
> Uncle Johnny told us after Mama died
> That God called the colonels and the generals,
> Not the privates and the corporals.
> What do you say about a ninety-eight-year-old lady who died?
> That after ninety-eight years,
> She finally got her promotion in Heaven.

The Women's Counsel at the parish also helped by getting together a small reception for us in the Lourdes Center after the funeral Mass.

From the funeral home, we brought Nana's body back to church for the Mass. Going or coming, I may have asked them to drive by our house, but I don't clearly remember it. Then, that afternoon or evening, the body was flown to Massachusetts. Uncle Joe, Patsy, and I flew up there, too. I had to leave Mikki at home. I had reason to think that perhaps Aunty Rene didn't want dog hairs in the Norton, MA house, which they were getting ready to sell. Uncle Joe tried to put a good face on it, by telling me that Aunty Rene was allergic to dogs. I didn't think that was the case, but I let it go. I told myself that enduring these trials was the last thing that I would do for Nana, aside from continuing to pray for her. As for how I knew that Nana was at peace, after she died, the only thing that kept going through my head was the sound of Nana laughing, as though at the greatest joke in the world! I think that God finally gave her all the answers to her questions, doubts, and fears!

Patsy and I spent the night in Uncle Joe's house. The next morning, we went to Sweeney's funeral home in Quincy. We had a brief viewing for the relatives in MA. Nancy and Dick, Great Uncle Bill, Uncle Joe, and Aunty Rene. I don't remember if Nancy's children came, but they probably did: Richard and Bonnie Jeanne. I don't think that any of the Abbiattis came, but at their age, it would be understandable.

Before they closed the casket, Aunty Rene took me up to it to say good-bye. "Cry," she urged me, putting my hand on Nana. "Tell her that you love her."

How much I wanted to break down and do just that, but, in light of the little these folks had done for Nana, leaving me alone with this problem, I was darned if I was going to give them the satisfaction of seeing me do that. When I used to ask Nana to tell me that she loved me, just to hear her say it, she would tell me, "If you don't know that I love you, you're one damn fool lawyer." Now, in answer to my aunt's desire to see an emotional display, I simply said, "If she doesn't know that I love her, after all we've been through, she's one damn fool grandmother!" and I turned away.

After the brief viewing, we took Nana's body to Mount Walleston cemetery, to be laid beside her husband. Before they interred the casket, they let me feel the beautifully detailed crucifix on the lid of the cover of the vault.

After the funeral, they took me to the nursing home where Aunt Riri was living to visit her. It was good to see her for what turned out to be the last time, but I wished that it could have been under happier circumstances. I gave her one of my personal pendant crucifixes on a chain as a gift, the one I had in my pocketbook. I don't know if she knew that Nana had died, and I didn't want to be the one to tell her. That sad duty probably belonged to Uncle Bill. He was the only one of my relatives to ask about my dog. He had throat surgery on account of cancer, and he spoke barely above a whisper. He may have been using the esophagus to vibrate to speak. He and Aunt Riri survived Nana, but they have since died. If I remember correctly, I heard about their deaths casually after the fact from Uncle Joe and Aunt Irene.

After my return from the second part of Nana's funeral in MA, the full force of grief set in. For a few days, all I wanted to do was to cry. I expected to feel relief, as I did with Papa, but the reality was that Nana's dying began so long before her death that the whole process was dragged out in an agonizing way. She was the pal of my baby days, the last of my parents to depart this life, and a big part of me was gone.

Mary Spellerberg expressed concern that I wasn't getting myself together better. The truth was that I felt stranded, that I didn't want to be left behind. I assured Mary that I would seek counseling if the anguish didn't abate after a reasonable time.

It all really hit me the first weekend that Patsy went out, as usual, and I was at home alone with my two furry pals. The house felt so empty! I let them out, and then I called them. I panicked, because I couldn't hear them. I thought that maybe one of the gates was left open. Then, they came running from somewhere, and I was so relieved!

Eventually, I understood that I had to accept God's will, and realized that Nana was in a better place, and go on with my life. This realization was reinforced on the Tuesday after Pentecost of that year, when I received another visitation from the Lord, similar to the one I described in the chapter discussing my work difficulties. It was one of those spiritual consolations that are totally unexpected.

I took the title of this chapter from a poem by Emily Dickenson:

> This is the hour of lead
> Remembered if outlived,
> As freezing persons recollect the snow --
> First chill, then stupor, then the letting go.

# HEROICS AND HEARTBREAKS

*T*he first few months after Nana's death were devoted to personal regrouping and to the settlement of Nana's estate. As with Papa, Mike Geltner helped me to make the necessary court filings and accountings. Nana's will divided her estate equally between Uncle Joe and me. As discussed in an earlier chapter, she made an exception and left her pendant watch and her wedding ring to me in her will. However, I decided that Uncle Joe should keep her watch, so long as it didn't go to Tom. We agreed to waive any appraisal, and that I would keep the ring, and he would get the watch. Aside from these personal articles, by the time the bills were paid for the nursing home and the hospital, very little of her savings remained to be divided between us.

I still had Mikki and Vincent. Mikki was a loving comfort as always. Vincent was starting to really show his age. He had trouble with one of his back legs, which eventually became both rear legs, with symptoms of arthritis. X-rays showed boney bridges in the spine, which pressed on the nerves and caused the problem. The condition is termed spondylosis. As discussed in this chapter, I would only have Vincent another year and eight months.

Vincent's idea of self-treatment was to go outside and lie on the ground under the azalea bush near the back door for a while, even in cold weather. He would come inside after an hour or so, and he seemed to feel better. One of my friends told me that he might have found the magnetic field from the ground therapeutic. I later took the hint for myself. I now have a magnetic chair pad for my home office chair and another one in the armchair in the dining room near the telephone. I also bought a magnetic pad that my previous guide, Teddy, my current guide, Ives, and I like. I find these items helpful for my own arthritis.

In addition to the spondylosis, we had some other health crises with Vincent. On one weekend, I had to call Ethel Stanulis for help in the small hours of the morning. Vincent kept having diarrhea. Fortunately, he managed to get outside, but I was up and down for several hours. He also got sick to his stomach. We found a pink hair roller in the mess afterwards, and swallowing that probably caused his problem. Ethel took Vincent and me to the vet, and they kept him for a few hours to give him IV fluids.

Vincent's needs still prompted positive changes in the house. On one occasion, I was in the basement working on art projects. I was finishing and starting to come upstairs. At the same time, Vincent started to come downstairs to be with me. He lost his footing and started to slide. I tried to catch him, but I couldn't. Vincent may have tried to keep from colliding with me. However it was, he went off the open edge of the staircase. Fortunately for him, an old file cabinet that Papa used to keep old pictures and negatives was still next to the stairs on that side. Vincent's fall knocked over the file cabinet with a horrible crash! I died a thousand deaths, thinking that I would find my pal seriously hurt on the tile floor. I was infinitely relieved when he stood up and calmly walked over to me. Needless to say, I decided that we needed to close up the open side of the stairs. Law School Judy's husband, Ed, constructed a partial railing on that side that went as far as the wall, with palings close enough together to keep a person or a dog from falling off the side of the stairs.

Mikki was very solicitous of Vincent, as well as me. As he grew older, Vincent would go out in the yard and bark; we never knew at what he was barking. Sometimes Mikki would ignore him, but sometimes he would sound lost, and whatever he said got Mikki's attention. She would jump up from her resting place beside me, give out a big "woof," run to the back door and push it open, and go outside with Vincent. The screen door would slam loudly behind her. Translation: "I'm coming, buddy!" Eventually, I'd get them back into the house. I really appreciated how much she paid attention to him.

We still had some good times together. I spent a couple of days at Trinity with both dogs. The sisters kindly came to get us and brought us home after the weekend. It was nice to be able to do something all together.

Changes were happening to the neighbors, too. In the late 1980's, Ellen was diagnosed with some kind of breathing disorder, possibly emphysema or what medical people now call COPD. The condition was aggravated by the curvature of her spine, which limited the room that her lungs had to expand. She had to start using liquid oxygen. She had a big tank in her house, to which she stayed connected by a hose that she had to pull around with her as she did her daily tasks. She also had little portable tanks that she filled and took with her on a frame with wheels, so that she could still go out on errands or to visit me and other friends. When she came shopping with Patsy and me, she would take two of those tanks with her, changing to a full one when the first became empty. She had to take two tanks if she were going to be gone for more than two or three hours.

On the other side of me, I heard through a secondhand source that Walter and Susan Graham had separated and eventually divorced. Walter continued to live in the house. Across the street, Helen and Wynn Alley sold their house and moved away. Eventually, Helen died, and Wynn remarried. He has since died, too. I still miss them. They were good neighbors. At some point, one of the Murdaughs died, and the other moved away; either the survivor or the estate sold the house behind me. The people who bought it began a major renovation project. The neighbor who lived there for a while was Tom Paulsen and his wife, married for over fifty years.

As for the Sheehans, their son and daughter married. They eventually both had children. Donna's two daughters, Kimberly and Jessica, are now married with little boys. One of them also had a little girl. Barbara was a great-grandmother!

During the period of 1988 and 1989, I had the roof replaced on the house. It was a major undertaking, with some leaks resulting from inadequate covering of the opened roof. Mikki hated all the noise from the work on the roof. Vincent took everything in stride.

I took advantage of not having to worry about Nana to take some trips. In the summer of 1988, I paid Jeanne and Bill Rhode another visit, this time to their new house in Redwood Valley, CA, near Ukiah. Dependable Patsy looked after Vincent while Mikki and I were away. I very much enjoyed seeing Jeanne and Bill, but the trip was memorable for another reason. Mikki piddled on Jeanne's back porch; rather, the urine was coming out of her involuntarily when she was lying down. We had to take her to the local vet, and he put her on antibiotics for a urinary tract infection. The first antibiotic had to be changed after the urine culture results came back. I'm glad that he was so competent and helpful!

After I came back home, I received unsettling news from Aunt Maria. She was back in Pittsburgh from her trip to IN, but now she had received a diagnosis of cancer. She was undergoing treatment, I think radiation and chemotherapy.

In the early fall of 1988, I accepted Sister Elizabeth Henry's invitation to go with her to Oxford, England, for about ten days to two weeks. It was a wonderful opportunity to explore a new place with someone who knew the area, and it was especially nice that this country also spoke English! In fairness, I will concede that the various accents and dialects in the UK can be hard for someone with a hearing loss or who isn't familiar with the way words are used and pronounced abroad.

I very much enjoyed my time in England. We stayed in a flat that the SND's use for visitors or when the Trinity students came to Oxford. We walked to most local places. I enjoyed shopping for sweaters and slippers in Oxford, and I found a nice Cardigan sweater. Although I liked the slippers, they are sized differently in the UK, and I couldn't find the size that would fit me and let me use my orthotics or arch supports in the slippers.

In Oxford, Sister found a museum that gave me a tour in which I was able to touch some things, and they told us about the process of making china. We went to London and visited the Tower, for which I didn't care too much, and Westminster Abbey. We also toured St. Paul's Cathedral, which I found much more pleasant and warm. We saw there a beautiful little statue of Mary holding the Baby Jesus in her arms. Both Sister and I thought that a woman might have sculpted it, because whoever did it knew how babies wiggle around in their mothers' arms. Of course, a man like Papa, who loved babies, would have known that, too.

Patsy liked complex puzzles with hundreds or thousands of pieces, so I bought her a puzzle to put together with hundreds of pieces, showing a girl trying to teach her dog about reading. The puzzle was called Compulsory Education.

We spent a day at Kew Gardens in London, and I wished that we could have spent more time there. They had plants from so many different habitats under climate control. It was wonderful! When we ate our lunch, we had to deal with the pushy, noisy geese that tried to persuade us to give them part of it. All in all, it was a very memorable trip!

Back home, the news about Aunt Maria wasn't good. Gretchen went to see her with daughter Sara. Aunt Maria gave Sara the old-fashioned doll that she had saved from her childhood.

Eventually, I got a call from my cousin, Jim, who said that Aunt Maria was now under hospice care, and she did not have long to live. I decided that I needed to fly up to Pittsburgh to see her. I think this was December of 1988.

Patsy and I flew up to Pittsburgh for a one-day trip. I left Mikki at home. I didn't think it was time to do any trail blazing with my dog. Jim met us at the airport, and we went to see my Aunt Maria. She could hardly talk, but I think that she was glad to see me.

"I didn't expect this!" she said.

"You've fought the good fight," I told her.

Jim took us to his house and served us lunch. We went back to see my aunt one last time before we boarded the plane to go home.

"Don't miss your plane," was the last thing that she said to me.

I was glad that I went to visit her. She had come to us when Papa needed her. Papa wasn't there to go to her, and I wanted to see her. We had become good friends.

Aunt Maria died around January 6, 1989. I agonized over this decision for a day or so, but decided not to go back to Pittsburgh for the funeral. I was torn, because part of me wanted to pay my respects to her, but I had seen her alive, and that was more important to me than trying to deal with the cousins.

Instead, I went up to Avalon with both dogs and Billie. I don't remember if Frances was still living at that point, but she may have already died, because I think that Billie was by herself. We had gone somewhere, and when we came back to the house, Vincent started walking toward us, and he defecated on the floor.

"Don't correct him, Linda," Billie said. "He's walking, and it's coming out of him!"

Needless to say, we went to the vet to check him out when I got home. Among other things that they did in the examination, they tried to express his anal sacs. One of them stayed firm and hard and didn't give out any fluid. For two weeks, he was on antibiotics, but the results were the same.

We consulted Dr. Anne Chiapella. He had anal sac cancer, and the tumor was inside the rectum. I agreed to have the tumor surgically removed.

After the surgery, the surgeon called with a report. He seemed angry that I had it done.

"The tumor was up inside the rectum," he told me. "He probably will be incontinent."

I didn't like that idea, but after losing Nana, I was just grateful to have him alive! However, I still had to decide whether to do chemotherapy or not. The doctors told me that doing chemotherapy would lessen the chances of the tumor coming back or metastasizing somewhere else, but I couldn't see making him sick with the chronic chemotherapy. Much as she loved Vincent, Billie was comfortable with my decision.

"Even some people refuse that treatment," she told me.

The next year was difficult. If I was in the house, Patsy insisted that I do the honors and pick up after Vincent. I would try to get up in the middle of the night to check on him, and get him outside. Sometimes, I would have to help him up from the floor. I would put my arms under him and say, "One, two, three, Lift!" and he would try to stand up. He understood what I was doing.

We had one memorable night, which was bittersweet. Vincent came upstairs to me, because he didn't feel good, and he ended up with the upper half of his body on the bed. I held him and tried to comfort him. There wasn't enough room for Mikki up there, too, and I made her understand that she had to stay on the floor, because I had to help Vincent. He never slept on my bed before, and, although I was very sorry that he was feeling bad, I was grateful to have this time to share with him and cuddle him on my bed. It was the only time we did that. Eventually, it became no longer safe for him to climb the stairs, and he spent his time on the first floor.

Law School Judy and I started talking about how nice it would be if I had a statue of Vincent. As already discussed, I had already hired a photographer to take a set of pictures of both dogs, but a statue would be something that I could feel. I consulted a sculptress, and she proposed doing a life-sized bronze statue of him, but it didn't seem very practical to me, and the cost would have been quite high. I began to think that I should try to do something myself. I couldn't see doing it with kiln-fired clay, because those statues can break so easily, and they remain breakable even if they fire successfully. I decided to try making a statue from modeling clay and having it cast in bronze. It may have been the sculptress, but, someone referred me to Wegner Metal Arts in Fredericksburg, VA. I successfully did a statue of Vincent, small enough to put on the mantelpiece. Of course, I also had to do Mikki. I did a large German shepherd, in memory of Nana's Leelo. Eventually, I stopped using the modeling clay, which added the expense of a mold, and I began making things to be cast in bronze or silver directly from wax. Thanks to Vincent, my artistic endeavors went off in a whole new direction. I have made bronze statues of all five of my previous dogs, and I arranged to get one cast of Ives a year or two after he came to me.

In the spring of 1990, Janice came over one Sunday afternoon. Mikki went outside, but Vincent came to us. We decided to put his harness on him, and I walked slowly and carefully with him down to church and back. Janice made a videotape of that walk. It turned out to be the last time that I worked Vincent.

In the summer of 1990, my big preoccupation was that I finally bought my first house computer, equipped with a program for converting text to speech, called a screen reader, SoftVert, from Telesensory Systems Inc., and a speech synthesizer, DecTalk, made by Digital. Chris Gregory referred me to a wonderful computer store, DMCC, which has since gone out of business. The folks came to my house and helped to set up the computer. As you might imagine, things didn't work smoothly right at first, and we had a lot of bugs and configuration issues to resolve. Folks had to come out from Digital, too, because of problems with the DecTalk. I am very grateful to all the wonderful folks who helped to make things work in the end.

Vincent still had my security and safety at heart. One day, when the computer folks were here, he tried to come upstairs with me, because he didn't know what these strangers were doing in my house.

During that summer, Patsy went back to Jamaica, as usual. Jackie came to substitute for her. Everything had gone well before, and I didn't expect any difficulties. Jackie couldn't drive, but she was a good cook and housekeeper. Unfortunately, unknown to me, this recovering alcoholic had a relapse. She may not have been able to drive, but she found her way, walking, to the local liquor store! Fortunately, she did not find the bottles that Nana missed in her clearing out sweep that were down in the basement! She held on until just before she was to leave. The first inkling that I had that something was wrong was coming home Thursday and Friday to find that Vincent was only picking at his food. I thought that it was his typical indigestion problem with pancreatitis. No, in retrospect, it was his only way of telling me that something wasn't right in Denmark.

Friday evening, I was trying to run a spell-checker on the manuscript of *The Unbroken Circle*. Jackie came upstairs to help me, and she actually was quite good. She had something in a glass with ice cubes, but I didn't think anything of it.

By Saturday morning, she was, as they say, three sheets to the wind! Very little of what she said in her now-fuzzy speech made any sense, except for one thing.

"I don't understand it," she complained. "But sometimes, I think that I can feel Nana in this house. I don't know why, but she's mad about something."

I went upstairs to the bathroom, shut the door, and quietly howled with laughter, while sitting on the toilet, in case I "watered the petunias." "Nana's mad!" I howled quietly. "Nana's mad? Teetotaler Nana! You bet your booties! Nana's mad!"

I called Margie. She came to get Jackie, and she took her down through the basement and out to Margie's car that way to drive her home. We didn't want the neighbors seeing her in that condition. Needless to say, it was the last time that Jackie worked for me. I'm not angry, but only sad. That sweet, intelligent woman could have done so much with her life if she didn't have this problem! She really did help me that night.

As for what she said about Nana, Margie, Patsy and I all agreed that she probably really did experience Nana. I'm sure that Nana's spirit wasn't happy about what happened in that house during those last few days! Eventually, I heard that poor Jackie died! A life is a terrible thing to waste on an addiction!

On another occasion, One of Patsy's young relatives came to visit her. He was staying in the house. One night, Vincent got himself upstairs to me. I thought that his stomach was bothering him, or that he needed to go outside. When I went down to the kitchen, I found the young man had been cooking eggs at 2 in the morning. I took care of Vincent and got him settled, and went back upstairs feeling very secure. He might not have been able to walk very well, but he wouldn't have let anybody burn the house down around my ears without coming to tell me! By the by, he May have wanted some eggs, too!

About this time, a gentleman from church began to express an interest in me. He dated me for a month or two, but we eventually decided to break off the relationship. I found him immature, and he subsequently told me some things about himself and previous relationships that made us both decide that a deeper relationship between us was not meant to be. One problem we had was that, when I thought that he came upstairs to help me with a manuscript, he proposed to make love. I hadn't known him long enough to even consider such a thing. When he left on that occasion, I went downstairs and sat at the dining room table.

"Please comfort me, Lord. There isn't anyone else." Again, I felt that sensation of being charged. God provided more consolation than I could ever have imagined. I found the gentleman's courtship so stressful that all in all I was glad when it was over.

Meanwhile, I hired a young neighborhood boy to take Vincent walking so that he would get a little exercise and wouldn't become too stiff. I explored other treatments for Vincent. In the fall of 1990, I decided to take Vincent to Dr. Anita Walton, to try acupuncture treatments. He seemed relaxed during the treatments, but she cautioned me that we needed to complete all ten of the sessions before we would know if it was helping or not.

Despite his difficulty walking, Vincent still wanted to be with me. He would follow me into the dining room if I was doing art projects on the table and flop down on the floor near me.

"Do you love me that much?" I asked him with tears in my eyes. I didn't feel deserving of love like that. How much more true that is for Jesus who died for me!

Shortly before Vincent's last trip to the vet that ended with his death, I was trying to call Mikki to get harnessed. Mikki was dilly-dallying around. Vincent came over to me and sat down. Translation: "If you need me, I'll go." All I could do was hug him, wanting to cry.

We never made it through the acupuncture protocol. On Saturday, December 1, Billie came to get me and take me out to dinner. Vincent didn't react very much when he saw Billie, and she thought that it was because he didn't know her. I didn't think it was so. I think he just didn't have much energy to express himself. After we came back from dinner, I tried to settle down for the night. I lay on the couch with Mikki at my feet and Vincent beside me on the floor. I felt secure and happy with my canine family. Patsy was away for the weekend.

Before going to bed, I tried to get Vincent outside one last time. He could hardly walk, but he played the old game with me outside, when I tried to get him into the house. I could hear his tags rattling, as he walked around, just out of my reach! It was after 11 P.M, going on midnight, and I was in a robe and my Daniel Green patio slippers! I was afraid that I was going to step in feces, and meanwhile, I just couldn't get Vincent. I went inside and put a leash on Mikki, to see if she would find him for me or help me to find him, but we didn't get to where I could touch him. He finally came inside. I went to bed, relieved that he was inside, but a little voice in the back of my brain was asking me how much longer I could do this. I came downstairs to check on him later during the night. I had to pick up solid matter from under his tail. When I tried to lift him up to get him outside, he, like Nana on that last occasion, was dead weight. In the morning, I put him out again. He walked around a little outside, and then he came into the house and lay on the floor in the dining room near the telephone. He didn't seem inclined to get up. I wondered if he was dying, but it was Sunday, and I needed to go to Mass. I left him lying on the floor, looking as though he were saying, "I love this floor!" and very peaceful. He also may have been trying to indicate that we should call someone for help by being near the telephone.

When I got home from Mass, he was still there and alive, and it was time to get to the vet. Janice came over, and one of the fellows from church helped us to lift him on a blanket into her hatchback.

Vincent was at the vet for the next week. They told me that they didn't think that he would walk again. However, I wanted the myelogram taken. I had to be sure that the situation was terminal and that we couldn't do anything else. I felt that I owed it to Vincent. They needed to wait for the mobile vet who did the procedure to come to Alexandria Animal Hospital. The day before the vet who did the myelograms was coming, I agonized as to whether I was doing the right thing. That night, Mikki slept on my bed as usual. She lay on my feet, holding my ankles tightly with her paws. I think that she may have been telling me to wait, and I took it as a sign that I was doing the right thing. The next day, when the vet who performed the procedures came, I went to talk to the vets.

They asked me why I wanted to do this for a fourteen-year-old dog. I tried very hard to explain to them that, like the dog in the K9 movie, Vincent was more than just a dog; he was my eyes. If it weren't for him, with my going in the subway when I was tired and not thinking straight, I might not be here! I told them that, if they found big bad cancer, not to let him come out of the anesthetic.

On Wednesday, December 12, the feast of Our Lady of Guadalupe, they did the procedure. That evening, they called me at home.

"The spinal canal is clear all the way down to his tail," the vet told me. "We will try prednisone to see if he can recover movement."

I went to bed that night happy over Vincent for the last time. All I could think of was that Vincent lived! I was very thankful.

The next evening, I went to see him. He was in Alexandria Animal Hospital, under the day vets' care in the daytime and the emergency vets at night. I knelt down next to the kennel crate in which he was lying. He was on soft blankets and things, and the staff had kept him very clean. He looked peaceful and comfortable, like typical Vincent. They had the door open. I think that if he had got up and walked out of that crate, everybody would have cheered.

I talked to him, and I fed him a piece of toast that I brought him from home. He seemed to enjoy it.

I did notice that, when I tried to talk to him and he tried to respond to me, he was panting a little bit.

The next day was the Christmas party at work. It kept me from getting the call from the vet right away, but I eventually got the message. Vincent was worse.

Patsy drove Mikki and me over there. Vincent hadn't eaten that day, and he was running a temperature. Worse, he had that horrible, rasping breathing that I remembered from Papa's last hours. The last thing that Mikki did with him was to try to eat his untouched dinner! Mikki was always the chowhound!

I spoke with the vet, Dr. Johnson. She told me that she thought that the cancer had spread to his lungs. He probably would die on his own in a few hours. She told me that it was time to say good-bye.

I tried to call Sister Elizabeth Henry, but I couldn't get her. In the end, I was alone with God and this decision. Part of me wanted to keep fighting, and the other half knew that we had lost the physical battle. I had to accept Dr. Johnson's judgment.

They asked me if I wanted them to lift Vincent onto the table for me to say good-bye, but I said no. I would talk to him where he was. I couldn't see disturbing him just to gratify my last desire. I told Vincent that I was sending him home to heaven. I noticed that when he tried to come alert and respond to me, his breathing was worse. I decided not to stay with him when the vet gave the final injections. Dr. Johnson told me that he might cry out, and I knew that, if he had, I would never be able to do this for another dog.

I went out into the waiting room with Mikki until it was over. Dr. Johnson came out and told me that he went quickly and quietly, and that he was ready to go.

From then on, Mikki didn't like going into the vet by herself, without me with her. I knew why. She had learned from that horrible day that, when Mama doesn't come, bad things happen sometimes. I knew that I would have to stay with Mikki when her time came. As described in the next chapter, I did.

After it was over, I decided to have Vincent cremated. I considered that it might be hard to handle a body, I didn't like the idea of pet cemeteries, and I didn't think that it would be wise (and it might have been illegal) to bury him on my property. After what happened to Nana, in the back of my mind was the idea that I might not be able to count on permanently staying in the house, and I wouldn't have wanted to leave Vincent behind.

I went home and called Janie McIver. She agreed that I had done the right thing in not letting him gasp away his final hours. He loved me, and I had to show my ultimate love for him by letting him go. As I told Vincent at the vet's, Jesus had a dog, and he let me borrow him for a while, and now I had to give him back.

Needless to say, that year, it was one of the more somber Christmases that I have spent. When I collected the little box with Vincent's final remains, a friend helped me do what I thought was right with them. I will not name her, in case what we did might be illegal. Early in the morning, we went to the cemetery where my parents were buried, when nobody else was likely to be around. We removed a square of sod from a spot below the large marker at the head of my parents' grave, and we put the little box into the hole and replaced the grass. As Tolkien says about Snow Mane's grave, the grass has since grown thick and high over the place, and only I know where it is. Vincent was my father's buddy, and he loved his people. His mortal remains should be there.

After Vincent died, we asked the boy who had walked him to come and walk Mikki, so that she would have someone paying attention to her. He walked her for many months, until his family moved away.

Vincent died thirteen years to the day from the date in 1977 when I brought him home from Guiding Eyes. One wonderful chapter of my life was closing. At that point, only God knew that He was going to open another wonderful chapter for me.

# THE PUPPY LOTTERY

God has His own ideas and His times. In *Whistling in the Dark*, Fred Lowery, a blind man who became a professional whistler, describes his life. In talking about his book, he said in an interview on a taped cassette magazine, *Newsreel,* that you don't know what is going to happen to you when you get out of bed in the morning. He was right.

When Vincent was sick and dying, Katie Nix, my friend from work who also likes dogs, had three dogs. All three had their purebred kennel names, but I'm only giving them here the informal names that she called them. She had a one-year-old German shepherd male, Rommel; a German shepherd female, Holly; and a four or five-year-old Australian cattle dog female, Pebbles. All three dogs were anatomically intact. Katie and her husband, Larry, did their best to keep the three dogs separated when the females went into heat. In retrospect, we like to say that God bred the dogs and was responsible for what happened. Within two or three days after Vincent died, Rommel, the busy man, got to both females. In the next month, it looked as though both were pregnant!

Katie told me all this at work as the weeks went by. We knew that all three dogs were intelligent, especially Rommel and Pebbles. Katie said that the vet wasn't sure if Pebbles was pregnant, but maybe one puppy. I said, half in gest, but really in earnest, "If she has one puppy, I want it."

On February 17, 1991, I was on the phone with someone else; either call waiting or the operator interrupted the call. "I've just taken Pebbles into the vet for C. Section, because after three hours of hard labor, nothing is happening," Katie told me.

Later that evening, Katie called me back. "We just picked up Pebbles and six screaming puppies!" Katie said. "Mama is out of it right now, and we are trying to feed them with an eye dropper!"

Once Pebbles recovered, she proved to be a good Mama, but meanwhile, I was talking to Janice. We both agreed that we were a little crazy, but we were both seriously considering my taking one of those puppies for training as Mikki's successor. After my experiences with Guide Dogs of the Desert, I wasn't exactly thrilled to go back there, and at that point, I still thought that I had burned my bridges with Guiding Eyes. Katie offered me the pick of the puppy litter as an Easter gift.

On Holy Saturday, Janice and I, with Mikki, drove out to Katie's house in Rockville, MD to check out and temperament test six puppies. Although the future owners probably changed the names of five of them, Katie and I had given them informal names, just to keep straight which one we were talking about.

There were the two twins, that we called Romulus and Remus, after the fellows who supposedly founded Rome. They looked a lot alike and hung out together. Remus turned out to be a girl, but we kept calling her by that name. (For all we know, in those snobbish days, maybe one of the twins was a girl, and she had to counterfeit to be a man to do anything spectacular.) There was a puppy that whined and vocalized a lot; I called him Leelo, after Nana's dog, and because he was so loud, we thought of him as Leelo the loudmouth. Another male seemed calm and laid-back, and we called him Aladdin; another male had stars on his head, and we called him Quasar; finally, there was a female with a white ring around her neck. We thought of the ads for Whisk detergent, the ones that talk about the "ring around the collar," and we called her Whisk.

Of the six, the two top scorers on the temperament test were the twins, Romulus and Remus, with Whisk and Aladdin as backups. However, I had my doubts. I went to Mass that evening, wondering if I really wanted any of those puppies.

In the next few days, I came up with one more test. The puppies were being kept in the basement. I asked Katie to bring the four upstairs, one at a time, and see how they reacted to someone pushing the vacuum cleaner around the floor. After all, I would need the candidate to be able to cope with moving vehicles. That test pretty well decided the issue. Aladdin hid under a chair; we wouldn't cross too many streets with that attitude; Whisk piddled on the floor, reacting with fear; Romulus let Katie bump him a couple of times with the vacuum cleaner before he learned to respect it: hard head, but could learn; Remus stopped consistently and let the vacuum cleaner go past her. Remus was it.

Once I had decided which one I wanted, Katie placed an ad to sell the remaining four puppies. She decided to keep Romulus and renamed him Bowser. Four potential owners showed up, and each one went home with a puppy.

Janice and I signed a contract for her to privately train Remus for me as my next guide dog. As it turned out, the project took a big chunk of my savings, but I have no regrets. At the time, we took a big leap of faith, because we couldn't know for certain that it would work out that Remus was suited to guiding or even that she would get large enough; her mother was around forty-five pounds, and Rommel was between eighty and ninety. As for the Parents, Katie had Pebbles' hips x-rayed when she had her spayed, and they were all right. Rommel's hips were x-rayed at the request of his breeder; they looked good, and they wanted him back for breeding. It was a good thing, because he had a tendency to jump and kept escaping Katie's property. Holly turned out to be sterile and only had a false pregnancy.

As far as the training was concerned, I was fairly confident that Janice could successfully train Remus, if she otherwise proved to be suitable for the guiding work and a good match for me. Janice had studied and taken an interest in guiding training. When we were beginning to think about the possibility of her doing private training of my next dog, even before the puppies became available, Janice had put a harness on Sheppy and Kelly and began to train her two dogs. One memorable afternoon, I went to her house and worked both relatively inexperienced dogs. It was a wonderful, interesting experience.

Sheppy, like Moose, was nice and tall. He realized immediately that I was the real thing, as opposed to Janice's simulating blindness. He blocked my path at the top of the steps from her house to the sidewalk, and he was very reluctant to take me down those steps. Kelly sat down at the top of the steps, and she was reluctant to take me down them, too. I really enjoyed this experience. We knew that both of her dogs could learn the work, but for various reasons, including age and Janice's need for them in her work, they would not have been suitable for me.

Remus was twelve weeks old before Janice and I had finalized our arrangements and found the first of her two puppy raisers. Katie brought that cute little puppy, Remus, to work and gave her to me to bring home. She was in my office for a few hours, and everybody fell in love with her, fortunately, including Mikki!

Mike Kigin had the van that day, and he drove the three of us home. A little later that evening, the puppy raiser came and picked up Remus. We were on our way! Later that summer, while the puppy raiser was away for a week or two, we decided that I would keep Remus while they were gone. We wanted her to get to know Mikki and me as a puppy so that later moving into my house, as an adult, would not be a big deal. Those two weeks were the best of times and the worst of times. On the one hand, Remus was a very cute puppy, and I wanted to love and spoil her. On the other hand, I knew that I must not, because I was so afraid of ruining her. Keeping track of a puppy if you can't see isn't easy. Remus had to be either at the end of a leash that I was holding or confined to the kennel crate. I didn't dare let her loose to run in the house, because she still was into the "chews" and not yet completely housebroken. Even as it was, she managed to pull a bottle of perfume out from under my high chest, to make a mess or two inside, and to chew up one of my telephone's cords so that it had to be repaired! God love Mikki, but she tried to play with and love Remus. "Tire her out, Mikki!" I would say. "That's right! Tire her out, so she will go to sleep!"

Fortunately, Margie fell in love with Remus, too. She was still covering me on the weekends, especially while Remus was there. I put the puppy in the kennel crate to go to church. When I came home, I found Margie, holding her on leash, comfortable on the couch watching sports on TV! It was an exhausting two weeks, but in retrospect, I was glad that I did it. It gave me a unique experience. Very few guide dog users ever have the experience of knowing their guides as puppies. [27]

Toward the fall, Janice had to find another puppy raiser, because the first one didn't want to go through a heat cycle. We had decided that we wanted Remus to go through at least one heat cycle before spaying her, because I wanted a fully mature adult guiding me, not an overgrown, arrested-development puppy! I didn't need a member of the Peter Pan Club!

In the fall of 1991, Jeanne Rhode and her friend, Frances, came east, and they came to visit me. About this time, I was having pain in one of my heels from bone spurs, and the podiatrist, Dr. Taylor, had put me on Advil. However, we still took our planned trip to Williamsburg. We drove in my new Mitsubishi Gallant. Dottie had taken me all over the dealers to buy my new car; I sold the Grenada to someone at work.

I very much enjoyed my trip to Williamsburg. Mikki worked pretty well, but she bumped me into an overhanging telephone booth. It hurt my shoulder, but fortunately it was not a serious injury.

When we got back from the trip, I had to let Dr. Taylor inject cortisone into the painful heel. Fortunately, it calmed down, and it hasn't bothered me very much since them, except if I put too much pressure on it at night. While Jeanne and Frances were with us, we went around doing fun shopping locally. It was wonderful to visit with Jeanne and her friend again.

Meanwhile, Janice already had begun the process of training Remus. The puppy raisers took her to Janice's obedience classes. Janice also began taking her out to stores and other public places, to get her used to being in busy crowded places. She brought her to church with me and Mikki at Sunday Mass. Remus learned early that church was a good, safe place to be. She may also have become aware of the Presence of Jesus there. Remus went into heat at Christmastime, and we planned to have her spayed in the spring of 1992.

In late 1991, Patsy retired. For a few months, I employed a lady recommended by Mothers Indeed. She needed a temporary job in northern VA, because her mother was in the hospital. She stayed with

---

[27] Pilot Dogs in Columbus, Ohio, or perhaps its founder, Stanley Doran, had a program at one point, one of a kind, in which some blind young people raised puppies that were matched with them as future guides, if they proved suitable. I think that it was called the Pathway Program. After my experience with Remus, I understand why it isn't generally done.

me until after her mother died. She was a pleasant, competent person, but housekeeping wasn't her forte, and we knew that the arrangement was only temporary.

In early 1992, Mothers Indeed sent me Mae Garrison. Mae was the closest that I ever had to a second grandmother. The year that we spent together was wonderful! Like Nana, she was a wonderful, plain cook. She had a warm, loving, fun personality. She enjoyed shopping in the goody stores, visiting and reminiscing over lazy cups of tea, and helping me with art projects. She was also a comfort and a moral support during my vicissitudes with Remus during her training.

When Remus was a little over a year old, she moved into Janice's house. In addition to the black cat, Fred, that I already described, Janice had Sheppy, the large German shepherd male, and Kelly, the black Labrador-mix. They all got along, but that was part of the socialization lessons that we wanted Remus to learn. She needed to be able to get along well with Mikki and to coexist with reasonable discipline in the presence of other dogs and cats that we might encounter, either loose or walked by their owners or in houses that we might visit.

Janice and I also began going out together on two-unit trips. She generally worked Remus, and I worked Mikki. Sometimes, these trips were fun as well as learning experiences. We would let one of my friends go off with me by ourselves and then Janice would tell Remus to find me, and she often did! Sometimes, the aim was to have Remus learn from Mikki. For example, Janice and I agreed that Remus should learn to use escalators carefully but confidently. Remus was OK with the shorter ones, but the taller escalators she found daunting. Janice hoped that she would learn from Mikki's example and follow her onto the escalators.

Another problem with which we had to deal was the behavior of young children and Remus's reaction to it. During the training, sometimes children would come up to try to pat and play with Remus, and Janice had to let them. She needed to make sure that Remus would handle these situations without becoming aggressive. Of course, I, like other guide dog users, try to tell children not to feed or pat my dogs, but sometimes it happens without our being aware of it in time to stop it. On one such occasion during training, Janice saw a little boy approach Remus as though he wanted to pat her, but then he hit her on the back with his fist. Remus fortunately didn't snap, but Janice said that she looked at him as though to tell him to get out of her face. Eventually, Janice intervened. However, from then on, if Remus encountered little kids, including the ones who shouted, "Doggy!" at the top of their lungs, she would try to go the other way to avoid the situation. However, she did try to read little kids. One of my friends brought a little child over to my house, and the little one actually played ball nicely with Remus, and she was OK with that.

Remus spent overnight and a day at my house when she was spayed, so that someone would be around to keep an eye on her. She had already demonstrated a propensity to remove stitches when we had to treat a cut paw, and we were trying to be extra vigilant that she wouldn't remove the sutures from the spaying surgery.

As the time approached for Remus to start working with me as my guide dog, I began actually working with Remus under Janice's supervision. In the summer of 1992, Janice came to my office area, along with another woman who was involved with service dog work. She had me try to cross some streets in the area. On one intersection, they were working on the street and had put metal plates over the work area. Remus became upset with the cars going across the metal plates, and she began to vocalize loudly. Katie was also there as an observer. The consultant wasn't impressed, and she told us that she didn't think that Remus would work out as a guide dog.

I went home that night and cried in bed. I didn't know what to do with this smart, intelligent dog, if she wasn't to guide me. She had too much potential to go bark in somebody's yard as just a pet. Janice and I prayed and talked about it, and we decided that we had to keep going, that we believed too much in her potential, and we had to keep trying. Yelling for help wasn't necessarily inappropriate if Remus didn't know what to do, and we thought that it was just a matter of her learning to deal with unexpected situations like the metal plates. Fortunately, we were right.

In the late summer or early fall of 1992, Billie invited Mae and me to go up to Avalon with her. We had a very pleasant beach trip. Mae bought me a beautiful shell as a souvenir.

In late 1992, Mae needed to leave me to return to Tennessee. She was doing this job to earn money to pay off a credit card bill, but she had to go home to take care of her husband when he became ill. For a few months in late 1992 and early 1993, one of the cantors at church, Rose Ingberman, came to stay with me and to be my housekeeper/assistant. It was the closest I've come to having a housemate, as opposed to a housekeeper, because Rose was closer to me in age and had her own outside activities. Rose was with me when Remus moved into the house as my guide in March of 1993.

Before the turnover, Janice and I took both Remus and Mikki on the train to Philadelphia, so that both dogs could be examined by Dr. Ruben. He pronounced Remus's eyes as all right. We also arranged to have Remus traffic-tested with a quiet, almost-silent, electric vehicle, to make sure that she was using her eyes to watch the movement of cars. Finally, Janice did a blindfold test with

Remus, with another dog trainer following behind. Remus went over an up-curb out of the street a little too quickly, and Janice tripped and fell. She had to get stitches in her hand in the emergency room. I was sorry that it happened, but Remus learned a valuable lesson. During our work together, she was always cautious on up-steps and curbs.

While Rose was with me, we got around to cleaning out the basement, and we had a yard/driveway sale to dispose of some of Papa's extra drill bits and tools, as well as old screen doors and old wooden storm windows. I was very gratified when someone took them off my hand to use on a house they were building. Rose's mother also sold some things with us, and I bought more 33 1/3 L.P. records from her to add to my collection.

Remus (February 17, 1991-November 8, 2008) moved into my house as my working guide on March 1, 1993, when she was a little over two years old. The transition was pretty seamless, as we had planned. We still had some adjustments to make, but we succeeded.

Like Mikki, Remus could jump straight up, high enough to try to nose me with her nose. I had to teach her to stay on the floor, and she had to learn to be gentle with me and my nose or I would have a nosebleed. To encourage her not to jump, I tried to bend down to her level so that we could gently touch noses.

I eventually had to move the couch from its erstwhile place in front of the picture window, because Remus was breaking down the back of the couch by lying up there to look out the window. We switched the couch with the piano, because both of them took up longer walls.

Like Mikki, Remus rarely barked when she was working, but she would bark or vocalize at home to indicate that a person or animal was in the vicinity or coming to the door. She had different sounds for different situations, and an incredible vocal vocabulary! Remus got to know and accept the mail people, because they spoke to us through the intercom. She was furious and frustrated with most of the UPS folks, because they dropped things on the porch and vamoosed without communicating with people inside the house. I think she thought that they were rude in not talking to us! On one occasion, though it was rare for her to vocalize while working, Remus barked at someone on the way home from church, because he was walking his dog without a leash. I guess she thought that they were out of order, too. Although I corrected her, I privately agreed with her. No matter how quiet the neighborhood or disciplined the dog, this kind of thing can be dangerous on account of traffic and other possibly unpredictable dogs!

Another time, in the office at the SEC, Remus let out one big, loud bark: "Woof!" No, she wasn't asleep and dreaming! We never found out why, and maybe she heard something that no one else did. In any event, it was such a rare occurrence that people came running from all directions to find out what was going on with Remus! After it was certain that nothing was wrong and everyone dispersed, my assistant, Judy, remarked that maybe it was a good thing it happened.

"Remus has learned now that, if she talks, people will come, and that probably is a good thing, especially in an emergency!" she told me.

I also had to get a higher fence put around the back of the yard, more like five or six feet, because Remus demonstrated the ability to jump, like her father. Even Janice's attempts to curb this behavior with a shock collar didn't work. Fortunately, although I'm sure that she could have jumped my higher fence, her sense of responsibility and loyalty to me kept her from doing it. She wasn't above going through the gate if it was left open. On one occasion, both dogs left together. They came back after a joy romp, and poor Mikki had to go to the vet for an arthritis flare-up. On the second occasion, Remus got out, but Mikki did not. When we got her back in the yard, Mikki chased Remus all over the yard by way of correction!

In many ways, Remus was everything I wanted. She was the shepherd that I longed for, and in fact, I liked her wider head and face, wide, large ears, and flat straight back much better than the conventional look of many German shepherds. Although she was smaller than any of my past or present dogs, she worked like a big dog. I mean that she conveyed a sense of stability and surefooted confidence and steadiness that I associated with my larger canines. Like Vincent, she could think outside the box and take initiative when required. Remus was excellent at following my sighted friends, and she would often circle behind them to get them out in front of us. As I tried to explain to them, Remus had inherited a high degree of herding talent from both parents. She knew that the harness connected me, one sheep, with her. She wanted the other people sheep out front, where she could see them!

Remus, like Vincent, was always looking out for my security. On one occasion, she howled and fussed in a doctor's office, until they let her come into the room with me while they were doing a procedure. On another occasion, I was lying face down on a table preparing for a massage. Remus thought that I looked vulnerable, and she jumped up onto the table to lie full-length on me so that she covered my back, with her head up near my head and her tail down over my legs! She felt a little heavy, but very soft, warm, and reassuring! The lady who was going to give me the massage laughed and joked about it. When Remus saw that we weren't serious or upset, she got down off the table and let us proceed with the massage, but she had to be sure that I was OK. Generally, when she realized I was finished with the doctors, Remus would go out into the waiting room to let my waiting companion know that we were done.

Remus and Mikki got along together fine. Remus probably remembered Mikki as the big Mama Lab that she encountered as a puppy. Although I'm sure that Mikki missed not accompanying me to places sometimes, unlike Vincent, she was content to surrender the responsibility. "It's your job, Kid, if you want it," she probably would have said.

Mikki and Remus often would lie on the couch, back to back, with just enough space for me to squeeze in between them. Then, Mikki would bark, by way of telling me that she wanted me to come and sit with them. I would squeeze in between their two tails. It is a very healing experience to sit bracketed by two furry, loving friends!

The two dogs reacted very differently to storms or other scary events. Mikki, typical Labrador, believed that wherever I was probably was the safe place to be, and she would stick close to me. Remus, on the other hand, knew about forty-five minutes ahead of time that bad weather was coming. She would either jump into the nearest bathtub (if the bathroom door was open,) run downstairs and sit against the cinder block wall in the basement if that door was ajar, or hide behind the couch until the thunderstorm was over. I used to tease her that we needed to teach her to dial 911, because she might be the only one left if the house fell down!

Remus loved to play ball, and Janice had taught her to retrieve the tennis ball and bring it back to my hand. For that purpose, the command was, "Give." If she got her hard exercise and play when not working, she was a model of decorum in the house and office. At work, we took her across the street to play a hard ball game off leash at lunchtime. Although the area wasn't fenced, she was so focused on the game that we didn't have to worry about her leaving us. This behavior on Remus's part is the exception that proves the rule. I would never do with any past or likely future guide dogs what I did with her. However, given her nature, we considered it to be a calculated risk.

If she got her exercise, Remus knew how to stay out of my hair if I was reading or working on art projects. Most important of all, when Remus was working her tail hung straight down, her ears went back as though pinned to her head, and she generally was all business. Unless she knew somebody, she usually did not go up to strangers to greet them or seek attention from them. If they patted her, she would submit politely to their attentions, and then she would shake herself, fluff up her fur, walk away and return to duty. "That's that!" she seemed to say.

Remus was not always "good as gold." We had to work on her tendency to jump excitedly if she saw someone that she knew. On a couple of occasions, she lunged against my leash, because she saw a dog, cat, or squirrel that distracted her. On the most serious of those occasions, I was afraid that she might pull me down. I pinned her on her back for a moment by way of discipline, to try to make the lesson stick that this kind of conduct was unacceptable. She was physically small enough for me to successfully use this form of discipline. Fortunately, she listened.

By way of explanation, my pinning her on her back was my effort to assert my alpha status. It's something to be done only on rare occasions, and it only should be done if you physically can do it, which I could do with Remus. If you try it and don't succeed, the dog thinks that he won, instead of you. I would think twice before attempting this with one of my Labradors. As described later, I only did it once with Teddy.

Because Remus tended to be a picky eater, she also wasn't prone to lobbying me when I was eating or to picking up scraps from the floor while working. The downside of her fussy eating habits was that she would sometimes go without eating for a day or two. If it was longer, it could be worrisome. We added some cottage cheese or yogurt to her food to tempt her appetite. Except for a taste of my banana in the mornings, unlike the labs, Remus did not generally like fruit. She developed a taste for homemade cranberry sauce. She also developed a taste for fish, and we sometimes added a little to her food. We called her the Fish Hound.

Rose and I eventually decided that our arrangement wasn't workable long-term. I hired a lady recommended to me by someone at work. She had a take-charge personality, and she did accomplish one good feat. She finished putting those loose pictures into albums, and I appreciated that. However, in other ways, it turned out not to be a good match at all! Like Moose, this individual had a very strong, assertive personality. I didn't like always having to be on my mettle and not being able to relax, and I felt overborne. The stress of the situation and (I later discovered) my eating little chocolate mint candies caused me to have a very severe nose-bleeding episode. Dr. Lynden had long ago retired, and the ear, nose, and throat doctor that I was seeing decided to hospitalize me, under sedation, to get the bleeding under control. It was one of the worst times of my life. I was afraid that I would never get out of there. I also didn't know how well the housekeeper was taking care of the dogs at home.

One evening in the hospital, I wanted so badly to break down and cry, and I was afraid that the nose would open back up again. Out of nowhere, this lady came. She said that her name was Aurora, and she supposedly was a nursing student or assistant. She brought me a drink of water and consoled me.

"You'll be all right," she told me. "Lindas are tough!"

I eventually was able to persuade the nurses to have the doctor cut down or stop the morphine pills, which I hated. I also got hives from them. Eventually I was discharged. When I called the hospital to thank them for their care and try to express appreciation to Aurora, they told me that nobody by that name was assigned to my floor. I'm cautious about jumping to a conclusion like this, but maybe God sent me an angel that night!

After a few more weeks, I concluded that I would have to fire the overly assertive housekeeper. I asked Mike Geltner to come to the house when I told her, because I expected (rightly) that she would get confrontational. On my side, I tried not to get antagonistic, just to let her understand that I liked her fine and could admire her in some ways, but I couldn't live with her. I offered her two weeks' notice, but she left immediately, in a huff, and I wasn't sorry. Margie covered for me short-term, and Patsy eventually came back for a few months. She got to see Remus work, and she agreed that she was much better at helping me to get around stores by following Patsy than Mikki had been.

Remus and Mikki also differed in their reactions to snow. Mikki liked snow well enough, but she wasn't so enthusiastic about it as Vincent had been. On the other hand, Remus thought that snow was put down especially for her playground pleasure, and she loved chasing balls and Frisbees in the snow. Patsy noticed that Mikki could find balls buried in the snow by scent and by following her nose. Remus lost them totally if she couldn't see them, because she was so focused on using her eyes to follow them. Snow also kept balls clean; if they got too dirty in the grass and mud, I've observed Remus drop them into the dishwasher rack if I had it open to load dishes. One ball actually went through the cycle and came out squeaky clean.

Remus's acute use of her vision helped her to be such a good worker. On one occasion, we were playing ball, and a friend told me that a bird flew into the line of direction of the ball in such a way that it looked to Remus as though the ball was flying away. My friend said that her expression of surprise and incredulity was priceless! Balls don't fly! Then she retrieved the ball that dropped on the ground. I would love to have seen that, but if I could have seen it, I wouldn't have needed Remus.

Over New Year's, 1994, I went back to Florida to see Aunt Murff, this time with Remus. I had a nice time again there, but Remus went off her feed for a few days. She started eating again one morning, when she heard Pattie's husband, Ronnie, crunching on cereal. Unfortunately, Murff's cat was more afraid with Remus than with Mikki, and Remus was a little too excitable over the cat. They didn't coexist so easily. I went back to the religious store to see what I could find. I don't remember what I bought for me this time, but I also bought a stable for Janice's nativity set, because she mentioned to me in passing that she didn't have one.

In 1994 through 1996, Tina McAllister worked for me as my live-in housekeeper and companion. She was just twenty when she came. She was fun-loving and energetic, and she shared my love of collectibles, dolls, fuzzy stuffed animals, music boxes, and jewelry, as well as artwork. I still have a cat figurine that Tina painted by hand for me.

Tina was a good, creative cook, and she knew how to use the microwave, stove, and charcoal grill to good advantage. A young lady of many talents, she also knew how to cut my hair in such a way as to take advantage of the little natural curl or wave that it has.

Tina also introduced me to some of the better modern music that she and her friends enjoyed. She read me the wonderful science fiction book, about a horrible future time in which it is illegal to own books! I think the title was *Fahrenheit* 451, or something like that. Tina also took the trouble to learn a little Braille, so that she could leave me a note or phone number if she needed to do so. Tina is a convert to Catholicism, and she and I also share a deep commitment to pro-life and the cause of ending abortions.

Tina had some difficulties in her life and childhood. I came to love this girl who was young enough to have been my daughter, and I wanted so much to make up for her past difficulties. I did what I could for her, including arranging for a complete physical with Dr. Morrissey. As with so many things, it is only possible for us human beings to love each other now, and we have to let the healing work be done by God.

Tina's friend, Patricia King, was often visiting at our house. She had stayed with Janice for a while when Remus was living with her, and she, like Tina, really loved Remus. Pat is a good musician and had played drums in a band. She told me some very interesting things about drums, including that you can vary the pitch of the sound by hitting drums in different places or with different things. I was pleasantly surprised when Pat and Tina agreed with me that the analog recordings on phonograph records conveyed more of the overtones and tonal quality of music than the digital recordings on CD's. The CD's have become better with time, and maybe I am adjusting to them better.

The girls taught Remus to play Frisbee, and after that, it was her favorite game at home.

One evening, Remus began making sounds as though she was choking. Pat put her fingers down Remus's throat and pulled something out. Then Tina, Pat, and I, with Remus, piled into my car and made it double-time to the vet. I told Tina that I was afraid that a policeman would pull us over for speeding.

"I wish he would!" Tina said, as she kept going. "I'd ask him to get behind us!" By the protection of Divine Providence and the lightly traveled roads that night, we made it to the vet all in one piece, and fortunately Remus was Ok.

For the Easter of 1995, the girls hid goodies all over the house and made me go on an Easter treasure hunt! After I found the goodies, I tried to find the crowing rooster to set him off, but we couldn't find that stuffed rooster, and everybody began going all around looking for that darn rooster! I hadn't done anything like that since Papa did it one year a long time ago!

In 1995, Jim Waeldner took another position in the SEC, and Judy Gechter became my assistant. The position was a permanent, Schedule A. posting at that time. I was able to interview the applicants who applied for it. Because an important part of the position involved assisting me with research, many of the candidates emphasized their paralegal abilities and credentials.

Judy's husband, Ruben, had moved to VA from San Diego, CA, to accept a position in the IT department with the Division of Corporate Finance at the SEC. Judy had been a school teacher. When she joined her husband in their home in Springfield, VA, she applied for my posting. Before the interview, Ruben came to my office to see me.

He told me that he knew Judy didn't have all the paralegal criteria. However, he also knew her intelligence, ability, and integrity. He asked me to consider whether I wanted someone with the paper credentials, or someone smart and loyal. After I interviewed Judy, I agreed that "smart and loyal" trumped everything else. I was sure that we could work well together.

Judy was excellent, and we made a good team for eighteen years! We found that it helped to put a spice in the hard work by keeping our senses of humor, and we laughed a great deal; it helped not to take things seriously that weren't that important! I became very impressed with Judy's quick learning of the substance of our work. She became a good researcher, with a good grasp of problems and analysis of how to get information to solve them. When her daughter, Ronit, eventually graduated from law school and became a lawyer, I asked Judy if she wanted to "read for the bar" while working for me, and then pass the bar exam to be a lawyer, too. Virginia was one of the few states that allows someone to do this and take the bar without a degree from a law school. I was confident that Judy could have done it. She declined, but I'm sure that she appreciated how much confidence I had in her. One of the most helpful things Judy did for me was to encourage me to quit stewing about difficult things, and "just do it."

Judy and I also became personal friends. Outside of work, we enjoyed going to lunch together and occasionally shopping and other outings. I had the pleasure of spending Passover evenings at her house for a few years, and celebrating the Passover meal with Judy, her husband Ruben, and other family members and friends has given me an even deeper appreciation of the Mass and Easter.

That year, 1995, I also finally followed my dream and got the kitchen expanded by ten feet out into the yard and renovated. I hired a contractor, Mickey Simpson Builders, to accomplish the project. When we were in the planning phase, I told Clarke Simpson that I wanted to use 5/8-inch drywall on the walls and ceiling of the addition, because I thought that it would better complement the original plaster. To dissuade me, Clarke took a kitchen knife and tried to make a hole in the wall. Tina sat there and laughed at him, because she knew that he wouldn't succeed. He couldn't even nick the plaster! I got my thicker drywall!

Clarke subsequently confirmed again how well built the house is. In order to enlarge the kitchen, they had to break through part of the original brick wall of the house. Fortunately, I was at work when they did it, because the noise must have been horrible!

"I never saw anything like this!" Clarke told me later. "First, of course, there was a layer of brick; then came the cinderblock, and behind the cinderblock were two-by-fours! I've seen two of those together, but never all three!"

"They built the houses well in those days," I told him.

By way of advertising, the contractor had signs on my property during the renovation. A real estate agent called us, thinking that I was fixing up the house because I planned to sell it. Tina answered the phone, because I was at work.

"Hell no!" she told the caller. "She isn't planning to sell! She's spending all this money to fix the house to suit herself!" One of the carpenters overheard her response and laughed like a fool!

Once the kitchen was enlarged, to complete the project I replaced the gas stove with an electric, had the dishwasher that Billie gave me installed under the counter, replaced the refrigerator and demoted the old one to the basement, had wooden cupboards installed, and put down a ceramic tile floor and ceramic tile counters. The work took several weeks, and we had to improvise while the kitchen was unavailable. By this time, a new combination microwave/convection oven had replaced the old, faithful G.E. toaster oven. We moved the oven into the dining room, we relied on the electric teakettle for hot water, and Janice lent us a hotplate. We had to make do with frozen dinners, tea reheated in the microwave after made with the electric kettle, and other dishes that could be cooked on these devices. I remember coming home from an outing one Saturday, and Tina trying to cook stir-fry Chinese on the hotplate in the living room. The difficult task was made more challenging, because the hotplate kept tripping the circuit breakers! Tina said that she would rather have been cooking over an open fire in the fireplace than using these electric appliances!

We were comfortable with all the folks coming into the house, and Remus even tried to invite them to play ball, except for the dry-wall guys. They also painted the kitchen after installing the drywall. When they were working, Tina and I stuck close to the house to supervise them. The dogs stayed protectively with me on the couch while they were there. When they left, Remus would bark at them, as though to say that they should keep on going!

It was a relief to get it all done. The kitchen is now one hundred square feet bigger than it was originally. Law School Judy's husband, Ed, made me a beautiful, unique table, with a tile work space inside a wooden frame, a shelf above the back of it, and a storage drawer underneath. I'm only sorry that Patsy and Nana didn't get to work in this nice space.

Mikki still literally gave us a run for our money sometimes. On one occasion, Tina was late coming to get me at work. When she told me why, I laughed. Tina brought Mikki with her in the car. En route, she stopped to let Mikki run off leash in a park near my house. Mikki had such a good time that she didn't want to come when she was called. As Tina told me, Mikki ran Tina's legs off, all over the park. Young boys and some men tried to catch her to help Tina, but nobody could catch Mikki, until she was ready to stop! I laughed and laughed!

In the fall of 1995, Jeanne Rhode came to visit again from California. I'm glad that she got to see the newly renovated kitchen and to meet Remus, Tina, and Pat. We had another good visit.

The girls and I celebrated my birthday in late October-November of 1995 by going to Busch Gardens near Williamsburg. Like Vincent, Remus was wonderful in the gondola. She helped me follow Tina and Pat all over that theme park. I also got to shop in the goody stores and to pat one of the big Clydesdale horses. Each of the girls also took turns holding Remus so that I could go on some of the milder rides with the other one. I considered trying one of the roller coasters, but I couldn't work up the nerve, and we fortunately ran out of time. We finished up by all riding together (including Remus) on the carousel. It was lots of fun!

We had another adventure when I decided to replace the asbestos tile on the basement floor with ceramic tile and to have waterproof paint put on the basement walls. I hired Melvin King, who had successfully paved my driveway with cement. He did a good job on the basement, but he didn't tell me ahead of time that he planned to use oil-based paints that gave off terrible fumes! Tina and I couldn't spend the nights in the house until the work was done. Fortunately, one of my friends put up the dogs and me. It was a very unsettling time, and it reminded me again how little I like changes!

When our parish decided to do a directory that would include pictures of parishioners, Tina and I went to get our pictures taken with both dogs. They both were wearing their harnesses. It gave me an opportunity to get pictures taken with my canine buddies and Tina.

I wanted to share one of my favorite places, Calvert Cliffs, with the girls. We tried to go one afternoon, but by the time we got ourselves together, it was too late, and the park was closed. We had both dogs with us, and we wanted to go to dinner. It was too hot to leave Mikki in the car. Fortunately, I had Mikki's gear with me. I harnessed up Mikki, and I told Pat to pretend to work Mikki, and I would work Remus, and we would tell the dogs to follow Tina. We got away with it, and we had a very nice dinner in a restaurant on Solomon's Island whose name I don't remember. I'm surprised that we got away with it. Both dogs gave the game away by lying at my feet. Tina tried to carry it off by reading both of us blind ladies the menu, but Pat kept forgetting and giving the game away. At the end of the meal, she wanted to go outside (maybe to smoke) and I tried to stay in part.

"Well," I said to Pat. "I guess that Mikki ought to be able to lead you out to the car." When Pat wanted to go to the ladies' room, I suggested that Tina take her. Looking back at it, the episode was hilarious! We went back to Calvert Cliffs another day, when we could go earlier and find the park open.

In 1995 or 1996, we learned that good old Woodward and Lothrop's, affectionately known as Woody's, was going to close. Judy, Katie, Debbie Abernethy (another friend at work) and other friends and I began going to the downtown store as often as possible, to buy some precious things "that came from Woody's" and have lunch in the tea room, and say good-bye. A few years before, Dottie helped me pick out the Seth Thomas Woodbury 1302 mantle clock for the living room from the store in 7 Corners, when Woody's was getting out of the clock selling business. Losing Woody's was like losing an old friend. A touch of class and elegance went out of the shopping scene.

As the time approached for Tina to leave me, I felt regret at losing her, but it seemed to be time for the girls to go on to more independent lives.

I don't remember just when it happened, but in June, sometime in the 1990's, Ellen finally succumbed to her lung disease. Patsy and I were able to go to see her in the hospital to say good-bye. I thanked her for all the fun that we had. She was turned over to hospice care, but she died a short time afterwards. Rose Ingberman sang beautifully at her funeral Mass. Ellen's house and family treasures came to her niece, Pat. Pat asked me if there was anything that Ellen had that I might like as a keepsake. I told her, yes, something that Ellen had made in a cathedral window style of quilt. Pat brought me a pillow that Ellen had made with that pattern. I removed the stuffing and had it put in a frame without glass, so that I could touch it. It hangs in the hallway of the stairway going up to the second floor. I still miss Ellen very much; she was a good friend.

This period brought other changes to family and friends, but I don't remember exactly when they happened. Sister Margaret James Dean, my cousin, had retired from teaching and was living in the Mother House in Allison Park, PA. She developed diabetes and lost much of her vision. She also began having trouble with her legs. Ironically, I could have given her tips to cope, but she didn't adjust well to losing her eyesight at all. She was angry and bitter over her loss of mobility and especially not being able to drive any more. Eventually, they discovered that she was having silent heart attacks. The doctors, with her consent, tried to do bypass surgery, but something went very wrong. They were unable to wean her off the respirator, and other organs began to shut down. She never regained consciousness, and they eventually shut off the respirator. She waited for the sisters gathered around her bed to sing a hymn, Cousin Jim said, and then she died within a few minutes. Ironically, at the time that she died, the religious community was having a "chapter" or big meeting, so many of her community sisters were there for the funeral who might not otherwise have been able to come. Gretchen told me that they found that she collected butterfly pins, a trait that she shared with me, (and I didn't know it.) At the cemetery, a black butterfly flew past her grave. I didn't go to the funeral, but I learned these details from my cousins.

Patsy eventually moved away from northern VA and went to Ocala, Florida, moving into a little house that Mrs. Bortnick allowed her to use. Dottie moved to Atlanta to be with her parents. I think that both of her parents have since died, but I have lost touch with Dottie. Ed Boehme took over the bill paying until he moved to Ashburn, VA, and then the bank had to help me. Since Ed, I have had a number of wonderful, competent, dedicated volunteers.

Doreen also moved to Florida to be near her son, Peter. She had surgery to limit her food intake, because she was fighting a weight problem. She eventually died. Chris Gregory's two adopted children are grown, and she and Chuck are grandparents through their daughter, but Chuck hasn't been well.

Michelle Howell, a wonderful volunteer, replaced Karen Goodlatte as the person reading me literature and less important mail, but she eventually died from esophageal cancer. I very much miss this good friend.

Billie's lung cancer recurred in another lung, but they were not able to get it under control. She asked me to come to see her, but before I did so, she died. I'm sorry that I didn't just call a taxi and go ASAP, but I was a little reluctant to take a taxi somewhere that I hadn't been by myself. Yes, I had been to Billie's house, but not on my own. I kept in touch with her sister, Eleanor, for a while, but I lost contact with her and the rest of the family.

After Tina stopped working for me, I relied on part-time help for a while. Shirley Collins, referred to me by a friend at work, came to clean once or twice a week. She fell in love with Mikki, who generally was home when she came, while I was at work. However, we had a funny incident on one occasion when Remus was there. I either took leave for something or was home sick. At that time, we had two braided rugs with pads in the kitchen, along with a throw rug near the back door. Shirley was trying to clean and work, and Remus wanted her to play. Shirley told Remus no, that she couldn't play. She put the three rugs and two pads outside to air while she cleaned the kitchen floor. When she looked outside again, Remus had dragged all five things up into the yard and was lying next to them, wagging her tail.

Translation: "Now you will have to come outside and play, Shirley! You have to come and get the rugs!"

We all split our sides laughing!

In 1996, I finally went to see Father Seamus in Peaks Island, Maine, in the monastery. Janice took care of Mikki while I was gone, and Sister Elizabeth Henry went with me. The trip was part retreat, and part vacation. I got to meet Father for the first time. He introduced sister, Remus, and me to the other monk, Brother Nicholas, his working guide dog, his retired dog, the ex-Seeing Eye golden retriever, and the resident cats.

When we first arrived, I had a nose bleeding episode, because I had a feather pillow on my bed. Sister Elizabeth Henry and I were alone in the guest wing, so brother Nicholas suggested to us that we should check the other beds in the wing. He felt certain that at least one of them had a fiber pillow. It's a good thing that we went exploring down the hall. We discovered that Remus had done so ahead of us, and she had stirred up the covers on all the unoccupied beds, her idea of a teasing prank! We hastily straightened out the covers!

It was a wonderful trip, with both a spiritual and a recreational side. I found Father Seamus to be a comforting spiritual adviser. He also used his Braille printer to prepare copies of hymns and prayers for me, so that I could follow the prayers and Mass more easily. I learned how peaceful and tranquil it could be to sit in the Presence of the exposed Blessed Sacrament! Also, hearing those monks praying together is truly inspirational! Lest some ask what is the practicality of the contemplative life, we really do need some people living this life, to pray for all of us who often lack the time and motivation to do it well ourselves, and to show the rest of us what it means to be devoted totally to God. They need more monks, so I must keep praying for vocations for them.

Father Seamus also arranged for some of the volunteers and friends of the monastery to show us around Portland, Maine. I bought a lobster pendant as a souvenir, as well as my first nautical clock for the kitchen.

In 2002 or so, the monks sold the property in Maine, because the climate was too hard for Father's arthritis. They now are located in Deland, Florida, in difficult living conditions, and they no longer have space to easily put up guests. They are trying to accumulate a building fund to make necessary changes and improvements. Meanwhile, in addition to the working and retired dog, the Seeing Eye reject (for security) and their pugs, they also have chickens, ducks, geese, and miniature goats. Someone gave them a donkey for a while, that was devoted to Brother Nicholas and named Noel. They had to find a new home for her, because they didn't think that the donkey would coexist safely with the dogs. They had alpacas for a while, and they sold yarn made from the wool and sheep's wool mixed together. I bought some and knitted myself a scarf with it.

About a year after going to Maine to see Father Seamus, Sister Elizabeth Henry went with me to the Trappist monastery in Berryville for a weekend retreat. I liked it very much. Remus did pretty well, but she did bark at the resident cat, when we encountered her one night when taking Remus out to park.

With Mikki getting older, I also needed someone to come in the afternoons to let Mikki out. Shirley's daughter, Sabrina, tried to help me part-time for a while, but I eventually hired Chris Oliphant to do this work.

With her arthritis, Mikki was having more trouble getting onto my bed. I knew how much she needed to be with me, and I loved snuggling with her at night. We put one, and eventually, two crib mattresses next to the bed, so that Mikki could get onto the mattress and then get up on the bed. The first time we put the mattress next to the bed, Remus proceeded to demonstrate how it should be used. Several times, she went from the floor to the mattress to the bed and back again, to demonstrate it to Mikki! She seemed to know exactly what it was for!

Mikki began getting more bladder infections. Eventually, they wouldn't go away, even on antibiotics. In the spring of 1997, we went for an examination of the urethra under anesthetic. The results and diagnosis in late March showed cancer of the urinary tract and bladder. Catheterization isn't practical in dogs, so surgery wasn't an option and would have left her incontinent. They told me that we had six to nine months, and that eventually the cancer would get so big that she wouldn't be able to empty her bladder! I told Mike Kigin about the horrible diagnosis on the way home from work. It was a gorgeous, mild March day. Mike said that it seemed so ironic to get such sad news on such a beautiful day.

I cried and cried to the Lord. I told him that I just wasn't ready to say good-bye to Mikki. I loved her, and I still valued her comforting presence on my bed. I put the two twin beds together to make a big bed so that there would be enough room for both dogs. Sometimes, Remus got onto the bed with Mikki, but she often preferred to be under the bed. Aside from how much I would miss Mikki physically, I also felt as though Mikki really didn't have a fair deal. I had retired her when she was around eight years old, hoping that she would have some time to enjoy her retirement, and here we were four years later with what amounted to a death sentence. Mikki had tried so hard to do what we asked her to do.

"Please, God! I'm not yet ready to say good-bye!" I pleaded, as I cried. I think I kind of stormed heaven.

God's answer to my prayers and tears was to encourage me to "give me Mikki." In other words, He wanted me to trust that He would take care of the whole situation, which I now can see that He did. He also helped us find ways to fight the disease. Mikki had to stay on antibiotics the rest of her life to combat chronic bladder infections. One of my vets said that sometimes the anti-inflammatory medicine, feldine, helped to slow down cancer. Mikki had arthritis anyhow, so we switched her onto this medicine. We also began to see a chiropractic vet, Dr. Jana Frohling, to treat her joint issues with spinal adjustments. On the days that Mikki had those appointments, I took leave from work, and Rita Lorenzetti, (now married to Jim Felkel, so Rita Felkel,) drove me to those appointments and spent the day with me.

Next, someone at South Paws referred me to Dr. Charles Loops, a vet in SC. who specialized in using homeopathic remedies. As he told me candidly over the telephone, "I can't promise to cure this, but we can slow it down."

He was right. We kept throwing different remedies at the cancer and monitoring the progress through the local vets. I had to mix the remedies he sent me into half-and-half or yogurt to give them to Mikki. When we were relaxing in the evenings, I sometimes made popcorn, and I shared it in appropriate quantities with both dogs. Mikki enjoyed it, and I hoped it would distract her from any discomfort she was experiencing. We gave it a good fight for almost two years.

In early 1999, we began to notice other symptoms. They x-rayed Mikki's lungs, and it looked as though the cancer was spreading there. We tried adding additional and different antibiotics to see if it was an infection, and not cancer. Mikki was already on medication for an enlarged heart. At some point, dr. loops advised taking her off the heartworm preventative and other medicines. I didn't want to admit it, but I knew the end was coming.

For a couple of weeks, as sometimes happens, we had a false recovery. Mikki's appetite returned, and I began to hope that God had given us another reprieve. One Sunday evening, we were watching the TV version of *Alice in Wonderland*, and Mikki was lying on the couch beside me. She put her head on me, and I got the distinct feeling that she was telling me that she knew that I was trying to fight for her. I teased Margie that Mikki, not President Clinton, was the real "comeback kid."

It was not to be. On March 4, overnight, I had to let Mikki out to piddle. Afterwards, we snuggled together on my bed for what turned out to be the last time. Chris came the next day as usual. She left in the evening, after I had dinner.

On the evening of March 5, 1999, it became clear to me that Mikki was in distress. I feared that she couldn't empty her bladder any more. Barbara Sheehan took Mikki, Remus, and me to the emergency vet at Alexandria Animal Hospital. I rode in the back seat, holding Mikki, and trying to comfort her. I could feel the rasping in her breathing as I was holding her. Mikki had tried to dig a hole in the yard, but she still came into the house to me. She trusted that I would solve her problem!

We thought that we were too late for our regular vet, but it turned out that the regular vet, Dr. Baxter, was there. She forgot her pocketbook and had to come back. X-rays confirmed that the cancer was huge. It blocked the urethra, and it wouldn't be possible to get a catheter in to relieve it. I asked Dr. Baxter to drain her bladder with a needle. I didn't want the last thing on her mind to be that she had to relieve herself.

"You can go home tonight, if you want to, but you'll be back in the morning," Dr. Baxter told me.

I would have loved one more night with Mikki, but I didn't know if I could get friendly transportation to come back in the morning. Besides, the previous night had been good. I didn't see any sense in further delay. I stayed with Mikki for the final needle. She died peacefully. I had her cremated, and I retain her remains in a wooden frame behind a picture of a Lab puppy.

I came home and cried and cried that night. I almost told Janice to come and take unresponsive Remus away! She was no comfort, and she spent that night on the couch, not with me. I realized afterwards that Remus was mourning in her own way, but I was too self-absorbed that night to really be objective. The next day, I called friends and cried all day. The Monday after Mikki died, March 8, we had a light snowfall, a bit of a consolation for Remus and me. I made a lady's head pendant out of Sculpy that afternoon, because I came home early from work on account of the weather.

The loss of Mikki was slow to heal.

Aside from the feelings that I already described, I felt especially bad because of something that I learned a little before Mikki died. Apparently, to see if bladders could be grown in a lab to help people, some scientists conducted an experiment using dogs. They grew bladders using a matrix in the lab, removed bladders from otherwise healthy dogs, and transplanted the new bladders into the dogs. The dogs survived and did well with their new organs, but to test the results, the researchers "sacrificed" i.e. killed -- those dogs to dissect them and analyze the results! It made me a little sick to think of killing a healthy animal to verify results. Couldn't they have let them live out their lives and then checked on death? I would happily have been a guinea pig and let Mikki get a new bladder under a trial similar to a person with cancer, but not to have her sacrificed afterwards! We trivialize animals and act as though they are ours to do what we want with them in the name of science, and I think that it's wrong! We are supposed to be stewards of creation, not to disrespect the life around us. If we think that we can treat animals like this, is it any wonder that we now trivialize the life of the unborn in the womb, in the name of expediency, or think that we can use embryonic human beings for stem cell research? Our dear old teachers were right when they said that ends do not justify means!

As mentioned in an earlier chapter, Mikki's legacy to me was that I found out about homeopathic medicine, and that it can be effective in providing alternative remedies for some conditions. Armed with this knowledge, I sought a homeopathic physician, and Dr. David Wember has helped me to find some vitamins, supplements, and other natural remedies that have greatly helped me to combat my arthritis and my nose bleeding problems.

Remus expressed her grief for Mikki by developing physical problems in one of her paws. It had to be opened two or three times, including once by a surgeon, but we couldn't find a cause of the problem. Fortunately, it eventually healed, after Dr. Loops sent me a one-dose homeopathic remedy for removal of a foreign body. We documented the results with pictures and sent it to him.

In 1999, Tina came to visit me with her little baby boy, Andre. We decided to go out to lunch. We put Remus in the back of Tina's station wagon, and we put Andre in the back seat in his car seat. As we were driving, we noticed that Remus was up in the seat area, standing between Andre and the door. At the next light, a lady began hollering at us from another vehicle.

"Your door's not shut! Your door's not shut!" she cried. It wasn't tightly secured. Remus recognized the problem and was being protective of the little kid!

At the SEC, things kept changing, too. At some point, around 2000, the agency moved some of the staff, including the Division of Investment Management, to a satellite building at 901 E Street

NW. They were vacating 450 5<sup>th</sup> Street to move the headquarters into Station Place I. Eventually, we moved into Station Place II when it was ready, but meanwhile, it added some inconvenience to Mike. He and I retained our parking permit in the 5<sup>th</sup> Street Building as long as he was there. Eventually, he had to drop me off at and go on to Station Place I. It was a time of upheaval and transition.

One advantage of the new location was that I was within easy walking distance of St. Patrick's Church. One year, I had the memorable opportunity of attending Mass in this church when the parish commemorated the feast day of its patron saint, St. Patrick. It was a beautiful Eucharistic celebration! I also began walking over there with Remus at lunchtime. We found a beautiful life-sized crucifix in the antechamber of the church. One of my colleagues at work, Bill Middlebrooks, helped me to get up on a chair, so that I could feel the corpus of this highly detailed crucifix. The experience formed the inspiration for part of the poem, "Face to Face", which I reprinted earlier in this book.

Meanwhile, Mike was anticipating that he would be retiring around 2007, and he tried to augment our carpool. Ken Cureton came to work for the SEC from one of the banking agencies. He and Mike began to share the driving. He also became quite fond of Remus, and he would come to my house in the evenings sometimes to play ball with Remus before going home.

In 1999 or 2000, I enlarged the office area upstairs to make it more comfortable with a convenient workspace. Because this meant moving the front wall of the upper story, it added some space to the front alcove in my bedroom, too. I also added outside stairs to gain access to the backyard from the second floor. That new exit has been a lifesaver in terms of getting older dogs out quickly when they need to park!

I remember the year 2000-2001 as the time when I tried very hard to get to Mass during Lent and Advent and even to daily Mass. Remus took me down to church diligently. Dee Artim and other friends sometimes walked with me. Although she hated thunderstorms, Remus got me speedily down to church for the 5:30 vigil Mass one Saturday evening, even though a storm was threatening. She still thought of church as a safe place.

As discussed more fully in another chapter of this book, 9/11/2001 changed a lot of things for many of us. Remus heard the noises of military jets and the ultrasonic frequencies of security devices, and she no longer felt safe downtown. Also, she was getting older, turning 11 in February 2002. In that year, I hired my last live-in housekeeper. A friend recommended her. Ruili (Lily) Zhang-Beck came from China to marry Donald Beck a few years before I hired her. When he died from Lymphoma, she sold their house in New York and came to the DC area seeking employment. She worked for me until around 2005. One year, her musician daughter, Phoebe, came to visit her mother and stayed at my house.

Lily loved Remus, especially because she thought that Remus resembled a German shepherd that she used to have in China. She said that government authorities took her dog away.

In 2002, with the support and a letter of reference from Father Seamus, I decided to reapply to Seeing Eye, and this time, they accepted me. In the period of October-November, 2002, I went to the school for three weeks of the program. Two instructors spent the fourth and last week at home with me. I knew that Lily would take good care of Remus while I was gone. I took the train up to Morristown, NJ; Lily and Remus saw me off at the station. As with the time that I left Vincent to go to Guide Dogs of the Desert, I cried, knowing that I was losing Remus as a working partner.

The class was very large, around eighteen people, and I had a private room, instead of sharing with a roommate. Otherwise, the program was very similar to that at the other two schools. We worked our dogs in residential and downtown areas of Morristown, stores and shopping centers, and one big-city day in New York City.

Seeing Eye assigned me an ex-breeder dog, a black Labrador female, named Jamaica. I did not like the name. I remembered what Nana said about her sister, Gemma, and her big brown eyes. I decided to change my new pal's name to Gemma. Gemma (December 13, 1997-June 20, 2012) was going on five years old when she started working with me. She was a wonderful worker.

As with the other programs, I found this training difficult. I didn't like the idea of pushing a dog through having five litters of 27 puppies and then putting her back in service afterwards. Judging by how good she was, I'm sure that many of her puppies made good guide dogs. In fact, one of her grown puppies, a male called Skip, was in our class. We teased him when he went out with his human, and we told him to "make your mom proud, Skip!" We had an arduous, steep route to walk as one of our routes, called the High School route, and for some reason they excused me from this route. I thought at first that it was an accommodation to my arthritis, but I found out later that, because she had so much kennel confinement with the breeding and the puppies, Gemma needed to develop more muscle tone in her legs with exercise and fish oil supplements when she came home with me. She might have had trouble with the High School route, too.

Another reason that I found the program difficult was that the large size of the class and the difficulty that I have functioning in large groups contributed to my sense of isolation. Also, Gemma was reluctant to cross some busy streets, and the instructor forced the issue, by pulling the collar high up on her neck and pulling her. I questioned the appropriateness of this behavior, but, as the satire about President Kennedy said, it was the school's ball, and I had to go with the program. As with my other two school dogs, all I wanted to do was get through with the formal training and get home with my dog! I might not have hung in there, if Janice hadn't kept calling me and talking to me in the evenings on my cell phone in my room. I had to use the cell phone, because I couldn't hear over the phone in my room, and I had to use the speaker on the cell phone. I also missed so much going to daily Mass!

It was such a relief to get back home to my normal routine! Gemma and Remus got along fine together. Perhaps Gemma reminded Remus of Mikki, and I'm sure that Remus sensed that she could trust Gemma to safely guide me. Both dogs liked to play ball, and sometimes they even played catch together in the living room. The first night that I was home, I teased the instructors about being a sandwich between two dogs in the bed!

The three years that Lily was with me were good years. We enjoyed the goody stores, or just sitting together, with me listening intently to the wonderful Chinese folk stories that Lily told me. Lily is a wonderful storyteller. She told me some of the legends of the Monkey King saga, and she also recounted a story about two little girls outwitting a bad, scheming wolf. I liked the story of the smart little girls much better than "Little Red Riding Hood." Eventually, I wrote my own version, called "The Wolf's Story", in *Flights of Fancy and Food for Thought.*

Lily cooked me some wonderful Chinese dishes and introduced me to authentic cuisine Chinese restaurants. Lily was a good driver and a very reliable person.

Lily also took some good pictures of me and the two dogs. With help of friends, and maybe her daughter, Phoebe, when she came to visit, she was able to get into some of the pictures with me.

Meanwhile, in 2003 at work, we got new computers. Eventually everything went from MS-DOS to WINDOWS! I also replaced my first computer with one that was compatible with the new one at the office. Both at home and at work, the new DecTalk synthesizers were smaller, and the new version of screen-reading software was JAWS, by Freedom Scientific, Inc. One of my volunteers, Jeff Gara, knew a great deal about computers, and he helped me with setting up the new system at home. At work, the effort by the community of employees with disabilities was to persuade the SEC to hire someone who would be dedicated to serving our adaptive technology needs. They finally hired a contractor dedicated to these needs. It made a big difference, but it was a long struggle to get to that point. Once everybody was set up with their new systems, they went back to having us rely on the IT helpdesk for assistance.

In the spring after I came home from Seeing Eye, we had to treat Gemma for an eye problem. The vet whose office is across the street from the SEC had seen us and cleaned the eye and given us medicine. I didn't realize how serious it was until I tried to walk to church with Gemma the Sunday after we saw the vet. It turned out that Gemma really couldn't see out of the problem eye. With only one good eye, she didn't have depth perception. She kept weaving back and forth on the sidewalk. We felt our way down to church, and I had to find someone after Mass to walk home with us or drive us home. We saw the local veterinary ophthalmologist, Dr. Cochran, who said that Gemma had scratched her cornea. She inserted a contact lens to protect the eye until it healed and gave us drops. Fortunately, the eye healed, and she was able to remove the lens.

Gemma was in the unique position of having an eye problem and recovering to guide again. She was a good, steady worker and guide. When she managed to find her way around the complicated Station Place complex at work, she would wag her tail in a self-satisfied way, as though to say, "I did it!"

I also call Gemma my registered furry nurse, because she was very sensitive to my emotions and moods. When she sensed that I was under stress, she would often encourage me to cuddle her on the couch, until I calmed down.

In 2002 or 2003, I began reading the Harry Potter books. I have read all of them, and I like them very much. Like C. S. Lewis's The Chronicles of Narnia or J. R. Tolkien's Lord of the Rings Saga, these books can be read on many levels. They address in very modern terms the struggle between good and evil. I strongly disagree with conservative Christians who say that these books are bad, just because they have major characters called witches and wizards. If the characters had been called Jedi or some other fictional name, these people probably would not have a problem with them. However, I think that parents should exercise good discretion and judgment about the age of their children as they read the books. I think that the first book in the series should be for children in third or fourth grade, and then the child should read one or two a year; the kids should grow up with the books. The last two or three books are definitely for junior or senior high school students, not little kids! Ideally, parents should discuss the books with their children as they read them, and the parents also should read the books. Parents need to provide this kind of guidance and judgment about other literature, plays, movies, and TV shows. However good or worthwhile these works of art may be, no substitute exists for good parental guidance!

In 2004, I replaced the Mitsubishi Gallant with my dream car, a white 2004 Prius, and Ken Cureton helped to test drive it when we picked it up from the dealership.

Lily left me, I think, in 2005. After she left, Shirley Collins came back to work for me part-time.

In the summer of 2007, Dot Milne, a friend of the Kigins, came to visit the U.S. from her home in Scotland. She stayed with me for a couple of months. We went on some outings together, including visits to Monticello, Luray Caverns, the National Cathedral, and the Shrine of the Immaculate Conception. At the Cathedral and the Shrine, Dot arranged for a special tour for us, and I was able to touch some things that otherwise would have been off-limits. In the Crypt of the Shrine, we found a wonderful statue of the Flight into Egypt, showing Mary, Joseph, the Baby Jesus, and the donkey, all tired out and resting from their journey. I also was able to touch the relic cover of Pope St. Pius X, one of Mama's favorite saints. At Luray Caverns, it just happened that we visited on the once-a-year day that a special room was open to the public, the crystal cavern, all lit up with candles. I bought a souvenir CD of the music from the wonderful, natural pipe organ in the cave.

At work, I eventually got settled into the Station Place complex at 100 F Street N.E., and most of the SEC employees were back together again. However, we had an accessibility problem in the Station Place I building's main lobby for many years. A flight of 11 steps connected the upper ground and lower ground levels of the main lobby. The only means of easily getting between these levels for anyone who could not use stairs was a lift. We only finally got a full elevator put in to connect the levels in 2010. To address this issue and others affecting SEC employees with disabilities, I was a member of the SEC's Disability Issues Advisory Committee for many years.

Ken Cureton retired before Mike, but another Ken joined our group, Ken Beals. After Mike retired around 2007, Ken continued to drive me for a while. Eventually, he decided to move out to California to be close to his aging mother. Fortunately, about that time I became eligible for telework up to four days a week. I wasn't able to find any reliable colleagues with whom to carpool, so I had to rely on paratransit for the days that I had to go into the office. It's an imperfect system, but at least I didn't need to use it very often.

After Lily left me, she began seeing Walter Graham, who still was living next door. They eventually married, but Walter died from cancer in 2008. Lily later sold the house to Amy and Derek, who were good neighbors, and she moved back to Fredericksburg, VA, where she has a house. The Graham house has changed hands several times since Amy and Derek.

# NO GOOD-BYES IN HEAVEN

*A*fter Lily left, I decided not to hire any more live-in housekeepers for a while. I wanted to save some money, and I needed an emotional rest from the roller coaster of bonding closely with employees who often turn out to be short-term or temporary. I know that I need to retain my role as "the captain," or the employer, but I formed a special bond with each of my housekeepers. Patsy, Margie, and Mae filled motherly or grandmotherly roles; Tina, as I said, was like a daughter; and Lily was a little like having a sister. All of them have helped me become a better person, but losing employees who become friends still leaves a sense of loss.

When I was by myself again, Shirley returned to work for me twice a week. I also hired a dog walker through Becky's Pet Care to walk Remus three times a week. Sometimes Larry Cohen, the dog walker, would take Gemma, too.

Remus was beginning to really show her age and slow down. However, she still remembered what it was like to go to church and that it was a good place to be. In the Easter season, 2007, I left the house to go to noon Mass with Gemma, and Remus slipped out the door. The first time she tried that, I stopped, caught her and put her inside, and had to miss Mass. On this second occasion, I decided to keep going, because I wasn't sure that I would be able to catch her, and I didn't want to miss Mass. We had a bell on Remus's leather collar so that I would know where she was.[28] All the way down to church, I could hear her bell! She was keeping up with Gemma and me. I just hoped that she would stay close to me on the street crossings. When we got safely to church, I was able to get the free end of the leash on her. Fortunately, our retired resident priest, Father Loftus, was saying that daily Mass, and he wouldn't have cared if I brought an elephant into church, so long as it behaved itself. Remus was good as gold during Mass. On the way home, a friend saw us going by, and she helped me get both dogs home in good order. I was glad that Remus had this opportunity, but I didn't want to temp Providence in the future. I learned to use my legs to block the entrance and keep the retired dog from following me when I left with the working guide.

Since 2006 or so, I started keeping the artificial Christmas tree in the living room after the Christmas season and decorating it with hearts for Valentine's day and Easter egg ornaments during the Easter season until Pentecost. Janie McIver's stepmother, Nancy McIver, made many of the hearts and most of the egg ornaments that I use. I kept in touch with Nancy after Janie's father died, but she went home to the Lord on September 4, 2021. I will miss her.

During Remus's last Easter season, in 2008, the landscaper man took a picture of the decorated tree and Remus and Gemma on the couch. I think that it's the last good picture of her that we have. That picture is at the beginning of this chapter.

---

[28] With new dogs, while they are adjusting to house rules, a bell on the collar can be useful in keeping track of what they are doing when they are in the house off leash. Usually, such a precautionary device becomes unnecessary when the working partnership is well established. However, as dogs age and retire, I have found a bell useful to find them in the house, especially once I stop using a choke chain collar and instead put a leather collar on my canine pal. In Remus's case, she could be quiet and hard to detect, remaining calmly in a crawl space when she went in to snoop for the squirrels she knew were there and I shut the door without knowing it. She also inadvertently closed herself in the upstairs bathroom a couple of times!

One of our vets found a heart murmur in Remus. We had it checked, complete with heart monitor, but it turned out not to be dangerous. Like the two first Labs, Remus developed spondylosis and arthritis in the hips. We tried various homeopathic remedies and aquatic therapy, but she became more and more finicky with her eating. I arranged to have exploratory surgery done, and they found ·indications of irritable bowel syndrome. They put her on a hypoallergenic food to try to control it. She seemed to like the food, and it helped for a while, but eventually, nothing seemed to work.

Remus began to develop chronic and recurring bladder infections, probably because her bouts with diarrhea meant that she was contaminating herself, and the antibiotics used to treat the infections caused more diarrhea. Eventually, she had so little control over her bowels that the aquatic therapist would no longer take her in the water tank. They could not risk it being unsanitary for their other users.

All that we could do was keep Remus as comfortable as possible. We teasingly said that Remus was the dowager queen, and Gemma was the young queen. What the dowager queen wants, she generally gets, we said. Larry, the dog walker, was a great source of comfort and support to me with my dogs.

The year 2008 was destined to be a year of partings. Janie McIver received an award in Chicago, and she decided that afterwards she would come and stay with me a day or two, to visit her father in the nursing facility where he was. However, he died before Janie could come. She stayed with me overnight on Friday October 18-Saturday, October 19, and we went to the funeral together. I'm glad that I was able to visit with Janie, but it was a sad occasion. At least, she met Remus before Remus died.

It soon was no longer safe for Remus to go upstairs. Toward the end, if she did get upstairs, I would have to help her down again, taking much of her weight on my arms. I would have denied her nothing, but it still was emotionally painful having to help her this way, but we couldn't risk her falling down the stairs and injuring herself. The last time that Remus came up, Jeff was fortunately there to help me with the computers, and he carried her back downstairs.

When she came up that time, before he brought her down, I told her, "Take a good look around, because you aren't coming back up here like this if I can help it!"

In October 2008, Remus was having more trouble getting up on the couch and began sleeping more on dog beds on the floor. As with Mikki, during Remus's illness, God encouraged me to "give her to Me!" Shirley kept arguing that I was prolonging things too much. Father Seamus also sent me a stern e-mail, warning me to pay attention to signals that my dog might be giving me that she no longer wanted medical intervention and was ready to go in peace. I understood their concerns, but I am aware of my own disabilities, and I didn't see that alone as a reason to say good-bye. Remus, for her part, still did her best to let me know when the mailman had brought the mail, even when she grew weaker and seemed to have trouble barking.

Gemma, like Mikki, liked to be upstairs on my bed. As we prepared to go to sleep, she would want me to pat her. If I stopped too soon, she would hit me with her tail, to tell me to keep on patting and scratching her. Gemma's antics made me laugh, and it's wonderful to be laughing as you go to sleep!

As Remus had more and more problems, however, Gemma began to spend more time downstairs with Remus at night. I will always remember how good she was to her! I felt bad leaving them and sleeping upstairs, because my hearing aids come out at night, but I felt that I needed to preserve as much normal living for myself as possible. I wasn't going to be able to solve the problem by stressing myself out, and being downstairs without my hearing aids wouldn't necessarily have allowed me to keep better tabs on what was happening with Remus. I may have kept the intercom upstairs in a listening mode to the downstairs, the way we sometimes did with Nana.

In the middle of one night, at the end of October, 2008, I woke up to find Remus up against the fireplace crying. She had trouble getting up after that. With a homeopathic remedy, Arnica, we were able to help her to get up and walk, but now her movements were erratic, and she could no longer settle down. She kept trying to walk off whatever was bothering her, but she couldn't do it.

On Saturday, November 1, I had committed to help at the white elephant sale at church. Another friend of mine, a different Chris, stayed with Remus while I went down there. It was one of the saddest birthdays I ever had, but at least Remus was still with me. The next day, Sunday, November 2, Nancy Thomsen, a friend of mine, drove Chris and me to the vet with Remus. They advised me to say good-bye, but I couldn't let go without being sure, and I didn't like the way that they were going about it. Remus confirmed my decision by reaching over and pulling out the IV needle that they had inserted. They sent us home with muscle relaxers and pain medication.

The next week was horrible. It was like the situation with Nana; there seemed to be no appropriate natural end to this wonderful life. I was resigned that Remus would die at some point, but I prayed that she would just quietly go to sleep on the couch or her bed. I didn't want her life in my hands like this. Chris and I tried to nurse Remus through this crisis. I stopped the antibiotics, hoping to get control of the diarrhea, but we soon had the reverse problem. Her systems seemed to be shutting down, but she still was eating.

I went to vote on Tuesday, November 4. That evening, we tried to get Remus comfortable under blankets. She seemed to want to be outside on the front porch, so I sat there with her. When Barack

Obama was elected, they started shooting off firecrackers and woke her up, just when she seemed to be going to sleep! I could have killed whoever was shooting off those firecrackers!

We were able to get in touch with Dr. Frohling, the chiropractic vet who used to treat Mikki. She had relocated to suburban VA to treat horses, but she came to the house to see Remus on Thursday, November 6. She told us that she didn't think that the sedatives and muscle relaxers were helping, and they might be making things worse. She tried an acupuncture treatment, and she said that she hoped that we might see improvement. If not, she agreed that it was time to say goodbye. She left me with a detailed article on degenerative myeloma in German shepherd dogs, which might have been the cause of this deterioration in Remus's condition. It was the first time that anybody had given me an explanation that made any sense, other than the truisms about getting old.

Remus didn't get any better. Larry understood that I didn't want to have to end her life. He, like me, was praying that God would intervene, but eventually, he told me, he came to the conclusion that maybe God wanted us to use the wisdom that He gave us to do what was best for Remus.

On Friday, November 7, Chris, Gemma, and I all went with Remus and Larry down to Our Lady of Lourdes church one more time. Larry had to support her back legs with a sling. I took her down to the altar, and then back to Mary's chapel. I pretty much had decided that the next day would end the agony for both of us.

"After tomorrow," I told Remus. "You can come here any time you want. You won't need anybody else to take you."

I called Dr. Rita Blacker to arrange for her to come to the house the next day. Friday evening, Jackie de Forge, another friend from church, came over to hold me and comfort me. I really appreciate what she did.

Shirley came Saturday morning to be with me. Saturday morning, Remus turned up her nose at the piece of chicken in which we hid the last muscle relaxer. Eventually, she took it. If she didn't want chicken, I knew in my heart that she was dying and that I probably wasn't preempting God in taking this final step.

We put her on the couch, with pillows under her head to facilitate the circulation of the medicines. I took off her collar, and I put her bell on Gemma. As with the others, the first injection was to render her in a deep sleep. I prayed. I tried not to cry, because I didn't want to upset her or Gemma. The last injection was an overdose of anesthetic and stopped the heart. The queen's spirit was gone, and only the shell remained. Like a queen, her body was carried out the front door.

Gemma tried to follow her out, and we had to call her back. Horrible as the whole experience was for me, in looking back, I had to concede that Remus died like a queen and had a royal sendoff.

Gemma wore Remus's bell for a few hours after Remus died, but I could not bear to hear the sound of its ringing, knowing that it wasn't Remus. I put the bell away, and I later used it during the first few months with my next guide, Teddy, until I was sure that I could trust him to behave well when he was loose in the house.

I had Remus cremated, and her remains are on my desk in a little wooden box. I made one more wax statue of her, lying at rest with her Frisbee under her paw, had it cast in bronze, and laid it on top of the box. Her statistics are on a little plate on the front of the box.

God always knows better than we do. Within a few months of Remus's death, Gemma began to slow down. She still tried her best to take care of me and comfort me, and Larry and I called her the Registered furry Nurse. However, she no longer tried to get up on my bed, content to stay on the lower dog beds. She also was getting really stressed out in the vans use for paratransit.

As discussed in a later chapter, I applied to the Seeing Eye for a replacement dog, letting them know that I planned to keep Gemma in retirement, and I asked for home placement. I asked that I be given a younger dog this time, if they could find a good match. In early September 2009, Rick Connell brought me a wonderful black Labrador male that I called Teddy (September 3, 2007-August 7, 2020). He was two years old, with a birthday of September 3, 2007. He was born on the anniversary of Mama's death, but maybe that just indicated that she is still praying for me and helped them to pick him out. His original name was Ronnie, but I had two friends by that name, and I thought it would be confusing, and I changed the name to Teddy. They were originally planning to give me a golden retriever-Labrador cross, named Shiloh, but at the last minute, they changed their minds and chose Teddy instead. I'm glad that they did. During the ten days that he was here, Rick spent the time getting me used to working Teddy in various settings, especially going to church and my work environment. We seemed to be a good match in terms of pace, pull, and personality.

It took me almost three years to heal from the loss of Remus. A big part of me died with this wonderful, unique friend, the puppy who loved the Lord and His house almost as much as I did. I visited Dr. Wember while I was still grieving, and Dr. Wember told me to remember that she has gone to a better place, and it is better for her to be there than to be sick and suffering. I am sure that I will see her again. From this horrible experience, I have learned that in such a time of crisis, I must try not to get too tired, and not to lose my sense of perspective. God knows that I wish that the lives of my canine friends were not in my hands, but since they are, I will have to continue to try to do the right thing for them with His help. One question that I find helpful in making these excruciatingly painful decisions is to ask whose problem am I solving, mine or my dog's. When it's the solution to the dog's terminal quality of life issue, then it's probably time to say good-bye. It never will be easy, but it's the double-edged blade in having such wonderful pals.

One serious difficulty that service dog users have is that the world at large does not understand our grief at losing our canine (or other service animal) partners. Pet owners bond closely with their pets and consider them to be family members, and they understand somewhat. Still, partners with service dogs or police canines take the relationship to an even deeper level, because they have an interdependent relationship with their buddies, and their lives often depend on the reliability, trustworthiness, and intelligence of these animals. However, the world at large kind of says, "Oh, you lost your dog? Too bad." And expects you to move on with life. It's even harder, because many people don't even think that animals have souls. I don't know of any Catholic liturgy that formally would let us pray our good-byes in a meaningful, healing way.

My only consolation is that there won't be any good-byes in heaven. We will only have eternal hellos and maybe an occasional "see you soon." I'll see all my canine pals again, along with Papa, Mama, Nana, siblings, relatives, and friends. As another friend, Leslie, said, "They will all jump on us at once, and it won't even hurt!"

As for the folks who try to make high-sounding theological arguments that dogs don't have souls, I can only say that I know that their ghosts have been back to my house, along with those of my parents and Nana. No, I don't live in a haunted house. If they come, they come with God's leave, for my comfort and benefit, and they probably will come to me wherever I am, and not the house specifically.

At times, I have gone downstairs in the morning to find a light lit that I thought I had turned off the night before; that would be the lamplighter, Mama. Sometimes, both Patsy and I found the front door unlocked, when we were sure that we locked it; that would be Papa. He always got angry when Nana would lock the door and keep him from getting easily back into the house when he was doing chores outside. Concerning Nana, I already mentioned hearing the refrain of her laughter in my head after her death and the episode with Nana and Jackie.

As for the dogs, Vincent has been back on at least three occasions. The first was one evening when I was by myself in the house with Mikki. I let her outside, and afterwards I opened the door to call her into the house. I felt a dog's tail go past my hand, heard claws on the kitchen floor, and then didn't hear anything more. That didn't surprise me, because we had a rug on the floor. I went into the bathroom, and then I heard Mikki bark from outside. I came out of the bathroom and let Mikki into the house. On the second occasion, Mae was with me. I went outside with Mikki, opened the door to let her inside, and thought that I felt her go past me. I came inside and prepared her dinner, but the chowhound did not come to eat.

"Where's Mikki?" I asked Mae.

"In on the couch!" Mae said.

I found no dog on the couch. I went upstairs, and no Mikki. I went to the back door and let Mikki in the house. Finally, during Mikki's illness, I heard Vincent shadowing me on the stairs as I walked down from the second floor. He couldn't stay away.

Years later, Shirley and I went somewhere and left both Remus and Gemma at home, which was unusual. As I was walking down the front steps to get in the car, I put out my left hand and felt a dog walking down the steps beside me. The fur was rougher than Vincent, and the dog was taller than Gemma.

"Shirley, did Gemma get out?" I asked. She hadn't. It probably was Mikki.

Once, both Gemma and Teddy were downstairs. I was upstairs in my bedroom, but I still heard a dog shake its ears. Maybe it was Remus. Sometimes, with Teddy beside me on the bed, when he was lying still, I have felt the bed shake, the way it did when Remus went under it.

These touches of comfort aside, it's hard not to feel marooned. Too many relatives and friends have moved away, lost touch with me, or died, including Barbara Sheehan's husband, Don, who died around 2006, and others to be discussed in a later chapter. Fortunately, God keeps sending me others.

And I keep winning the puppy lottery and ending up with these wonderful, faithful canine friends! Blessed be God and His Holy Name!

As discussed in the previous pages, each of my dogs came into my life at a special time. Vincent came home from Guiding Eyes in time for Christmas, 1977, and I think of him as my white Christmas dog. Mikki came into my life during the Easter-Pentecost season in 1987; Remus was an Easter gift in 1991. I was at Seeing Eye in training with Gemma for my fifty-first birthday in 2002. My previous guide, Teddy, came into my life shortly after the forty-fourth anniversary of Mama's death in September, 2009. My present guide, Ives, came into my life on October 9, 2020, a little over two months after Teddy died. My friend, Dan, was right when he called my dogs manifestations of God's great love for me.

# BECOMING A ONE-DOG HOUSEHOLD

*A*s described in the previous chapter, Remus retired when I went to the Seeing Eye for Gemma, a wonderful female black Labrador retriever. She got along well with Remus, and they even sometimes played ball together. Remus died on November 8, 2008. Gemma began showing signs of slowing down and not wanting to jump up on my bed a few months later, in 2009.

Seeing Eye accepted me for home placement of a second dog from their school, and this time, Rick Connell came to my house for a week or so of home training. In September 2009, he brought me a male black Labrador retriever, that the school named Ronnie. I didn't like the name, so I call him Teddy. He showed the same intelligence and initiative that Remus and Vincent had. Like Gemma, he was very good at reading my emotions and moods, and he did everything that he could to calm me down and cheer me up. He loved to snuggle on my bed with me at night, and he got along well with Grandma Gemma. In fact, because Gemma was a breeder with Seeing Eye and had her last litter of puppies in late 2001 or early 2002, it is possible that she was, in fact, Teddy's great-grandmother or grandmother. Teddy knew my complicated work building at 100 F Street NE better than many of my sighted colleagues did. He also showed a tendency to vocalize when we were riding in a vehicle if he thought that we were going somewhere different or had taken a wrong turn. He generally was right about that! None of my other dogs paid as much attention to where they were going in the car! I called him, by way of descriptive nickname, Sir Teddy, my Squire and Navigator. I will speak more about Squire Teddy in a later chapter.

So long as Gemma continued in relatively good health, we were a two-dog house. We had a scare with Gemma in or about 2010. She had an intestinal problem, and the emergency vets nursed her through a serious crisis. However, she didn't like the bland diet that the doctors wanted her to observe. Without my realizing what was happening, Gemma began swallowing the stuffing out of one of my elephants, including a piece of the electronic mechanism. Fortunately, the wire showed up in the x-ray when she began vomiting, and she had surgery in August of 2010 to remove the debris. She had a difficult recovery from that episode. WE began exploring issues with an irregular heartbeat. Like her predecessors, Gemma developed spondylosis, trouble with her joints, a heart valve problem, and some control issues with her bowels. We didn't know how long we had to be together, but we were determined to enjoy our friendship as long as it lasted in this life and make the most of it.

On August 23, 2011, we experienced an event that reminded us of how unexpected events can be and how we need to keep relying on Divine Providence! Gemma was home alone. Shirley and I had gone for a medical appointment. We returned with Teddy riding in the back seat of my car. After 1 P.M., we were pulling into the garage when we felt the car shake, and at first, I thought it was Teddy moving around in the back seat. It wasn't. As we got out of the car, the shaking continued for several seconds. Shirley said that Teddy had big eyes! It was an earthquake centered in Virginia, felt over several states and Washington, D.C. In fact, it did damage to the Washington monument and major damage to the inside and outside of the National Cathedral. Repairs to the Washington Monument took a long time, and they still may be doing restoration on some parts of the National Shrine for this and other reasons. As for the National Cathedral, I'm told it has taken the last ten years to make progress on the repairs, and it probably will take ten years more and cost $17 million to finish the painstaking work!

Meanwhile, when I went upstairs to my office to resume teleworking, I discovered that a figurine or something else heavy had fallen off the top of one of my bookcases or file cabinets! I am so thankful to divine protection that I wasn't upstairs then with Teddy. I wouldn't have known what was happening in time to duck, and I could have been seriously hurt! Gemma probably was downstairs when it happened, and she was all right, too. Fortunately, we didn't find any other damage to the house.

The spring of 2012 was difficult, as far as the health of my canine buddies was concerned. In late April or so, Gemma got sick with an infection resulting in diarrhea, and the vet put her on antibiotics. Fortunately, she seemed to recover from that. In early May, Teddy stopped eating and had diarrhea, possibly attributable to an anal sac infection. He scared me with his symptoms and resisting taking pills, and his loss of appetite led to a barium test that fortunately found nothing serious. He seemed to recover all right with the help of antibiotics and medicine to help with his digestion. To deal with Gemma's arthritis and joint discomfort, Dr. Frohling had put her on an herbal remedy called Body Sore, which seemed to help. We wanted something more effective to use with it, but the typical pain relievers seemed to make her sick to her stomach. We decided to try one ascriptin (aspirin buffered with Maalox) pill twice a day, and for a few weeks, it seemed to help. To protect against stomach troubles, we also gave her Pepcid AC twice a day. Dr. Frohling cautioned me to watch out for signs of possible stomach problems with this medicine, such as loss of appetite.

On Pentecost Sunday, May 27, Gemma refused her breakfast. She did eat that evening, but I became concerned and consulted Dr. Frohling. She advised trying to cut back on the ascriptin to one pill a day, and we tried to set up an appointment for the vet to come to see Gemma at home. I hoped that the ascriptin was the problem, and I knew that Gemma got very stressed out when she went to see vets at the animal hospitals. Eating was touch and go for the next couple of weeks, so we stopped the ascriptin altogether. Dr. Frohling had to postpone her appointment on account of medical life-and-death emergencies from some of her equine patients. Gemma seemed to get better for a while, but then the appetite fell off again.

By Saturday, June 9, Gemma seemed very weak and sluggish. I feared that I was going to lose her that evening. Fortunately, Dr. Frohling finally came on Sunday, 6/10. Dr. Frohling was concerned that Gemma's heart murmur was worse, and we might have to consider heart medication. She performed acupuncture, gave us a different painkiller to try, and drew blood for testing. Initially, the painkiller seemed to help Gemma to feel better and want to eat. The blood test results showed problems with the liver values. Dr. Frohling recommended milk thistle and Sam E, natural remedies that might support the liver, but then Gemma developed diarrhea. I was afraid that it was a side effect of the medicine and the pain pills, and I finally stopped everything except the Pepcid AC, but now Gemma was not only a picky eater, but she also was resisting taking pills.

Monday morning, June 18, after a difficult weekend, I suspected that something serious was wrong with Gemma and that we might be running out of time to treat it. Shirley and I went to a vet that could get blood test results done in house quickly. They confirmed problems with the liver values and an enlarged liver shown in the x-rays, along with low red cell and high white cell counts. They gave us anti-diarrhea medicine and antibiotics as a stopgap, and meanwhile we scheduled an ultrasound with Columbia Pike Animal Hospital, our regular vet, for June 20. The results showed a mass on Gemma's intestine, probably cancerous, touching and impacting the liver and close to the pancreas. Gemma was now down to 64 pounds from the mid-seventies, and she had lost two pounds since Monday, even though we were getting her to eat some favorite things, liked cooked ground beef and eggs. The only possible workable solution would have been surgery, but there could have been complications, including possible damage to other organs, the operation might not get all the cancer, and they told me that it probably would recur in the best of scenarios. Although we might have tried to nurse Gemma back to health after surgery, it would have been an ordeal. I kept thinking that Gemma would not have been happy if she couldn't help me anymore. I didn't think it was fair or kind to put Gemma and me through this agony without better odds. AT best, it might have bought us only six to nine months, and Gemma's quality of life would have been a real concern.

Shirley and I took Gemma home. Gemma ate some ground meat and seemed to enjoy it. We ordered Chinese lunch, and the dogs enjoyed sharing the fortune cookies with us. I was distressed that Gemma was having trouble getting comfortable on the couch, and I could feel her bones on account of her losing weight.

Larry Cohen, the dog walker, got to our house in time to see Gemma once more that afternoon, between 3 and 4 P.M. Soon after, the vet arrived. She and Larry lifted Gemma onto the couch on which she liked to lie so much. I sat beside her, with her head in my lap. When she was well, Gemma and I liked to snuggle together on the couch, and she often hit me with her tail to encourage me to keep patting or scratching her. She often encouraged me to pat her, to calm me or to comfort me when I was emotionally distressed at losing Remus or otherwise upset.

Larry took Teddy for his regular walk. While they were gone, the vet administered the last injections. Gemma died peacefully with my arm around her and her head in my lap. Teddy came back with Larry in time to see the doctor carry Gemma out to her vehicle. Gemma was born on December 13, 1997; she died on June 20, 2012, at the age of 14.5 years. It's a long life, especially for a large dog like a Labrador retriever, but the time never seems long enough for us who lose our canine partners and friends.

Teddy and I needed some time to recover. I had a big hole in my life and my heart, and I'm sure that Teddy was sad, too. I thank God that loving friends were with me and that others were praying for us. I know that God helped us to have a peaceful, dignified end to Gemma's loving life, but these reflections never make it any easier to say good-bye. Thanks, God, that we will have no good-byes in heaven!

# FAREWELL TO THE SEC: ADDING YEARS AND RETIREMENT ARE NOT FOR SISSIES!

*T*rue to Patsy's saying about bananas, the troubles that started with Gemma's death continued to build. In 2013, my assistant, Judy, was diagnosed with a benign brain tumor. She had surgery to remove it, which set in motion her decision to retire toward the end of that year. She came back after surgery long enough to help to transition to someone else performing other duties that she had besides reading for me. As part of the transition, I was assigned a new reader/assistant.

Meanwhile, we gave Judy a good sendoff, and as later discussed she and I have remained friends and stayed in touch. It was a very bittersweet occasion for me when Judy retired. I was glad that she would get to relax, enjoy herself, and spend time with family and friends, but I knew how much I would miss her!

Concerning my new assistant, unlike when Judy was hired eighteen years before, they did not post the position as a Schedule A posting. Instead I was assigned a very nice young lady as part of a separate governmental contract with an agency to provide this kind of assistant. The person was paid only when I was there and she was directly working for me. This put pressure on me when I knew I had to take leave for doctor's appointments, for which I was paid, but the assistant was to be sent home if I was gone for more than a short period of time. This arrangement was a big contrast with my partnership with Judy and my other full-time government—employee assistants. In the case of Judy and her predecessors, if I were out of the office, I left the assistant with something to do in my absence. I didn't like the independent contractor system and thought that it was unfair and unjust. The lady was very competent and helpful, but it was an uncomfortable situation for me.

About a year after Judy retired, in About the same time, the nature of the work I was doing changed, and I needed to rely more and more on the help of the assistant. The signposts seemed to be pointing toward my leaving the SEC to begin my retirement soon.

In September, 2014, I accepted a buy-out of a certain nice sum of money and retired from the SEC, after almost 37 years. They gave me a little sendoff brunch party, but it was also very bittersweet for me again. While I was there, I gave it everything I had. I would like to have been able to hold out for forty years, but as the song says, "Go while the going's good; knowing when to leave may be the smartest thing anybody can learn."

Being retired, like growing older or accumulating years, is not for sissies. It requires a whole adjustment to a change of life. You have to decide how to handle Medicare and government health insurance programs, your whole life schedule is different, and you generally have the fixed income from the government retirement annuity and any other retirement savings that you access from time to time, especially after you turn 72.5 or 73 and take required minimum distributions, or RMD's as they are called. Gone are the hopes for grade increases or possible promotions. Except for cost of living adjustments, what you see is what you have. You also have to learn to restructure your time and schedule and self-manage. I think the fact that I was teleworking during my time at the SEC helped me to do this, because I had to learn to be a self-starter.

Katie told me to expect to be tired after retiring. For the first couple of years, I kind of took things easy. I tried to walk down to Mass on Sundays and as much as possible at noon on weekdays, and began wanting company and assistance from others to accompany me, as I noticed some balance issues when I was walking. I'm sure that the situation was aggravated by bouts with cellulitis in my left leg and later in my left wrist, probably in late 2016 and 2017, requiring treatment with antibiotics, wound care therapy in the case of the leg, and physical therapy. Nana had cellulitis in the leg that wasn't treated surgically in her younger years from time to time, too, and it was regular enough that all we had to do was tell her doctors that the leg was red and they would prescribe the antibiotics. My bouts with cellulitis gave me a better appreciation of what Nana endured. Conversely, I took encouragement from her experience: if Nana could come back after these infections, so could I.

Meanwhile, because I considered them to be special friends, I tried to keep up with Patsy, Jeanne Rhode, Mae garrison, and Janice Morton by phone. One way or another, all of them were out of town. Jeanne was in Redwood Valley, California, Mae was eventually in Roanoke after moving there from her original home in Tennessee, Patsy was in Ocala, Florida, and Janice eventually moved to Georgia to be close to her son.

Father Seamus continued to be a wonderful friend and comfort. We kept in touch by phone and e-mail.

In 2012, Barbara finally sold the house at 823 25th Street S. and moved into an assistive living apartment in the Hermitage, in Alexandria. I could understand that she felt the need to simplify her life, but I very much missed being able to walk to her house to visit her, especially on her birthday, Christmas, Easter, and Mother's Day. Shirley was working for me part-time when Barbara first moved, about two years before I retired, and at first we were able to take Barbara out to lunch sometimes when Shirley drove me to visit her. Otherwise, I tried to call Barbara in the evenings to have a visit over the telephone. As she requested, I tried to remember to remind her when Sixty Minutes was coming on CBS in the evening on Sundays. She also let me know if she found out about a special program that I might like. It eventually became harder to go out to lunch, but Shirley continued to drive me to visit her in her nice assistive living apartment, especially on the holidays and her birthday.

I also kept in touch with Tina, and occasionally with her friend Pat. Tina lives in Vienna, VA; she has four children, two girls and two boys.

I don't remember when it happened in the years since my retirement, but I gradually began losing these long-distance friends. Jeanne had health issues. She eventually had to go into a care facility. I got her number and tried to stay in touch. I knew that she wasn't doing well. A few days after I last spoke to her, I could no longer reach her. Eventually someone from the facility told me that she died. Despite my attempts to keep in touch with them or contact her two sons at their last addresses, neither Ken nor Clifford ever wrote to me about their mother's passing.

Janice had lost her two dogs and Fred before she moved. In GA, she was lonesome for a dog and eventually found a Chihuahua named Yoda. Janice began having health issues, and she was diagnosed with cancer of the liver. Then Yoda developed his own health problems, including seizures, and she had to say good-bye to him. Janice went into the hospital and then into a rehabilitation place. I did my best to keep in touch with her by phone, but she died. I was able to go to her funeral, because her remains were placed in Arlington Cemetery on account of her husband's veteran status. I lost touch with our mutual acquaintances and her adult son, Roger.

Mae and I did our best to keep in touch by phone. Before I retired from work, she came to visit me for a few days, which we enjoyed very much. Before she left, her daughter, Janie Weaver, and she took me to dinner. Mae moved into a mobile home in Roanoke, but eventually she had to go into an assistive living place. She lost her dachshund, a little dog named Gretchen, but she had a cat for a while before she went into assistive living. We kept in touch as well as we could by phone. She died in 2019, at the age of 100.

Margie came over sometimes and we still were able to go shopping together. For a while, she also was busy trying to help get our friend, Seldin French, to his medical appointments. Eventually, he died. Margie and I enjoyed our little excursions together, which reminded us of old times, but eventually, she seemed to me to be less mentally alert. On our last trip together, she got lost coming back to our house, and I then knew that it was no longer safe to go out with her. She eventually developed serious health issues and went into a care facility. I think that she died in June of 2019.

At some point, Mrs. Bortnick needed the house in which Patsy was being allowed to live. Patsy moved into a rental facility. When I was talking to her by phone, I became aware that she seemed less mentally alert, including forgetting to keep a rendezvous to go to church with a friend, something completely uncharacteristic of her. Eventually, that last phone number I had no longer reached her, and someone else answered who knew nothing about her. I don't know if she still is in the land of the living. I hope she got the care that she needed, or went to live with one of her children if she still is alive. All I can do is pray for her.

As I was losing some old friends, I tried to make new ones and keep in touch with others. I still call Margie's friend, Mary, to keep in touch, and I had another telephone buddy through my neighborhood association for a while. Kate Desch, one of the ladies who used to sell me jewelry through Ross-Simons, before they closed their store in Potomac Mills, in Woodbridge, VA, still keeps in touch with me as a friend. She is busy looking after in-laws and grandchildren. Sometimes, we still go shopping for jewelry and other goodies. I still keep in touch with other friends, such as Cindy Goble and Peggy Clark.

Gretchen still kept in touch and gave me news of her family in TX and OK and the Pittsburgh side of the family, until she died in the spring of 2023 from cancer. Her younger brother, Tim Dean, is fighting a battle with lung cancer. He has survived with one treatment, but now the cancer is spreading, and they had to change the treatment protocol to infusions of chemotherapy and some genetic immuno-therapy. He had a setback, and the last I heard he was trying to recover his strength enough to resume the immune-therapy treatment. He has done better than Papa, thanks to timely diagnosis and new, better treatments, but his struggles with the illness are still hard and require a great deal of prayer, faith, and trust in God and His Providence!

The oldest of the Dean Cousins, Jim Dean, still lives in the Pittsburgh area, but he moved into a senior assistive living center. I keep in touch with the Deans through his daughter, Molly Bitner. I wondered why I didn't hear from Paul Nolan at Christmastime, and Molly recently told me that he died in 2023.

Tom Calabro and I called each other to pray for each other and keep up with our health vicissitudes. He had a knee replacement. Last year, he suffered a serious health crisis and died in December of 2023. So far his wife, Arlene, is in good health.

I keep in touch with Nancy and Dick through her. Both of them have been dealing with health issues. In particular, Dick had a great deal of trouble with a knee replacement and eventually had to have a leg amputated. He and Nancy are living in San Antonio, TX, to be near their daughter.

I still talk to Lily, who still lives in Fredericksburg and sometimes comes to visit. Mary Spellerberg and I talk by phone, as it's a long way to drive up to Arlington from Culpepper. She and Peter are busy with daughters and their families, especially the grandchildren. Mary did come to visit me on November 1, 2018, to help me celebrate my birthday. I was especially glad to see her, because as discussed below I was getting ready by then for hip replacement surgery on my right hip.

Over the years, Aunt Murff lost her hearing. I had to communicate by e-mail and telephone with her daughter, Pattie. Aunt Murff also was fighting breast cancer. I found out that Aunt Murff died suddenly on December 22, 2022. I will miss her.

I keep in touch with Katy, Debbie, Lelia, and Judy and her husband, Ruben. Before COVID19, Judy and Ruben would sometimes come over to my house to share lunch or dinner on a weekend.

We used to grill hamburgers and knackwursts on my little charcoal grill for July 4. The Pandemic interrupted these activities, but in 2021 with all of us being fully vaccinated, we felt safe enough to get together for Independence Day. Because of Ruben's health issues, we grilled inside on my little electric grill. It was wonderful to get together. In addition to the hamburgers and knackwursts, we had Shirley's delicious potato salad, three-bean salad in a jar, and lemon squares for dessert.

Katie's husband, Larry, died a few years ago. She still lives in her house with one of her two sons, Chris. She lost all her dogs and cats over the years and doesn't now have any animals.

Debbie and her husband, Tom, have been traveling around the country in their RV. Their son, Steve, is married to Sarah with two little girls. Tom used to keep bees, but he gave it up after some disease, possibly colony collapse disorder, killed his hives. When I asked him for the leftover wax to use in making things to be cast, he told me that insects called wax moths came and completely cleaned up the hives! I never heard of them before he told me about them!

Lelia is the last of us five to retire from the SEC in 2023.

Before the disruption caused by the pandemic and all of us retiring, the five of us liked to get together for lunch in Thunder Grill in Union Station arcade. I would go downtown by taxi and meet Judy in front of our old SEC building. Then we would enter the public lobby and walk across the connector to meet the others at the restaurant. Sometimes, Judy and I did a little shopping, but it was somewhat difficult, because we had to make sure to get Teddy out to park, and it was hard to do that with no good place close by. The last time we met for lunch was, I think in 2018 before my hip surgery. The picture in the front of this chapter is the group picture taken of the five of us and Teddy. It may have been on an earlier occasion, because I'm not sure that Teddy came with me in 2018. Going around the table from right to left, we are Linda, Judy, Lelia, Debbie, and Katie, with Teddy under the table.

At Thunder Grill, I really liked and enjoyed their bison steak, which they eventually stopped having, and their bison burgers.

In between all of my attempts to keep up with friends, I have kept busy with my writing. As discussed in a later chapter, I published other short story collections and a revision to *Heir to the Dragon* King with Author House after I retired. I also brought out a compilation of my short stories in 2024 through Amazon: *Diamonds, Nuggets, and Pearls: New Stories and Old Stories Retold.*

My frustration with retirement is that nothing turned out as I had hoped. I thought that I might have been able to regroup for the first two years and then maybe plan some trips and such. However, as they say, reality bites. I began having telephone issues with static on the lines or sometimes interruptions in service. I was repeatedly calling Verizon for service, but they kept telling me that they were retiring the copper lines. They had little incentive to maintain the existing land lines, and they kept encouraging me to jump to a different kind of system. About that time, the price of copper went up, and some people were actually stealing copper for scrap metal. I didn't like the way the company was treating me and other customers. I also didn't like replacing human operators for directory assistance with automated computers that don't understand what you want half the time!

At some point, I wrote a letter for the 2016 Shareholders' meeting in Albuquerque, NM. I decided that I would have to go there as a shareholder and put in my complaint in person. A friend, Jen Carter, flew out with me and Teddy. We stayed overnight in the Hotel Albuquerque and went to the meeting in the morning.

Teddy worked well on the trip, following Jen through the crowded airports and the hotel. The Southwest Airlines outgoing flight was difficult. They didn't put us in the bulkhead seat, which would have had more room for Teddy and me. We ended up back in the crowded seats of the plane. Teddy had to be up on the seat next to me some of the time. When we deplaned in NM, the passengers gave Teddy all kinds of sympathy.

"Poor Teddy was stuck in the back of the plane!" they said. Fortunately, we were in the bulkhead seat section on the return trip!

We made a good presentation, with me able to walk independently into the meeting following Jen and working Teddy. I think I was able to convey my concerns that the company was not adequately maintaining the lines, and they were intent on forcing everyone to FIOS, which fortunately isn't tied to the internet but does require electric power to run. It was a good experience, inasmuch as I got the company's attention about the need to help me get accessible service. In the end, after coming home, I did sign up for FIOS and resigned myself that the old copper lines were being retired. I didn't want to go with Comcast, because that would have put me entirely at the mercy of the internet for everything, including telephone service. So, with FIOS, I have the phone off internet, but the computer and FIOS TV would require the internet to run. To maintain phone service during a power outage, I must rely on a battery backup, with batteries that have to be replaced from time to time. One must sometimes concede to the inevitable.

Meanwhile, I also had to face the inevitable when Donald J. Trump was elected president of the United States in November of 2016. This chapter is not meant to be about my political views, but what follows is a discussion of how recent events have impacted me emotionally. I also want to set the record straight in light of the unfair accusations that some of my conservative friends have made that I hated President Trump.

When President Trump was elected, some of my more liberal friends asked me what I was going to do. (Some of the more incensed were making rumblings about moving to Canada or some other place.) I said repeatedly in response, "I'm going to pray to be protected from the wrath to come!" No, I didn't necessarily think the wrath was from God, but I thought it might follow from the consequences of human folly! As discussed below, I felt vindicated by the events of the last administration. Between the ongoing COVID19 pandemic and some of the ineptitude and mistakes of the current administration, I think we still are in "the wrath."

I was revolted by Mr. Trump's bombastic manner and speech, rudeness, and apparent lack of consideration or courtesy for his fellow-Republicans who were running against him. He also behaved that way toward some of our international allies. I also didn't like his being so anti-immigrant and clearly biased against Moslems, ignoring that extremists and terrorists are the exception not the rule in that faith. I also want to point out to those opposing abortion that abortion is considered wrong under Islam.

I understood that Mr. Trump appealed to some angry and frustrated people, because he dared to say some of the angry things that they were thinking, and he exploited our worst emotions and fears instead of encouraging our better instincts. In this regard, I consider him to be an emotional catalyst, who somehow managed to facilitate conflict instead of defusing it, even when he might not have meant to do it! Mr. Trump also took advantage of pro-birth and pro-life voters who desperately wanted to defeat pro-choice and pro-abortion-on demand candidates and who were desperate to avoid Hillary Clinton being president and to oust pro-choice democrats! I agreed with former President Obama's assessment that Mr. Trump didn't cause the deep division in our country, but he accelerated them. I disagree with those who blame Mr. Obama for causing our divisions as president, but I recognize that as a president with a bi-racial background, his election and administrations exposed many latent and developing conflicts and buried prejudices. [29]

Ironically, I also sometimes perceived that Mr. Trump could be like the suave, beguiling wizard, Salomon, in the *Lord of the Rings* Saga, able to charm and persuade people into accepting him

---

[29] I recall that during his two terms, Mr. Obama was criticized by whites and majority voters as tilting too much in favor of blacks and other minorities. I also heard criticism from some people in the black community that he wasn't doing enough for them. That seems to me to indicate that he was trying to walk a fine line and do the right thing.

despite his underlying flaws and evil and devious intent. I sometimes almost succumbed myself, even finding him a little comforting during the first days of the pandemic. In any event, I was grateful that President Trump was pro-birth, but I don't consider him pro-life. No one who can separate families without blinking, even illegal immigrants and asylum-seekers, really cares about children! Many of those poor children still have not been reunited with their families, even after the awful policy was ended! You can't argue that unborn children in the womb should be protected without supporting policies to help, nurture, and protect those same children after they are born! He also was too tolerant and fond of the death penalty! [30] In the 2016 election, I couldn't vote for him, but I couldn't vote for pro-abortion Hillary Clinton. I wrote in two Republicans. After Mr. Trump won, I began having nightmares of Nazis and Hitler, and trying to hide in my cedar closet upstairs! I hope I won't experience them again if Mr. Trump is reelected in November of 2024!

Despite my uneasiness at Mr. Trump's election in 2016, I did want him to surprise us and succeed as well as he could, but even his better attempts fell flat. I was glad when he tried unsuccessfully to come to an agreement and détente with the dictator of North Korea, but I was disappointed that he was comfortable flattering the dictator in his remarks, even after the talks failed! I was relieved that the president fired missiles at Syria to punish them for using chemical weapons in the civil war with the opposition, but I was very disappointed that he didn't attempt to enforce compliance and pursue the issue, despite the Syrians' false claim that they gave up all of their chemical weapons. I applauded his galvanizing research and other efforts to come up with vaccinations against COVID19, but he forfeited an opportunity to promote the use of the resulting vaccines by being too focused on overturning the results of the 2020 election. Once it was clear from the court decisions and the evaluation of the Department of Justice that any possible irregularities in voting that may have happened were not sufficient to change the results, the country's interest lay in a smooth

---

[30] While our church concedes that the state does have the authority to administer the death penalty, recent statements and Pope Francis's changes to the catechism strongly indicate that we no longer consider it consistent with the respect for life of every human being, from conception to natural death. I personally consider that the infliction of this extreme punishment also is harmful to society as a whole and to those people who need to flip the electric chair switch or administer fatal drugs.

transition and transfer to the next administration. [31] In my opinion, a great leader reveals character by being a gracious loser, even if he doesn't always win.

Meanwhile, on June 24, 2022, in Dobbs v. Jackson Women's Health Organization, the Supreme Court finally overturned Roe v. Wade and held that the case was wrongly decided and the Constitution does not confer a right to abortion on demand. I become angry when the news media still speaks of these issues as revolving around "reproductive rights," which prejudges the issue of how and to what degree abortion or the termination of pregnancy should be regulated. In the fall of 2022, the Republicans didn't win as many seats and elections as they hoped, partly because of their strong pro-life stand. Unfortunately, the public and the national conscience consensus haven't kept pace with the direction of the Supreme Court's ruling. The voters will get another opportunity to speak through the ballot box in 2024, and it looks as though it will be a rematch between President Biden and former President Trump. My problem with Mr. Trump is that he still is engaging in the same behaviors of the 2016 election, including making negative and derogatory remarks about his opponents and members of the Justice Department and the judiciary, and he shows no remorse for his actions in not facilitating a smooth transfer of power. He also encourages his gullible supporters to believe that he alone has the perfect solution to fix all of our foreign and domestic problems. That kind of blind faith and trust should only be given to God! Mr. Trump maintains the impossible position that the President and even a former president is immune from prosecution for violations of our laws, which I consider to be sheer nonsense. We are supposed to be a government of laws, not of fiat and flawed human beings! I cannot vote for Mr. Trump in good conscience!

However, I will hesitate to vote for President Biden because of his failure to defend the lives of the unborn. He unrealistically speaks of wanting to codify Roe v. Wade into federal law, which I do not think most people really want, and he fails to recognize the value of pregnancy crisis centers in giving disclosures and support to mothers who may choose to carry their babies full term. Because of the Democrats' favoring abortion on demand, I may be forced to write in two more candidates this November. I would consider supporting a third-party set of candidates, if they had enough

---

[31] Some of the lawyers who continued to file what have turned out to be frivolous lawsuits contesting the election are being disciplined by their bar associations for filing frivolous claims. Lawyers are allowed and should be zealous in advocating for their clients, but there is a line that they should not cross by filing claims that have no merits. I won't go so far as to say that no voter irregularities took place in 2020, but I am convinced that they weren't sufficient to overturn the results. Some Republican election officials endured threats and hardship protecting what they saw as legitimate vote counts.

support to possibly carry the day without giving the likely victory to President Trump. I will have to pray very fervently for guidance as the election approaches!

On balance, President Trump's first term fulfilled my worst fears, especially his dehumanizing treatment of immigrants and failure to tell the public the truth about the seriousness of the pandemic. He claimed in an interview with Bob Woodward when he was writing his book that he didn't want people to panic, but "positive talking" doesn't justify a lie, and Americans will not panic and will rise to the needs of an emergency if they are given accurate science-based facts, not a sales pitch! All this conflict and discord about the facts has exacerbated the public's distrust of their government and even scientists who testify to the safety and effectiveness of vaccines! Measles that was almost eradicated has now rebounded, because some parents are not getting their children vaccinated without a justifiable reason.

Concerning his policies while in office, I also was distressed that Mr. Trump considered that he could abrogate accords and agreements from earlier administrations, such as the Paris Accord and the agreement with Iran. The serious environmental crisis requires diplomacy and international cooperation, not "America alone for America" showmanship and brinkmanship! No, the Iranian agreement wasn't perfect, but nations should honor their word, and enforcing Iranian compliance might have bought us more time for a stronger agreement in the future. If you are going to break off an agreement, like the one with Iran, you need to have strong evidence of their non-compliance, which we didn't have at the time.

I was especially incensed that the president abandoned the Kurds, who were faithful allies with us against ISIS. He also was in too much of a hurry to withdraw from Afghanistan without doing enough to secure the peace and a smooth transition to Afghanistan standing on its own without us.

I also came to believe that the president tried to involve foreign governments in our 2020 Presidential election and that the President disregarded the rule of law and encouraged the insurrection on January 6, 2021 to attempt to stop certification of the election and perpetuate himself in office. Despite the violence clearly visible in the Capitol, he delayed telling the rioters and protesters to disband until late in the day, or to adequately condemn their actions. No, I didn't rely on commentators to come to these opinions, and I don't do Facebook, Twitter, or other social media platforms! I prefer to get straight facts from the news and make up my own mind and not to have the news filtered through someone else's opinion or prejudgment. Although some valid commentary and opinion may be useful, I wish that they would restore the so-called fairness doctrine, which required opposing points of view to be given equal time.

I listened to the debates for the 2016 and 2020 elections and the hearings for the two impeachments. I also listened to the testimony in the Congressional committee's investigation of January 6, which convinced me of President Trump's role in facilitating and instigating the insurrection. I like to focus on primary sources as much as possible. [32]

I agreed with both President Trump and President Biden that it might have been time to start withdrawing from Afghanistan, especially when most of the population didn't try to support the government before the Taliban takeover. I wish that we had delayed drawdown and made it contingent on a negotiated peace. If such negotiations didn't succeed, I am most distressed that they didn't plan better for an orderly withdrawal and evacuation of civilians and service dogs who saved the lives of many soldiers. I can't help believing that more could have been done to keep from leaving American citizens and green card holders, as well as endangered Afghanistan citizens who helped us, behind when we left. Now we must make every effort to keep President Biden's pledge to get them out somehow. I see plenty of blame to go around, but all we can do now is go forward by God's grace and with His help and keep praying. Unfortunately, although the pandemic seems to be receding for now, we are being distracted and preoccupied by the hardships of inflation and high prices, as well as the serious war in Ukraine and the crisis in Israel's war in Gaza. Although I can understand that citizens are upset at the domestic economic difficulties we are experiencing, I am distressed that some people and legislators are willing to turn a deaf ear to Ukraine's pleas for our help. I feel as though I am living in a similar era to the late 1930's before World War II. I don't want someone in the future to write a book called *Why and How America Slept!*

While I recognize that we need to control our border and regulate immigration, I also wish that President Biden and Congress would come up with a way to fix our broken immigration system and let asylum seekers and legitimate refugees come expeditiously into the country. Mary, Joseph, and Jesus were refugees when they had to flee into Egypt to escape from murdering maniac Herod! I find

---

[32] Years ago, I read about an interesting study meant to examine how people absorb and evaluate information. The researchers conducted staged interviews of a group of students; half of them answered honestly; the other half pretended to be cheaters. After the interviews were conducted and recorded, three groups of subjects were exposed to them. One third only heard the interviews; one third read the transcripts; the final third saw the video of the interviews. Those who read the transcripts and heard the interviews were better at picking out the "cheaters."

no mention of entry visas in Scripture! What if the Egyptians had sent them away? Everybody in this country, including the native peoples, has come from somewhere, however long ago! Nobody has any right to boast about elitism and prior claims! Although I recognize that seeking economic opportunity in the U.S. plays a major part, the extreme weather events, tyrants, and climate crises are making it all worse by encouraging people to flee from dire conditions in their homelands! As St. Paul has said, God has imprisoned everyone in disobedience to show mercy to all! If we say we follow His laws, we can do no less than show mercy to our fellow human beings, especially children and the most vulnerable!

For me, the Trump years were déjà vu, Richard Nixon all over again, but with no good ending! In my humble opinion, as I perceived them, both of these presidents shared an attitude that normal rules shouldn't apply to them and that people were out to get them and against them and persecuting them! At least, President Nixon had the good sense to appoint Henry Kissinger as Secretary of State to advise him on foreign policy and to reach out to China. Although, like Former President Trump and President Biden, he failed to have an orderly withdrawal that protected civilians and service dogs that worked with our military, he did bring an end to the conflict in Vietnam, a war in support of a government that wasn't supported by the people in the end! President Nixon did have enough healthy embarrassment mixed with patriotism to spare the country the ordeal of impeachment proceedings by resigning when he did! Unlike the democrats who slavishly defended former President Clinton despite his sexual misconduct (which amounted to sexual harassment in my opinion and merited removal from office) and the Republicans who mindlessly backed former President Trump during his impeachments, the Republicans in former President Nixon's time, especially Senator Lowell Weicker of CT, condemned Mr. Nixon's misconduct. For me, one of President Trump's inadvertent achievements was to rehabilitate the reputation of Richard Nixon!

We had another horrible choice in the election of 2020, especially for those of us who do not favor abortion on demand and used for birth control and who do not want our taxpayer dollars used to fund it! While President Biden favors some good proposals for people and the environment, I am very disappointed that he has not resisted the push by other liberal democrats to expand the availability of abortion and to federally fund it here and overseas. All we can do now is to support good social policies, oppose wrong-headed notions and proposals, and continue to speak out strongly in favor of life and the dignity of every human being. As Dr. Seuss quoted one of his characters as saying in *Horton Hears a Hu*, a person is a person, no matter how small! We will make the best of a difficult situation and hope and pray that some good comes from it, in God's way of writing straight in crooked lines! By way of consolation to some of my friends who also were distressed about President Trump and his policies, I sometimes told them that I believed that God had something for Mr. Trump to do, and when it was accomplished, he would leave office. Maybe his mission was to appoint judges to the Supreme Court who overturned Roe v. Wade! While I believe that The Roe v. Wade case was wrongly decided, I recognize that some non-constitutional privacy protections may be appropriate for enforcement purposes during the very early stages of pregnancy, in which termination often happens through oral medications, some of which like the "morning after" pill may be legitimately used for other things. The "War on drugs" illustrates how difficult it is to regulate prescribed drugs taken orally, and the experience of other countries like Brazil show how hard and controversial it can be to get between patients and their doctors. For me, the focus needs to be on regulating medications and treatments for safety and making sure that patients have the benefit of full disclosure about the nature of procedures and side effects. I wish that we would at least retain the ban against sending oral abortion drugs through the mail. I would like to see the Supreme Court justify taking one of these medications off the market in its pending case. In any event, disclosure needs to be provided about the perils and dangers of abortion in general and these medications in particular. In the Federal securities laws, we require disclosure of material facts to investors about companies and securities in which they are going to invest. In regulating disclosure to parents we should apply the same standards of material disclosure to information about drugs and procedures impacting the lives of mothers and their unborn children.

However, from my work with dogs, I know the perils of giving a command that you cannot enforce! The fiasco of the attempt at prohibition of alcohol demonstrates that laws not accepted by the conscience of the majority in society are doomed to fail.

Of course, we need to have an exception for the protection of the life of the mother. Rape and incest also need to be legitimate legislative exceptions, because these circumstances often involve coercion, and we legally cannot ask people to be heroines. These dire or traumatic circumstances aside, we still need to work with the emerging public conscience against taking unborn life, especially in the later trimesters. Advocates of so-called pro-choice emphasize their idea that the mother should decide whether to carry her pregnancy to term, but this argument ignores the humanity of the unborn child and doesn't acknowledge that the baby isn't given any choice and has no ability to exercise any say about life.

Enforcement of laws legitimately regulating abortions, especially during the second and third trimesters, needs to focus on the providers, not the women who have these procedures. Otherwise, pro-life advocates weaken their cause. The old legal adage reminds us that "hard cases make bad laws." We can take moral stands, but we have to recognize the practicality of enforcement to avoid greater evils. [33]

The Texas recent law, which allows private suits as its enforcement mechanism especially in crossing state lines to obtain an abortion, risks creating a vindictive, vigilante system if it is abused! As such, it is a clumsy, inept, and inappropriate means toward a legitimate end. Some pro-life advocates have argued that suits against providers of transportation like Uber and other such scenarios are unlikely, and that they would be dismissed by the courts. However, I am concerned that suits could be brought by ex-husbands or boyfriends for harassment purposes and to coerce settlements, even if the litigation is eventually dismissed. Also, unlike criminal cases that require proof beyond a reasonable doubt, civil suits only require a preponderance of the evidence for a plaintiff to prevail. We need to work carefully to support the pro-life views of so many of our population, and to recognize that even many doctors and nurses in the medical profession have to reawaken their consciences and medical ethical standards now that the Supreme Court has ruled.

For me, this issue is deeply personal. I accept the Church's teaching that human life begins at conception, and certainly by implantation when the individuality of the developing embryo is set, because that is when potential "twinning" occurs. If that isn't true, what is the significance of the Annunciation? Jesus suddenly didn't begin being God's Son incarnate after four months of Mary's pregnancy. Besides, I and my brothers were premature, possibly as much as two months, and very small. At one time, we wouldn't have been considered "viable." Did we suddenly become human just because science developed all the then-extraordinary things that were done, including feeding tubes and oxygen in incubators, to try to save our lives? I shudder to think of what would have happened to us in a different time and with different parents, when children too often are seen as burdens, economic drains, and career interrupters, instead of blessings. After all, from a crass, materialistic point of view, how would two people with limited incomes be expected to support

---

[33] The Fourth Amendment of the Constitution protects the right of people to be secure in their persons, houses, papers and effects from unreasonable searches and seizures. That provision could have been construed to include a right of privacy in the early stages involving oral medications which may be hard to regulate, (witness the often unsuccessful "war on drugs,") and to protect against results like those in Brazil where abortions are illegal and prosecutions often are contested as to whether a pregnancy terminated naturally as a miscarriage or from an abortion.

three babies, especially if they had disabilities? Instead of looking to abortion as the solution to problems, we should put our efforts and resources into finding ways to help mothers the keep their babies or to facilitate adoption if necessary. Politicians who promote abortion from convenience and expediency ignore the fact that we thus penalize disadvantaged and vulnerable people. Yet some of these same leaders promote and seek to protect ibf treatments to facilitate having children, which generally only will be available to higher income people or people with good health insurance policies that will cover these expensive procedures!

While I support overturning Roe v. Wade, which has returned regulation of life issues to the states where the conscience of the community can speak and express itself, I am concerned that the conservative justices on the Supreme Court will also overturn civil rights gains, legitimate gun control, and campaign reforms. Unfortunately, we have to seek the greatest good, whatever the price. "Packing the court" is a useless solution on either side; the party in power will change, and justices will keep being added. That way madness lies! Term limits for judges don't make sense to me, either, in view of the wording in the Constitution that they serve for life during good behavior.

In light of all this difficulty and controversy, I can only do what I can, which is to keep praying. I also try to offer up my sufferings and frustrations for an end to abortion on demand and the good of the country, as well as for the intentions of family and friends.

In 2015-16, I made two other new friends. Marilyn Fluharty and her husband, Denny, were in our parish for a while. Denny had a temporary job in the DC area. Marilyn sometimes walked with me to church, or drove me other places I needed to go. We became friends. She and Denny were also Teddy fans. We did some fun things, including going on a dinner cruise out of Alexandria on the cruise boat, *Dandy,* and taking a trip on the barge on the restored C&O Canal.

We attended a baseball game in Nat's Park, too. I always said that I would attend a game if baseball came back to Washington, DC. I think the home team won, but I especially remember that the man who sang the national anthem at the beginning of the game had a wonderful, strong, operatic voice! It was a hot day, and our seats were not under cover. Teddy was with us, and some nice people allowed us to come and sit in empty seats near them which were under the roof and much more comfortable. I learned from that experience that it isn't wise to go to the baseball park with your canine when it's very hot! *Needless to say, I was ecstatic when the Nationals won the World Series in 2019!* I kept in touch with Marilyn after Denny's work here ended and they went back to Kansas.

Another church buddy, Lisa, also came with me to church and enjoyed visits over lunch and tea. She and her husband, Dan, have been very helpful in many ways. Lisa found me a beautiful azalea bush to replace one of the original ones that died. It blooms twice a year, one of two or three that I have like that.

When I was still working, I noticed some discomfort in my right hip, and Dr. Chu had used it when called upon to write a justification for my using para transit instead of Metro. As 2016 turned into 2017, I eventually became aware that my hip was the worst of my arthritis problems. I tried acupuncture, but it didn't resolve the situation. Eventually Dr. Robert Stinger took x-Rays and concluded that I needed to have my right hip replaced, but he was retiring after July of 2018. He had me scheduled in July, but when I mentioned the HHT condition, they did a genetic test, which confirmed that I had it. The need to make sure about all of that delayed the surgery until after Dr. Stinger withdrew from doing surgery, and I wasn't able to do it until December, with Dr. David Romness. Meanwhile the resulting disability and discomfort cut down on my ability to be independent. As discussed in the next chapter, although willing to work with me slowly if necessary, Teddy was also having his problems, too. I had his eyes examined, and Dr. Corcoran noticed age-related changes, but she also put him on antibiotics for lime's disease. Sometimes, the blood tests for it aren't accurate. The medicine may have helped, but he still seemed less confident in the evening or low lighting. We were winding down like old clocks.

As my hip became more uncomfortable before surgery, I made modifications to the house to make things safer. I already described the change to the staircase going to the second floor, but I also had two railings installed on this staircase and the one going to the basement. I also had to resort to a quad cane and Nana's walker, and to a couple of other walkers to have one on each of the three floors. In the kitchen, I bought a serving cart on wheels to use for support and to help me transport things from the kitchen to the dining room. A blue power recliner replaced the regular one in the living room.

I had to resort to going downstairs backwards, especially the basement stairs; I replaced the first-floor tub with a walk-in shower; and I put a battery-operated lift in the second floor tub. I eventually obtained a medical alert device to keep handy if I am doing something possibly risky, like getting in and out of the tub.

The hip problem really cut down on my independence. It wasn't safe for me to go with other people to church, and I could no longer be an active lector. The parish put me on the list for at home Holy Communion visits.

When the day of the surgery, December 3, 2018, finally came, Shirley took me to the hospital, and picked me up the next day after I was discharged. Judy and Ruben came to the hospital and were with me in the recovery room. Judy spent the night in the hospital with me.

Needless to say, it took a while to come back from the surgery. Shirley stayed with me for a week, and then another friend, Marilyn Fluharty, came from Kansas to stay with me for the second week. I had in-house and then outpatient physical therapy during the recovery period.

It has taken much physical therapy and practice to be able to ditch the walkers inside the house, and I still use a straight cane in my right hand, with my dog or a person on my left, when I am outside. Shirley now works for me three days a week, instead of only two. I also have to do more medical maintenance things, including jell shots every six months in both knees to prevent or postpone any knee replacement surgery. From Margie, Debbie, and Tom Calabro, I know that knee replacement is much more complicated than the hip replacement. Like Nana, I also now need to see the podiatrist every three months, not to mention dental cleanings every six months, too!

The Pandemic has complicated the physical recovery. On the one hand, it has allowed me the necessary time to be at home, and I have learned to appreciate the televised Masses on EWTN. But Oh! How I wish they would dispense with the Latin which I find so distracting! It also gave me leisure for more prayer and reflection! I continued to participate by telephone in another Scripture group which I joined while still at the SEC, after Dan Savitsky died and his group eventually disbanded.

On the other hand, I had to do without Jesus in Holy Communion while the lockdowns took place. I still took consolation from the fact that, in the springtime, both Papa's wonderful azaleas and the cherry blossoms on the tidal basin continued to bloom and brighten our world with color and beauty! In 2024, the cherries came into peak bloom by St. Patrick's Day! In 2021, the seventeen-year cicadas returned with their comforting wave of warm sound and the thought-provoking saga of their long life cycle![34]

Now that the COVID restrictions have been relaxed, I was eligible to go back on the visitation list, but now I have found buddies to drive me to Mass in my car. Although my current working dog, Ives, is very patient and works slowly when walking with me, I still don't feel comfortable walking to church independently on my own yet. To walk, I still would want company for now. Ives isn't the problem; my balance and the pain from the arthritis especially in the knees are the difficulties.

---

[34] See "The Short, Sweet Season," *Tying up Loose* Ends, Linda Anne Monica Schneider, Author House, Bloomington, IN.

Of course, I keep in touch with my friend, Janie McIver, who now lives in Oregon, by telephone and e-mail. We commiserate about our tilts with computer windmills and our frustration with the slow recovery and reemergence from the pandemic.

Overall, things are opening back up, but I still feel as though I am living in a nightmare. Too many people are not taking the COVID vaccine, and I am concerned we could have a serious surge again if they don't keep up the "herd immunity." During the first year or so, the numbers of COVID cases and hospitalizations, including younger people and children, were going inexorably back up again in many places, following initial improvements in the spring, but the trend may be turning downward in places with high vaccination rates. I have taken the Pfizer boosters, as well as the flu and RSV annual vaccines. The Moderna vaccine booster was approved under similar circumstances and is available as an alternative.

I still am concerned that another resurgence or a shutdown may come if people don't start behaving more responsibly and don't give up the vicious "them against us" mentality that seems to prevail everywhere! God has helped us by allowing the COVID virus to mutate to behave more like the seasonal flu.

We are like Germany now: it isn't safe to speak of politics in polite company. Regardless of how wrong we may consider other people's ideas and behavior, I believe that charity requires us to try to listen to others. We cannot possibly understand others' points of view or hope to persuade or change any minds without loving, receptive dialog with them! Even though I sincerely believe this, I still find it very hard sometimes to "keep my powder dry!"

The result of all of this uncertainty is that I feel very frustrated, bereft, and cheated of what I hoped would be a pleasant retirement! For me the so-called golden years are years of brass. Judy's husband, Ruben, keeps quoting Winston Churchill and reminding me to "Keep calm and carry on," but I still am struggling with a great deal of anger, which prompts me to pray to follow Father Seamus's advice to give the anger to God and try to reaffirm my faith and Easter joy, despite everything.[35] I try to remember what St. Augustine said: that Jesus made us for Himself and our hearts are restless until they rest in Him! Francis Thompson in "Hound of Heaven" put it another way. He quoted the Lord as saying that all He took from him, He took, not for the poet's harms, but

---

[35] For a discussion of my emotional turmoil, see "I'm Holding on Tight by God's Grace and the Tips of my Fingers!" in *Tying up Loose Ends*, Linda Anne Monica Schneider, Author House, Bloomington, IN.

so the poet would seek it in the Lord's arms. 'Ah, fondest, blindest, weakest, I am He Whom thou seekest! Thou dravest love from thee, who dravest me.'

I'm grateful to be able to offer up my discomfort and frustration for the good of others! At least, I can do <u>something</u>! My friend, Janie McIver, keeps reminding me to "hold onto the Lord, the King, and keep asking for His protection!"

These conflicting emotions and feelings have been intensified by the loss of two other very dear friends. On April 9, 2019, Father Seamus went into the hospital for surgery to remove a cancerous tumor from his esophagus and died from complications of the surgery. I now have a huge hole in my life. Brother Nicholas, as prior of the monastery, still is trying to find "a few good men," as they say in the Marines, especially a priest to say regular Masses, to keep the monastery going. They have some new candidates, but I don't think they have a priest yet. I have to remember to keep the monks in my prayers, the living and the departed. I've also asked Father Seamus to keep praying for me in heaven, and I will remember him! I only wish that I could have visited him while he was alive in his new monastery in Deland, Florida.

A few days later, on May 2, 2019, Barbara Sheehan died from an untreatable sepsis infection in one of her legs at the venerable age of 103. My only consolation is that Shirley and I went to the care facility of the Hermitage to visit her to bring her Easter goodies around Easter time, when she still was alert and strong enough to visit with us. Barbara was a priceless friend and my surrogate mother! I'm grateful that at least she never had to deal with the lock-downs, anxieties, and restrictions of this pandemic!

I'm working very hard to stay thankful for all of God's blessings, especially Ives and the friends that I still have.

I'm glad to be fully vaccinated against COVID19 as of early April, 2021, and I have taken boosters to stay current, including the flu, COVID, and RSV vaccines last fall. I still think it's prudent for me to continue wearing a mask in public, at least until people are not crowded together so much in the summertime.

Because I was concerned about another possible COVID19 shutdown, I was frantically trying to get medical appointments and new hearing aids in 2021, while things seemed a little better. Yes, the wonderful folks at G.W. Speech and Hearing Center have found a pair of digital hearing aids that actually work for me. I am glad that they do, because my present analog hearing aids are getting older, and I need to have new ones before my present aids break or cannot be repaired! Unfortunately, they just aren't making analog aids anymore! I tried the new aids beginning on Wednesday, September 1, 2021. They may need adjustments, but I think that they will work. So far, so good!

I'm also very distressed about the progress of climate change, with the extreme weather and the fires and floods in the world. I fear that people aren't doing enough to try to overcome the disaster that hangs over so many people and the planet. It seems that too many people and businesses don't want to sacrifice present convenience, pleasure, and profit to avoid the looming catastrophe in the future! I'm grateful for the strong environment stand that Pope Francis took.

Writing this revision to my autobiography has been beneficial to me, because it required me to relearn and review many of the coping mechanisms that I have needed in other emotional crises. I revisited a poem from my poetry collection, *The Ivory* Pyramid, "The Other Side of Anger," and reprinted it here at the end of this chapter.

# ON THE OTHER SIDE OF ANGER

Linda A. M. Schneider
June 15, 2005

On the other side of anger
Is an unexpected place,
With a calm, untroubled sky,
Where we meet God face-to-face,
The undisturbed center of the universe, the EYE!

Around the eye, the hurricane winds whirl,
With anger, fury, and strife.
If we deal with them ourselves,
They will tear us apart.
The only sane rhythm for this dance
Is the beating of His Heart!
But, if we give it all to Him:
The anger, conflict and turmoil,
By the miracle of His Love,
He transmutes them into the energy of Life!

Beneath the calm blue of the eye,
The stirring waters boil
The energy of Love remaking all our world.
We either add to or hinder it:
The choice is ours to make--
We either surrender to the power of Love,
Or on its rocks we break.

# PRINCE TEDDY: MY SQUIRE, MY NAVIGATOR, AND MY HEALER

Mrs. Schneider & "Teddy" at the IA Compliance Forum 2010 in Washington DC

by René Bettschen

*E*arlier I mentioned that Gemma had to retire in 2009. Seeing Eye brought me Teddy as my fifth dog and a home placement. This chapter begins with two pictures. The first was taken during a meeting that I attended as part of my work outside the office, and it was taken by one of my fellow conferees. The second was taken after I finished training by Rick Connell in front of my house. I described our home training with Teddy in the earlier chapter. He was a beautiful big black Labrador retriever. I felt that I had a mental bond and communication with him. When

I first was matched with him, I told him that he would be my squire and go everywhere with me, like the knights of old. He worked competently and confidently, and he could take initiative and think outside the box. For example, he took me up onto the green divider in the middle of 26th Street when he thought a car was coming, instead of only stopping like my other dogs. As I mentioned in an earlier chapter, he knew the complicated hallways of my former work place in the Station Place complex better than many of my colleagues. Once he knew where we wanted to go, it was better to let him pick his own route, because often alternative hallways went to the same destination. Teddy also learned to brace beside me on stairs, so that I could use him for support, especially if the stairs didn't have a railing. He also displayed an amazing ability to keep track of where we were in traveling in the car. If he thought we were going home and we were driving somewhere else, he would vocalize and let us know. He did this, too, on one occasion when the taxi cab dropped me at the wrong place at work. We had to get back in the car and go to the right place. I told the driver that he should have listened to Teddy! Sometimes I felt sorry for Teddy, because I sensed he wanted to say many things, and not just about basic needs. "Um, um," that people mistakenly call whining is not a big vocabulary. Sometimes Teddy like Vincent, resorted to body language to communicate. One day in the springtime, Marilyn and I were discussing the possibility of putting azalea flowers in a keepsake locket. When we returned from church, she let us out near the end of the driveway. Unlike Mikki who liked to put her nose in plants, it wasn't characteristic of Teddy, but he put his nose in a bunch of blooming white azalea flowers, as though to say, "If you want to get them, you better do it now!" We followed his advice and took a spray of them!

The first winter after I had Teddy, 2009-2010, was the year of the huge snowstorms! A friend helped Teddy and me to walk to church in all that deep snow in the first snowstorm! He had to learn by doing! I enjoyed all that glorious snow, but even then I was worried enough about the warming climate to wonder whether the snows of 2009-2010 were the last big snows I would see in my lifetime! [36]

When we were going to the airport to go to Albuquerque, I told Teddy, "Put that GPS away. We are going somewhere you have no idea!" He listened to me. He didn't start talking again until we were coming home from the airport after we came back!

Although when she was alive Gemma tried to demonstrate for Teddy retrieving a ball and bringing it back to me, Teddy never became a ball player. His idea of play was different. Teddy had

---

[36] See "Meditation on Christmas Carols: Why We Like Snow on Christmas," *A Walk in the Park with Friends*, Linda Anne Monica Schneider, Author House, Bloomington, IN.

a quirky sense of humor. He would pick up articles of clothing or other things that he found in the laundry basket or on the floor and either put them under my computer desk in the office or hide them under the artificial Christmas tree in the living room! I didn't scold him, because he didn't damage or chew up anything valuable. It was his idea of a game or a joke! Because he was very consistent, we knew where to look if something was missing!

We had some issues that we had to work out with Teddy. He seemed to need to go out to urinate very frequently. He would cry when he felt that he needed to go outside to relieve himself and sometimes get anxious and urgent about it. The result was that we had to schedule an extra park at work, and to make sure that he was "empty" before we came back from lunch or errands. I didn't want to cut down on his water intake, especially with the heat and humidity we get in the summertime. Eventually the vets diagnosed suspected diabetes insipidus, and they put him on lignin extract, (which is derived from flax seed hulls,) which he had to take for the rest of his life. Fortunately, it helped.

The other problem that we had was that Teddy tended to lunge sharply at some dogs. Rick Connell, the instructor who brought him to me for home placement, and I suspected that he might have been attacked as a puppy. I guess dogs can have PTS, too. The school sent someone out to work with us on this problem, but of course it didn't happen when we were walking with the instructor, although we saw lots of dogs! A few times, this lunging resulted in my falling. Fortunately, I wasn't seriously hurt, but I'm sure these tumbles didn't help the deteriorating right hip! With the passage of time, I did get a clue of something that might have been bothering Teddy. When we walked to church, we passed a dog that usually barked ferociously at us, fortunately behind a confining fence. One day as we walked by, the dog and his master were outside, and I found out later they were preparing to move away. The dog barked at us again, but the master made no attempt to correct or remonstrate with his dog, notwithstanding the fact that he should have been able to see a service dog harness on Teddy! I subsequently learned from someone that the dog had a nasty, aggressive temperament and reputation and everyone was glad he was leaving the neighborhood. It may have been a German shepherd. The breed is irrelevant, but I found it unconscionable that anyone would keep a dog like that in a private neighborhood under inadequate control. Yes, people need protection, and police canines and security dogs go home at night, but control, discipline, and proper social behavior are essential for everyone's safety!

The last time Teddy lunged at a dog was when we were walking around after our canal barge trip. Fortunately Marilyn and Denny were with me. He lunged at a dog, whose owner indicated might have been the problem, and I fell. Because I was, by that time, fighting angry and in a position to do it, I flipped him on his back and pinned him!

"Don't you ever do that to me again!" I told him. He didn't.

As I said, Teddy worked beautifully during our trip to Albuquerque. (No other dogs were in the hotel or shareholders' meeting!) However, the other issue that he had was that he was hit a couple of times by electronic doors going into church, because people let go of them and they didn't stay open. He became very shy of approaching those doors! The last time this happened, Teddy wasn't with me, and the door hit me, causing me to fall. I think that it was in 2019, on my birthday, and it turned out to be the last time that I went to church before the pandemic.

Teddy was very patient and solicitous of me as my hip and arthritis became more problematic. He would snuggle with me on my bed, so that I could relax and go to sleep despite the pain. If Gemma was the registered furry nurse, I thought of Teddy as the doctor. I would tell friends that "the doctor still is in the house!" Once, for no apparent reason, I tripped over my toes and went down in a heap on the kitchen floor, fortunately on the rug. Although I didn't say anything or make any sound that I heard, Teddy was there in two seconds, checking on me to see if I was all right and asking what he could do. I patted him to reassure him and calm us both down, and then I asked him to sit and held onto him to get up. At other times, Teddy would sit beside me on my bed and just look at me, as though he were making his own assessment or evaluation of me. Often he would lie next to me and put his head on the left side of my chest, and I would ask him, "Teddy, are you listening to my heart?" Ives has done this on occasion to snuggle, but Teddy seemed thoughtful and serious when he did it. As Marilyn and I say, in this house we take care of each other.

On one occasion, I was waiting for someone to drive me to church, and she was late. I was getting frustrated, because I don't want to go in late. Teddy came over to me and just about said that I should hook him up and he would get me down there somehow. I couldn't do it, but he understood what the situation was.

In the spring of 2020, Teddy couldn't seem to get onto the bed anymore. He started sleeping on the floor near the head of my bed. One night in March of 2020, when I started to cry out of discouragement and frustration that I wasn't getting better after the surgery, he forced himself to get up onto my bed one last time to comfort me!

After I was working him less, I had Becky's Pet Care come back to provide us with a walker for Teddy. Larry wasn't there anymore, but George walked Teddy. George said that he saw Teddy behave gently and with pleasure when a butterfly landed on his nose. Before Barbara went into assistive living, she had a cat. Teddy also got along well with Smoky.

A wonderful lady named Sara became our walker when George took a different job. As the pandemic dragged on in 2020, I began to think that more was going on with Teddy than just arthritis. He was having pain in his back legs, and especially in one of them. I went into Columbia Pike Animal hospital in July, but I didn't find the doctor I saw that day very helpful. He kept saying, "well, it's an old dog!" I thought the vet to be insensitive! Teddy wasn't "an old dog." He was my best friend and my eyes! I'm disappointed that the vet didn't trust my judgment as the owner and handler that something serious might be happening! I thought that something serious was wrong, because he was deteriorating too quickly for normal arthritis, and pain inflammatory medications weren't helping after a while. I'm incensed that after a certain period of time, for people and for dogs, the medical people want to dismiss everything as old age, instead of looking deeper.

In order to try to get answers, I wanted a neurology consultation, but I couldn't get an appointment with Bush Neurology or even with Friendship Animal Hospital before September. I didn't think that we could wait that long. As Teddy's condition deteriorated, Sara and I didn't think it was safe to take him down the front steps for his once-a-day walk, and we started taking him down the grassy hill to the sidewalk. Eventually, she was coming several times a day and friends were helping me in the evenings to get him relieved in the backyard. He couldn't seem to be able to enjoy the couch anymore, and his favorite place inside now was under the artificial Christmas/holiday tree in the living room.

I went into friendship Animal Hospital on Thursday, August 6, In Washington, DC, on an emergency basis. COVID19 made it even worse, because they came and got him from the car; we had to go home and wait for a telephone call. It was horrible but very important to me. They did an examination. I had to know for sure whether Teddy could come back from whatever it was, as I was trying to do with my arthritis. The neurologist thought she felt a swelling through the rectum, and she did a scan. They found a tumor in the sacrum of the spine and nodules in the lungs indicating that the cancer had metastasized. Because of Teddy's laryngeal paralysis and the spread of the cancer, surgery was not an option. How much I wish that we could have found the cancer in time to try to do something for him! They sent Teddy home with pain meds, with the hope that we might have a few days to say good-bye.

By the next day, Friday, I knew we couldn't wait. He was in too much distress, with pain and some difficulty breathing. He also was having increasing trouble getting up the hill outside in the backyard to relieve himself, and Sara was afraid that he would fall and get hurt or break a bone. She stayed with me for much of that horrible last day! I needed help to make sure that he came inside safely.

During that last horrible day, Teddy was comfortable outside in the grass. Like Vincent before him, he probably found the magnetism in the ground soothing and therapeutic. Fortunately, the weather wasn't impossibly hot as it often is here in August. During those last few weeks, a brown rabbit buddy had been in the yard with Teddy and hanging around our house. I'm glad that he had a friend to comfort him. According to Sarah's observations, that last day, the rabbit was close by, and birds sat up in the branches and sang to him.

I found Dr. Juan Villar, from Home Veterinary Care. He came to the house, and he reviewed the results of the tests from Friendship that I sent to him. He confirmed that we couldn't do anything to help Teddy get better. We said good-bye that evening on my back deck. We did it there, because I didn't want Teddy to be embarrassed if his bladder or bowels emptied involuntarily during the procedure. He wouldn't have wanted to void in the house!

Before the final injections, I told Teddy what was happening and that he would see Papa, Mama, Nana, and my other previous dogs, including Grandma Gemma. It hurt me horribly, but I tried not to break down too much for Teddy. What also hurt me was that physically I couldn't get down on the floor to hold him, which I would have wanted to do, but I sat in a chair nearby. Dr. Villar was very gentle and compassionate! While the vet was trying to administer the medicine, Teddy kept struggling. To the last, he didn't want to leave me! I think he was especially reluctant to let go, because he knew that I didn't have any other canine in the house! After he was gone, I took off his collar and bell and put them in the closet. However, for about an hour afterwards, I still inexplicably heard his bell.

"Go in peace, Teddy," I finally said out loud, and then it was silent.

My only consolation was that Teddy wasn't hurting anymore, and now he can say anything he wants spiritually and make himself understood! I had Teddy's body cremated, and his remains are in an ornate maple box, which also serves as the pedestal of the bronze statue of him that I sculpted of him. It is on the mantelpiece with the other four statues that I did of my previous dogs and the one I recently sculpted and cast of Ives!

# IVES THE DANCER

*A*s Teddy began slowing down, I applied to Seeing Eye again for home placement in 2018. Because of my increasing difficulties with balance and arthritis, the school knew that I would need a special dog who could do some of the things that Teddy already learned. As I recall, they decided to wait until 2019 or early 2020 after my hip surgery to send an instructor to do a Juno walk at my home. When they eventually did, they were concerned about whether I would have enough use for a dog, given my restricted mobility.

In 2020, the pandemic struck. Eventually, Seeing Eye and all the major schools had to suspend their in-building classes on account of fears of spreading the virus among the staff and students. For a while, the school even closed their kennel facilities and sent their breeding dogs and trainees to puppy raisers and other volunteers who could take care of them until it was safe to resume operations at the facility. Also, many states began to impose quarantine requirements for travelers going and coming from their jurisdictions. That meant that it would be difficult for them to send someone to Arlington, VA from Morristown, NJ, because the instructor would have to quarantine after returning home when he/she finished training me.

For Two months after Teddy died, I was completely without a dog, for the first time in forty-three years. Seeing Eye knew that I needed to retire Teddy, and they said they were trying to find the right, special dog for me. They knew about my physical limitations. I was very afraid that they would give me a marshmallow dog without initiative or personality, but as things turned out, I was wrong. I didn't know when the quarantine window would open up enough to let someone come from the Seeing Eye, and I knew that if they started classes in the meantime, they couldn't necessarily keep a dog in reserve for me. Also, no one knew when the vaccines might be developed. I even reached out to other schools, to see if there were any openings, but everybody seemed to be in the same boat, and it would have taken longer to start all over again with the application process for a different place.

I desperately wanted another canine partner. Despite my own concerns about my mobility and stamina, I told God in tears that I really wanted to have another good dog again!

After Teddy died, Seeing Eye kept looking for the right dog.

The Lord must have intervened. The quarantine window opened up for a short period of time. The school called to say that they had found a possible good match. On October 9, 2020, Tom Pender came to my house for another home placement. It turns out that he was the instructor who trained me at the school with Gemma in 2002. He brought me Ives, a black Labrador/Golden retriever cross. Ives was born on January 26, 2018, and he was almost three when he came to me. The delays in training schedule caused by the pandemic might have resulted in his being the oldest non-breeder guide with whom I trained. Ives, for whom he is named, happens to be the patron saint of lawyers.

On the following week, Tom worked with us on the route to church and some walking in the neighborhood, as well as trips to Pet Smart for supplies and an ID tag. Because I'm now retired, we did not have to practice anything to do with a work environment.

We just had the window of opportunity in time. The quarantine was imposed again while we were training. Poor Tom had to isolate for a period of time at home after he came back from training us!

Ives is a very gentle, loving dog. He works conscientiously and patiently with my slow pace, and he is very solicitous for my welfare. I call him my dancing partner, because he seems to sense intuitively how we need to move together. He knows when to lead and when to follow.

He shares qualities with my other dogs. Like Vincent, he keeps close track of what I'm doing and where I am, reminds me of what I usually do, and seems to understand what I say to him. Like Mikki, he has an upbeat, happy personality and loves company. Like Remus, he knows how to bring me a ball in my hand when we play in the living room. Like Gemma, he is prompt to comfort me or calm me down if he thinks that I am unhappy or upset. Like Teddy, he provides solid support for me on steps and curbs.

He also is a big snugly, cuddly bear and likes to love me and be loved and patted! He is another manifestation of God's love. I have won the puppy lottery yet again!

# ABOUT MY OFFSPRING, THE BOOKS

*I* shall conclude here and discuss the ten books that I have published with Author House, in Bloomington, IN, not including the earlier edition of this autobiography. As mentioned earlier, in 2024, I brought out an additional short story collection through Amazon, which contains many of the earlier stories from other books and some new ones.

By way of background, I liked to write as a child. I made some childish first attempts that fortunately never found their way into print. As mentioned in an earlier chapter, I wrote another story in Braille about a relationship between a young boy and a doctor who became his mentor; I read this one onto tape, and I have reason to think that my cousin, Nancy, used it as a reason to hide out in her room to await Dick's call. I never finalized this story or tried to get it published. In grammar school and high school, I wrote for creative writing assignments. I was doing a multi-part story about a boy who lived in arid North Africa, but I never finished it. Nana teased me mercilessly for years, reminding me, "You left that poor guy stuck in the desert."

In grammar school, I also wrote a story about candidates for the religious life who attempt to find themselves in the real world before deciding about their vocations. I fortunately gave it to Sister Eileen Ann to read. She lovingly and honestly told me, in effect, that I was writing about things about which I knew nothing, and that it wasn't a good story. I remember how hard it was to swallow my teacher's criticism, but I loved and trusted her and respected her judgment. I distinctly remember taking the rolled-up, typed manuscript and throwing it into the trash! It was one of the harder things that I have done in life, but I'm glad that I did it, and I have no regrets about it.

Because I came to understand that I needed to know something about the subjects of my creative endeavors, I sometimes got help with a story, such as one in *A Second* Helping about a girl taking flying lessons, or I built on research that I was doing for a history class, such as in "The Unsinkable Liberty M." I also turned to fantasy and science fiction to provide a scope for my imagination and to express truths in a symbolic way. At least one friend has criticized some of my works as not adhering closely enough to realistic details or what probably would happen in similar circumstances. My answer is that I, like Robert Kennedy, prefer to dream things that never were and say, "Why not?" In these flights of fancy, I usually am not trying to write historical fiction, stories with realistic details about ancient or modern customs, or pieces grounded in reality. I ask my readers to fly with me into a world of wishful hoping and possibilities and let their imaginations soar! Although we all must come back down to earth eventually, maybe we will be happier, freer, and wiser for the experience!

As I mentioned in an earlier chapter, when Nana was beginning her descent into dementia after Papa's death, I started thinking about a story of a Princess named Gertrude. I had conceived this idea as a child, but now I wanted to develop it into a novel. Drawing inspiration and formatting ideas from other books that I read, including *The Thorn Birds*, by Colleen McCullough, as well as the *Lord of the Rings* books, by J. R. Tolkien, I conceived the idea of turning my story into a multi-part fantasy, allegorical novel. Working on the book gave me a way to escape for a little while from details and circumstances in my real-life situation that I found hard to understand and accept. The book also gave me a means to externalize in allegorical, fictional, and fantasy form my attempts to makes sense of the bewildering and devastating loss that Nana's mental decline represented for me. I worked on the book by dictating it onto cassette tapes. When it was finished in rough form, I had to find someone to type the manuscript from the tape. Sister Elizabeth Henry helped me to find a Trinity student, Sekethia Smith, who typed up the first draft.

When Patsy went to Jamaica for one of her yearly trips, Anna Mae Herrington came to stay with Nana and me. She came again after Nana died, and on this occasion, I was recovering from one of my nosebleeds. We used the time of my enforced inactivity for her to help me with the book. Anna Mae helped me to make corrections in the manuscript. This novel became *The Unbroken* Circle.

Anna Mae found out that I like jewelry, and she introduced me to one of her daughters, Peggy, who sold jewelry. In addition, Peggy is a wonderful Christian, optimistic lady, and she has taught me the value of remaining joyful and happy in the Lord, regardless of whatever adverse circumstances you may have. Her lessons reminded me of the hymn that we sang during my Cursillo retreat. Its theme was, "Every day is Resurrection Morning from now on. We are the Easter people!"

In addition to *The Unbroken* Circle, I also began to compile various short stories I had into another manuscript, including one of Mama's stories, the story I wrote in the '70's about the War of 1812, some other stories from my grammar, high school, and college creative writing assignments, and Nana's story of "The Three Little Pigs." Judy and I at work began talking about what it might be like to land on another inhabited, strange world, and I wrote a science fiction piece on this theme, *Diary of an Unwitting Explorer.* By the time I was doing some of the later stories and the science fiction piece, I was using the computer to do my rough drafts. Debbie Abernethy, one of my friends from the SEC, helped me in proofreading my drafts in her spare time.

I became friends with Nancy Thomsen in the 1980's. She saw a copy of my poem "The Madonna of the Tear," in the parish bulletin of our church, and she also had seen the painting. She wanted to meet the author of the poem. The folks at our parish helped her to find me.

About this time, Nancy had published a wonderful story, *The Christmas Deer,* with Author House, known at that time by the name of First Books Library. She encouraged me to consider publishing a book with them. At the time, I had the three manuscripts: *The Unbroken Circle, Diary of an Unwitting Explorer,* and the short story collection, *Slice of Life,* and I was trying to decide whether and which one to publish.

I was very happy to see the year 2000 go away. I hoped that the bad, evil 20th century ending would mean that Satan's power would be waning, and that an era of peace would be on the way. Then, in 2001, 9/11 happened.

I had just arrived at work. We began to hear the terrible news about the planes hitting the two towers. At the time, as I may have mentioned in the previous chapters, I was carpooling with Mike Kigin and Ken Cureton. Ken didn't drive with us that morning, so Remus and I went into work with Mike. Ken saw the plane hit the Pentagon, and he turned around and went back to VA.

After these horrible events, nobody knew what to do. Judy was waiting to confer with Ruben, to decide when and how they were going to get back to VA. Some other folks that I thought were friends vamoosed without giving me the time of day. Mike checked in with me, and he drove Remus and me home by way of MD. We stopped at the Mormon Temple to pick up his wife, Judy Kigin. On the way home, Mike was involved in an auto accident; he pulled out without looking and collided with another car. It broke the rear window next to Remus and me, but we weren't hurt. Mike's poor old car was never to go again after it limped home with us. By the time we got home, all of us were shaken.

That evening, the phone rang. It was Manfred Begert from Frankfurt, Germany. Of all my relatives, he was the only one who called. He knew I worked for the government, and that was enough to make him worried when he heard of the Pentagon being hit.

"Linda, are you all right?" he asked. He made my day.

For once, I also was glad that Papa had died. It would have grieved him to see these events, especially the Pentagon being hit. From the safety of heaven, I'm sure that he was sad to see them, but he has the eternal joy of the Lord!

As briefly described in an earlier chapter, after that horrible day, Remus no longer enjoyed playing ball at lunchtime downtown. She just wanted to go out and park and then go right back inside. She only gave us one good game on the very last day that she worked, in late October 2002, before she retired. Shortly after it happened, she may have smelled lingering fumes from the jet fuel after the plane crashed into the Pentagon. I think that she also heard the high-pitched ultrasonic security devices and the military planes flying around, which sound very different from commercial jets. She surely remembered the automobile accident on the way home on 9/11. She knew that all wasn't well.

For my part, it dawned on me that I might not have a long life, and that I could die, with all these books unpublished and in my drawer or on my computer. Consequently, I sent Author House all three books. I decided to put my picture with Vincent on the back of those three.

In the years that followed, I have continued to publish more books with them, although at my own expense. The next book was another short story collection, *A Second Helping*, followed by the poetry collection, *The Ivory Pyramid*, a third collection of short stories, *Cream Puffs and Other Goodies*, another fantasy novel, *Heir to the Dragon King*, the fourth collection of short stories, *A Walk in the Park with Friends*, the fifth short story collection, *Flights of Fancy and Food for Thought*, and the sixth one in 2021, *Tying up Loose Ends. I think that Vincent was on the second short story collection, and* I put Remus' picture on two of the others, Gemma on one, and Teddy on the fourth short story collection. I think Teddy was on the fifth short story book, too. We put Ives on the sixth one. I'm keeping Mikki's picture inside this revised edition of my autobiography, introducing one of the chapters. She deserves to be in one of my books. Despite the expense, it's important to me to get these books into print. They will do nobody any good sitting in my drawers or in outdated files on my computer.

In the introduction to this book, footnote 1, I cautioned my readers that I did not intend to explicate the origins of all my novels and short stories, but I have mentioned the source for some of the ideas in the course of telling my personal story. I do want to amplify the record concerning "My Real Pal," the first story in *Cream Puffs and Other Goodies*. Some similarities admittedly exist between Sara, the main character in that story, and me. Like me, Sara is blind, lives with a working and retired guide dog, has arthritis, collects dolls, and writes stories. Like me, Sara's father disposed of her dolls when she was a child. However, Sara isn't I. What I was trying to do in this story, among other things, was to project into the future the life of a lonely old lady in similar circumstances to mine, in a world that doesn't respect elders or reach out to the vulnerable people among us. In such a world, an imaginative old lady might tend to think of her dolls as real, as many children do, and she might read genuine intelligence into the actions of a sophisticated robotic doll. I leave the readers to figure out the rest of the puzzle!

Some of my stories indeed are taken directly from real life experiences. In the Author's Note to "The Short, Sweet Season" in *A Walk in the Park with Friends,* (reprinted in *Tying up Loose* Ends,) I describe my experiences with the seventeen-year cicadas, including their distracting Mikki. I actually found a live mouse in a bag of dog food kibble and released it, and I decided to tell that story from the mouse's point of view in "The Sky's the Limit" in *Cream Puffs and Other Goodies.* That short story collection also contains "The Oak Tree's Story" about my big white oak in front of my house, as well as "What Remus Knows," told from her point of view. I have written other imaginary stories told from the points of view of dogs, cats, robins, flamingos, other mice, a monkey, Biblical characters, and even the seventeen-year cicadas! Of course, my poems in *The Ivory Pyramid reflect many of my thoughts and beliefs, and the* essays and religious reflections in the short story collections are my personal opinions, thoughts, and meditations.

However, I caution my readers not to draw conclusions about my personal or political opinions from the reactions or statements of fictional characters in my books, including my heroes or heroines. Even my idealized characters have feet of clay. For the most part, my goal has been to tell a compelling or interesting or entertaining story.

Some people have asked me if I regret not having any children. In some ways, I do, because I don't have anyone with whom to share my experiences, the things that I have learned, and the truths that I consider valuable. I love my dogs and my employees, but they have been more colleagues and team members than children. In some ways, my books probably are the closest to being my offspring, because I have put so much of myself into them. Because it was the first to come to completion, *The Unbroken Circle* is probably my firstborn. This book, on the other hand, is my story.

In some ways, I consider my books to be my apostolate. In addition to having my books published in print by Author House, which used to be called First Books Library, I have tried to put some of them into an accessible form for people unable to read printed material. Aunt Murff arranged with a volunteer Braillist to put five of my previous books into Braille, and I used the Braille copies to read the books onto CD's. Mae Garrison, who lived to the age of 100, lost much of her vision, and she used the CD's to read my books.

As Mama used to say, life and growing up are the medicine in Mary Poppins' songs. I hope that the spoons full of sugar or the dollops of honey that are my books will help the medicine of truth to be communicated in a more palatable, if not a more delightful, way.

# FINAL REFLECTIONS

$\mathcal{L}$ike the character, Damian, in *The Unbroken Circle,* I find it useful to ask myself sometimes a few basic questions: "Who am I? Where do I come from, and where am I going?"

Put in those terms, I think that I know the answers. I wrote these thoughts in 2011, and I still consider them valid and true!

"I am the child of a loving God, made in his image. I am the human sister of His Son, the Resurrected Jesus, and a member of His Mystical Body. I am a temple of the Holy Spirit. I belong to the Trinity. I came forth from His hand, through the interaction of my parents, to sojourn on this planet for a little while. I hope to return to Him forever after death and to rise again with Jesus on the Last Day. I am an Easter person, because my life, perspective, and world view have been profoundly changed by my faith in the Trinity, the life, death, resurrection and Ascension of Jesus, and the coming of the Holy Spirit! [37]

As Margie liked to say, "God is not through with me yet." To quote Phyllis McGinley in *Confessions of a Reluctant Optimist*:

> Less a woman than a mouse
> To alter fate I would not bother.
> I like my plain suburban house.
> I like my children and their father.

Writing this book has afforded me an opportunity to remember the many wonderful people, events, dogs, and other blessings that God has bestowed on me. It has reminded me of the lessons that I have learned during my time on this planet, and it has given me the freedom and space to

---

[37] For more discussion of the concept of being Easter people and retaining Easter joys, see "The Children of God Should Rejoice at Easter!", *Tying up Loose Ends*, Linda Anne Monica Schneider, Author House, Bloomington IN.

mourn for those who no longer grace me with their physical presence, yet to hope for a reunion with them in eternity. Writing this book also has been an opportunity for me to consciously will to forgive all those who hurt me, whether on purpose, inadvertently, or by honest mistakes.

I don't know what the future holds, but I have learned, among many other things in this blessed life, that my safety, peace, and happiness ultimately depend on the Lord, but it remains for me to internalize and realize this fact and to continue to trust him. If my life has been filled with these blessings described in this book, it is not from any merit of mine, but from the great, overflowing abundance of God's love. Whatever good I have attained or managed to accomplish has been with His help and represents a feeble attempt on my part to respond with love and gratitude to God's care for me. I hope that my story will help others to appreciate and perceive the blessings in their lives that ultimately come from God and to respond with praise, gratitude, and love to Him.

As I approached my 72$^{nd}$ birthday in November of 2023, I tried to remember that I then would be about ten years older than Nana was soon after I was born. She surely had no idea of what was in store for her when my parents brought a tiny, five-pound baby girl home from the hospital.

To paraphrase a hymn that we sometimes sing in church, whether I live or whether I die, I belong to the Lord. Fanny Crosby, in *Blessed Assurance, says it another way:*

> This is my story!
> This is my song:
> Praising my Savior
> All the day long!

It's time to say "so long" again to my patient readers. As mentioned in the Author's Note at the beginning, by necessity, this autobiography will close open-ended and unfinished.

Linda Anne Monica Schneider

March 31, Easter, 2024